# AREN'T WE DUE A ROYALTY STATEMENT?

# AREN'T WE DUE A ROYALTY STATEMENT?

*A Stern Account of Literary, Publishing and Theatrical Folk*

## Giles Gordon

Chatto & Windus
LONDON

First published 1993

1 3 5 7 9 10 8 6 4 2

Copyright © Giles Gordon 1993

First published in the United Kingdom in 1993 by
Chatto & Windus Limited
Random House, 20 Vauxhall Bridge Road, London SW1V 2SA

Random House Australia (Pty) Limited
20 Alfred Street, Milsons Point, Sydney.
New South Wales 2061, Australia

Random House New Zealand Limited
18 Poland Road, Glenfield
Auckland 10, New Zealand

Random House South Africa (Pty) Limited
PO Box 337, Bergvlei, South Africa

Random House UK Limited Reg. No. 954009

A CIP catalogue record for this book
is available from the British Library

ISBN 0 7011 6022 5

Printed in Great Britain by
Mackays of Chatham PLC

'It is personalities, not principles, that move the age.'

Oscar Wilde

'Those who tell their own story you know must be listened to with caution.'

Jane Austen, *Sanditon*

*To the memory of my father*
*Alexander Esmé Gordon*
*1910–1993*
*who died as the proofs*
*were being corrected*

# Cast list and order of events

# Who's Who

Because this book is about anyone but myself, I had no intention of providing autobiographical details. As the pages progressed, however, I realised that they might only be fully intelligible to readers if, at the back of the book, as an appendix, I presented some basic biographical 'facts' about myself. By the time I finished the manuscript, I accepted that this unremarkable if inevitable résumé should be available for the reader, either before he or she plunges in, or to refer to as he or she pads along.

The following is reproduced, more or less verbatim, from my entry in *Who's Who*.

GORDON, Giles Alexander Esmé, FRSL 1990; *b* 23 May 1940; son of Alexander Esmé Gordon, 1910–93, and Betsy McCurry, 1910–1990; *m* 1st, 1964, Margaret Anna Eastoe, children's book illustrator as Margaret Gordon, *d* 1989; two *s*: Callum Giles, *b* 1968; Gareth Alexander, *b* 1970; one *d*: Harriet Miranda, *b* 1974; *m* 2nd, 1990, Margaret Anne McKernan, publisher, two *d*: Lucy Frances McKernan, *b*. 1991; Clare Esmé McKernan, *b* 1993. *Educ*: Edinburgh Academy, 1948–57; (briefly) Edinburgh College of Art. Trainee publisher, Oliver & Boyd, Edinburgh, 1959–62; advertising manager and commissioner of jackets, Secker & Warburg, 1962–64; editor, Hutchinson, 1964–66; editor of plays, sociology, business books and ancient classics, Penguin Books, 1966–67; editorial director, Victor Gollancz, 1967–72; literary agent and director, Anthony Sheil Associates, 1972–90; literary agent, Sheil Land Associates, 1991– ; *Transatlantic Review* erotica awards: runner-up, fiction, 1974; runner-up, poetry, 1976; C. Day Lewis fellow in writing, King's College, London, 1974–75.

Secretary, then Chairman, The Society of Young Publishers, 1963–65.

Member, Literature Panel, The Arts Council of Great Britain, 1964–68. Committee of Management, The Society of Authors, 1973–76. Council, The Royal Society of Literature, 1992–   . Committee, The Association of Authors' Agents, 1989–91. General Council, Authors' Club, 1992–   .

Lecturer in creative writing, Tufts University (London program), 1970–74; lecturer in theatre criticism, Hollins College (London program), 1983–86.

Editor, *Drama* quarterly, 1983–85. Theatre critic, *Spectator*, 1983–84. Theatre critic, *London Daily News*, 1987.

Publications: short stories: *Penguin Modern Stories 3*, 1969; *Pictures from an Exhibition*, 1970; *Farewell, Fond Dreams*, 1975; *The Illusionist*, 1978; novels: *The Umbrella Man*, 1971; *About a Marriage*, 1972; *Girl with Red Hair*, 1974; *100 Scenes from Married Life*, 1976; *Enemies: A Novel about Friendship*, 1977; *Ambrose's Vision*, 1980; children's (with Margaret Gordon): *Walter and the Balloon*, 1974.

Editor: (with Alex Hamilton) *Factions*, 1974; *Beyond the Words*, 1975; *Prevailing Spirits*, 1976; (with Dulan Barber) *Members of the Jury*; (with B. S. Johnson and Michael Bakewell) *You Always Remember the First Time*, 1975; *A Book of Contemporary Nightmares*, 1977; (with Fred Urquhart) *Modern Scottish Short Stories*, 1978; *Shakespeare Stories*, 1982; *English Short Stories 1940–80*, 1982; (with David Hughes) *Best Short Stories* (annually), 1986–   ; *English Short Stories: 1900 to the Present*, 1988.

Bibliography: *The Twentieth Century Short Story in English*, 1989.

Recreations: theatre, opera, walking, travelling, eating, drinking, book collecting, paintings.

Clubs: Garrick, Pen.

# I

The difficulty with autobiography is that you are expected to begin at the beginning and go on until the end; or to whenever you think your life ceases to be interesting, at least to the reader; or until you peg out with boredom, bemused by the self-indulgent vanity of the exercise. There is, of course, an intrinsic arrogance in attempting the form at all: not in *reading* other people's lives as you may learn something about the rest of humanity which hadn't occurred to you, but in adding to the tomes on the bookshelves by writing your own.

It is a curious phenomenon that autobiographers seem to have a detailed recall of their early years, and readers are content to be intrigued by interminable details of idyllic or (you take pot luck) ghastly childhoods. Maybe autobiographers get away with mind-deadening minutiae about their early days because, since they are writing relatively late in life, few people from their formative years are around to contradict them.

Then there are the statutory photographs which every autobiographer miraculously seems able to produce of him or herself as a baby, an alien and dangerously shawled object frantically clutched on an ancient relative's capacious lap. These days, mercifully, publishers are unlikely to allow autobiographers more than sixteen pages of blurred images, stretching it perhaps to thirty-two pages if they are politicians or terribly famous. But, above all, unless someone – usually yourself or a publisher – thinks you are famous enough, you are unlikely to be permitted an autobiography.

An exception, I suppose, as we British are obsessed with childhoods, is someone who isn't famous but who poses as a poet and remembers, or pretends to remember, his or her childhood in sufficient unctuous detail – 80,000 words perhaps – to make a book. Maybe, if the book reaches its concluding page when the author is, say, eleven and life thereafter is all downhill and a disappointment to the memoirist, there is little reason to inflict upon the reader a stultifying account of the subsequent sixty-odd years. Be grateful for modest mercies.

My problems as a would-be autobiographer are twofold. First, I am not famous, although I have always wanted to be. To achieve what others perceive as fame has long seemed to me the only justification for the mediocrity of my life. I only slipped into *Who's Who* along with 28,000 others in 1991 when I was half a century old, a generation after my father got in. For years he'd been asking me, about once a year: 'Haven't you made it into *Who's Who* yet?' which was hardly balm to the ego. When I did make it into the august double-column pages and told him so, he asked if I'd send him a photocopy of my entry as he'd no intention of purchasing the latest edition, given the frightful price it was. I suspect he hadn't purchased the book, an annual publication, since 1958 when he was admitted to its pages.

On reading my entry his only comment was that it was too long; it was much more dignified to keep the vital statistics of one's 'career' and the facts of one's life to the minimum. You should be in *Who's Who*, but there's no need to tell the world all about yourself. I suppose the length of my entry (I've just measured it, with a ruler; it's exactly the same length as my male organ, which I've also just measured for confirmation) is greater than my father's because I have two marriages to declare while he restricted himself to one, and not having had a vasectomy, in spite of the butcher's advice and his assurance that the operation is reversible, I have fathered five children – three by my first marriage, two by my second – whereas I have but one brother and one sister. I've no idea if my father had a go at my younger brother, Christopher, for not being in *Who's Who*, but I'm confident he'll make it there 'ere too long. In any case, what does it all matter? Most people, the yawning majority, in *Who's Who* either have double- or triple-barrelled names, or you haven't heard of them, or both. The people you want to read about are frequently not there. Billy Connolly, for one, isn't there and he's famous.

The second impediment to my writing a proper, or even an

improper, autobiography is that I cannot recall much about my childhood. Maybe I do not choose to do so, but that amounts to the same thing. My earliest memory is of sitting on a crocus in our garden in Edinburgh when I was about three. Well, I don't actually remember that much remarked upon incident – much remarked upon by my late mother – I remember being shown a photograph in the family album of a thriving, thrusting, vigorous crocus and myself standing by it, and being assured that I was about to demolish the innocent flower. Would a psychiatrist or psychologist assert that my remembering this incident, or at least the rather attractive photograph, was a formative influence, with penile connotations? No doubt, no doubt at all.

The next picture I recall in the album is of my father in khaki having returned from the war, and myself climbing up his legs. You will already have grasped the message that the 'significant' events of my childhood are meted out according to the pages of my parents' photograph album, depicting events, still lives, in which I am said to have participated, or which perhaps were enacted by child thespians hired for these tableaux because they physically resembled me, my cousin Jamie and, eventually, my brother and my sister Celia. But there again I have to display a degree of scepticism because I cannot, when parted from the photographic images, truly remember what I looked like as a child, and take it on trust (my father was not a liar) that the boy depicted in the photograph album is indeed myself. Presumably I didn't – like the mythical warriors, sown from dragon's teeth – spring fully grown from the ground, having missed out on infant and early childhood years? And if you ask me what I look like now, I cannot describe my nondescript appearance with much precision. If I attempted to do so, I would be interpreting the image as I see it in the shaving mirror, or even in a photograph.

I remember as a child (but what age?) not having many friends, and feeling a bit worried about that because people ought to have friends; I suppose I thought most of my contemporaries had them, or perhaps I just imagined they did? Was I good at playing with myself (and I do not mean in a masturbatory way)? Did I enjoy it or just do so because there were few other children to play with or because I didn't want to play with them?

I discovered the subscription library at Douglas & Foulis in Castle Street, which had in the basement a treasure trove of a room devoted to children's books. Nearly all of these seemed to be published by T. C. & E. C. Jack, later to be subsumed into Thomas Nelson, whose printing works and offices nestled below the Edinburgh landmark of Arthur's Seat, a mile or two from my parents' terraced house in Albert Terrace. (When I was eighteen, I went there for my first interview, with Van Milne, who published Nkrumah. I did not land the job. I don't think there was a job.) Most of the thick, chunky books, printed on paper with the consistency of blotting paper, seemed to be fictionalised biographies by G. A. Henty which, for junior readers, celebrated the heroes and very occasionally heroines of Empire and Commonwealth. Other authors who attracted my attention included Baroness Orczy (but why couldn't she have had a Christian name like other authors?) and Alexandre Dumas (whether *père* or *fils* I can no longer recall, but I puzzled for months, maybe years, over why this exciting novel wasn't called *The Four Musketeers*). I also enjoyed Arthur Conan Doyle's historical romances, particularly *The White Company*, *Sir Nigel* and, later, *The Adventures of Brigadier Gerard*, but I couldn't – still can't, really – see what was so heinous about cutting up a fox with a sword if the poor creature was to be killed anyway. I couldn't make much of Sherlock Holmes: nothing seemed to happen. I secretly liked Enid Blyton best but knew even then that it wasn't done to say so. The 'Famous Five' books were about characters and a world I could easily identify with (unlike Richmal Crompton's 'William' books, where the eponymous hero seemed to aspire to being scruffy and unidealistic). I could and did discriminate within Enid Blyton's books: Noddy and Big Ears, for instance, were stupid, for babies, but the 'Famous Five' series evoked a recognisable world, where things happened, unlike my world in Edinburgh where nothing seemed to happen and adults seemed to sleepwalk, ever so politely, through life, visiting church once a week. Reading wasn't an escape; it was a discovery.

I remember the horror of John Crabbie (his family manufactured Crabbie's Green Ginger) snatching my obligatory Edinburgh Academy navy and silver braided cap on the upper deck of

the 23 bus one morning on the journey to school and hurling it
across the seats. I was terrified of being 'reported' by some Edinburgh worthy for not wearing the wretched cap in the street,
which was a punishable offence. I remember despising the boys
from Watson's and George Heriot's for not being obliged to wear
caps and thus (a touch of the William Browns?) looking scruffy.
I think it was more that I was afraid of the realities of life,
the playground of the world, than that I was simply weedy and
priggish.

And so it continued, childhood, seemingly for ever. I failed to
concentrate upon my lessons at school, and hated the façade like
that of a Greek temple, the school motto in Greek, Homer's head
in profile everywhere (as if anyone knew what *he* looked like) and
the fact that nearly all the masters were English. Was there something wrong with the Scots, with Scottish education? Why wasn't
it good enough for us? Why, near the end of their school careers,
did the more able boys – the Academy wasn't, of course, co-ed
in the fifties and sixties, although I gather the progress of the
century has persuaded it now to harbour some token girls – sit
English A-levels rather than Scottish 'Highers'? Such questions
were not to be asked, or if they were they were not adequately
answered.

The first 'event' or 'incident' in my life which I really recall –
and in important respects I feel I have never fully recovered from
the outcome – was when, aged fifteen, I casually informed my
parents in the kitchen of our house in Greenhill Gardens (to which
we had moved to become more upwardly bourgeois) that that
Easter I would, with thousands of others, march from London to
Aldermaston to protest against the Bomb. Oh, I knew a thing or
two about the world by then! My father clenched his fist and, his
voice trembling (like me, he lost his cool when crossed), asserted
that I would not; I insisted that I would. My mother, with tears
in her Ulster eyes, slowly shook her head and told me to obey
my father. Eventually, like the dominie that in many respects he
instinctively was (he taught architecture at the College of Art in
addition to being senior partner of a well-known architectural
practice with offices in Heriot Row in the Georgian New Town),
he pronounced: 'If, young man, you insist on marching to Alder-

maston you need not think you can return to live here.' He made it plain that until I was in a position to earn my own living, I would do what he and my mother thought was best for me.

I didn't go to Aldermaston, that year or any other. Something in my spirit snapped, and I deeply, fundamentally regret not having had the courage of my convictions. When I reminded my father of the little kitchen contretemps more than thirty years later he professed to have no memory of it.

My father obviously influenced me. Fathers, for better or for worse, particularly if they are 'strong' characters as mine was, cannot avoid this fate, of judging their children and usually, in return, being silently judged by their progeny. And so the wheel turns and is never still.

To me, the pleasure of autobiography is writing about people I've known, people who have influenced me in the sense that their lives have come into contact with mine and left an indelible impression. They do not have to be 'famous', but it obviously helps if they are because the reader will recognise their names and thus it won't be essential for me to describe them, define them, create them out of the ether as the novelist has to do with his or her characters (unless, that is, he or she wishes to encourage a libel suit). What I am required to do is, simply, record my response to them, evoke them to you as I see them. For whatever ideas are about and in the wind, it is people, individuals, who give shape to those ideas, to history.

As the American historian Will Cuppy wrote, 'Biography is about chaps'. And history, unless you are a Marxist, is caused by a concomitance of chaps. Our relationships with other people are what make us what we are, or aren't. Even Samuel Beckett's solitary, life-soiled characters have, for most of their lives, been part of society, even if not necessarily society as many of us recognise it. Their memories, their tape recordings and mouthings, are of relationships – or a lack of relationships, positive memories in themselves – with other people. If man is an island, life is about discovering other islands and learning about them, even if ultimately, to retain our sanity and humanity, much has to be forgotten.

I did badly at school. Why, I do not know, although I have

always been bad at rote. For this reason, if for no other, I could never have been an actor, which in other respects I'd have liked to be. I could never have held the lines in my head, and I'd have been bored by giving the same performance twice. My mind wanders too easily, speculates. The high spot of my time at the Edinburgh Academy was when, in 1955 and with my alto voice on the verge of breaking, I sang the Queen of the Fairies in *Iolanthe* opposite the Private Willis of Gordon Honeycombe, later to find fame as a reader or 'caster' of the news. Each summer term the Academy alternated between mounting a Gilbert and Sullivan operetta and a play by Shakespeare. In 1953 the operetta had been *The Mikado*, with six feet four inches of Honeycombe in the title role and me in the chorus of schoolgirls as well as understudying a pretty boy – particularly svelte in his rugby shorts – Ronald Sinclair, who sang Pitti-Sing. I did not have a crush on Sinclair, though he appeared to do brilliantly at everything and was a few years older than me. (I'm delighted to see he's not in *Who's Who*, although I hope he wasn't killed in some war or other. He was the sort of person who might have seen it as his duty to enlist, wherever the war.) A few years later he became Regimental Sergeant Major of the Combined Cadet Force and displayed a reddish-blond down on his exposed knees when, as was *de rigueur* during the summer term when battledress trousers were banished, he sported the kilt. Maybe I did have a crush on him after all.

Those who had proved competent in Gilbert and Sullivan were, almost invariably, awarded a part in the subsequent year's Shakespeare. The year after *Iolanthe* the play was *The Merry Wives of Windsor*, and to my shame I was not offered a part, quite possibly because my dialogue in *Iolanthe* was creatively altered on each of the four nights of the run. On the third night, when stardom had begun to turn my head, I skipped two pages of dialogue, but some kind junior fairy noticed this and guided me and the rest of the company back to the straight and the narrow, where it was necessary for me to repeat a line or two about how disgusting it was to live at the bottom of a slimy stream with only frogs for company. (As to *The Merry Wives of Windsor*, I have never thought much of the play. Who, other than Queen Elizabeth, would have wanted to see Falstaff in love?)

## Chapter I

My hired costume for *Iolanthe* was like an enormous Victorian lamp-fitting constructed over wire hoops. No sooner had I climbed into it – feeling a bit like one of those French knights at Agincourt, in the Olivier film of *Henry V*, being almost welded into his armour before being winched up on to his caparisoned horse – than I realised that the dress was built for a singer, presumably female, with a more voluptuous bosom than mine. I stuffed my socks into the cups, the gaping cavities, and when they failed to provide ample cleavage I added tissue paper. 'Take those ridiculous things out,' squeaked Mrs 'Beanie' Read, the wife of the senior maths master, who was assisting behind scenes. She looked like a babushka doll, her husband like a garden rake. He spoke in strangulated tones, lacking, I think, part of his voice box, and sounded like a ravaged Dalek. If a boy so much as dropped a rubber in class, let alone a pair of dividers, a metal ruler or a book, 'Beanie' would leap into the air like a scalded cat, plunge towards his desk, take out his thick, unsinuous tawse and thrash the recalcitrant youth on his quivering outstretched palm.

Quite a few of the masters seemed to relish using the tawse. The most dangerous was a master named George Fletcher. Unlike most of the others, he beat regularly for bad work, for not having mastered the map of Brazil, or (in my case) temperature charts. He would beat you after class too. Most masters beat you during the class, in front of your fellows, which meant you had to adopt a stiff upper lip. At the end of the lesson, after the rest of the class had departed with relief, the vile Fletcher would order – there was no invitation about it – you to bend over or project your palm (I seem to recall that, liberally, he gave you a choice). He would saunter, as if he detested what he was about to do, to the far end of the classroom, remove his sports jacket, then *run* at you, the full length of the room. If memory serves, he invariably meted out six of the best, and equally invariably – I can see him now, in my mind's eye, Horatio, and smell his cowardly sweat – began foaming at the mouth. He exuded real sexual foam, like phosphorus glistening at the edge of the sea as waves lap in and pull out, and his thick dry lips would pant and pout, and he'd lick the dryness with the point of his tongue. He was, I believe, a horrible man, whose fingers would be coated with white from writing on the blackboard, and whose gown would be shrouded in chalk. Why, under the pretext of being educated, did we have to put up with the likes of George Fletcher, the French master 'Scabby' Scott and 'Beanie' Read?

Masters could and, as I have indicated, did beat with the strap, mostly for misdemeanours. The prefects, embarrassingly known as ephors – the Greek word for prefects, to underline the school's classical foundation – beat naughty boys with a large flat wooden spoon known as a clachan. Its primary use was in the school game of hailes, in which every player wielded a clachan and used it, like a hockey stick, to beat a small hard ball into the opposing team's goal mouth. The game was played in the school yard, and anyone unfamiliar with the game must have paused in bemusement when passing the front gates of the playground in Henderson Row.

The head ephor when I graduated from the 'Prep' school to the 'Upper School', aged eleven or twelve, was a *very* old boy (I believe he was nineteen, but he may only have been eighteen) called C. D. L. Clark. We were invariably called by our surnames, and used our initials. In the mid-seventies, when as Charles Clark he was running Hutchinson, he was to publish two of my novels and a collection of stories, as well as the book which I was to have edited jointly with my friend B. S. Johnson, *Beyond the Words: Eleven Writers in Search of a New Fiction.* (I was obliged to undertake this on my own as Bryan Johnson, in 1973, cut his wrists in the bath before we had seriously begun to compile the anthology). R. G. Honeycombe was another senior ephor the year I graduated to the Upper School (I think there were only six, or it may have been eight). Senior ephors had their own common room, a room in the masters' lodge, where, after school each Friday, they foregathered to 'try' boys for reported misdemeanours and walloped those found guilty.

I cannot remember what my offence was, but I do remember that I was petrified, confronted in a tiny room by six or eight old boys who seemed almost as grown up as my father. I pleaded my case and the opposing view was put, then I was dismissed from the room while the ephors decided whether or not I was guilty as charged. Boys, I believe, were rarely let off. When I returned, I was told solemnly – there was no jollity or light-heartedness about

9

the proceedings that I had been sentenced to two strokes of the clachan.

Those sentenced had to stand at the head of the hefty rectangular table in the centre of the room, thrust their heads below the table and grasp the top firmly with their hands. Then they were beaten hard on their posteriors with the ridiculous, if lethal, wooden weapon. Ephors took it in turn to admonish boys and, as a victim, you were not permitted to observe who handed out the punishment. Judging by a look of complicity when next I passed him in the playground some days later, I think one of my two strokes may have been meted out by Honeycombe. It was all extremely painful, as well as humiliating. I looked with anguish rather than pride at my purple bruises each night and each morning, and for a week or so I was all too readily reminded of them whenever I attempted to sit down.

Nearly a quarter of a century later I saw Honeycombe walking up Charing Cross Road. I'd seen him the previous evening on television reading the news. The climax of the relationship in *Iolanthe* between the sentry Private Willis, who stands guard outside the Palace of Westminster, and the Queen of the Fairies (not once does Gilbert call her the Fairy Queen, leaving that to Spenser and innumerable others) is the following piece of scintillating dialogue:

> *Queen of the Fairies*: Private Willis!
> *Sentry* (coming forward): Ma'am!
> *Queen*: To save my life, it is necessary that I marry at once. How should you like to be a fairy guardsman?
> *Sentry*: Well, ma'am, I don't think much of the British soldier who wouldn't ill-convenience himself to save a female in distress.
> *Queen*: You are a brave fellow. You're a fairy from this moment. (Wings spring from Sentry's shoulders) . . . Then away we go to Fairyland.

By which time, the entire on-stage cast, including the chorus of Peers, has sprouted wings, Private Willis's being scarlet to go with his Guards tunic. We then indulged in an absurd dance, holding hands, with the principals at the front of the stage, the Queen of the Fairies and Private Willis in the middle.

'Private Willis, how would you like to marry a fairy?' I said quietly to Honeycombe in Charing Cross Road. He looked taken aback, but quickly regained his composure. 'Don't be such a bloody fool, Gordon,' he said, looking down at me from his great height.

After he'd left the Edinburgh Academy and graduated in English from Oxford, he decided to become an actor and in 1962 joined the young Royal Shakespeare Company. One day the *Scotsman* announced that the RSC were to visit Edinburgh with Friedrich Dürrenmatt's thoughtful, fashionable, and elegant play *The Physicists*, directed by Peter Brook. In the cast were such luminaries as Michael Hordern, Alan Webb, Cyril Cusack, Irene Worth and Diana Rigg. Cast to the hilt it was, as in those days RSC productions were. But the *Scotsman* was more excited by the fact that local boy Gordon Honeycombe was returning to his home town in the cast. I seem to remember it was mentioned that Honeycombe's formidable mother still resided in the Scottish capital. I was terribly envious of Honeycombe for having made it to the ranks of the great RSC. I bought my ticket and, on the appointed evening, mounted miles to the gods of the King's Theatre. The programme ('refuse this programme if the seal is broken') listed a large cast and at first glance I thought they'd left out Honeycombe's name. 'Police doctor', played by Gordon Honeycombe, was, I think, the last name on the cast list. The evening was nearly over before Honeycombe's chance came. After hours of the play, Nurse Monika Stettler (Diana Rigg) keeled over. 'Fetch a doctor,' someone cried. Honeycombe, looking taller than ever, walked quickly in, wearing a heavy dark coat and homburg and carrying a medical case. He leant over the nurse, felt her pulse, then solemnly announced: 'She's dead, sir.' And that was that. The line was clearly spoken, the words ringing up to the gods, but I don't believe Honeycombe's career with the RSC advanced much further. He went on to cultivate an interest in the darker aspects of the police, publishing *The Murders of the Black Museum* in 1982, and a royal book or two.

# II

My life has been much concerned with authors and books, and in these pages it is mainly of authors that I speak and their books that I celebrate.

Jonathan Griffin – how exotic the name seemed to a seventeen-year-old Scot; how heraldic; so romantic that it might be pseudonymous – was the first author I met. He was also the first author to inscribe a book to me. The flyleaf of my copy of *The Hidden King*, somewhat battered now and much reread, is embellished by his spidery scrawl in mundane blue biro:

> For Giles Gordon, whose fresh approach and warm response encouraged not only me but the whole cast at Edinburgh in 1957; gratefully,
>
> Jonathan Griffin

Born and bred in Edinburgh, I was theatre-struck. The International Festival each August was the three weeks to wait for, and nothing ruined my summer more than when my parents booked a family holiday which meant that I'd miss a week or even two of nirvana.

I had a particular addiction to the Church of Scotland's Assembly Hall at the top of the Mound which, each Festival for three carnival weeks, was transmogrified into a playhouse, with thrust apron stage devised years before by Tyrone Guthrie. The intimacy this theatre afforded between actors and audience was thrilling, pulsating. I had, prior to 1957, seen a number of productions there, usually try-outs by the Old Vic on the way to Waterloo Road. I remember a spring-like *Twelfth Night*, with John Neville as a palsied Aguecheek. I especially remember sitting

12

in a front row pew while a fleshy male bottom clad in stretched black tights pronounced a soliloquy in a dreamy nasal Welsh voice above me; I was not impressed as the proximity of the buttocks to my face distracted from the poetry. This was Richard Burton essaying Hamlet.

It was disappointing to learn early in 1957 that there would be only one production at the Assembly Hall that Festival (in previous years there had been two or more) and that it would not be a Shakespeare, it wouldn't even be a classic. Still a schoolboy, I only really approved of the 'classics', for they had stood the test of time. Anyone, in a sense, could write a new play, and I wanted something special. The new play, by a hitherto unknown dramatist and poet, was being mounted for three weeks because it was so expensive to put on, and was the first major dramatic production at the Festival to be presented by the Festival Society itself (albeit in association with the impresario Stephen Mitchell).

*The Hidden King* by Jonathan Griffin opened to terrible reviews – so bad that I hope no playwright ever received a more severe verbal beating than poor Jonathan did. The driven, destiny-ridden Kenneth Tynan particularly disdained the play. On the other hand, J. C. Trewin, that sound appraiser of literary excellence, albeit in largely unread publications, much admired it. Having read some of the appalling notices, I went expecting the worst, and had what is probably the most engrossing and enriching evening I've spent in a theatre.

I wish I could assume that anyone reading these words is familiar with Griffin's masterpiece, a 'poem for the stage in the form of a trilogy'.

They do not, certainly not at the RSC or the National Theatre (neither of which had been founded in 1957), make casts like that one any more: the actors included Iain Cuthbertson, Frank Thornton, Derek Nimmo, John Bennett, Míchéal Mac Liammóir (sulphurously sinister), Ronald Harwood, Hugh Cross, Bernard Horsfall, Clare Austin, Rosalind Atkinson, Sebastian Shaw (a lecherous villain), Richard Dare, Ernest Thesiger (the most emaciated, glittering, corrupt Cardinal imaginable) and Pauline Jameson (radiance itself). The leads were Robert Speaight, who gave the play rather a good write-up in the *Tablet*, and the ethereal, Christ-like

Robert Eddison as Dom Sebastian, claiming to be the King of Portugal, generally assumed to have been killed at the battle of Alcazar twenty years earlier.

I cannot, at this distance in time, recall whether 'Bobby' Speaight, as I wouldn't have dreamed of calling him, was theatre critic of the *Tablet* (I think he was, but how did he cope with reviewing the plays in which he appeared, and when he wasn't 'resting' how did he manage to see other plays?) or simply a regular columnist, but I do remember that, in his article about the excitement which the production of *The Hidden King* generated, he remarked that *some* people were enthusiastic about it, including the saintly John Trewin and someone described as 'a straightforward ordinary schoolboy', an appellation which reappeared years later in Speaight's autobiography. The description smarted at the time and smarts even more now. Maybe if I had not been wearing my kilt when I attended the performance with the Griffins I might not have been so dully solemnised. On the other hand, Speaight was a Roman Catholic, and perhaps any descendant of John Knox might have been regarded as 'straightforward' and 'ordinary', and there was no denying I was a schoolboy.

Who cares about the critics? (Certainly I never did when I became one for the *Spectator*, a quarter of a century later.) I'd read in an Edinburgh newspaper that Jonathan Griffin was in Edinburgh for the première of his play. I wrote him a letter, telling him how good his work was, and that he really wasn't to worry about the critics, who were clearly morons. Unable to find a door that opened at the Assembly Hall during the day, I pinned my note – not thinking of Luther and the church door at Wittenberg – to a barred entrance of the Assembly Hall, watched by the statue of dour, bedraggled, finger-pointing old John Knox as I did so, and hoped that my envelope would reach Mr Griffin.

I can't remember, thirty-five years later, whether I received Jonathan's letter the next day or the day after. I can still recall the thrill of reading the letter. I remember feeling dizzy, nearly fainting at Jonathan's suggestion – nay, assumption – that I accompany him and his wife to a matinée of the play within the next few days.

I cannot, to my shame, remember anything about that second

performance, so awed was I at sitting next to the playwright and his wife (yet whether I sat between Jonathan and his wife Kathleen, or next to one of them I cannot recall).

After the performance, Jonathan and Kathy took me backstage to meet the actors. They weren't, of course, interested (except, I remember, Míchéal Mac Liammóir, who, with mascara sweating all over his unwholesome visage, was too interested), as they wanted to steal a few minutes' relaxation between matinée and evening performances: the production, when it opened, ran for nearly four hours. By my second attendance it had been shorn of, I think, nearly an hour and was artistically diminished.

After this Jonathan and I began to correspond – 'Dear Mr Griffin'; 'Dear Mr Gordon' – which lasted for five years until I came to live in London. His letters were an illuminating crash course in drama, with particular reference to the minor Elizabethan and Jacobean playwrights. (Jonathan had a relish for, not the second-rate, but the less fashionable, the less well-known). I dread to think what I wrote to him, but the sweet, selfless man continued to undertake my theatrical education. 'You really should read *The Dutch Courtesan*,' I remember him telling me. The trouble was, and is, that I have always preferred plays in the playhouse to the naked texts in the study, which no doubt says a great deal about my frivolity.

Jonathan tried to persuade me of the riches of opera, but I was unconvinced: a mélange of art forms by those who can't achieve complete success with any one of them, I sullenly wrote back. Quietly he admonished in his next letter: you will come to appreciate opera when you are older. This, of course, irritated me but, as almost always, he was right.

When, in 1962 I came to London to work for his own publishers, Secker & Warburg, he and Kathy invited me and Margaret, my wife, to dinner at their jewel-box of a house in Markham Street, Chelsea, before King's Road had become something approximating a seaside pier. The white terraced house was a feast of theatrical, operatic, poetic and literary *objets*, a sort of miniature, personalised Garrick Club. Did Kathy, with cats in tow, always serve fish? So I remember it. My memory of Jonathan, no doubt unfair, is of his talking and talking, blinking and smiling like a vole presiding over the meal of a lifetime, brooking comment from his guests without much enthusiasm. Not that he was rude – on the contrary – but any guest who made a pitch for a paragraph or two would not always be encouraged.

As the years went by, I saw less of Jonathan and Kathy, especially – rather surprisingly – after they came to live near us, in Sharpleshall Street. In the last few years, we only exchanged Christmas cards. 'We must get together next year. Love Jonathan and Kathy.' But most years we didn't.

I have two small mementoes of him. First, at an auction at the National Theatre a decade or more ago I bought a watercolour costume design by Leslie Hurry of the Venetian Ambassador to Portugal in *The Hidden King*. The character does not appear to be listed among the dramatis personae; but no matter. Second, in 1963, after Fred Warburg had more or less ordered his partner Roger Senhouse to exile himself from Secker & Warburg (Roger had published a collection of Jonathan's poems, *The Rebirth of Pride*, in 1957), I published, from my bedsitter in Ridgmount Gardens, a pamphlet of elegant poems by Jonathan, *The Oath and Other Poems*. It was the smallest repayment of an impossible debt.

In the late fifties, Dame Edith Sitwell gave a poetry reading at the Lyceum Theatre one weekday afternoon as part of that year's Edinburgh Festival. She was pretty famous then, as were her two brothers. She knew Dylan Thomas and had written the libretto for William Walton's *Façade*, and thus was a terribly important artistic figure, a neo-Romantic when they were all the rage, before Kingsley Amis, John Osborne and the Angries erupted.

When the curtain rose (plush curtains still rose and fell in those days, lending magic to theatregoing) she sat there on stage, against the set for *Gammer Gurton's Needle*, a knockabout early English play which Birmingham Rep would perform rumbustiously that evening. To my youthful eyes, Dame Edith resembled nothing so much as Nefertiti's mother, or possibly grandmother. She was swathed in purple, almost buried in it, the upper part of her strangely crumbling body hung with vast gold discs that looked as if they had been purloined from the tomb of an Aztec sun god, her wizened, stick-like fingers encrusted with rings the size of mammoth rhinestones. She began reading, as though she were on her own in the lavatory, in a ridiculous upper-class voice which barely carried to where I was sitting, in the upper reaches of the gods. Eventually someone had the courage to shout, 'Please speak up,' and others repeated the exhortation until there was something of an unruly chorus.

At first the poet ignored the outburst, and meandered on, apparently muttering to herself, like old Nilus, oblivious to everything except her 'art' and her self-absorbed arrogance. Eventually, the row from the auditorium was so great she was forced to stop. She peered up towards the gods, all Lady Macbeth's daggers. '*What* did you say?' she demanded, sepulchrally. Her interrogation reduced the audience to a cowed silence. She repeated the question, and people began to shout back at her, 'Dame Edith, we cannot hear you.' Everyone was terribly polite in a way they wouldn't be today. The poet's response, when she eventually decided to understand the question, was a haughty admonishment: 'If you can't hear, why not invest in a hearing aid?' And she continued to read, this time a little more distinctly.

People kept coming into the stalls late, and staggered around in the semi-darkness searching for their seats. This was beginning, noticeably, to irritate her. After ten or fifteen minutes of disturbance (she was an artist, after all), she directed her hooded eyelids at some poor soul who was stealthily trying to scramble his way into his seat, and withdrew from somewhere within the folds of her voluminous garment a huge timepiece. 'Am I mistaken,' she intoned like a cantor, 'in having commenced this reading at 2.15? A large number of you seem to think it begins at 2.30. I apologise if *I've* misread the time.' Then she read on in her strangely remote and utterly condescending way.

I think it was the same year, but late at night, that four young men named Miller, Cook, Moore and Bennett made a bit of a splash, also at the Lyceum, in a show I didn't particularly approve of, *Beyond the Fringe*. That sort of undergraduate jollity (I, of course, had never been an undergraduate) was all very well *on* the Festival's unofficial and unruly Fringe, but there was no need to promote it to the official Festival, which should be concerned with *art*. Edinburgh, I fear, is a very earnest city in which to grow up; or perhaps my memory maligns the place and it was only I who, no doubt with buckets of self-consciousness, indulged myself in the importance of being earnest.

Looking now at the published text of *Beyond the Fringe*, I see that it must have been 1960 when it opened in Edinburgh. Michael Frayn, who provides an introduction to the text, begins: '*Beyond the Fringe* first fell upon London like a sweet, refreshing rain on the 10th May 1961.' In his subsequent four and a half pages he doesn't once mention that it started life in Edinburgh. Satirical justice then that on the dust wrapper, in heavy black type, his own name is spelt 'Michael Frayne'.

# III

Stratford-upon-Avon has always been very special to me. When I first paid homage at the shrine, in 1958, it was still a modest Midlands market town, where the world's greatest writer happened to have been born and brought up and died. The people seemed to have a self-absorbed serenity, to go about their lives aware of the fact of Shakespeare but not allowing it to influence them. Most emphatically, the citizens of Stratford weren't mute, inglorious Shakespeares. You did not, then, have to pay to view Shakespeare's monument and grave in the lovely fourteenth-century Holy Trinity Church with its confident spire. And the walk to Ann Hathaway's cottage at Shottery was still across fields.

I went for a week on my own to celebrate having sat, if not necessarily passed, my A-levels. The following year, the one-hundredth anniversary season, I went with my friend Charley Dodds. I had an introduction, through friends of my parents, to one of the leading actors in the company (still the Shakespeare *Memorial* Theatre, with the emphasis very much on reverence). This was Cyril Luckham, the sweetest and gentlest of men, whom I'd seen the previous year playing Polonius to Michael Redgrave's Hamlet (he told me that as Redgrave gave a different interpretation almost every performance the rest of the cast was constantly kept on its toes), Friar Laurence (who married Dorothy Tutin's joyous, squeaky teenager of a Juliet to Richard Johnson's saturnine and lithe Romeo), and Feste (in Peter Hall's ravishingly mature first *Twelfth Night* with Lila da Nobili's Watteauesque sets). I felt very famous, very reflected glory, having been invited to lunch in the garden of Hall's Croft with Cyril Luckham, and no doubt boasted of it incessantly to poor Charley Dodds.

Cyril, sitting under an apple tree, greeted me in a loud, actorly voice. I recall being somewhat embarrassed by the stentorian ring of it booming out for all to hear, and being vaguely aware of visitors to the Elizabethan mansion, which served as the Festival's club house, realising who Cyril was, and staring.

The one-hundredth season has gone down in the annals as probably one of the greatest. Paul Robeson played a dark-voiced, lyrical but underpowered Othello to Sam Wanamaker's Method Iago. Laurence Olivier was magnetic as a sullen, utterly aristocratic Coriolanus: his headlong, eighty-foot plunge to his death from the top of the set to within a millimetre, or so it appeared, of the stage boards, twisting and dangling upside down on a leather thong, was electrifying. Edith Evans played the Countess in *All's Well That Ends Well*, all nose and autumnal haughtiness. Peter Hall directed many of the best actors in the country in *A Midsummer Night's Dream*, and that legendary film star Charles Laughton had returned to England to essay King Lear (as well as Bully Bottom in the Dream). I can remember every detail of all five productions, including Cyril's transformation from playing Shakespeare's old bores to a vigorous and mustachioed Parolles in *All's Well*.

He had invited me for lunch at noon as there was a matinée that day. The matinée play was the *Dream*, in which Luckham played the benignly bossy Athenian amateur thespian Peter Quince. As we walked from Hall's Croft by the banks of the Avon, past the Black Swan (the actors' pub more familiarly and appropriately known as the Dirty Duck), Cyril asked me if I'd like to go on stage. *Would I like to go on stage, of the Shakespeare Memorial Theatre?* Was God in His heaven? Is the Earth round?

I followed him through the stage door, where he collected a letter or two and chatted with the doorman. We then wandered backstage, avoiding vast pieces of scenery: in those days, sets for all five of the season's productions were stored there, hanging and flying, and props all over the place. To me, it was the ultimate treasure trove, theatrical gold unimagined. Suddenly we were on the stage. As I write these words I can feel its rake, almost a magnetic pull projecting me towards the footlights. However the stage looked from the auditorium, the angle of the boards when you were treading them at Stratford then was incredible, not so much dangerous as impossible, I thought, wondering how any actor could move about and remain upright. A stage hand or two were finishing things off. The odd prop was put in position. A hammer banged nails. Spotlights were tested and briefly Cyril and I were lit up in a blaze of lights, then they dimmed. Around us, Lila da Nobili's opening set of Theseus' palace with its central staircase seemed a blur, out of focus, the brush strokes crude. There were voices about the place, details being finalised. I was awestruck.

Then I was vaguely aware of a large presence, like a mountain bear, a great, slow animal, human no doubt, on the tilt of the rake. He was vast, and wore what looked like a shiny cheap suit, but was probably silk and expensive. He seemed to spread, like ripe Brie, quite beyond the physical space he occupied, as he greeted Cyril with a cursory clipped but friendly word or two. 'Good morning, sir,' said Cyril. 'How are you?' He frowned, concernedly.

I was appearing on the same stage as Charles Laughton. *King Lear* had opened ten days or so earlier, the last production of the season. Laughton, that most experienced of actors, had been unable to sleep each night after he had played Lear, so affected was he by the role. Cyril knew this, and that Laughton had been to London to consult a Harley Street specialist. Laughton explained matter-of-factly, in that mincing, somewhat thin voice, that the specialist had given him pills to enable him to rest after going through the torments of Lear, but if they didn't work the production would have to be taken off, or his understudy would have to replace him. This, of course, was completely shocking, and as news sensational, although I was oblivious to that.

Charles Laughton looked as weary as William Blake's Ancient of Days, with his great flowing beard. (Or so I remember him: yet in photographs of him as Lear the beard is much longer than that which he wore as Bottom. I suspect I am grafting my memory of his performances on to that of my brief meeting with him, and that he was in fact clean-shaven.) He shambled back into the wings, waddling duck-like. Cyril smiled at me, understanding the thrill I had experienced.

Although Charley Dodds (whatever happened to Charley

Dodds, I wonder?) and I had seats to see the *Dream* later in the week, I managed to secure – for, was it sixpence? – a standing position at the back of the stalls for the matinée in half an hour. The young lovers included Vanessa Redgrave and Albert Finney, the monarchs of fairyland were Mary Ure and Robert Hardy (there was none of the later, cost-saving doubling of Oberon and Titania with Theseus and Hippolyta). Ian Holm was Puck and others in modest parts included Julian Glover, Roy Dotrice, Peter Woodthorpe, Zoe Caldwell, Michael Blakemore and Diana Rigg. They don't cast Shakespeare like that a generation on. No wonder it rarely rings and sings as it did in those golden years, the end of Glen Byam Shaw's era as director of the Memorial Theatre, the beginning of Peter Hall's vision of the RSC.

In the first mechanicals scene, Cyril was benign and gentle and well-spoken as Quince, but how would Laughton manage Bottom? No understudy had been announced, and yet, and yet . . . I knew what no one else in the audience did.

Suddenly, as I was having these thoughts, an actor burst on to the stage, every inch the young Bully Bottom. I have seen many actors play Bottom (and this was the only one whose face was entirely uncovered, his later ass's head only ears), but to this day I haven't witnessed a more youthful, energetic, lively, seemingly spontaneous, eager one, desperate to please. He cannot, that afternoon, have been a day older than seventeen. The 'translation' was absolute. I didn't need to look at my programme to see that Laughton was playing him.

The critics disliked Laughton's Lear, with few exceptions (one, surprisingly, being Milton Shulman: 'A brilliant Lear – by any test'). Dressed at first in a vast green smock or dress as if he were a female blues singer, he was to me a druid monarch whose terrible weariness emanated from the responsibilities of kingship, the journey of a thrust-upon living soul. Later, in white, cradling his dead daughter, he was like a giant blubbery baby, the natural order of birth and death reversed. His death was heart-breaking. Even Paul Scofield's great, grizzled, leather-clad Beckett-begotten Lear at Stratford a few years later did not dislodge from my mind Laughton's cruelly destroyed innocence. But what a play. Of all of them, it is surely the most difficult to come to terms with.

22

As the Stratford season meandered on towards winter, Laughton looked heavier and heavier, an actor who was with the company later told me. His capacious suit seemed almost literally weighed down; and so it was. It was only at the end of the season that eight months of pay packets were found in the pockets of Laughton's jacket, all unopened. The Stratford salary was to him just so much loose change.

# IV

I link together two of the *grandes dames* of post-Second World
War literary London, Elizabeth Smart and Sonia Orwell, no doubt
because soon after I arrived in the English capital in 1962 I was
introduced to them in turn by the glorious Anne Graham Bell,
who was publicity manager at Secker & Warburg and my boss,
my title (or tittle) being advertising manager.

Anne was first married to Graham Bell, the Euston Road School
painter, who was himself a descendant of Alexander Graham Bell,
the Scotsman who invented the telephone and whose dubious
achievement is commemorated by a plaque upstairs in Bianchi's
restaurant in Soho's Frith Street, in whose premises the momen-
tous invention took place, though not, I suspect, over lunch.
Anne's second husband, from whom she is divorced, was Gerald
Reitlinger, the historian of cultural and artistic values. 'My husband is a horrible man,' she once confided noisily to me.

Anne Graham Bell was both brilliant and eccentric at publicity.
Like all the best publicists in publishing, she had an understanding
of the *angst* of authors, the hang-ups of each, without necessarily
reading their books deeply. I remember once being in her tiny
office in Carlisle Street (almost directly opposite where *Private
Eye* is now) when she telephoned Hunter Davies, the then influential gossip columnist 'Atticus' on the *Sunday Times*, a mention
in whose column sold books the way an author's appearance on
*Wogan* or some such ghastly chat show today does not. 'Hunter,
I've something to tell you,' she began, in her booming, emphatic
voice. Her arms and hands flapped and waved about a great deal
when she was on the telephone, as if to emphasise her words. She
then asked the gossip columnist how he was. Clearly he was
busy, a deadline approaching perhaps, or lunch, because after ten

minutes or so he gently asked her what she'd rung him about. There was a pause, and Anne's eyes filmed madly over. 'Hunter, I've forgotten.' Then a sweep of an arm. 'I'll ring you back. Goodbye.' Somehow Anne managed to give the impression that the two syllables of 'goodbye' were one, and she didn't do it by losing the first. To this day, in the era of bimbo and yuppie publicists, when two older authors gather together and find they were published by Secker & Warburg, they reminisce about Anne Graham Bell, now living in Richmond, Surrey, with a lascivious poodle.

I first met Elizabeth Smart, the mother of four of George Barker's extended family of children, in Gaston's, the French Pub in Dean Street, not to be confused with Gaston's of Chancery Lane, who bought review copies and kept many otherwise impoverished writers in readies. I had to be told that her slightly drawly, soft accent – which evoked Irish whiskey – was Canadian. I'd taken it for Devonian or French. She was a lovely serene person, always smiling, making you feel you were the only person who mattered, interested in everyone, and never ceasing to marvel at the possibilities of humanity. It was hard to accept that this apparently daffy lady had written that exotic verbal fruitcake (which I have to admit is not to my taste, being too celebratory of the senses rather than the sense) *By Grand Central Station I Sat Down and Wept* (1945), reissued in 1966 with a triumphant foreword by Brigid Brophy. But the moment you try to relate the mere mortal, a writer met in the flesh, to the *œuvre*, or one particular book or even poem, you are usually in trouble, confronted with schizophrenia. I also see Elizabeth Smart (I never knew her well enough to call her 'Liz'), in the French Pub with a cigarette in one hand, smoke drooling everywhere, a glass of Pernod in the other. It was also in the French that I met the painters Colquhoun and McBride, or perhaps it was only one of the Roberts. No, I believe it was both, unless I was seeing double. Certainly he, or they, had a strong working-class Glasgow accent, which rather shocked me, coming as I did from middle-class Edinburgh. Those forty miles, between Scotland's two great cities, divide a world; and I should know, as my second wife, Maggie McKernan, hails from Glasgow.

Also in the French I met Frank Norman, then at the height of his fame after Joan Littlewood, theatreland's baglady of genius, took the blueprint of his *Fings Ain't Wot They Used T'be* and transmuted it in Stratford, E17, into iron pyrites. Norman, caricatured in *Private Eye* as Fred Normal, was a rather alarming man, with bulging eyes and an angry slash down his face, presumably the legacy of some criminal encounter. He was writing the words for a book on Soho for Secker & Warburg with moody, grainy photographs by a sullen young friend and protégé, Jeffrey Bernard, son of the architect Oliver Bernard and the opera singer Fedora Roselli. Bernard looked as if he'd never seen a stage set, let alone a drawing-room, in his peripatetic life. I remember thinking how good-looking he was, in a Brylcreem and leather-jacketed way and how properly spoken – BBC rules – compared with Cockney 'Fred Normal'. Frank invariably addressed you as if you were completely deaf, stabbing his face into yours for emphasis. (Was he the first person to base his conversation around the imperative 'Know wo' a mean?' which has, like 'Cheers' and 'Take care', become so louchely commonplace?) He was a warm-hearted, likeable man of whom I was surprisingly fond. He was generous too, and trusting, and I do not think I shall look upon his like again in our sour, post-Thatcher society.

Then there was David Wright, the tall and stocky deaf Yorkshire poet. At a poetry reading given a few years ago by my friend and client Dannie Abse, Wright's deaf aid started to clatter out urgent words, obliterating Dannie's reading for those of us situated, for modesty's sake, at the back of the Poetry Society's room in Earl's Court Square. But it may have been Wright saying the poems out loud, by way of endorsement or concentration, after Abse, or reciting Milton as an alternative, or even a poem or two of his own. Among the audience bribed by the Poetry Society's vile wine, this led to confusion and hysterics. I sincerely hope Dr Abse didn't think I was laughing at him; I saw him looking at me once or twice and I had to try to straighten my contorted features immediately.

I have always had problems controlling my laughter, always seeing the funny side of things, sunny side over, when it is there to be seen, and sometimes when it isn't to other people. Occasionally, if you are that way inclined, tears are taken for laughter, as at funerals or memorial services (I missed Robert Maxwell's). This, I'm afraid, goes back to childhood when my parents took us children to Sunday service at the High Kirk of Edinburgh, St Giles' Cathedral, and I used to while away the achingly dull time by laughing at ladies' hats and people dressed up in their Sunday best, with faces like Daumier caricatures, and getting my younger brother and sister and particularly my poor mother into trouble by making them laugh too. My father, as well as being the architect to the fabric of St Giles', was an elder of the Church and was, after boiled egg for breakfast and before roast beef for lunch, conspicuous in his striped trousers and tails each Sunday, although, unlike the lawyers who were elders, he declined to purchase a top hat (the accountants donned bowlers, the born-again turf accountants cloth caps).

I continue, as I begin the plod to my second half-century, to find funerals and memorial services both funny *and* touching, which can lead fellow mourners (or celebrators, depending on their feelings about the deceased) into thinking that I'm not being sufficiently respectful, or had one too many at the wake. I remember sitting behind the rolling fat neck of a revolting-looking creature, male, at Cecil Day Lewis's memorial service at St Martin-in-the-Fields in 1972. His hair, such as it was, all greasy and too long, like a rat's tail, covered the top of his neck and oozed out on to his collar. When he moved his head slightly I could see that his skin was sallow, as if he were constructed of tallow candle and candle grease. When he twisted his head further round, to search the pews and identify who was present, I recognised the bulbous saggy face of Cyril Connolly, author of two books – *Enemies of Promise* and *The Unquiet Grave* – which had thrilled me as I aspired to Pooterish heights still unknown. The books were not remotely diminished by my recognition of the guttering Connolly, unpleasant though he was to behold. I think as they grow older people attend memorial services to see who's still up and about. Did Connolly think, as his eyes searchlighted the congregation: Good God, I'm likely to be next. Will this lot all be there?

In the Nellie Dean, the pub on the corner of Dean and Carlisle Streets, Anne Graham Bell introduced me, or tried to do so, but the lady wasn't much interested, to Sonia Orwell – *née* Brownell

27

– who, virtually on his deathbed, married Eric Blair, toothbrush-mustachioed ex-Burmese policeman who wrote as George Orwell. The pub seemed empty except for the rugby scrum at the fireplace where everyone crowded round Mrs Blair, or Mrs Orwell as she preferred to be known. I didn't remotely take to her. She was like a screen goddess who had come out without her false eyelashes and was offended at not being recognised. She'd met Orwell when working as Cyril Connolly's secretary on *Horizon*, a proper literary groupie before the term was known. I've always – what else do I have to go on? – trusted my instincts with people, and the litmus paper came up blue with her. She was alkaline, a phoney. It wasn't, I insist, because she was less than interested in me when Anne Graham Bell tried to introduce us ('Sonia, I want you to meet a brilliant young man from Scotland'), but she might have made the minimum of effort to be polite. Anne was her friend, or at least the publicist of her late husband's publishers, and no doubt she made the most of the royalties. Fred Warburg, as literary history records, snapped up *Animal Farm* when Victor Gollancz had rejected it as not being sufficiently friendly to Comrade Stalin, and T. S. Eliot at Faber and Faber had ducked out too, not surprisingly given his political circumspection. But people sniffed around Sonia Orwell as though she were a fragment of the true Old Etonian socialist cross. She smoked incessantly, and her body odour was redolent of nicotine along with alcohol. She wore a fur coat, perhaps to protect the Orwell estate. She had a voice like an elderly actress who had, when nineteen, played Lady Anne in *Richard III*, since when she'd had far too much, and yet too little, of everything. I've never been good with literary hangers-on and she was one with a vengeance, indeed all vengeance.

In 1962, Warburg sent me a proof ('Dear Gordon – You might like to read this before you join us') of Günter Grass's *The Tin Drum* after he'd telegraphed to say, subsequent to my interview with him, that he was going to provide me with employment. It was the first proof copy of a novel I'd seen and I regarded it as something miraculous: a printing of a book, wrapped in plain green paper covers, before the proper first printing. It was, of course, only the English, or rather American, translation, by the late Ralph Manheim, but in the subsequent three decades I haven't read a more tremendous novel. So excited was I by it that, when I started work at Secker & Warburg, I persuaded Fred (said to be taken on a dark night for Humphrey Bogart) that we should use Grass's jacket design of Oskar Matzerath beating his drum (a phallus, in a manner of speaking, clutched in each paw) as Secker's device or colophon – it did not, surprisingly, have one – to be used in advertisements, catalogues and on all publicity material. It was the hallmark of Secker & Warburg for some years.

Günter Grass was a charming man of thirty-five. All he wanted in London, I recall, was a raincoat, as he thought he'd obtain a better one here than in Germany (though I see from the blurb that he lived in Paris at the time), and the indefatigable Anne Graham Bell went with him one Saturday morning to buy it. (And here is where the past dangerously blurs, great writers merge. The following year Secker published Donald Keene's translation, this time from the Japanese, of thirty-eight-year-old Yukio Mishima's novel *After the Banquet*, with a jacket designed by Margaret Eastoe, soon to be my wife. It was Mishima who came to London for a raincoat, not being able to purchase one to his fancy in Tokyo where he lived. Seven years later Mishima disembowelled himself and then had his head chopped off. What happened to the raincoat is not recorded.)

I wish I'd asked poor, tragic, mad Mishima to sign my copy of *After the Banquet* but I didn't. I treasure my copy of *The Tin Drum* which Grass inscribed to me and dated. (Although when I mentioned my proud ownership to him at the Frankfurt Book Fair, thirty years on, in 1992, his only, gruff comment was 'So?' In the early sixties German writers smiled more at Brits than perhaps they do now.) It makes a nice Germanic pair with the copy of *Dr Faustus*, in its American translation, which Thomas Mann inscribed to his British publisher, Roger Senhouse, in 1949. At the end of the novel, there is an 'Author's Note', which suggests there was a wrangle over publication involving Messrs Sue, Grabbit & Runne, or some equally competent firm of lawyers.

It does not seem supererogatory to inform the reader that the form of musical composition delineated in Chapter XXII, known as the twelve-tone or row system, is in truth the intellectual property [is this the first time that invaluable phrase has been used?] of a contemporary composer and theoretician, Arnold Schoenberg. I have transferred this technique in a certain ideational context to the fictitious figure of a musician, the tragic hero of my novel. In fact, the passages of this book that deal with musical theory are indebted in numerous details to Schoenberg's *Harmonielehre*.

Roger Senhouse has written in his neat pencil hand above this note: 'Schoenberg insisted on being named as the true author, jealously reclaiming his property from the Devil himself.' Anyone who knows this great twentieth-century novel will be delighted by Senhouse's remark. Below the note he has written, 'I never asked TM whether he knew – or even knew of – Ludwig Wittgenstein (sic)', followed by his initials and the date.

The house of books, it has to be said, is a small world. I bought Roger Senhouse's copy of *Dr Faustus* for £35, a substantial sum at the time, from bookseller George F. Sims, whose thrillers I was to publish at Gollancz. George Sims had bought much of Martin Secker's library, and it was Secker whom Warburg and Senhouse bought out in 1936, when Senhouse provided the money to establish Secker & Warburg, which should really have been called Secker, Warburg & Senhouse. The last, I take it, lacked the ego necessary for his name to appear above the credits.

Roger Senhouse was the first publisher I met, in 1957, at a party given by Robert Ponsonby, the director of the Edinburgh Festival, in a handsome Georgian house in Ann Street, one of the city's most desirable streets. I recall that there was a large stain on the wall in the main room in which the party was held, and that Senhouse, a tall, bald and slightly doddery individual who invariably had stains on his crumpled clothes, wore a white linen jacket, the month being August. People in Edinburgh then wouldn't have dreamed of going to a lunchtime buffet wearing anything other than a staid suit. I don't imagine that the state of Senhouse's clothes concerned him at all. He was above, or below, such petty matters. By the time I arrived at Secker & Warburg in 1962, he'd become utterly eccentric, if he wasn't always, and he and Warburg had ceased to communicate. Roger worked away at his translations of Colette, and that was about it. A few weeks after I started, he departed, but until then he was delightful to me.

The last time I saw him was when he, Anne Graham Bell and I shared a taxi to go to some Secker launch party. The taxi was becalmed in Oxford Street. I turned to say something to Roger but, abstractedly, he'd slipped out without a word to either of us, disappearing into the crowd. When he died in 1970 a hoard of valuable French Impressionist paintings was found under his bed; he hadn't the wall space to hang them. And there were thousands of books, all marked in his fastidious hand in pencil, which continued to enliven booksellers' catalogues for years. You can still pluck a book down from a bookshelf and find it was one of Roger's, annotated with his script and usually initialled RGS or RS on the flyleaf.

You rarely find genuine bargains on booksellers' shelves these days, but I found one in the late seventies when for a fiver I picked up at a book fair a copy of John Collier's lovely edition of one of my favourite books, *The Scandals and Credulities of John Aubrey*, illustrated with trenchant wood engravings by Helen Knapp. The edition, published by Peter Davies in 1931, is not particularly rare but it is handsome. Why, to me, this copy was such a find was because on the inside cover it bears Roger Senhouse's book label (which I take to be smaller than a book plate). But even better than that, on the flyleaf, in neat ink, is the signature of Lytton Strachey. Infuriatingly, someone, probably the anonymous book dealer from whom I acquired the copy, has rubbed out Senhouse's lengthy pencil remarks below Strachey's autograph. I thought Michael Holroyd, who published the first volume of his monumental biography of Strachey in 1967 (brief lives are not Michael's forte), might have something interesting to say about my book: 'Strachey left part of his library to Roger Senhouse in his will. So you have got something that was at the Mill House Tidmarsh and at Ham Spray House, and that Strachey used when writing his essay on John Aubrey for *The Nation and Athenaeum* (15 September 1923). There's scholarship for you.'

Collier's edition is a small but enticing selection from Aubrey's *Brief Lives*. Later, in 1982, my client the genial, courteous and scholarly Alan Watkins was to write a book entitled *Brief Lives*, biographies somewhat in the Aubrey manner of individuals he'd known, all referred to in the past tense, which seemed to annoy some of those still alive, although they should have had the nous to realise that they were, in a manner of speaking, being written into history.

When I met Roger Senhouse at that party in Edinburgh, I was introduced to him by Jonathan Griffin, whom I'd met only a day or two before, and who in a way made me realise that I was desperate to work in publishing, or with authors (I didn't then know that there was such a 10 per cent being as a literary agent), and as a writer.

The first author I edited was Richard Chopping, better known as a meticulous illustrator and painter of plants, very much in the John Nash manner, and designer and illustrator of the *trompe l'oeil* dust jackets for Jonathan Cape's hardback editions of Ian Fleming's James Bond novels. Chopping, who taught plant drawing at the Royal College of Art, lived with a painter named Dennis Wirth-Miller. His constant reports of the relationship made it sound like the kitchen scene, with dough and utensils flying, in pantomime. Indeed, Dickie Chopping resembled a pantomime dame in more ways than one, and relished playing such parts in Royal College of Art end-of-term or Christmas shows. He was a friend (part of the East Anglian mafia) of Angus Wilson and Francis Bacon, and it was Wilson who urged the manuscript of Chopping's first novel, *The Fly*, on his editor, David Farrer, at Secker & Warburg. Farrer, with cigarette ash bespattering his brown and comfortably lived in suit, wandered into my office one Friday afternoon and asked if I'd give the manuscript a read over the weekend. 'It's a perfectly disgusting concoction by a friend of Angus's,' he chortled, obviously not trying to influence my judgement. Dear David, who was something of a moral coward in these matters, probably wanted to be able to say to Wilson that even the younger generation was repulsed by the book.

I was determined to like the novel. This, clearly, was my opportunity to nail my editorial credentials or aspirations upon the masthead. If I made a success of it, I was confident that more, and no doubt better, books would follow. *The Fly* was indeed disgusting, with much about used condoms and dirty underwear. Chopping, a most fastidious person with flaring nostrils and an apparently hairless body, was revolted by the detritus, the muckiness of everyday life, hence presumably his preference for plants. *The Fly*, I thought, was sufficiently sordid to appeal to voyeurs, and if Chopping were to adorn it with one of his famous dust jackets it could be a *succès de scandale*; and so it proved.

I decided, with the arrogance and ignorance of youth, that I needed a weekend with the author in which to edit the book. The weekend I chose, with a typical lack of sensitivity, was the first after my wife and I returned from our honeymoon in 1964. There was only one bed in our two-room flat in Belsize Park Gardens, and I cannot recall where Chopping slept. He brought with him a crate of champagne, something utterly exotic in our young and love-struck lives, and as a result probably very little editing was achieved. Chaos was compounded by Chopping rushing out every few hours to telephone Wivenhoe where poor Dennis was apparently suffering from a cold. In a sense my first marriage, which lasted for nearly a quarter of a century, didn't ever quite recover from this first peculiar weekend at home *à trois*. Chopping's second novel, and mercifully the last to be published, *The Ring*, albeit embellished with a revoltingly clever cover, was a much more mundane affair than *The Fly* and sank with very little trace, even in the second-hand bookshops.

The bed in the Belsize Park flat was so big, or the flat so small, that life seemed to revolve round it. I can remember the young and angelic-looking Heathcote Williams, in those days a superb writer (*The Speakers*), before he discovered elephants and whales and poetry and the planet, smashing a whisky bottle into the interstices of the bed, between the mattress and the metal structure. We were still removing shards of glass months later.

The same year, when we were on holiday, we lent the flat for a week or two to the mesmerising Canadian poet David Wevill, and his wife Assia. We had arranged to meet the Wevills at the flat on our return, but by the time we returned they had departed. They must surely have left in a hurry, for the sheets they had used were still on the bed and a hole had been burnt, almost definitely by a cigarette, in one of them. Assia was a rather tight-lipped blonde who, centuries before, would undoubtedly have been suspected of being a witch. Later she left Wevill (who, I believe, went back to Canada) to spend some time with Ted Hughes and, in the horrific footsteps of Sylvia Plath, eventually committed suicide.

# V

I have always enjoyed doing journalism. There are considerable satisfactions in seeing your words, or more usually approximations of these, in print as soon as you have written them, and being paid more or less on the nail and, at least theoretically, being read by legions of readers. I was particularly pleased with a series of ten interviews I conducted with women writers which appeared on successive Saturdays in the *Scotsman* in 1965. They included Edna O'Brien, Nell Dunn, Margaret Drabble, Brigid Brophy, Ann Quin, Penelope Mortimer and Stevie Smith.

In *Ivy and Stevie*, her book of conversations with Ivy Compton-Burnett and Stevie Smith, Kay Dick writes of the poet: 'Like Ivy she had not much good to say about formal newspaper interviews, and approved only two short ones – one by Giles Gordon in the *Scotsman* (April 24th, 1965), the other by a poet she much admired, John Horder, in the *Guardian* (7 June 1965).' This, to say the least, is disingenuous.

When I wrote enquiring of Stevie Smith – whose quirky poems and particularly her zany readings of them amused me – if she would allow me to interview her, she replied: 'I should be only too happy to oblige, provided I could see proofs. I have had to make a rule of this as I have had the experience of being badly misquoted and though I am sure that would not happen with you, you can imagine one feels nervous.'

She asked me to suggest a venue in central London (she famously lived in the northern suburb of Palmers Green, with her 'lion' aunt). I suggested Bertorelli's in Charlotte Street, which I thought would have the right atmosphere. She responded: 'May I suggest Brown's Hotel, Albermarle Street, instead of Bertorelli's? It is much easier for me to get at and much more peaceful for interviewing! If you will book a table, I will join you there about one o'clock, or meet you in the lounge just before one.'

To be honest, I can barely remember the lunch, but only that Stevie Smith was scarifying in a minor way, quite severe and hermetic. I was, though, rather pleased with my interview, over which I took great trouble. When sending her the typescript, I apparently invited her to make any alterations she wanted. This was but a courtesy and I hadn't expected her to do anything but dot an i and cross a t, if that.

The interview came winging, or whingeing, back. Her typescript, not mine, and on the thinnest of copy paper. 'I'm afraid I've taken you at your word and made some suggestions. Do hope you don't mind and can stick them in without too much bother . . . I'm afraid where I have actually altered your comment (as about not seeing the disturbing laughter in the sad poems), and the edgy sphinx and the fox bit, you may think I have gone Too Far. But the trouble with my ghastly face (as is but too obvious on television) is that it is really too un-sphinx-like, positively grimacious, hence the word "edgy" I have put in.'

I rewrote the interview, in accordance with Stevie's changes (we remained 'Miss Smith' and 'Mr Gordon'), and, feeling humiliated, incompetent and frustrated, sent her the new version. I had told my friend the poet John Horder, who then as now was forever scrabbling about in search of literary journalism to pay the rent, that I was 'doing' Stevie Smith for the *Scotsman*, and he thought he'd do her for the *Guardian*. She replied to me: 'Many thanks for sending me the typescript, with the alterations I suggested, so kindly-like embodied therein. John H came to interview me yesterday and now I feel rather worn out. I only hope the two interviews won't be too much alike, but it is difficult to say different things and still stick to the truth. However, he wanted much more personal stuff, not calculated to make the interviewee feel easier, especially after the interviewer has left and one remembers how much one has said one shouldn't have. I think I shall now write up an entirely fictitious biog, full of relatives one never had, and places one never lived in, and use that in future. Like Lemprière on Helen . . . "The circumstances of her birth were peculiar; she was born from an egg".'

And that was that. The reason she approved of Horder's and my interviews was, presumably, because we were the only interviewers whose work she rewrote. As Horder opined later, and rather grandly, in the *Listener*: 'I have refrained up till now from commenting on Glenda Jackson's performance in the play and film, *Stevie*. Suffice to say, the Stevie I knew never lost contact with her child-self till the day she died. Who else but an adult, tyrannised by the omnipotent child, would have dared to have completely rewritten my interview with her for the *Guardian* and Giles Gordon's for the *Scotsman*, and got away with it?'

Stevie Smith was completely crazy, I think; so batty and subversive that she came through to sanity; a female Spike Milligan, but more disciplined and certainly more talented, and a heartaching and true poet. Her verse, like Blake's, like Lear's, will last, as will her stunning 1936 *Novel on Yellow Paper*.

The literary editor of the *Scotsman* who hired me to write a weekly letter from London under the pseudonym 'Boswell', was William Watson, later to write a play (*Sawney Bean*), in collaboration with Robert Nye, and a number of intelligent novels, some under his own name, some pseudonymous. By the time I delivered the typescript of my last interview, with the biographer and historian Lady Longford, Watson had departed and been replaced by Christopher MacLehose, a son of the manse, whose previous job was as a sub-editor and football reporter on the *Glasgow Herald*. MacLehose has an extraordinary voice like crystal permanently muffled by a velvet cushion. You have to interpret what he says rather than try to comprehend the vowel sounds. His wife, Koukla, also speaks a curious English, but she is French. It is not surprising that they converse in French at home. Anyway, in 1965, and out of the blue, the new literary editor of the *Scotsman* telephoned to say that the interview with Elizabeth Longford wouldn't do because nobody would be interested in reading about her. He was not impressed when I pointed out that her biography of Queen Victoria had made some waves. To MacLehose in those days, Burroughs and Mailer and Genet and Beckett were where it was at. He then made it clear that as the new literary editor he wouldn't be requiring my services in London.

He went on to become just about London's best literary publisher, and for some years has run HarperCollins' Harvill Press with inspiration and distinction. In person he is tall and gangly, closely resembling a slightly bashed about question mark, and used to smoke a reeking pipe. His voice, though, is his most marked characteristic, and should be preserved in aspic for future generations to marvel at. In his headier youth, MacLehose rushed around London in a Land-Rover and spent much of his free time parachuting with the Territorial Army. One evening at about ten o'clock our telephone rang and the unmistakeable voice of MacLehose asked to speak to Sir Michael Levey, then director of the National Gallery. I replied, without revealing my identity, that he must have the wrong number. 'But that *is* the National Gallery, isn't it?' he half enquired, half insisted. I then came clean, and told Christopher that, for reasons best known to himself, he'd rung my home number, to which his response was: 'That explains why I can never get a reply from the National Gallery.' Clearly it explained nothing of the sort, and why he thought the National Gallery would be open to callers at that hour of the evening, and that Sir Michael Levey would be in his office, and why he'd dialled my home number are also, in a MacLehosian way, inexplicable.

Once we invited MacLehose to dinner. He was over an hour late (he always has problems with the time) and when he arrived the meal was well advanced. He sat down briefly next to the literary agent Lois Wallace, our American guest of honour, who had asked for him to be invited. He nibbled at something or other, then stood up, presumably bored, and began washing the dishes which the rest of us had already used. He is, all in all, an eccentric in the first league, particularly difficult to interpret because the verbal semaphore he indulges in bears so remote a resemblance to speech as commonly understood. It will be intriguing to observe how Koukla's and Christopher's children speak.

# VI

When I moved from the literary excellence of Secker & Warburg to the middle-brow mediocrity of Hutchinson, because I was determined to become an editor and had been offered a job there, almost the first author I met and had to 'edit' was Dennis Wheatley, whose reputation and sales in 1965 were, I suppose, something akin to those of Jeffrey Archer today. I'm afraid I had nothing but contempt for his supernatural and historical ravings, or so I thought of them, perhaps because I hadn't taken the trouble to read more than a very few paragraphs. *The Haunting of Toby Jugg*, the title of one of Wheatley's best-known novels, seemed to sum up the ludicrousness of his *œuvre*. Hutchinson was one of those publishing houses – much rarer then than now – in which editors were not supposed to 'waste their time' reading manuscripts until they'd been vouched for by outside readers.

Hutchinson's chief reader was a wonderful old bookman named Frank Morley, younger brother of the then well-known writer Christopher Morley. An American, he came to Britain as manager of the London office of a New York publisher and was eventually lured to the fledgling firm of Faber and Gwyer before it became Faber and Faber. 'Had I had £100 in 1929,' Morley told me, 'it would have been Faber and Morley.' There was a long pause. Morley was given to long pauses. 'Do you know who the second Faber was?' I shook my head. 'There never was one.' Morley shared an office with T. S. Eliot, and wrote the blurbs for the great writer's books. He was the most gentle and discriminating of publishers' readers, and usually tried to temper my excessive enthusiasm for a manuscript by asking how I thought it stood up in comparison with . . . and he would name a famous novel, a work of literature which invariably I hadn't read. Actually, it's well nigh fatal for publishers to make such comparisons. Posterity must decide.

Frank teased me quite a bit, and would take me out at 11.30 a.m. on the day of the week he came up to London from Jordans, the Quaker village where he lived, to have a sustaining glass at the Green Man public house at the top of Great Portland Street, where Hutchinson's hideous premises were.

Hutchinson at that time had an imprint called New Authors Limited, which existed to publish first novels. (It was, surely, historically doomed to failure as it only published first books. The idea was that the author, for his or her second successful trick, would move to Hutchinson.) I published four writers under the imprint, three of whom made quite a splash. One manuscript I examined with particular care because it had come all the way from Greece, and after leafing through the typescript and being sure it was literate I gave it to Frank. 'You've got something here,' he said of *The Partnership* by Barry Unsworth, when he brought the manuscript back seven days later. And so it proved. Unsworth's first novel, about two homosexuals making plaster gnomes in a cottage in Cornwall, was the first of ten remarkable novels by one of the most honest and craftsmanlike writers I've known. When I left Hutchinson, Unsworth followed me to Gollancz, and when I became an agent he signed up with me. We nearly parted company over his ninth novel, *Sugar and Rum*; one of the potential difficulties in the relationship between agent (or publisher) and author is that if the agent (or publisher) doesn't take to a book, doesn't think it works, the author who has just completed it (and, almost inevitably, believes it's the best thing he's written) is bound to be unamused by the carping, superior criticism. But with his tenth, *Sacred Hunger*, Barry wrote one of the finest, most readable and all-encompassing novels written this half-century. Unsworth is the ultimate professional novelist. His whole adult life has been dedicated to ensuring that the quality of his books is as fine as it can be. For many years he and his family, when his three daughters were growing up, led an itinerant life, Barry teaching English for a living in Greece, Turkey and elsewhere. His novels should all last (except for *Sugar and Rum*!) and in *Sacred Hunger*, a novel about slavery and Liverpool mercantilism in the nineteenth century, he has written his masterpiece, which advertently or inadvertently provides sardonic criticism of Thatcherism. In 1992 it won Barry 50 per cent of the Booker Prize whereas it ought to have won him 99 per cent.

The second New Author I published was an unpleasant, ambitious and talented young man named Edward Lewis, who looked like a cross between an anaemic pig and the actor Hywel Bennett. He was northern working class and proud of it, and for this reason I persuaded him to change his Christian name on the title page to the name he was called by his friends, Ted. *All the Way Home and All the Night Through*, the Hemingway echo being intentional, was a tender account of a northern love-affair, lyrically written. Ted Lewis was to become much better known for writing *Get Carter*, but success did for him.

The managing director of Hutchinson, Robert Lusty, was a comedown after Fred Warburg. He was a publisher less by instinct and 'flair' than by slide-rule and balance sheet. I had to plead ridiculously to be allowed to publish 'my' third New Author title, Archie Hind's *The Dear Green Place*, one of the steeliest of novels about Glasgow. I'd spent years (long before I went to Hutchinson) nagging at Hind, in those days an inarticulate Glaswegian of little hope and education but with a Dostoevskian drive, to complete his rich if inchoate manuscript. The sentences needed thinning, chopping up like worms, and punctuating, but it was, I felt sure, the authentic article. Even Frank Morley failed to see what was remarkable about it, and so of course did the more superficial English readers. It was unintelligible to them. Lusty said: 'If Mr Cowan can sell 2,000 copies, then you may publish it.' Bob Cowan, Hutchinson's Scottish representative, was down in London for a sales conference. That night I took him out to the Green Man and plied him with whisky. By the end of the evening he readily agreed that he could sell 2,000 copies. *The Dear Green Place* went on to win both the *Guardian* and the *Yorkshire Post* novel of the year awards.

I would not have insulted Morley by giving him Wheatley's latest manuscript to read. Hutchinson's bestselling novelist came in one morning to deliver it, and insisted upon handing it over to me in person. I do not know whether it ever dawned on Wheatley that the reason he changed editors so frequently was that the junior editor at Hutchinson was always assigned the responsibility of processing his work, and as soon as the most junior editor was promoted (there was quite a turnover, the firm employing more editors or 'book processors' than most), he or she could pass Wheatley down the line to his or her successor. I remember that Wheatley wore a raincoat, of the kind labelled 'dirty', and his surprisingly black hair (it was probably dyed) was slicked back with Brylcreem. I think it was parted down the middle, always a give-away as to lack of liberal stance and even, in my experience, latent fascism in the wearer. He didn't smile or indulge in small talk. The meeting must have lasted less than a minute. I staggered hysterically back to my office with a huge pile of typescript. It was said that each of Wheatley's novels was longer than the previous one, but this may have been because as he grew older he used, or his secretary did, a larger and larger typeface. The novel I took delivery of (I cannot recall the title, if I ever noticed it) had type such as is used in large-print books for those with failing eyesight. There appeared to be but a hundred or so words on the page, and many, many hundreds of pages.

In traditional Hutchinson manner, I prepared to send it to a reader, selecting one Jan Siegler, the most acerbic and intolerant. I thought it would be instructive (and amusing) to send her the typescript without revealing the identity of the author. Thus I removed the title page before sending it to her. I waited impatiently for the report. Eventually it came in. 'This author can tell a decent, if irretrievably old-fashioned story, and his (it must be a he) plotting is sound. The book is terribly hackneyed, and it is hard to imagine that it would appeal to readers today. Above all, he cannot write. Regretfully decline,' was Mrs Siegler's verdict.

I was more pleased with myself than I can say about this, and requested a meeting with Lusty (you didn't just walk into the great panjandrum's office). Why I thought it would do me any good to show him a report which said that he who was then Hutchinson's bestselling author (Harold Harris was to pick up Frederick Forsyth a few years later) couldn't write I have no idea, but as an ever so serious young editor I resented having to soil my brain cells with the likes of Wheatley, and now he was exposed.

Literature and integrity would triumph. Lusty, of course, went spare. He had a curiously strangulated voice at the best of times – the one-time *Kent Messenger*-boy trying to rise to the ranks of the country's rulers – which made it difficult for him to speak loudly, let alone shout. This may, in fairness, have been at least in part due to his deafness. Nevertheless, when he realised what I had done he went red in the face and shrieked at me: 'Mr Wheatley's books are not to be read; they're sent straight to the printer.' He sat there, behind his vast desk, conspicuous as always by its lack of paper, manuscripts, books. 'What other manuscripts have you elected to send to readers, Mr Gordon?' he asked, terrified of the answer. I confessed there was no one he would have heard of, since they hadn't previously been published by Hutchinson. Somehow in spite of my best efforts Dennis Wheatley's career continued to prosper.

There is, in a manner of speaking, a coda to my Hutchinson experience, or inexperience, with Wheatley. When I began seriously to collect books, I tried to acquire – in a fairly haphazard, arbitrary way – English novels which employed the aesthetics of the book as object, the look of the page, to enhance and embellish the 'literary' content. I was initially reminded of this with B. S. Johnson's first novel, *Travelling People*, which used one or two of the typographical devices employed by the Reverend Laurence Sterne of Coxwold in his uniquely original novel, *Tristram Shandy*, a first edition of which I bought at Sotheby's, this copy having belonged to Auberon Waugh's uncle, Auberon Herbert, and bearing his book plates. (I use the plural as the book is in twelve volumes.)

At a book fair, a year or two after I had left Hutchinson and moved to Penguin, I came upon a curious paper-covered printed dossier, tied together with red ribbon. The front cover reads like a tabloid newspaper, and the type is almost as large:

DENNIS

WHEATLEY

PRESENTS

A

NEW ERA IN

## Chapter VI

CRIME FICTION
A MURDER MYSTERY
PLANNED BY
J. G. LINKS
MURDER
OFF MIAMI

Inside the front cover is a lengthy Author's Note (which is actually an Authors' Note):

> We have pleasure in presenting to the public, between these covers, what we believe to be an entirely new departure in Crime Fiction.
>
> Cablegrams, original handwritten documents, photographs, police reports, criminal records, and even actual clues in the form of human hair, a piece of blood-stained curtain, etc., are all contained in this folder, each in its correct order as received by police headquarters, thereby forming the complete Dossier of a crime.
>
> The mystery is presented to the public in exactly the same sequence as that in which it was unravelled by the investigating officer, without any extraneous or misleading matter; photographs of living people taking the place of the descriptions of characters which appear in an ordinary detective novel. Clues to the identity of the murderer are scattered liberally through the investigating officer's reports, and are also to be found in the photographs.
>
> On reaching the end of the investigating officer's fifth report all the available evidence is to hand, yet he finds himself unable to solve the mystery. He then receives instructions to arrest the murderer from his superior, *who has never seen any of the people concerned, but reaches the correct solution of the mystery solely upon the evidence in Dossier form, exactly as it is presented to you here.*
>
> The murderer's confession as to how the crime was committed follows, and the clues which enabled the officer at headquarters to fasten the crime upon him.
>
> We hope that you will find the story a good one and wish

you lots of fun in deciding who [sic] *you* will arrest for the
MURDER OFF MIAMI.

We dedicate this original presentation of a Crime Story to
Walter Hutchinson, who always has the courage to back a new
author of promise or a new idea.

Dennis Wheatley
J. G. Links

The dossier sold an astonishing 200,000 copies, 'if you add the
French, German, Swedish, Dutch, Italian, Danish, Hungarian and
Finnish editions to the known bestseller figures of its sales in the
Empire and the United States', a note on the back of the cover of
the second dossier declares. Altogether there were four of them,
produced probably in consecutive years from 1936 (there are no
publication dates on the dossiers themselves).

Later, I acquired a set of all four dossiers, and sold my first
copy of *Murder off Miami* to George MacBeth, who was as
delighted with the concept and execution as I was. Reg Gadney
wrote an article discussing the Wheatley-Links dossiers in the
*London Magazine* (March 1969), and as I had in 1974 published
*Girl with Red Hair*, a 'crime' novel, using the same kind of
techniques, albeit in two dimensional form but also published by
Hutchinson, I ventured to write to Links, whom I knew as the
Queen's furrier, the husband of Mary Lutyens, and an authority
on Venice. He replied (17 October 1978):

I was fascinated to receive your letter and to find someone who
buys those ghastly dossiers at today's prices and who read Reg
Gadney's article (I still don't know whether it was meant as a
send-up or not) and even knows Hutchinson are reissuing them
(I think they need their heads examining) although I had the
contract only last week.

Alas, I have never even heard of novelists' non-linear techniques (or B. S. Johnson). The only things I know about, except
of course for God and Life and such certainties, are furs, Venice
and Canaletto – and I don't really *know* about these, only
enough to write books about them. Oh, and I know that the
professor of medical microbiology in Cardiff, whatever his name

is, is an ass. As for Dennis, well, you knew him: can you see him planning a book with non-linear techniques in mind?

Hutchinson's reissue of the first of the dossiers in 1979 was, I think, a flop. Forty years on, the idea may have looked jaded. The original dossiers, browning and crinkled though they are, take their place in the history of picaresque literature in English, and that Dennis Wheatley is there at all must be entirely due to the wit and wisdom, not to say modesty, of J. G. Links.

# VII

The qualities that make a first-rate publisher cannot be pinned down. Who would have thought in 1965, when, recently arrived from Australia, she landed her first job in publishing as secretary and assistant to Tom Dalby, a shiny-faced automaton of a man who ran the sponsored books division at Hutchinson, that a decade or two later Carmen Callil would prove one of the three or four most influential British publishers of the century? She used to come into the office at Hutchinson which I shared with Daniel Brostoff (who edited the scientific and academic books and looked and behaved like the Romanov who got away) during the coffee-break each morning, and sit dangling her legs on the third desk. It was used only one day of the week by John Hadfield, who edited the *Saturday Book*, a much-collected, slightly raffish annual of the period. Hadfield popped in briskly to conduct his business, dictate a few letters, make the occasional telephone call and leave, usually having said only 'Good morning' and 'Good afternoon' to Brostoff and me.

There wasn't a tea-break as such (or if there was, no one told me), although a woman in an overall came round with a trolley twice a day and administered tea and coffee. Carmen and I got on, perhaps because neither of us has any English blood, she being an Irish-Lebanese Australian. She laughed a lot, as she does now, quite raucously, with the well-lubricated throat of an actress who has possibly played too many major roles in the classics and certainly smoked too many cigarettes. With hindsight I see that she regarded what in a very modest way I was doing – taking on the occasional new writer when permitted to; editing proper books and being utterly committed to it – as what she wanted to do.

Her vision, a few years later, in realising that there was a crying need – a gap at least the size of a publishing company – for an imprint specifically to publish books by women, just when the so-called women's movement was beginning to make inroads, was both judicious and an indication of proper publishing flair. Another reason why the Virago Press was so successful, and in its early years so discriminating, was that Carmen has read almost everything, unlike many younger publishers who have read almost nothing. Well, too little and, like me, usually the wrong books. (I once complained to Angus Wilson that I had read too few of the classics of English literature and gave as my excuse the fact that I hadn't been to university. He offered me, there and then, a year at the University of East Anglia, where he was a professor of English. I couldn't take up the offer as I had a wife and young children, but whether, had I been fancy-free, I would have had the courage to take such a year out of life in my early thirties, I rather doubt.) Carmen used to be a great scourer of second-hand bookshops, and has a formidable library of her own. She knew when she began Virago in 1972 which books would or should find a market, a new readership.

Although she is still chairman of Virago, she ceased to be managing director in 1982, becoming the boss of Chatto & Windus – original publishers of so many of her beloved authors – the following year. In my view, she had done her work at Virago, established the principle that women could and did write as well as and often better than men, and laid down not so much the agenda as the vine. I think there is today a problem, probably insoluble, for Virago. The classics, the great books and the worthwhile slightly-less-than-great books, mainly fiction but some non-fiction too, are available in Virago. The backlist is almost as comprehensive as Penguin's. For a woman writer to want to be published by Virago today, she must have a keen sense of identification with other women writers, and the women's movement. In practice, most ambitious women writers would, if truth be told, prefer to compete with men or be published with men. The tragedy of Virago (like Hutchinson's New Authors) is that as soon as it became successful it was bound to be ghettoised.

Two other publishers who have changed the world of publishing, and thus to some extent the world, are Allen Lane and Paul

Hamlyn. (Most publishers, to a greater or lesser extent, are merely exercising their own tastes and egos.) I only met AL, as he was known by most of his employees, a few times during my eighteen months at Penguin, but he was forever to be seen bustling about the fragilely partitioned, eggbox compartments of the glasshouse at Harmondsworth. It was a frightful place to work. When the offices were built in 1937 they were obviously state of the art and set down in a green belt area. It was hardly Allen Lane's fault that somebody had the idea of siting Heathrow airport almost next door a few years later. As a result, whether the Penguin building today has double or triple glazing, it is virtually impossible to conduct a coherent telephone conversation because of the relentless roar of aircraft taking off and landing outside the window. The first, a Lancaster, lifted off the runway on 1 January 1946. Still, people who have worked at Harmondsworth for years seem almost immune to the conditions, and there is a canteen and a fountain or two.

For many years Penguin editors, who are clearly important people and simply *have* to work in London, where the action is, have only had to visit Harmondsworth for meetings and, in my time, only on one day a week. I used to travel on 'the Penguin bus', an ancient coach stencilled all over the outside with images of Penguins, which left the Notting Hill end of Kensington Church Street at, I think, 8.30 a.m. If you missed the bus, you either had to wait hours for a service bus or hitch-hike, assuming you had no access to a car, or didn't drive. I remember the first morning I had to go to Harmondsworth, greeting those colleagues I knew as we all waited for the Penguin bus, but they each looked away, as if being addressed by a stranger or a lunatic. Everyone buried him or herself behind a newspaper, usually the *Guardian*. Just under an hour later, as the bus swept into Harmondsworth, papers would be folded away and everyone would begin to chat to everyone else in animated fashion. It was all very self-conscious, very British.

Two or three times I deputised for Tony Godwin, the chief editor, at meetings to decide the print run and price of books, and I was each time surprised that the founder and architect of Penguin Books, by then in his mid-sixties, could be bothered to while away the hours tediously discussing print runs and prices. Like Hamlyn, Lane was not a great reader, but he was a successful publisher to his fingertips; understanding, as Tony Benn would say, the isshoes.

Paul Hamlyn, who founded Books for Pleasure in 1949, made it possible for the man in the street (in educational and social terms probably somewhat below the average Penguin buyer, and probably a bit older, at least when Hamlyn was at his peak in the sixties and seventies) to acquire mouthwatering illustrated books, superbly printed and, in comparison with the cost of colour books from all other publishers, at bargain prices. In his early years he had his books printed in Czechoslovakia, whose printers needed the work and charged him Soviet bloc prices. Thus he could always easily undercut British publishers printing in the UK, before publishers here discovered Hong Kong and other Far East printers. His taste and judgement were exemplary. I once applied to him for a job and came away without the job, though I may have given him a good idea. This must have been in the early sixties, when he was running in parallel with Books for Pleasure a company called, naturally enough, Prints for Pleasure. It was the first company to make available at incredibly low prices reproductions of well-loved masterpieces by Van Gogh, Cézanne, Degas, Monet and other Impressionists. The colour reproduction may not always have been the most subtle, but these prints brightened many a wall, educated many a young mind. I suggested to him at my self-requested interview that certain people, such as myself, would prefer black and white prints for our bedsitter walls, and what about blowing up Thomas Bewick's wood engravings of animals? Hamlyn, whose secret was to say little but always have his antennae alert, smiled. Within a year, Prints for Pleasure was marketing black and white Bewicks.

I went to see him later with the suggestion that he should publish illustrated novels, a mix of new titles and classics. If he were to publish, for instance, John Braine's hugely successful *Room at the Top* with stills from the film alongside the latest Alistair Maclean and the latest Anthony Powell, the two latter with specially commissioned illustrations from leading contemporary artists, together with classics illustrated by the best artists, he'd be doing something worthwhile and also stand to rival Penguin, then still the reprint publisher of most of the 'literary' fiction, in the market-place. Only the conservative Folio Society, then as now, was routinely publishing illustrated novels, though only titles that had stood the test of time and thus would have an assured readership. Hamlyn, looking shy behind a vast unladen desk in an immense mostly empty office, asked me to draw up a paper and send it to him. I did so within a few days of our meeting but I didn't ever hear anything further from him on the subject.

Hamlyn is mercurial, shy and modest; oddly likeable, as people who keep their own counsel frequently are. If they rarely express opinions, it is difficult to disagree with them. In later years he seemed to become very much the tycoon, buying and selling companies and people, and I for one was particularly cross, denouncing his behaviour in *Punch*, where at the time I wrote about the book trade (not that it's a particularly hilarious subject, but then neither was *Punch* a particularly hilarious object), when he sold on Secker & Warburg, which he had briefly owned as part of his Octopus Group, to Reed International. David Godwin, the volatile publishing director, was resisting leaving Secker's offices in Poland Street and moving into the characterless hutches in Michelin House, handsome from without but enervating within. Men like Hamlyn apparently cannot understand that certain kinds of publishing need particular environments. Secker & Warburg, while still publishing marvellous books, no longer has the aura it did. As for Godwin, ironically he went to Jonathan Cape, to work in a conglomerate building only a little more congenial than Reed International's.

Hamlyn's brother is the interesting poet and translator from the German, Michael Hamburger, although they do not broadcast their relationship. Hamlyn has a slight lisp, and sometimes when I'm the worse for alcohol, I'm likely, and not only when requested, to give my Paul Hamlyn rendition. It used to go down a treat.

David Godwin, although he went to public school, is in the Tony Godwin mould, although they were neither related nor knew one another. He was an instinctive publisher who, like the other Godwin, disdained to wear a tie, preferring jeans, billowing white shirts and sneakers. Now aged forty-four, he looks younger.

He appears to be doing nothing about an author's work for weeks then, when it's necessary that he respond so as not to lose the author's confidence, he'll suddenly tell the writer what he thinks of his book. Almost invariably when this happens he is both perceptive and inspiring.

Until recently managing director of Cape, he started in publishing at Routledge & Kegan Paul, introducing general books (notably Stephen Pile's *Book of Heroic Failures*) into an academic list, then went to Heinemann as editorial director before moving to Secker & Warburg. He wheeled about with him three talented individuals. Georgina Capel sells rights (serial, paperback, American, foreign: any rights she can put her hands on) and thus generates income to enable publishing houses to continue. This is much more important than the sale of copies of books, in the same way that advertising revenue is crucial to the survival of newspapers. Maggie McKernan, who now has her own imprint, Phoenix House, in the Orion Group, specialises in nurturing new authors (and I have to declare an interest here as she is my wife and the mother of our baby, Lucy). Peter Dyer was the third of Godwin's troubleshooters, the art director who in the last few years has quietly revolutionised British publishers' approach to jacket design. His pupils and disciples now occupy the art directors' drawing-boards in many of our publishing houses, though some of the more 'commercial' houses continue to prefer the hackneyed, unsophisticated approach they have relied upon for decades.

One day the veteran travel writer Norman Lewis made an appointment to meet his new editor, David Godwin, at Heinemann. He arrived at the preordained hour, and courteously told the receptionist that he had an appointment to see Mr Godwin, and that his name was Lewis. The receptionist telephoned Godwin's secretary (they were on the cusp of being called assistants then, to allow them more status but no more salary) to say that Mr Lewis had arrived. A minute or two later a gangling youth tripped downstairs to collect Lewis. The lad chatted pleasantly enough, and the distinguished travel writer was quite impressed that he seemed to know who he was, and a bit about his books. After a while, with the boy by then sitting behind the editorial director's desk (and his feet, no doubt, upon it), Lewis asked, ever so pol-

itely, when David Godwin would be joining them. The far from
callow youth admitted to being Godwin.

From the charismatic and hard-working to the hard-working
and horrible. Robert Maxwell, proprietor, employed me, although
he was surely ignorant of the fact, as theatre critic of the *London
Daily News*. The night he died in 1991, I said in passing to the
*Evening Standard* news-vendor in Gray's Inn Road when I bought
my paper and saw that Cap'n Bob had bobbed over, 'I'll never
get the money he owes me now.' 'That's what they're all saying
tonight,' he replied, and laughed. In truth, legally Maxwell didn't
owe me anything, although morally he should have done. He
declined to renew my contract at the *London Daily News* after
the initial months, even though, for the last two months of the
dying paper's life, I was reviewing plays every night. It seemed
that he knowingly declined rather than neglected to renew any
journalist's contract which had expired after a year (although the
paper did not make it to its first birthday, there had been months
of preparation and dummies before the first issue). By not renew-
ing contracts he avoided having to pay redundancy, and obviously
he knew that he was going to pull the plug on the paper, an apt
metaphor given the nature of his own demise.

I first encountered Maxwell in 1966 when I was chairman of
the Society of Young Publishers, and invited him to address the
Society. In those days he was ostensibly a man of the Left, Labour
MP for Buckingham. He had previously acquired Simpkin Marshall, a wholesaler of much influence and reputation which had
supplied books from publishers to booksellers pretty efficiently
until it fell on hard times after the Second World War, and had
ceased to trade profitably. Maxwell put the final nail into its coffin.
Although no one else was inclined to shoulder the burden and
legacy of Simpkin Marshall, the book trade had had it in for
Maxwell ever since, and thereafter he was known, to begin with
in semi-jocular mode, as the bouncing Czech. The nickname was
to rebound with a vengeance akin to nemesis. He had founded
the scientific, technical and academic publishers Pergamon Press
in 1949, although as a serious publisher he was, possibly unjustly,
always regarded as something of a rogue elephant.

The evening he was to address the Society of Young Publishers (which in those days was a bit of a power in the book trade), the room in which monthly meetings took place at the National Book League in Albemarle Street was crowded. There was standing room only, and many stood. Others, including some of the senior statesmen of the industry, seemed to be hanging on the walls. The atmosphere, indeed, resembled the House of Commons when a boisterous debate was anticipated. The secretary, Jill Mortimer, and I led the way through the centre of the room to the table at the top, elbowing people aside. Captain Robert Maxwell, MC, MP, dragged himself after us with some difficulty but with not too much indication of distress. When it was seen that one of his legs was encased in a large plaster cast a fair quantity of human sympathy went out to him. A few nights before when hurrying into the division lobby to vote the Member for Buckingham had fallen heavily to the ground (even in those days there was a lot of him) and broken his leg.

With difficulty, but smiling all the while, he lowered himself down at the table, and listened as I introduced him. There was a kind of hiss in the air, an atmosphere of distaste, scepticism. I have never witnessed a crowd that was so hostile, so aggressive towards a speaker before he had opened his mouth. From my vantage point behind the table, it was as if I were seeing a mob of dissenters painted by Rowlandson or Hogarth come snarlingly alive.

Maxwell apologised for not standing up, indicating his plastered leg stretched out in front of him below the table. Then he began to flatter his audience, the Society of Young Publishers, saying that in spite of its comparative youth (to be a member you had to be under thirty-five), it was the most worthwhile, galvanising body in British publishing, the only organisation which was asking the questions that needed to be asked and endeavouring to find solutions. He went on, and on. Within a few minutes nearly everyone in the room was grinning, almost purring, certainly supping at the captain's table. It was an extraordinary and frightening example of demagogy, and the ease with which an intelligent bunch of people may be wooed and won in the minimum of time by an opponent they have come to boo and put on the spot. Sitting there next to Maxwell, I could observe the faces of those in front of me change from thunder to sunshine. What he said thereafter hardly mattered, but it was, I vaguely remember, about the resurgence in Britain's scientific publishing, entirely as a result of the activities of Pergamon Press. Most speakers had supper with the committee of the Society afterwards. Mercifully Maxwell, like Philoctetes, dragged himself and his broken leg away without socialising.

The next time I met him was in 1970 after he had, infamously, been declared unfit to run a public company and had his treasured Pergamon taken away (it was later returned to him). He was trying to put Humpty Dumpty together again, and had purchased the old Book Society, once run by Tony Godwin from Bumpus in Baker Street, but dormant for some years. Britain, unlike America, has never taken wholeheartedly to book clubs, but Maxwell believed, or said he did, that if publishers would supply him with quantities of the right books at large discounts he would persuade readers to purchase the books, dispatched to them by post once a month, and bookshop sales would not suffer. As part of his act of rehabilitation, he arranged to visit the publishers he needed to assist him. He came to see Livia Gollancz, John Bush and me at Gollancz one evening. I was in Bush's first-floor office which looked out on Henrietta Street, and observed the Captain's sleek chauffeur-driven limousine park on the other side of the street. Maxwell got out and, standing on the pavement, consulted a clutch of index cards, which he then deposited in the back of the car.

When he was escorted into Livia's room, where we all were by then, he shook hands with each of us – a bear grasp – and immediately summoned up memories of the last time he had met us. With Livia it was at some event connected with her father (even Maxwell wouldn't have had the gall to suggest it was Victor's funeral or memorial service, surely?). With Bush it was at some publishing sales function. With me it was at the SYP meeting. Again, this was an assured, cheeky performance, flattering people with whom he hoped – needed – to do business that he remembered them, that they mattered to him. It would have been more impressive had I not observed him checking those index cards.

The last time I saw him was at a publication party for a novel by Michael J. Molloy, who had been editor of the *Daily Mirror* when Maxwell bought the paper but who was eventually kicked upstairs to be editorial director of Mirror Group Newspapers, an elevation more akin to being consigned to the Tower than translated into the House of Lords. Maxwell regarded Molloy, one of nature's most amiable beings (except when torridly drunk), as a sympathiser. Molloy had written his fourth novel, *The Century*, a saga about a newspaper dynasty, a most readable fictional account of Fleet Street seen through the eyes of one twentieth-century paper: its proprietors, journalists, editors, cartoonists, printers, the lot. It was also what is known in the trade as a blockbuster. Molloy's first three thrillers had been gently published by Hodder & Stoughton, but his new proprietor wanted in future to publish his editor-in-chief's literary outpourings himself. Maxwell, of course, had a handy publishing house, Macdonald, part of his modestly titled British Printing and Communication Corporation, later to be elevated to Maxwell Communication Corporation, which, although known by its initials, was never, but never, confused with Marylebone Cricket Club.

For a period, one of Maxwell's three sons, Kevin, was put in charge of Macdonald, and it was with him that I had to negotiate the publishing agreement for *The Century*. The way in which agents negotiate deals with publishers on behalf of the authors they represent is a fairly relaxed business, often if not invariably conducted over a lunch, naturally paid for by the publisher. The agent will know the publisher well and the 'correct' figure for the book will be arrived at relatively painlessly, but probably not before the coffee stage is reached. Brandies used to follow to celebrate the deal but not so frequently in these days of Perrier water.

Kevin Maxwell wanted to use the telephone, not the lunch table, and whenever I tried to reach him and occasionally got through he suddenly began selling (or was it buying?) a football team.

Eventually I was summoned to his office, aghast to find myself accompanied by my author. It was too late to explain to either Mike or Kevin that *this wasn't how things were done*. Agents do not negotiate with their authors sitting beside them.

Kevin asked me what I had in mind and I named an outlandish figure. Mike's previous three novels were perhaps best-known for not having topped any bestseller lists. A football team was then bought (or sold) on the telephone, and we settled on a figure somewhat larger, or smaller, than I had suggested. A few more football teams and empires were bought and sold and we were still sitting there.

'What about the publicity budget?' I piped up. 'What about it?' said Kevin. Publishers usually expend the price of a few bottles of plonk and a plate of canapés to toast the author and his chums on publication day, preferably out of sight of press, booksellers and Joe Public so that they can relax and curse the lack of publication reviews.

I thought quickly. 'Four times the advance.'

'Too much,' riposted Kevin. 'I'll agree to half that.'

'Done.' The result was the most stunning poster campaign in every railway station between King's Cross and Cleethorpes.

We stood up to go. 'What about Australia?' barked Kevin.

'Australia?' I said, in a knowing tone of voice.

'Can I have Australia?'

I looked at Mike, who hadn't uttered a syllable since we sat down, the only time I've seen him silent for so long. He looked at me beseechingly, even alarmed. Give him Australia, his look seemed to say; for God's sake, let him have Australia. 'Okay, you can have Australia.'

We left the office.

'What was all that about Australia?' asked Mike.

'British publishers get it anyway,' I said. 'It's still part of their exclusive territory. Commonwealth, you know.'

'Gosh, I didn't know that's how it's done,' said Mike.

'It isn't how it's done. I've never done it that way before,' I replied.

'Well, that's how you negotiate with the Maxwells,' said Mike happily.

Molloy was a rarity among authors because, if his publishers wouldn't give him a publication party, he would give himself one and invite his friends. His publishers began to understand this and thus Mike found himself footing the bill approximately once a year as he published a novel most years. The party for *The Century* was held at the Quo Vadis restaurant in Soho. His journalistic friends were there, including it seemed half the staff of the *Daily Mirror*, male to a man, all squat, truncated and sawn off, journalists of the same proportions as the *Mirror*'s tabloid format.

The party also marked the farewell to Molloy as editor of the *Mirror*. Maxwell, looking as if he'd been hired from Transylvanian central casting, delivered a hectoring speech telling everyone how brilliant the book was (he didn't read books; he hadn't read Mike's) and ordering all present to review it. Then he departed, a vast unquivering hulk of flesh with a voice like a guttural foghorn, booming out in the relatively small room as if he were addressing an audience in the Albert Hall. The novel received, I think, one review in a national newspaper, which was tough, and unjust.

At the party Molloy gave in 1991 at the Groucho Club for his next novel, also published by Macdonald, the presence of Maxwell was not evident, although it was rumoured that he might put in an appearance. The author made a brief and modest speech welcoming everyone, and beseeching them to do with the new book what Bob had ordered them to do with the last – to wit, review it – 'and you *all* disobeyed him'. There were gales of laughter. When standing in a room in which Maxwell was present, you invariably had an uneasy sense of menace, of a sinister life going on which you couldn't understand, of a Jacobean villain, someone dreamed up by Webster, too big and dangerous and *bullying* for everyday life.

Maxwell gave a party each summer at Headington Hill Hall, his council home and almost stately mansion at Oxford, to which he invited authors, agents, booksellers and printers. I now regret that I always declined the invitation. In 1972 the agent George Greenfield went accompanied by his client David Niven, shortly before *The Moon's a Balloon* was published. 'Where are the booksellers?' the actor asked his agent. 'Over there,' said Greenfield, nodding in the appropriate direction. Niven strode over to them, introduced himself, talked about his book and generally flattered and chatted them up for half an hour before leaving the party, having not even met his host. The book was one of the biggest sellers in the history of the book trade. Jeffrey Archer, years later, also saw the point of flattering booksellers.

Another tale frequently told of Maxwell's annual party is of the anonymous guest who arrived and stood at the top of the garden stairs, surveying the scene. People seemed to be bunched in groups in the vast acreage.

'Who are those sleek-looking people?' the newcomer asked, and was told, 'Those are the publishers.'

'Who are those affluent-looking people?'

'Those are the printers.'

'What is that motley crew over there?'

'They are the booksellers.'

'And who are those poor, downtrodden-looking creatures over there?'

'Ah, those are the authors.'

# VIII

I was astonished in 1964 to receive a letter from Eric Walter White, literature director and assistant secretary-general of the Arts Council of Great Britain, inviting me to become a member of the Council's newly constituted and first ever advisory panel on literature. Until then, in Arts Council terms only poetry had been considered worthy of subsidy. There had been a poetry panel since 1949, and in its last year of existence it had meted out just under £5,000 to worthy poets and poetic events: the Little Festival of Poetry at Cley-next-the-Sea received £11. I was chairman of the Society of Young Publishers at the time and I think I was invited in that capacity, although it was a personal not an *ex officio* invitation.

The literature panel was a bigger, grander affair than the poetry panel, although many of its original members had served on the last poetry panel. Its chairman was Cecil Day Lewis, the Poet Laureate, who also wrote thrillers under the name Nicholas Blake and put in time as a director of Chatto & Windus. In fact, many of the panel members seemed to be published by Chatto. The panel of twenty-one people – far too many for anything other than 'democratic' decisions to be made, and literature is anything but democratic – comprised Day Lewis, Patricia Beer, Charles Causley, Leonard Clark, Reg Davis-Poynter (a publisher, whom most people bewilderingly called Poynter-Davis, and a buddy of Lord Goodman), Patrick Garland, John Hall, Ted Hughes, Frank Kermode, myself, Edward Lucie-Smith, Julian Mitchell, Iris Murdoch, Ian Parsons (chairman of Chatto), Peter Porter, V. S. Pritchett, Alan Ross, Stevie Smith, Charles Tomlinson, C. V. Wedgwood and Angus Wilson.

The panel met in the Arts Council's elegant premises in St

James's Square. (I was disconcerted a few years later when doing my only stint of jury duty to find that the amply proportioned rooms had been subdivided into cubicles to accommodate extra courts of the Inner London Sessions, the Arts Council having decamped to grander but less attractive offices in Piccadilly.) We met five or six times a year, at 2.30, to allow panel members to have a decent lunch beforehand, and it was all terribly British and civilised. Waiters in white coats served tea and cucumber sandwiches. I had, in my energetic innocence, expected that large issues ('The issues of Literature') would be discussed, that we'd decree whither the novel, or was there point any more in poetry? Instead the discussions were trivial if practical, and almost entirely to do with the equitable carving up of the panel's annual budget.

Alan Ross would leave the room when a discussion was to take place, which it did once a year, on how large a grant the then monthly *London Magazine*, which he owned and edited, should receive. Charles Osborne, the Australian thespian and poetaster, who had recently been appointed assistant literature director, had previously been assistant editor to Ross on the *London Magazine*. As year followed year, the grant (or grant-in-aid, to give it its full, ludicrous Council appellation) to the magazine increased. I can't remember whether we asked searching questions over the sandwiches. Do we *really* think the magazine's that good, or do we agree with John Berger, who has called it 'a monument to triviality'? Do we feel Alan Ross is doing all he can to increase circulation? And is it right that he should use the Shenval Press, one of the most expensive printers in the country?

At least the panel paid lip service to the concept of excellence, which I do not think it can do today, judging by a speech I heard the Council's present secretary-general, Anthony Everitt, deliver to a private dining club some months ago. 'Elitism' – of which I'm a confirmed adherent because by definition it leads to high standards in the arts, and the arts have to be about 'the best' – elitism is out; and art for everybody is in. Community art. Black art. Ethnic art. Women's art. As if art can be categorised, sectionalised. The literature panel today – its director is an ex-teacher – is more concerned with finding readers, who do seem thinner on the ground than would-be writers. I had thought that it was the responsibility of the Book Trust, previously the National Book League, to find readers for the product, and for the Arts Council to try to maintain standards of writing, but perhaps majorism aspires to minorism.

While on the panel, I argued endlessly that if we were rewarding excellence Mr Beckett and Mr Golding (as he then was) and even Mr Greene should be given handouts. Day Lewis, who was a sweetie and tended to treat me as a recalcitrant pupil, would wearily explain in his mellifluous voice that, under the terms of the Council's charter, we could only recommend the offering of grant-in-aid to those who, through sponsors, had applied for loot. If Mr Beckett or Mr Golding, or even Mr Greene, were to apply, no doubt they would be seriously considered; but they hadn't applied.

The business of sponsorship, a legal nicety to do with accountancy practices, was preposterous. It tended to be writers of stupendous mediocrity, who mightily fancied their literary prowess, who brazenly collected sponsors of genuine distinction and thus filed up for state handouts. The more distinguished the sponsor, the more likely his or her applicant was to receive cash, although I do remember a lengthy discussion when we daringly turned down some third-rate writer and agonised as to how the *sponsor* could tactfully be told. Some members of the panel, the Gloucestershire sub-Georgian poet Leonard Clark, for instance, seemed invariably to want to back safe mediocrity. Others, such as Karl Miller, who joined the panel after a year or two, would, cheroot between his fingers, correct the proofs of the literary pages of the *New Statesman* as the meeting meandered on, and offered no opinion. The poet members of the previous panel would always want to give money to poets, feeling either that prose writers made enough anyway or that prose wasn't, in any case, worth endorsing. The publisher members would want money to go to publishers to subsidise books that didn't sell. They were often Chatto & Windus books, although in later years John Calder got in on the act.

Of all the panel members with whom I served, Ted Hughes was the most dedicated to seeing that justice was done, virtue rewarded. He went to infinite trouble to ensure that little known and young writers whom he believed had talent and originality were assisted. He read all the papers submitted to the panel (they were legion) and thus was in a stronger position than most members to offer a positive, even comparative viewpoint. He never said a mean or bitchy word, and kept his peace when a writer he didn't especially admire was being discussed.

Brigid Brophy, who joined after a year or two, rarely spoke, but when she did it was always devastatingly to the point. Iris Murdoch, William Sansom (a subtle short-story writer and very funny man with a limp, who once missed a bus he and I were attempting to catch after a panel meeting because, instead, he elected to pursue a pretty girl down the street), V. S. Pritchett and the other Chatto & Windus authors said little. I don't remember Stevie Smith turning up once.

The liveliest member of the panel was Julian Mitchell, in those days a novelist rather than the playwright he was sensibly to become when he realised he'd never be able to make a living from his somewhat arid books. He bubbled and squeaked effervescently with enthusiasm and ideas. I think it was during the second or third year of the panel's life, when Day Lewis had retired and been replaced as chairman by the much more effective and political Angus Wilson, that Mitchell had the brightest single idea – they were hardly ten a penny – that anyone had during my four-year stint.

This was the proposal of the writers' tour. A group of four contrasted authors would be brought together and sent for a week to an area of the UK. During the day they would divide into two groups, one pair visiting a school or two, the other pair another school or two. The pairing would usually change from day to day as would the schools. The writers would read and talk to schoolchildren, sometimes together, sometimes each talking to different classes. The permutations were innumerable. The children found it stimulating, or at least something different from their everyday lessons. The writers found it intriguing to see how young readers, or hoped-for readers, responded to them and their work. In those days, the late sixties, writers hadn't become the public property and even Aunt Sallies it has since become *de rigueur* that they be. They rarely met a reader then, or even a potential reader. W. H. Smith ruled then as now.

During the evenings, the four writers would come together to read, speak and answer questions in a town hall, church hall, college of further education, art gallery, theatre. They were each paid £150 for a hard week's work (the tours were the opposite of a sinecure), the equivalent then of an advance on a first novel. They were put up at a wide range of hotels and provided with meals. The cost to the Arts Council was relatively low – it must have been about £1,000 per tour, although Charles Osborne tended to accompany the writers, presumably to vet their performances, and this must have added to the bill. Arts Council 'officers', as they like to call themselves, have always enjoyed and attempted to justify their perks.

I was lucky enough to be chosen (could it have had anything to do with my being on the literature panel?) in May 1970 as a member of a writers' tour to Cheshire and High Peak, Derbyshire. In six days, in the company of Iris Murdoch, Paul Bailey and Paul Ableman, I visited Chester, Northwich, Sandbach, Wilmslow, Glossop and Buxton. The advance arrangements, as may be imagined, were complicated and took months of organising. Osborne, who administered the tours, had three on the go that week in the North-West, the other groups (visiting Central and North-West Lancashire) comprising Nell Dunn, Olwen Wymark, Peter Porter and William Trevor, and (visiting Blackburn and the mid-Pennine area) Tony Connor, my dear friend Ronald Harwood, David Lytton and Paul Scott.

Osborne, who had recently been appointed literature director upon the retirement of Eric Walter White, is a man who likes a quiet life with things going according to plan. He looked aghast when, as we assembled to board a train at Euston, Paul Ableman arrived with his very new and young girlfriend, Sheila Fox (whom he was later to marry, and who was to become a senior editor at BBC Publications). Single bedrooms had undoubtedly been booked everywhere, and place settings at tables strategically devised weeks before – everybody would want to sit next to Dame Iris, as she then wasn't. As it happened, in quite a few places Sheila Fox was taken for an Arts Council secret weapon or supernumerary, an unrecognised surprise poet, or poetess as she'd have been called then. The star of our group was obviously Iris Mur-

doch, who was simply adorable. She was earth mother, protectress
and goddess to us three lost boys. One day she and I had an hour
or two in the middle of the day between schools, and I suggested
a private visit to nearby Jodrell Bank. Somehow the starkness, the
pitilessness of that naked lunar landscape, with scores of crows
gliding parabolically about the great concave bowl of the telescope,
Lear's kingdom re-enacted, was enhanced by being experienced in
the presence of Iris Murdoch. We were both, I think, over-
whelmed, humbled, rather frightened.

During our six days in the North-West we seemed to meet
innumerable mayors (whereas vicars might have been anticipated).
They always, male or female, wanted a quick photograph with
Iris, but she would never allow it unless the two Pauls and I were
included in the picture as well. Most of the questions during the
evening sessions were, inevitably, directed to her, and she coped
with them admirably, honestly and sensibly. No attempt at flash
or wit. She treated every question, however sycophantic and foolish, with the utmost respect. Indeed, her humanity, her simple
respect for anyone and everyone encountered was awesome, and
she never seemed to tire. I only once saw her annoyed, when a
young woman asked a question about a novel from the Murdoch
canon, which she said she was studying for A-levels. 'But you
shouldn't be,' said Iris, in her terribly cultured, English, super-
educated, middle-class tone. 'You shouldn't be studying . . . me.
You should be reading Jane Austen. Now Jane Austen . . .' and
she was away, far happier expounding on the greatest English
novelist than commenting upon her own work. The poor girl who
had posed the question looked quite crestfallen. After all, it wasn't
(or was it?) her fault that she was having to read Murdoch not
Austen; and Iris must have been aware, although she seemed not
to be, that her novels, or some of them, are set by some boards
for A-levels. Like a good teacher, she loved talking about the great
nineteenth-century English novelists, nearly all female.

Paul Bailey, night after night, would retaliate by talking incessantly in praise of Dickens. Whereas the majority of the most
intelligent English novelists are female, most of the finest playwrights are men. Bailey had started out as an actor, and he articu-
lated and read as if to the boards born. He relished the theatrical

over-the-top, melodramatic quality in Dickens, the three-dimensional, tuppence-coloured evocation of characters which, for better or worse, leaves less than nothing to the reader's imagination. The pinnacle of Bailey's theatrical career, perhaps, came in 1961 when he was promoted out of the ranks of spearholders at Stratford-upon-Avon to play Denis, servant to Oliver, a previously little regarded character in *As You Like It* in Michael Elliott's production with Vanessa Redgrave. In the final production of the season, *Othello*, Bailey was back to playing senators, soldiers and/or Cypriots. He is mightily funny in mimicking how, in Zeffirelli's catastrophic production, Gielgud playing the Moor started the evening chocolate-colour, but by the end of the play had left most of his make-up liberally deposited on the pillars of the set. (Stratford continued to play host to novelists of the future, for Margaret Drabble appeared as a fairy in Peter Hall's production of *A Midsummer Night's Dream* the next year, and three months later Gordon Honeycombe was a lord in William Gaskill's *Cymbeline*.)

Like Paul Ableman, who has written a bit about nudity and spent time in a nudist colony, I tend to be naturally scruffy, though we both tried to look as presentable as possible in the North-West. Paul Bailey, on the other hand, looked from dawn to dusk as if he were ready to play Noël Coward. He changed his wardrobe entirely, or so it seemed, at least twice a day, including his scent or aftershave lotion, and never was he seen in the same tie, shirt or suit more than once.

On the last evening of the tour, after our evening session (were there two mayors in the audience, or had I mislaid my spectacles or had one too many to drink?) in the Town Hall at Buxton, we returned wilting to our hotel. Iris Murdoch commanded us, in the nicest possible way, to bring our tooth mugs into her room for a final drink. Each of us, armed with tumbler, crowded into Iris's tiny bedroom. She produced from under her bed a huge plastic jerry can; tilting it at a reckless angle, she slopped great cascades of whisky into our glasses. We toasted each other and the Arts Council. Charles Osborne had long since gone to catch up on another tour.

Someone commented favourably upon the trouser-pressing

machines in the bedrooms. They were fairly unusual twenty-odd years ago. Iris looked puzzled. She had not known what the upright wooden device in her room was. Paul Bailey graphically demonstrated to her how it worked. (I recall that Ableman and I both wore corduroy trousers, or even corduroy suits, and thus would not have had recourse to it.) 'But I never press John's trousers,' said Iris, as if she'd just been informed of one of the cardinal facts of life. The rest of us fell about laughing. Anyone who has had the pleasure of meeting Iris's husband, the critic and until recently Warton Professor of English Literature at Oxford John Bayley, would immediately recognise that his trousers were unacquainted with iron and ironing board.

Paul Bailey then said he had something to tell us, and he insisted we paid attention as, during the week, we'd become such friends. 'I'd like you to know that I'm gay,' he announced. The only extraordinary thing about this was that he seemed crestfallen, even hurt, when we all said that we'd realised as much from the first evening. 'It's all right, Paul, it's quite all right,' Iris soothed.

I was chary of Bailey before the tour because he'd reviewed one of my books severely in the *Observer*, and I found his much admired neo-realist early novels, festooned with prizes, overrated. Subsequent to the tour, he reviewed a collection of my stories in the *Observer* more temperately, although I can't believe he thought well of them. It's virtually impossible, unless you have a skin thicker than most writers do, to review a book unkindly if you know and do not dislike its author. For my part, I was much relieved to be moved by Bailey's scenes from childhood and beyond in *An Immaculate Mistake* (1990). Paul is a wonderful mimic, and lethally waspish.

He reviews theatre sometimes for *Kaleidoscope* on BBC Radio 4. I remember encountering him at Stratford some years ago when he was there to review *Julius Caesar* for the programme and I was doing it for the *London Daily News*. I was about to sit down in my seat in the stalls when Paul, a few rows in front, noticed me and said in a clear actor's voice which must have been heard in the gods, 'Did you have a good holiday last week, Giles?' I admitted that I had and enquired how he knew that I had been away. 'Bookworm in *Private Eye* was so *very* dull,' he said impishly.

When the literature panel was set up, members were appointed for an initial period of two or occasionally three years, with the likelihood of the appointment being renewed for a second period of similar length. I thought, for reasons which I cannot now recall, that I was not going to be asked to serve a second term and thus, near the end of 1967, I accepted the invitation of Sean Day-Lewis, Cecil's son and discoverer of a previously unknown hyphen, to write an article for *Socialist Commentary*, of which he was arts editor, on what I thought was wrong with the Council's policy for literature. It is surprising now to recall the extent of interest there was, at least in the media, in the way in which money was being doled out to writers. Charles Osborne quotes extensively from my article and comments on it in his hilarious and indispensable *Giving It Away: Memoirs of an Uncivil Servant* (1986). Because Osborne thought that the quality of writers who submitted work for grant-in-aid tended to be lamentable, and that the writers would be more advantageously employed not being published, he permitted the Literature Department's budget to be much reduced.

Undoubtedly Osborne was right: most art – not least writing, because it doesn't, prima facie, require any specialised (as opposed to special) skills – at any period of history is bound to be mediocre or worse, but this was not a judicious stance for an arts bureaucrat and civil servant to adopt. The point of arts functionaries is perceived within the arts community as being to argue the case for more rather than less money from central government each year, irrespective of the quality of the work requiring support. It is all very British. Osborne, an apoplectically reviled fellow, promoted the case not for more but for less, since if writers need the money, they can't be very good at earning it. And if they can't live off their writing, why don't they get up in the middle of the night (as Osborne himself did) and write their books then, before clocking into an office job at 10 a.m., or whenever the Arts Council wakes up. Anyway, a writer who begs for a state handout like Oliver Twist, can't have much self-respect; so let's not give him or her anything. When did Jane Austen last apply? That was roughly the Osborne philosophy.

I think it was the day on which *Socialist Commentary* was published, and the national press reported my criticisms, that I received a letter from the Council's secretary-general, a former civil servant named Nigel J. Abercrombie, inviting me to do a further two years on the panel. So surprised was I by this cordial invitation that I accepted by return of post, before Lord Goodman, the autocratic chairman of the Council should have my article 'drawn to his attention' – assuming he wasn't an enthusiastic subscriber to *Socialist Commentary* – and rule against my re-appointment. Dear old Eric White, however, later told me that he himself advised Abercrombie that there would likely be a row, which the press would make the most of, if my invitation were withdrawn.

The late Eric White, although he was enough of a mandarin to like being addressed as Eric *Walter* White, was, by inclination, an old-style arts bureaucrat, ready both to 'serve' the arts and to promote what he thought of as excellence within them. He was really a music man (as was his successor as literature director, Charles Osborne), his Faber and Faber monograph on 'Ben' Britten being highly regarded.

Arnold Goodman, named Arnold Abraham by his parents, and made a Life Peer in 1965 by Prime Minister Harold Wilson, whose solicitor he was, with the title Baron Goodman of the City of Westminster, was chairman of the Arts Council from 1965 to 1972 and was undoubtedly one of the most powerful people in the kingdom. He was physically a dauntingly large and hairy man who had a brother, to whom he was said to be devoted, who was smaller in stature. *Private Eye* lampooned the solicitor as Two Dinners Goodman, more because he was assumed to be a big eater than because he had been observed behaving greedily at the trough. The one time I had a meal at his flat near Broadcasting House in Portland Place, with half the literature panel, he seemed to eat nothing. Maybe he'd dined before we arrived. He spent most of the time on the telephone to Buenos Aires. Once I had to travel with him in his chauffeur-driven limousine and was about to get into the back of the car when the chauffeur politely pointed out to me that I was entering the vehicle on the wrong side. The back seat had been adjusted so that approximately two thirds of the seat (there may have been an arm rest in between; I was too alarmed to notice) was reserved for his lordship, the other third for his passenger, presumably expected to be of slender physique, but probably not of slender means; or maybe the space was devised for the more modest-sized brother.

Goodman was a curious cove. He entered public life suddenly, or so it seemed, when Wilson became Prime Minister. He also seemed to be Wilson's guru rather as Sir Laurens van der Post is thought to be the Prince of Wales's. He could easily have played a Jewish Cardinal Wolsey, all the way from the Ipswich butcher's shop, had he had a red gown poured over him, which presumably he had when he was inducted into the Lords. He had an insatiable passion for and a cultured knowledge of the arts and therefore I never could understand his enthusiasm for Jennie Lee though it would have meant instant social lynching to have said so at the time when she was Minister for the Arts. She was a rather silly, self-righteous person – like so many Labour politicians of that era – who could only have been given the job, such as it was outside the Cabinet, because she was highly regarded in the Labour 'movement' as Nye Bevan's widow. Her previous known interests did not extend to the arts.

Maybe Goodman, the most silkily courteous of men, liked her because she seemed persuaded by his ideas. Maybe he genuinely liked her. Since he was a bachelor, and she a widow, they were seen at many arts events together, and undoubtedly the subsidised and public arts did well in Britain when Goodman was chairman of the Arts Council and Miss Lee the Arts Minister. The arts did less well, much less well, when, for instance, Lord Rees-Mogg (only in Britain could someone with a name like that be taken seriously, or take himself seriously) was boss of the Arts Council. Rees-Mogg, in private life a successful antiquarian bookseller after he ceased to be editor of *The Times*, is essentially a literary man, whereas the chairman of the Arts Council needs to go through the motions at least of being an enthusiast of dancing, singing, opera, chamber music, the fine arts and all the less fine arts (if not pottery and weaving and basketwork, although I suspect that such pastimes will soon, in the days of 'ethnic' and 'community' and 'regional' art, be eagerly embraced by the present levellers at the Council, but not, I think, by the property developer chairman Lord Palumbo).

Goodman had his detractors, but they were mostly on the other side in legal disputes and he usually won. During my four years he appeared only once at a meeting of the literature panel, and that was to try to persuade us to reverse a decision, agreed at the previous meeting, to give a grant to the rather cheeky but otherwise reasonably respectable literary magazine *Ambit*, owned and edited by the wan-looking paediatrician Dr Martin Bax. The talented editorial staff of *Ambit* included J. G. Ballard, who didn't win the Booker Prize, the children's illustrator Michael Foreman and, later, the theatre critics' theatre critic, Irving Wardle, who should never have been allowed to leave *The Times*. According to Goodman, who buttonholed us over the cucumber sandwiches and watery tea as if he were a barrister addressing a jury, a recent issue of *Ambit* had included a story which, if you read it carefully enough, advocated the taking of drugs. We prissily bleated that the grant we had recommended to *Ambit* was because of the quality of the writing, and it was not for us to decree what that writing should, or shouldn't, be about. Most writing in *Ambit*, poetry and prose, was 'about' old-fashioned, straightforward heterosexuality. Boots and bosoms certainly came into it. Brigid Brophy, who as I have said rarely pontificated at meetings, was stern in argument with Goodman, puffing a cigarette (Turkish, I'd guess) through a holder and displaying her painted fingernails. Indeed, the spontaneous dialogue between Brigid Brophy and Lord Goodman should have been recorded for the BBC Third Programme, so learned, witty and stylish was the repartee on both sides. Goodman, crouching lower and lower over the long Arts Council table, facially resembling a Titian if not a pope by Bacon, as if dissolving like a jelly in the heat, would begin each argument: 'If I may say so, Miss Brophy . . .' and she would respond, sitting bolt upright against the back of her chair as if electrocuted: 'Forgive me, Lord Goodman, but . . .' I don't think any other member of the panel had the courage to join the game of intellectual badminton (who the shuttle? who the cock?), and honours were more or less even. I cannot remember if *Ambit* had its grant withdrawn. But Goodman was, as I have said, a powerful man who did not take to being crossed.

When Charles Osborne was literature director it was his responsibility to edit and prepare for press the Arts Council's annual report, and to pass the proofs. He couldn't dispatch the final proofs to the printer until the chairman had read the report, approved it, and appended his introduction. One year Goodman left it impossibly late and the usually debonair and detached – most would say cynical – Osborne began to grow agitated as the printing presses waited to roll. In those days publication of the report was a national event; maybe akin to a small volcano that failed to ignite, but still newsworthy.

Osborne was eventually requested by the chairman's secretary to be at a particular bar at the Savoy Hotel at 12 noon where he would be met by Lord Goodman with the marked proofs. Maybe Goodman was having the first of his lunches that day at the Savoy Grill and would first waddle in to deposit the proofs with his literature director. The telephone rang in the bar where Osborne attended his chairman. Osborne was asked if he'd very kindly wait; Lord Goodman would be a bit late. Goodman *was* late, Osborne reflected. The day went on and on, thus: innumerable apologetic telephone calls – Lord Goodman was almost on his way, he really was; please would Mr Osborne not leave. Whether Osborne got more and more drunk, whether he ate a meal or two or just a sandwich, I do not know. But come midnight, or shortly before, twelve hours after he entered the Savoy bar, Osborne observed, through a glass sullenly, the huge figure of Goodman padding into the Savoy bar. In his high-pitched, clipped voice, he addressed his literature director: 'Mr Osborne, I realise that you've had an appalling day, and I can only apologise for keeping you waiting. I informed the gentleman who has been detaining me for so many hours that you wouldn't accept my humble excuses and that you might only forgive me if he accompanied me to proffer my apologies.' Goodman does speak in this way, in formal, orotund paragraphs, purple prose blown a bit dry, immaculately modulated with always a Jewish Cockney twang whining in the background. In the Savoy bar, his lordship stood aside to reveal the, in comparison with him, modest, indeed diminutive figure of the Prime Minister. Harold Wilson, then at the height of his powers, shook Osborne by the hand, apologised for detaining Lord Goodman, and vanished into the woodwork, leaving the Arts Council men to discuss the proofs.

I last saw Goodman at the memorial service held, on 25 September 1991 at St James's, Piccadilly, for Angus Wilson. He sat at the back of the church, infinitely diminished, having lost stones in weight. He walked with the aid of two sticks and two helpers. His biography, I think, will not be published until after he dies. Some years ago the writer and solicitor James Morton put it about that he wanted to paint Goodman's portrait in words, and Richard Cohen at Hodder & Stoughton offered a contract. Soon after, Goodman telephoned Morton and said that he'd be grateful if Mr Morton desisted, as he didn't want his biography written. Morton tried to persuade him that the book would, on the whole, be appreciative, but Goodman still declined to co-operate. Not only that but, as Morton soon found out, someone had telephoned his Lordship's friends and other sources Morton would have consulted, instructing them, in the nicest possible way, not to co-operate.

To those who knew him, Angus Wilson (how he must have relished his knighthood) was one of the characters of the age. As an innovatory novelist, he is disgracefully underrated. The difficulty, for readers, is that each of his novels is quite different from the last, in tone, stance, construction, content. When you read the new Anita Brookner, say, or Mary Wesley, you may have every confidence that it will be similar in tone to the last novel you read by these writers. There is nothing wrong with this. A great deal of writing has to do with reassurance, a preservation of the *status quo*, or of what is perceived to be the *status quo*. A book, the physical object, is a comforting, conservative beast. Some bite – the content, that is – but most don't.

The novel, like the railway train, the charabanc and even the aeroplane, is a familiar vehicle. You can only, really, do certain things with it. This is why the 'experimental' novel is more or less bound to fail, although I thought otherwise in my heady youth when I was taken to be trying to write such things. Most critics vaguely assumed that Angus Wilson was merely updating Dickens for our times (that he wrote a book called *The World of Charles Dickens* made the assumption easier to adhere to). Others, including me, thought he was revivifying the *form* of the novel – and the novel, analytically, is as much about coping with form as it is about plot and character – to deal with the mores of his time. Thus form plus content, if the two may be separated, equated, in Wilson's work, to a passionate fictional response to the changing life of post-war Britain.

When I was at Secker & Warburg I'd designed the jacket for a little book of his, *The Wild Garden,* a series of lectures on writing which compared it to gardening, an activity which gave Angus enormous and sustained pleasure (and I take satisfaction in having persuaded Peter Carson of Penguin to include the book in Penguin's reissues of the Wilson *œuvre* in the early nineties). The front of the dust wrapper consisted of a photograph of Angus, wearing what looked like a blue rinse. When David Farrer, his editor, first saw the proof he said, 'Angus looks more like Margaret Rutherford than ever,' and as he grew older and more flamboyant – floppy ties, floppy suits, floppy hair and, no doubt, floppy everything – he increasingly resembled the glorious actress, except that her voice was low and Angus's in the upper octaves.

When I was on the literature panel I suggested that Michael Moorcock's magazine *New Worlds,* which in the sixties was publishing some of the most interesting 'experimental' prose (and, it has to be said, some of the least interesting, or worst) in the country, should receive a grant as well as the usual roster of more staid 'literary' publications. No other panel member even knew the magazine; probably, this being little Britain, because it didn't publish them. (I knew it because it published me.) Angus Wilson took the trouble to read some issues and was intrigued. He asked me if I could arrange for him to meet Moorcock, from whom I had at Gollancz recently commissioned a book. I took them to lunch at a then terribly chic Covent Garden restaurant, The Garden in King Street, with carpet designed by David Hicks (it looked like a field of liquorice allsorts) and wine cellar selected by John Higgins, then arts editor of *The Times.* I remember this latter fact because the first time I took Higgins out to lunch in his

capacity as literary editor of *The Times*, knowing his reputation
as a grape sniffer, I grappled uneasily with the wine list, determined to come up with a bottle that wouldn't betray my lack of
knowledge, while at the same time not making it obligatory for
Victor Gollancz Ltd to mortgage its offices. Higgins, across the
table, quietly suggested a particular bottle, and there was no more
nonsense. He later admitted his authority in the matter. The lunch
with Wilson and Moorcock was a great success and these two
most forceful and energetic of novelists became friends and mutual
admirers for life, and *New Worlds* received its grant.

Visiting Angus Wilson at his cottage at Felsham Woodside near
Bury St Edmunds in Suffolk was an experience. His companion
and 'partner' (what a horrible *nouveau pauvre* word that is), Tony
Garrett, provided a gargantuan tea, with lashings of jams and
cream, and more varieties of cake and biscuits than you could
imagine. Angus ate virtually nothing and neither did I, but Tony
didn't seem hurt or offended, only perhaps slightly surprised that
his lavish spread had not proved more of a bribe. After tea, Tony
drove us around the Suffolk countryside, with Angus sitting up
front beside him, and me lounging in the back. As we passed a
particular house or church or bridge or tree, Tony would comment: 'Angus did a great deal to see that that house [or church;
or bridge; or tree] was renovated, or saved from destruction.'
Whereupon Angus would say, trillingly: 'Oh, Tony, you do so
exaggerate. I didn't really do anything. All I did was have a word
with Mrs Tiggywinkle [or whoever it was] and suggest this and
that.' 'Oh, Angus,' Tony would respond, 'you're being too
modest.' 'Modest?' said Angus, giggling away, and tut-tutting.
'Certainly not. What an idea!' And a few moments later Tony
would point out another monument which Angus had saved for
the nation, or for someone. Perhaps he should have been appointed
Lord Lieutenant of the County, though if the office involved fox-
hunting I suspect Angus wouldn't have been good at it. He'd have
fallen off his horse.

Sadly, and confusedly, Angus and Tony exiled themselves to
France in the early eighties, it being said at the time that Angus
didn't feel he was sufficiently appreciated in this country. His last,
rich and poetic novel about England's 'heritage', *Setting the World*

*on Fire* (1980), alas did not set literary England alight. If this was the reason why Wilson departed it is a shocking indictment of how we treat our senior authors, not to mention those who've done the state some service. For myself, I'd be happy to be exiled to France, but the sad point about Angus's exile there is that, by all accounts, he did not enjoy it in spite of being a connoisseur of matters French, not least French literature: he had even published a book on Emile Zola.

Finding, I suppose, that the French were no more gushing to him than the British, he returned to Suffolk to die, and it is exceedingly poignant that his address is given in *Who's Who* for 1991 as Pinford End Nursing Home, Hawstead, Bury St Edmunds, Suffolk. He and Tony were virtually penniless too. Angus's novels and short stories (*The Collected Short Stories of Angus Wilson* is an irresistible book, more instructive than any social history of post-war England) were earning hardly any royalties and he was too ill to produce new work (he was suffering from senile dementia). Michael Moorcock went to visit him, when Angus's mind had almost completely gone. Tony Garrett whispered to Moorcock – the scene is like that in the last act of *King Lear* with Cordelia trying to comfort her father and Kent urging her away – after a certain period of time had elapsed that Angus was tiring and that Mike really ought to leave. Angus insisted upon accompanying the large bearded novelist to the door of his room. After thanking him for coming, Wilson paused and, drawing himself erect, said: 'I was particularly touched to learn that the writer Michael Moorcock wanted to come to see me. Do you know him? He hasn't been yet, but wasn't that nice of him? Goodbye.' Mike, an emotional man at the best of times, unsurprisingly could only just control his tears until he was out of the room.

Angus's memorial service seemed in many ways to be yet another occasion for homosexuals in the arts to make a public display of solidarity. The previous day the actor Sir Ian McKellen had, according to newspaper reports, spent forty minutes with the Prime Minister at Downing Street telling John Major (you couldn't imagine him telling Mrs Thatcher) that the government should try to be more sympathetic to gays. McKellen read a poem by Auden and Sonnet 116 by Shakespeare. It has to be said that he read them perfectly. The service was a good one, as memorial services go, but the highlight was Margaret Drabble's five-minute memoir of Angus, a wonderful character study and, in my view, quite the most incisive and rigorous thing that redoubtable woman has written. She told a story of how, visiting Angus for (cream) tea, she kept interjecting, as she does enthusiastically in conversation when concentrating on what is being said: 'You're quite right, Angus; that's quite right.' Eventually, irritated by these interjections, he said to her: 'Margaret, I do wish you'd stop interrupting me and saying, "Yes, you're quite right." Of course I'm right. I wouldn't be saying what I am saying if it wasn't right.'

# IX

One of the most hotly debated issues among bookpersons during my lifetime was why Graham Greene (or GrinGrin, as he was sometimes familiarly known) didn't win the Nobel Prize for, presumably, Literature; although it might, perhaps, have been for Peace. For me there could have been two reasons. First, highly entertaining novelist though he was, the chattering classes, who like to believe in their own influence in these matters, invariably overrated him while he was alive. Second, I seriously question whether the novelist, Roman Catholic or otherwise, actually existed. Let me provide at least three reasons, three anecdotes, to support my Doubting Thomas position.

In the sixties, most of the reading public, including his own readers, had little idea of what the tortured novelist looked like. His facial image did not appear on the back flap or back of his dust wrappers, as most authors' mug shots did by then, and if it did appear on the occasional orange Penguin the postage-stamp-size reproduction had plainly been snapped many years before.

One November morning in, I think, 1974, my wife and I were booked on a flight from Heathrow to Nice, Côte d'Azur, as the flight announcements had it. We were on our way to spend a fortnight's holiday in Châteauneuf du Pape, the one and only time I have watched men with bare feet trampling and tramping the grapes, fruit and sweat into wine. The plane was late departing (and in those days that was not a matter of course as it is now), apparently because one passenger hadn't shown up. We were disdainful: if flights were held up because one passenger was late, he or she must be some passenger. Perhaps because of the time of year, and the biting cold, we had few fellow passengers – maybe fifteen for a plane intended to carry one hundred or more. Eventually an announcement over the tannoy in the departure lounge requested us to board.

My wife and I settled down near the front of the plane. Since there were so few of us, passengers were not being directed to the seats marked on their boarding cards. A few minutes after take-off, I walked through the plane to the lavatory. (It was, of course, called 'toilet', a euphemism I cannot bring myself to speak or write, except here in quotation marks – something my older children find perverse. Ah, how language is debased as it is mis-used.) I returned in some excitement to whisper to my wife that I was pretty sure that the man on his own three or four rows back was Graham Greene. She was sceptical, remarking, correctly, that I was forever imagining I was about to have close encounters with the famous. (My second wife is depressed by what she sees as my passion for spotting 'minor' celebrities, usually morons from television, but occasionally politicians.)

At that time Greene was very famous indeed, an idealogue of somewhat elusive hue, renowned almost as much for penning tetchy, imperious letters to *The Times* and other publications on the rise and fall of a dictatorship as he was for his novels, entertainments or otherwise, or for the many films made from them. My wife hardly required an excuse to walk through the cabin to check up on my sighting, but the usual one served. She returned to say, 'You have to be wrong. That's a seedy American businessman drinking whisky.' The line was too Greene for words, but why she thought the man was American I do not know. Certainly she did not hear him speak. She went on: 'And he's reading the review in the *New Statesman*' – another power in the land then, the *Staggers* – 'of the new Muriel Spark novel,' which review I had just read. Why a 'seedy American businessman' would be reading a review of Muriel Spark in the *New Statesman* I could not imagine but there it is. 'And,' she added, as the *coup de grâce*, 'there's a Bodley Head book on the seat beside him.'

She had been much more observant than I had. Here was docu-mentary evidence indeed; and to me it virtually clinched the matter. Mrs Spark was a fellow Roman Catholic novelist, although it wasn't yet publicly known that Greene had supported her financially in her early struggling years. Greene, at the time, was a director of the Bodley Head, which firm had recently become his own publishers. (Euan Cameron, the imprint's publicity manager then, told me that Greene, who lived mainly abroad, rarely attended a board meeting, although he sometimes recommended promising new writers to Max Reinhardt, the managing director and proprietor. The board had something of a theatrical bent, probably because Reinhardt had been married to the actress Margaret Leighton. Directors included Anthony Quayle and Ralph Richardson. Cameron, who was later on the board himself, told me that Richardson would roar up to meetings each month on his motorbike, and comment shrewdly on the previous month's publications, all of which he'd have perused with care.)

I found a further excuse to wander down the aisle, noticing this time that the man was surrounded by (airline) miniature whisky bottles – it was still earlyish in the day – and reading a volume of that excellent edition, *The Bodley Head Ford Madox Ford*.

Soon we arrived in Nice and disembarked. Outside the airport, the sky glowed a zinging blue, as if painted by Raoul Dufy; and palm trees added to the impression. The seedy American businessman had, I swear, a mischievous look in his eye as we passengers stalked and prowled about, waiting for our luggage to be disgorged on to the baggage carousel and eager to leave the airport. His luggage, presumably because he was the last passenger on the flight to check in, appeared first. The tall (as he proved), anonymous-looking but curiously imposing man leant forward and plucked his bag off the moving belt. Then, deliberately walking in front of my wife and me, he raised his passport in front of him, to chest height, almost insisting that we read the name thereon. It was 'Mr G. Greene'. He then hurried towards passport control where he was nodded to, almost genuflected at (was I imagining this? I think not) and smiles were exchanged, mostly by the customs officers. Mr G. Greene walked out of the glass doors of the airport terminal, greeted an elegantly dressed young woman with, as I remember it, long blonde hair, opened the door of her red sports car (he seemed a size or two too large to fit in such a vehicle), and was driven speedily away.

A few years later, in 1966, I joined Penguin Books, to be responsible editorially for business books (about which I knew less than nothing; Penguin did not do well with business books), sociology, ancient classics and plays. The chief editor, Tony Godwin, was keen on the occasional weekend get-together and 'think-tank' (although I don't believe the phrase had been invented then) at which a dozen or so Penguin editors would hole up at a hotel in the country to discuss editorial policy, strategy and progress. At the first of these I attended, somewhere in Gloucestershire, he asked me one afternoon if I would accompany him on a walk. Like me, he enjoyed walking. Tony made little effort at small talk and I knew he didn't like small talk to be lobbed at him. Thus we walked for a while in silence. 'I have decided,' he eventually announced, in his nasal asthmatic voice, 'that there is only one person who can end the war in Vietnam.'

In an unusual moment of modesty, it didn't even occur to me that he might have me in mind. Tony said everything with such fundamental conviction that you were, at least until you thought the matter through, inclined to believe him. 'And that's Graham Greene.' I said nothing by way of response; for had I agreed, Tony would probably have dissented, demanding: how could a mere novelist halt a war? But that was the thought whirling through my mind. 'Of all the Penguin editors,' he went on, 'you are the one most likely to be able to persuade him to write a Penguin Special which will result in a cease-fire.' Thus was I picked out as the Pérez de Cuellar of the time.

I was to find out where Greene was, and visit him – and in the next few days. Nothing was to be put in writing, for Max Reinhardt would undoubtedly wish to wheel himself in and have the Bodley Head co-publish the book, and if Graham Greene on Vietnam was to achieve its purpose – to end the war – it had to be published as a Penguin Special paperback original. I protested my inadequacy, my lack of grasp of the details of the Vietnam conflict; my elementary schoolboy French (Greene lived mostly in France); my perfunctory command of the novelist's *œuvre*. I'd read *Brighton Rock*, and that was about it. Oh, and I'd seen *The Potting Shed* at the old Birmingham Rep. All I remembered of that experience was the peculiar smell in the auditorium, like mothballs that had gone off. Tony would have none of my protestations of incompetence. I was his man.

I established by stealth that Greene had a flat in Paris, and the address, and that he was there at the time. I flew to Paris as soon as the Penguin weekend was over, and tracked down the front door of the apartment house in the Boulevard de Malesherbes where the novelist was said to reside. I peered at the names on the brass plates by the bells and frowned. No Mr, or even M., let alone G. Greene. I looked again, and was amused. There was a M. Verdant.

I pushed the heavy, high front door open and asked the concierge if Monsieur Greene was at home. I felt emboldened to make this full-frontal assault having seen a shelf of the great writer's novels, in French, at the back of the concierge's lodge. Besides which, had I attempted to mount the stairs without declaring my intent, I might have been expelled from the building. There must be some mistake, the concierge said, shrugging wearily. No Monsieur Grin lived here. What about Monsieur Verdant? I asked. The concierge shrugged again as concierges do, and shook his head. Monsieur Verdant he hadn't seen in months.

My mad mission had already failed. I discovered later that Greene had the previous evening left Paris for some foreign location, I think in South America, where his novel *The Comedians* was being filmed with Elizabeth Taylor and Richard Burton, the well-known comedy act. Had Greene been at home, had the concierge admitted to it, had the novelist agreed to see me, might he have agreed to write a Penguin Special and, as a result, might millions of lives have been saved?

My third non-encounter with Greene was more modest, more pedantic. At Gollancz, in the early seventies, I signed up Maeve Gilmore's sensitive and touching memoir of her late husband, Mervyn Peake, author of the *Gormenghast* trilogy and artist grotesque. Maeve wanted to reproduce in her book a letter to her late husband from Greene, praising his play, *The Wit to Woo*. I wrote to the novelist, at the address where I'd failed to locate him, requesting permission. A few weeks later, having had no response and with time moving on, I wrote again, suggesting that perhaps the first missive hadn't arrived (always a tactful thing to say) and that, to avoid troubling him any further, I'd assume he'd have no objection to his letter to Peake being reproduced in Maeve's book unless I heard from him to the contrary.

By return of post he replied, most sternly, pointing out that the copyright in a living writer's words is his alone, and that my being prepared to send the book to press without his written approval to reproduce his letter was both unprofessional and a breach of copyright. I was properly rebuked but still wasn't quite convinced that Graham Greene existed. Even this letter could have been forged.

Greene described the *Spectator*, in the days when the effervescent Alexander Chancellor was editor, as 'the best-written paper in English'. He occasionally added to its distinction by addressing letters to the editor, and by the odd short story. Encountering Chancellor at the Garrick Club one day, I offered him a drink. He had just come from Greene's memorial service. 'The Abbey?' I muttered pompously, without thinking. 'No, the Cathedral,' said Chancellor, meaning of course not St Paul's but Westminster, without for once emitting his shoulder-shaking, explosive laugh, which sounds as if a cork is being routinely ejected from a bottle of champagne. Among the speakers, he said, had been Muriel Spark, whose homage – Greene had not only sent her regular cheques in her struggling years, but the occasional case of wine as well – was most gracious. Greene's niece, the Canadian publisher Louise Dennys, also spoke. She told what is, perhaps, the ultimate publishing story. In 1968, Greene sent the manuscript of his latest book, *Travels with My Aunt*, to his American publishers. After reading the manuscript they cabled him: 'Terrific book but we'll need to change title.' Greene cabled back: 'No need to change title. Easier to change publishers' – and proceeded to do so.

# X

I moved from Hutchinson to Penguin as the result of a telephone call from Anne Graham Bell, who had recommended me to Tony Godwin. In 1966, Godwin, Penguin's chief editor, was looking to add an editor to his team, she said. I hadn't met him, but was in awe of his reputation. Some thought he was akin to a genius, and was re-energising Penguin which, in recent years, had rather lost its way; others, almost invariably those older than Godwin, thought he was a demi-gorgon.

My 'interview' took place in an Indian restaurant in Hampstead. It was mid-winter, I remember, and thick snow lay on Haverstock Hill and Heath Street. I was in such a state by the end of the evening – Godwin was like a manic jack-in-the-box until you got to know him and learned to disregard his impossible social behaviour – that I left my treasured Russian fur hat (Harold Macmillan had started the fashion) in the restaurant, never to see it again.

Godwin insisted upon ordering enough courses for about five people. Whether he did it deliberately to test me – to see whether I'd try to stop him, or to discover the size of my appetite – I do not know, but most of it, saffron rice and curries of divers textures, was left comatose on the tablecloth as we departed.

He asked me what I would like to edit at Penguin, whereas it seemed to me that if he was looking for an editor he should tell me what subject or subjects were available. I tentatively suggested fiction. He exploded. 'You can't edit the fiction list. Oliver Caldecott edits it.' Ask a stupid question. 'What else?' he growled. I didn't want to put my foot in it again. 'Poetry?' I ventured. 'No, of course not,' he sighed, spluttering rice. 'Tony Richardson does poetry.' What else did I know *anything* about? 'Art books, then?'

I asked, by now expecting the answer No and receiving it, this being a further part of Tony Richardson's empire. 'Plays,' I suggested, a last thrust. 'Plays?' he said. 'That's hardly a job.' More stuffing of his little mouth with rice and curry. 'I'll tell you what.' He took out a pen and began writing on a paper napkin. 'You can do plays but only as a perk at the end of the day when you've done the ancient classics . . .' He paused, then, looking me in the eye as sometimes disconcertingly he did, he said, 'What's your Greek like? What about your Latin?' and honked and hooted with laughter. 'Ancient classics. Sociology. Business books.' He spent most of the rest of the evening, as more and more curries arrived, explaining to me his ambitions for the business list, and how I was to go about finding an advisory editor. But for me that evening was the beginning of my unanticipated professional involvement with plays and the theatre which was to lead to my becoming a theatre critic.

In those days the sale of plays was reasonably big business, a burgeoning side of publishing. Geoffrey Strachan and John Cullen, his boss, chose the plays for Methuen, and Charles Monteith and Frank Pike for Faber and Faber, which was at first the market leader. Faber had Osborne and Beckett, and quickly snapped up teenager Christopher Hampton when the Royal Court did his first play. They had Genet and Simon Gray. Methuen soon stole a march with Pinter, Arden, Orton, Bond, Brecht, and the learned Mortimer. Penguin had Wesker. My predecessor but one, Tom Maschler (between us was the scholarly Jim Cochrane, from Edinburgh, who mainly looked after the Latin and Greek classics and who years later saw the point of Nikolai Tolstoy's Arthurian trilogy, which he put under contract at Bantam), had had the lively idea of putting three plays by three playwrights between one set of covers, and calling the series Penguin Modern Dramatists. Thus Penguin plays were less rarefied than Methuen or Faber volumes, and usually – even with three plays for the price of one – less expensive, the print runs being appreciably longer. I added quite a few volumes to the series, including one of radio plays (starring Giles Cooper, Alan Sharp, Jeremy Sandford, Barry Bermange, Cecil Taylor and – this in 1968 – Caryl Churchill), and one of six plays, four by poets – B. S. Johnson, Stewart Conn, Ian

Hamilton Finlay, George MacBeth – the other two being by Peter Terson and David Storey. As three of the playwrights were Scottish, I asked Edwin Morgan to introduce the volume.

I also began a series called Penguin Modern Playwrights, which published single new plays, the object being to make them available for sale by first nights. The first volume was Charles Dyer's quirky two-hander *Staircase*, which opened at the Aldwych, then the London home of the RSC, in the autumn of 1966, starring Patrick Magee and Paul Scofield as homosexual hairdressers, directed by Peter Hall. Hall took exception to the text being published, because the script as presented by the playwright underwent so many rewrites during the rehearsal period. Whether the changes were the author's doing, or the director's or the actors', I do not know.

Certainly it is the case that most previously unperformed plays undergo drastic surgery during the rehearsal period (although I'm sure Pinter's do not) and playwrights, if only to save face, prefer their scripts to be published as they are staged. Similarly, directors want texts published which they have, to a greater or lesser degree, been responsible for orchestrating. A few playwrights though, who loathe what directors have done in rehearsal, would pay a great deal to see *their* words rather than other people's rewrites published. There were, I think, about ten titles in the series – including two sets of television plays, *Talking to a Stranger* by John Hopkins and the *Nigel Barton* plays by the pitiless Dennis Potter – but the series as conceived was probably doomed to failure from the start. There were quite a few 'political' plays which stand up today, including Charles Wood's *Dingo*, Michael Hastings' *Lee Harvey Oswald*, Jean-Claude van Itallie's *America Hurrah* and, undoubtedly the most successful volume in the series, Barbara Garson's *Macbird!*, a somewhat lumpen verse parody of *Macbeth* set somewhere between Dallas and Dunsinane by a more earnest than angry young American woman which suggested that Lyndon Baines Johnson, the then President of the United States, had had more than a little to do with the assassination of his predecessor, John F. Kennedy. It was good dirty fun, and Joan Littlewood staged it with some success at Theatre Workshop in 1967. The play became national news, which plays don't often do, being regarded by many as in bad taste, which undoubtedly it was. Penguin had published the text some time before the first night at Theatre Workshop, Stratford East (a small press, Grassy Knoll, had been set up in the States to publish the text in 1966), but subsequent to the furore caused by Littlewood's production some of Allen Lane's friends made it clear to the elderly and increasingly out of touch publisher that *his* bird had given birth to an unsavoury egg.

Lane leaned on Tony Godwin to have *Macbird!* put out of print, pulped or burnt; in short, got rid of. I do not know what happened to it as I'd left Penguin by then. I think it escaped the fate which befell the Penguin edition of a collection of the acerbic, indeed scatological, French cartoonist Siné's work. Another friend of Allen Lane's, or perhaps the same 'friend', persuaded the King Penguin that the drawings were rude, which they were, and that thus the book was not worthy of Penguin plumage. Upon being asked to do so, Godwin declined to withdraw the book. Allen Lane summoned up a pantechnicon and, at dead of night, burgled his own warehouse at Harmondsworth, purloining all the remaining pallets and parcels of the Siné volume, drove them back to his farm in Hertfordshire and is said to have joyously witnessed with his friends and family a great conflagration.

To be an editor at Penguin in the sixties was a heady experience. Now, for better or for worse – and for my money it's for worse – Penguin is just another publishing house. Penguin used to be almost a national institution, and what it chose to publish was part of the country's agenda. This was the heyday of Penguin Specials, original paperbacks dealing urgently with social and political issues, at a time when television in this respect was still in its teething stage. Colour supplements and dismayingly large newspapers hadn't yet come into being. Most of the Penguin editors were aged well under thirty, and Tony Godwin was simply the best publisher in the country.

He was an irascible, abrasive, shock-haired little man, a kind of pocket grey-haired Struwwelpeter, from ever so ordinary origins, who had been plucked from the obscurity of bookselling – and to publishers in the early sixties little was more obscure and infra dig than bookselling – by the shrewd Allen Lane. Godwin had run

Bumpus in Baker Street, and the influential Book Society, before starting Better Books in Charing Cross Road where, daringly, you could pick up a cup of coffee and, even more revolutionary, listen to authors reading from their work. Better Books advertised in the Underground too, with well-designed, arresting posters. Godwin was proudly self-educated, and much resented by the mediocrities, time-servers and mandarins who surrounded Lane, all hoping to succeed him: not only was the King Penguin beginning to resemble busts of Julius Caesar but, like the mighty Julius, he was obsessively prone to flattery. Godwin's undoing was that he couldn't flatter.

Articles were written about the Penguin editors, not least in the glossy monthly magazines, *Queen*, or *Tatler*, or *Harpers*, christening us 'the Whizz Kids'. Books mattered, and good books mattered particularly. We all took infinite care over poetry, plays, classics, economics, history, art, sociology. Most of the books were originals, commissioned for Penguin, fiction alone being bought in from hardback publishers. It has, of course, to be conceded that most of any month's turnover derived from fiction. Most contentiously, and probably wrongly, Tony Godwin insisted upon doing away with the orange, blue and green covers, the Penguin grid devised by Edward Young, and its familiar slabs of colour starkly adorned by Gill Sans-Serif Bold, and gave full rein to the art director, flaxen-haired Alan Aldridge (surely a relative of the 'Straw Man'), and his band of unpolished airbrushers. Penguin covers became as controversial and as sought after as record sleeves.

Tony was an intuitive editor, and sartorially as well as intellectually unorthodox. Even in his fifties he wore blue jeans and a blue open-necked shirt. If he had to wear a suit and a floral tie he did so with some disdain. He woke up very early in the morning – his widow, the photographer Fay Godwin, tells me it was usually about 5 a.m. – to read. He used as much nervous energy in a day as most people expend in a year. It was always risky to invite him to dinner, particularly if the meal was likely to continue latish into the evening, because Tony, sitting at the table, would all at once fall asleep. I do not know anyone who can fall asleep so suddenly. He would be eating away, using his fingers fastidiously, talking strenuously to his neighbour, and then you'd be aware he was asleep, his head having fallen down slightly on to his chest, causing him to resemble a doormouse at bay.

He cajoled and inspired writers, persuading them to produce better work than they had imagined themselves capable of: ask John Berger, Margaret Drabble, Edna O'Brien, A. (as opposed to, presumably, The) Alvarez, Philip Knightley, among others. He could and almost invariably did analyse a manuscript, whether outline, specimen chapter or finished script, as if he was the ultimate physician or arbiter, with in-built X-ray. He knew instinctively rather than analytically what was wrong, and orally conveyed precisely to the author the manuscript's shortcomings. He couldn't do this in writing. He was no good at writing, and embarked upon letters or reports only as a final resort, when there was no alternative. He didn't suffer fools lightly (he and I never really got on: he made me too nervous) and was moodily intolerant, stamping his foot like Rumpelstiltskin, with those who weren't on his wavelength. He despised the publishing establishment, and the trivial ways in which it tried to put him down. I remember once, at about seven of an evening, at the London Penguin editorial office in John Street, hearing him having an argument with Jock Murray, the seventh or so Murray to run John Murray, about the value to Penguin of Philip Magnus's latest biography. 'Look,' sighed Tony nasally as he berated Murray, 'tell Mr Magnus . . .' He was stopped in mid-flow. 'What did you say, Jock?' Then another pause at Godwin's end of the line. 'Oh, all right then. Tell *Sir Philip* . . .' He had no time for this kind of banter, this obsession with etiquette, social convention. When he replaced the receiver he laughed hysterically.

Eventually mean-minded, smaller men – lacking lean and hungry looks – poisoned Allen Lane against him, and Tony Godwin left mighty Penguin to join the formidable George Weidenfeld. He had quite a successful career at Weidenfeld & Nicolson, particularly replenishing the fictional coffers, which had for some years dwindled, and then he went to work for Harcourt Brace Jovanovich in New York, where, the last time I saw him, he was having a blazing row with an art editor about a jacket design. He died far too young, although he was older than his silly sense of dress and roving, engaging, quizzical mind suggested.

I am lucky to have served two such publishing masters as Warburg and Godwin.

# XI

Soon after I arrived at Gollancz in 1967, Livia Gollancz took me to have tea with Ivy Compton-Burnett, easily the firm's most distinguished 'literary' author. In those days I found her arid, smugly upper-class, incestuous novels pretty well unreadable, composed as they are almost entirely of dialogue. (Interestingly, they didn't dramatise particularly well. Julian Mitchell adapted *A Heritage and Its History* for the stage and it was at best a *succès d'estime*.) When we arrived at the block of mansion flats in Cornwall Gardens, Kensington, the housekeeper opened the door and said, surely mischievously (she must have been put up to it by Dame Ivy), 'It is Mrs MacGibbon, isn't it?' 'No, it's Miss Gollancz, Dame Ivy's publisher,' Livia boomed back. Mrs Mac-Gibbon was, no doubt, Jean MacGibbon, wife of James MacGibbon, my predecessor at Gollancz, who had resigned in a fit of pique a few months earlier when he wasn't appointed head of the firm on Victor's death. MacGibbon had dealt with Dame Ivy in recent years.

The ancient novelist (she was born, improbably, in suburban Pinner, Middlesex, in 1884; and was to die in 1969) sat by the fire in her drawing-room in a capacious armchair which looked as if it could house at least two of her. Probably it was less that the armchair was substantial than that she was so frail. She looked like a character from Henry James, someone left over from another era who had not been permitted to die. There was another elderly female party present (was it Madge Garland, Lady Ashton?) and Livia – rather rudely, I thought, but perhaps she was terrified of Ivy – spent most of the time talking to this other visitor while Dame Ivy engaged me in conversation. 'Come and sit close to me,' she said after I was introduced to her, and I felt like Pip with

Miss Havisham. I distinctly remember her saying, as she proffered a bag (not a plate) of extremely sticky buns or teacakes: 'Do you take crumpet, Mr Gordon?' I was terrified that she'd ask me what I thought of her books, or grill me on their content, always a publisher's occupational hazard with authors, though the more distinguished or successful they are, the less likely they are to be inquisitorial. Vanity makes them assume that their work has been noted and absorbed. It is inevitably the unpublishable first novelist who desires you to deliver an hour's lecture about his or her book.

I remember Dame Ivy asked me, having requested information about my background, how I found London; and I think we spoke, improbable though it seems, about the weather. And all the while I kept wondering why her first novel *Dolores*, the only one which hadn't been published by Gollancz, had been 'suppressed'. I couldn't see her as a D. H. Lawrence or even a Henry Miller. I was relieved when Livia said it was time to go. The flat seemed to have remained unchanged down the decades, and I couldn't imagine Dame Ivy having done anything but sit by that fireside throughout her life, like a praying mantis, her hair in its strange captive net, flickering her eyelashes and shooting her tongue out occasionally, taking in gobbets of gossip about the upper middle classes to be translated, cold and classical, into her lethal, ritualistic novels.

Gollancz's most popular author at that period, perhaps ever (though there was A. J. Cronin and the TV spin-off from his novels, *Dr Finlay's Casebook*), was another Dame, Daphne du Maurier. The firm published two novels by her when I was there, *The House on the Strand* and *Rule Britannia*. Neither was any great shakes, but the second was an embarrassment. I tried to suggest to Livia that Daphne, as she was familiarly known to everyone in the firm, should consign the manuscript to a bottom drawer, but this idea was not met with approval.

One of my jobs at Gollancz was to sell our authors' books to soft cover, and this occasionally meant reselling titles to paperback when the previous licence period, usually five or seven years, had expired. Victor Gollancz had disapproved of paperbacks, which in his lifetime meant little more than Penguin and Pan with Corgi publishing some rather more 'popular' or 'down-market titles', as we would say today. (The pejorative 'middle list' hadn't been invented.) Somehow Gollancz had been persuaded to sub-license the paperback rights in the best du Maurier novels – *Rebecca, My Cousin Rachel, Frenchman's Creek, The King's General, Jamaica Inn,* and so on – to Penguin for a seven-year period. Penguin published them as modern classics, which presumably pleased both hardback publisher and author. They did not sell as well as they should have done, and it occurred to me that they'd sell infinitely better if they were marketed simply as great romances or romantic novels. I made this suggestion first to Livia, who was shocked by the vulgarity of the idea ('Daphne would never want to be published in paperback other than by Penguin'), and then to du Maurier's agent, the supercilious Graham Watson of Curtis Brown. He tried to put a dampener on my enthusiasm, echoing Livia's point about Daphne not wanting to leave Penguin. Besides, he was sure that neither Pan nor Corgi would be interested. I had taken soundings and was certain that both would undoubtedly be interested, and at quite a high financial level, something that naturally would interest Watson. But he persisted in his line: Daphne was a classic, Penguin published classics, Pan and Corgi didn't.

I couldn't resist asking the respective editorial directors of Pan and Corgi, Clarence Paget and Alan Earney, to make offers. They proposed generous sums, way above what Penguin would have earned in a few years. When I told Livia she was embarrassed, as if I'd indulged in sleight of hand, but I think rather pleased. She discussed the matter with the chairman of the firm, John Bush (Bush, who was the sales director, was also chairman, that title being inferior to Livia's as governing director, but they were also joint managing directors). Bush's wife, Sheila, who later wrote the history of the firm, had been Daphne's editor for years, and was close to Victor, hence the Bushes' influence over all aspects of the company. Everyone was agreed that Daphne must be told, if only because of the amount of money involved. What I did not know and had not guessed was that Dame Daphne felt she was, if not exactly on her uppers, exceedingly hard up, in the way that those who have lived affluently and are used to the good life frequently say they are.

Agents have to be adept at guarding their flanks, and are not renowned for eating humble pie or admitting they have misread a situation. Graham Watson gave me the impression that he had been behind the idea of garnering other offers, and I was told to go back to Penguin and inform them that if they wished to keep their classic author for another seven years they would have to offer more. Christopher Dolley, the head of Penguin at the time (post-Allen Lane, pre-Peter Mayer, and whose background was the marketing of soap powder), declined to increase significantly the modest advance against royalties which Penguin had already suggested. I'm sure he thought I was trying it on, and that darling Daphne would never leave Penguin. In 1972 that was still very much the Penguin attitude. Both Pan and Corgi then offered more than they had previously done, each of them determined to win the books.

Livia asked me to telephone the author, and explain to her the pros and cons of the respective paperback imprints. I marginally favoured Pan because I thought it would sell more copies. What clinched it, though, was my telling du Maurier that Corgi was owned by Transworld, an American company, whereas Pan was owned in equal parts by three British hardback houses: Collins, Heinemann and Macmillan. As far as the Dame was concerned, there was nothing further to be said. She would in no circumstances be published in Britain by an American firm.

I delivered the bad news to Alan Earney, a thoroughly decent man, telling him that the decision had nothing to do with the terms offered, since Corgi's offer was to all intents and purposes the same as Pan's. It was because she insisted on being published by a British house. Within minutes I received a telephone call from the managing director of Corgi, a man I had seen in slick action but did not know, Pat Newman. He asked if it was true that Corgi's offer had been rejected because its proprietorship was American. I said that it was. 'In that case,' said Newman, 'will you kindly ask Lady Browning' – the down-to-earth and risen-from-the-ranks Newman was having none of the 'Dame Daphne' nonsense – 'why her late husband, General "Boy" Browning, was prepared to have me fight in his battalion during the war, but she doesn't think I'm good enough to publish her?' I didn't pass on the question. There was too much emotion in it, too little logic.

In 1992 Daphne du Maurier was, distantly, to re-enter my life. One of my colleagues at our literary agency represented the novelist Susan Hill, who was chosen by the du Maurier estate to write a sequel to *Rebecca*, the kind of idea dreamed up late at night which should, I suspect, be consigned to the trash can at the following morning's breakfast; except, of course, being so meretricious that all concerned would stand to make a great deal of money. And Susan Hill has a simple, straightforward prose style which is not a million miles from that of Daphne du Maurier.

At the 1992 Frankfurt Book Fair, the only titles nudging publishers from the lethargy of Maastricht were *Sex* by Madonna and the sequel to *Rebecca*. When I suggested on a number of occasions that a prequel to *Rebecca* would be more apt (my publisher wife's idea), heads nodded sagely; and when I further suggested that the *Rebecca* trilogy could then be marketed in a slipcase as by Susan Hill and Daphne du Maurier I was regarded as something of a savant.

Another author represented by our agency, Jean Rhys, has a great deal to answer for with her *Wide Sargasso Sea*, a prequel to another novel (*Jane Eyre*) and a minor classic in its own right.

In my five years at Gollancz I published a number of Scottish authors. It was depressing in a way to find that Scottish writers published by well-known London houses did significantly better than when published north of the border, and were treated with more deference or seriousness by the critics. This was, and sadly still is, partly because, too often, the Scots are only impressed when their writers are seen to have 'made it' by being published down south, and partly because Scottish publishers seem incapable of selling their books in other than modest quantities outside Scotland, particularly in England. And this, in its turn, is not least because the Scottish firms are habitually undercapitalised. If James Kelman and Alasdair Gray were not these days published by leading London imprints they would probably be prophets without honour in their own country (rather than merely novelists).

I was particularly pleased to suggest to the Orcadian poet and short story writer, George Mackay Brown (his novels don't seem to me to be in the same class), that he should put together *An Orkney Tapestry* (1969), a book of great beauty, and to Iain

Crichton Smith that he should have a go at a novel. The result was the masterly *Consider the Lilies* (1968), which sensitively explored the poignant, terrible life of one old woman during the Highland Clearances. Since then Iain has not stopped writing novels and short stories as well as being, at his prolific best, a masterly poet. All his work is highly intelligent, hard-edged, bleak, Calvinistically honest. There is no flab, no sentiment, no fine writing for the sake of fine writing. One of the books I was proudest of publishing at Gollancz was his translation from the Gaelic of Sorley Maclean's 1943 sequence of love poems, *Dain do Eimhir (Songs to Eimhir)*, which surely paved the way for Maclean's work to be substantially translated into English and for him to be now ranked with MacDiarmid, Auden, Eliot, and Laura Riding. Crichton Smith is, among authors, the world's worst typist, and strangely for one who is such a clear-headed and incisive critic of the work of others, does not seem to have any in-built critical apparatus when analysing his own work. It is so easy, relatively speaking, to criticise anyone else's writing if you are an experienced reader, virtually impossible to be objective about your own, at least until years after you've written it, when you're almost bound, if you are honest, to find it at best mediocre. Let others declare that you are a genius. I've yet to meet the Scottish author (maybe Allan Massie is the exception, but he is more a European) who isn't deeply suspicious of the way his or her work is regarded, especially by publishers, and who doesn't look for deviousness and perversion in reactions to it and usually finds it; and by extension Scottish publishers are surely to a man and woman the most paranoid, aggressive and self-righteous in the Western world.

# XII

George Mackay Brown was and is known to his initiates as simply George Brown, and the first politician with whom I dealt as publisher, and grew to know well, was George Brown, or Lord George-Brown, as he had rather fatuously by then become. When I arrived at Gollancz in 1967, the left-wing publishing house, still owned and controlled by the Gollancz family, was going through the doldrums. The anarchic Victor – to whom I was once introduced at some book trade celebration when I was chairman of the Society of Young Publishers, and he confined to a wheelchair having suffered one of a number of strokes – had died only a few months before I took the Gollancz ticket. He ran the firm – latterly, ran it down – almost to his dying day. Nearly everything I have heard about him and his treatment of his fellow human beings, including his daughters, makes him seem a martinet and a brute. As with Robert Maxwell, at least until his death and subsequent exposure, those who suffered personally as a result of Gollancz's boorishness – and his vanity was petty compared with Cap'n Bob's – talked after the event of his being 'a great character'. I found particularly distasteful the following anecdote, recorded at the first staff Christmas lunch after his death. Subsequent to his first stroke (his various strokes were spoken of as if modern history was recorded by them, as if they predicated subsequent events) he had found himself sitting on the bowl in his specially doctored lavatory at the top of a flight of stairs in the Gollancz offices in Henrietta Street (if it sounds like the stinking privy in Ben Jonson's *The Alchemist*, in truth it was not unlike that) without a toilet roll to hand. The ancient philanthropic publisher kicked open the door and bellowed and roared until some cringeing menial, no doubt trembling in terror and anticipating dismissal, lobbed a toilet roll, hand grenade-like, up the stairs for Sir Victor to use. This was all found terribly funny in retrospect. It has never ceased to bemuse me how people employed by bullies obtain a certain frisson, if nothing more, from the experience, and this of course encourages the brutes to bully more. If they are outstanding individuals, as VG must have been, it makes their nastiness the more reprehensible.

Why people become, or became publishers – when publishing was still an occupation for those who liked to think of themselves as gentlemen – is a book in itself. It must disclose some psychological need, to communicate your enthusiasm in and through the printed word to those who mostly couldn't care less. Certainly Gollancz harboured a need to humiliate. Godfrey Smith, whose first novel, *The Flaw in the Crystal*, was accepted for publication in 1954 by his Oxford contemporary and friend Hilary Rubinstein, a nephew of Gollancz and a young editorial director, was told that the head of the firm would like to meet his newest author. Lunch was arranged at the Savoy Grill, the socialist Gollancz's home from home, for the three men. At the end of the meal Gollancz, who had ignored the presence of Rubinstein throughout, asked Godfrey Smith if he'd like a cigar. Smith replied that he'd very much like a cigar, and the waiter was summoned. Smith took what he wanted, and Gollancz his usual. As the waiter made to depart, Smith said, 'What about Hilary?' 'What, him?' barked Gollancz, scornfully; and then to the waiter: 'Give him the smallest you've got.'

In his review for the *New York Times Book Review* of Victor Gollancz's last, posthumously published book (for literate publishers in those days fancied themselves as writers too), *Reminiscences of Affection*, Kingsley Amis told a tale which reveals a great deal about Gollancz's philosophy as a publisher. When in 1954 he received a letter telling him that Gollancz would be delighted to publish *Lucky Jim*, Amis was over the Swansea moon. A letter from a leading publisher indicating that he wishes to publish your first book is an event which cannot be transcended in the life of an aspiring author. And that, in addition, the publisher is offering money for the privilege is a bonus, a bonanza. Amis, if I recall his review accurately (and the sum would be in line with the times), was offered an advance against royalties of £50. Gollancz's letter concluded by asking young Amis to ring his secretary (note how from the beginning of the publisher-author relationship the publisher makes himself superior to the author by possessing a secretary) to arrange a luncheon date.

Amis, of course, would have caught the first train up from Swansea, where he taught, to have lunch in London that day, but Mr Gollancz didn't have a free date for three weeks. Thus, again, does the publisher exercise power (he is such a busy luncher) over the mere scribbler.

By the time the appointed day arrived, Amis had readily persuaded himself that if the novel was worth publishing it was worth considerably more than £50, and he'd ask, perhaps, for £250. He arrived at 14 Henrietta Street, in the middle of Covent Garden – in the fifties still awash with vegetables, the lorries conveying them thither and away, blocking the streets around for much of the working day. (Even in my time – and up to the firm's departure from Henrietta Street near the end of 1992 – the offices smelt of wooden packing cases.) Amis looked up at the peeling fascia board and thought that perhaps £250 was pushing it. He'd suggest £200. In his mind the bold sum he had intended proposing diminishes as he is led through the crumbling, carpetless old fruit warehouse which constituted Gollancz's offices, until he reaches Victor's room on the other side of the building, above Maiden Lane; by which time Amis feels almost obliged to take out his cheque book and ask Gollancz if he'd accept £50 for publishing *Lucky Jim*.

Today, with many imprints bunched together disagreeably in conglomerates, having been acquired by larger imprints during the 1980s in a possibly terminal game of literary Monopoly, the whole face of publishing has changed. Overheads resulting from purpose-built or adapted office blocks are such that even discriminating publishers can only infrequently chance their arms on what they believe could be the *Lucky Jim* of tomorrow. The process has, generally speaking, become bland, slick and cynical.

Gollancz, still not part of a conglomerate, was purchased in 1989 by the 'gentlemanly' Boston, Massachusetts, imprint Houghton Mifflin, and was more or less left to its own devices; in the autumn of 1992, it was sold on to Cassell. Until the end there were no carpets on most of the floors, although there was the odd lick of paint and the Maiden Lane side of the building had been sold. When Lord George-Brown paid his solitary visit to his publishers at the end of 1970, he had a part-time job as 'productivity counsellor' at Courtaulds, the textile manufacturers, presided over by Sir Frank (later Lord) Kearton, a staunch Labour man. Observing immediately the scruffy Gollancz floorboards which always smelt of linseed oil, Brown offered Livia Gollancz a keen discount on Courtaulds finest carpets.

Livia – who before being bullied into his publishing house by her father had been well known for playing the French horn in the Hallé Orchestra and a number of other major orchestras, including that of the Royal Opera House, Covent Garden, and the London Symphony Orchestra – was not amused. 'Our firm' (she always referred to it thus, the possessive clearly applying to her family rather than to the salaried directors and staff), 'our firm has survived for forty years without carpets and there's no reason why we should have to have them now.' After this rebuff, Brown asked me, in a stage whisper (he was incapable of anything quieter), if he could have a second glass of sherry. Livia, who didn't much approve of alcohol in the office, or anywhere else (although she bottled her own elderflower wine), said he could have one more glass but that was it. She'd bought in a bottle specially as George-Brown was known to like a drink.

The acquisition by Gollancz of Brown's autobiography (or 'political memoirs', as the title page of *In My Way* has it) in 1970 was at the time regarded as something of a landmark for the firm. VG, as he was universally known, hadn't 'believed' in paying large advances, or any advances at all if he could get away with it. Thus, I suppose, he was more readily able to indulge his comfortable lifestyle.

When I arrived at Gollancz the firm was, to put it politely, living on past glories. Like all the best 'English' publishers, Victor was a despot who since going into business on his own in 1927 had employed many talented young men (and infinitely more women, as slaves), including John Gross, later to edit the *Times Literary Supplement* and write a thrilling book about Shylock; John Rosenberg, who went on to have a successful career in television including producing, for Anglia, *Tales of the Unexpected*; Hilary Rubinstein, who was to run the world's oldest literary agency, A. P. Watt (founded 1875), and represent more than a few authors, notably Nadine Gordimer, published by Gollancz, as well as Michael Holroyd and Edwina Currie; James MacGibbon, who founded MacGibbon & Kee with broadcaster, historian and old charmer Robert Kee and who was an agent with Curtis Brown, the world's largest literary agency.

This was the era when most of the better-known Gollancz novelists, including Amis, Lionel Davidson, Gordimer and John le Carré, were inveigled away with offers of greater glory or money bags or, more usually, both. Gollancz would 'make' these authors and more businesslike publishers would benefit. Many of the best gravitated (in his heyday he was quite a magnet, later to become a magnate) to Tom Maschler at Jonathan Cape, generally assumed to be (there was little competition) London's leading literary publisher and the person sometimes credited with 'devising' the Booker Prize – not necessarily as an annual award for Cape authors, though more novelists published by Cape have won it than writers published by any other house.

Literary agents were beginning, just beginning, to become influential in authors' lives and thus in the book trade. This was entirely due to the fact that publishers, either through short-sightedness, meanness or business incompetence, had treated them less well than they should have done, given that they were hand in glove with the only begetters of the product. In 1968 we at Gollancz urgently needed a big book or two to make a splash, and I thought that George Brown's memoirs might do just that. Given how volatile the Foreign Secretary and Deputy Prime Minister was, he couldn't last for ever, any more than could the Harold Wilson era, with which, symbiotically, George Brown was identified. He had threatened to resign many times before, and sooner or later Wilson was bound to pull the plug on him. I wrote to Brown at the Foreign Office, telling him how much I admired him and asking could we commission his memoirs? (One of the reasons I admired him was that, like me, he had made his way without having been to university.) I was frustrated to receive back a letter politely requesting that I contact his literary agent, George Greenfield of John Farquharson.

I wrote formally to Greenfield, expressing interest in George Brown's autobiography if and when he came to write it. Greenfield rang me up and, ever so politely, made it plain that either Cassell or Collins would publish, and that both firms would be asked to bid. I don't think there had at that time been any 'auctions' for books in the UK (they ordered these things differently across the Atlantic, where agents had ruled the roost for some time). I said to Greenfield just two things. First, to remember that Gollancz was, and had every intention of continuing to be, *the* socialist publishing house; and second, that when the time came we should be allowed to bid.

In due course, Greenfield – whom I always found straight and honourable – gave us an opportunity to offer, and no one, I think, was more astonished than he that the Gollancz offer was the largest. George Brown naturally wanted to meet his publisher to be, and one day Greenfield and I went off to the club where his lordship (as he had become on leaving the Government) liked to lunch near Courtaulds' Hanover Square offices. Brown had indeed threatened to resign once too often, and in March 1968 Wilson had hurriedly accepted the offer. So in awe was I, aged twenty-eight and editorial director of Gollancz, that I can remember nothing of what was said, but the occasion was pleasant enough. We mainly talked about how the book would be written, Greenfield providing the ghost writer (not that that was how his name appeared on the finished book), the long-time industrial correspondent of the *Manchester Guardian*, J. R. L. Anderson. In his acknowledgements, George Brown declares that without the involvement of John Anderson 'the book would never have been finished'. In truth, the book would never have been started. Brown had kept no diaries and did not possess the kind of mind – Iain Macleod having famously described him as possessing 'the best untrained mind in British politics' – which could discipline and structure such a memoir.

At the end of lunch, Brown offered to show us his office at Courtaulds. It was surprising how much the job, presumably a sinecure, meant to a man who almost became Prime Minister, but important men (or men who have felt important) need to feel needed. We spent a few minutes in Brown's office, then shook hands and were on our way. His office was at the end of a long corridor. As we walked back towards the lift, passing the chairman Lord Kearton's office, Greenfield said out of the corner of his mouth: 'I think that went off all right, don't you?' I was about to agree when the large voice of George Brown was heard, bawling down the corridor behind us: 'Don't steal the carpets, you two!' In spite of myself, I at once looked round. Brown was standing outside his office door, hands cupped round his mouth, swaying backwards and forwards, for all the world like Toad of Toad Hall. Greenfield seemed alarmed. 'I think we ought to hurry,' he said as we speeded up our pace. The subversive discretion of the 10-percenter. I had visions of Lord Kearton popping out of his door and setting the police on us.

Publication was enormous fun. I see, looking at the guest list, that my fellow guests at the top table at the Foyle's luncheon on 30 March 1971 included, in addition to a clutch of ambassadors, George Woodcock, Lord Balogh, Baroness Gaitskell, Lord Longford, Robert McKenzie, Aubrey Jones and Mr Robin Day. The ravishing Liz Calder, Gollancz's first ever publicity manager, whom I inveigled from the film world (not that it was difficult) and who was much later to co-found the publishers Bloomsbury and become a star in the publishing firmament, and I accompanied George Brown on many of his publicity jaunts around the UK. He had to have a chaperone or two. I remember getting out of the train with him and Liz Calder at Doncaster where he was to speak and sign books, preferably his own, at a *Yorkshire Post* Literary Luncheon at the Racecourse Restaurant. He proffered his BR ticket to the collector at the barrier, then the benediction of a little nod, the merest tilting of his cranium, followed at once by the mumbled utterance of the word 'Brother', the word of familiar address he had used when meeting the public – voters, Labour voters – throughout his political life. George's fleshy, open, gullible, honest face froze. It was as if he wished he had not parted his lips, for the ticket collector had not recognised him: George Brown, every man's friend. He found it difficult to come to terms with reasonably private life again, not that he could ever return to obscurity. He was, at the very least, always value for money (which can't be said of every human being, let alone most politicians), invariably invigorating and stimulating to be with. His mind never seemed to be turned off, and even when he was the worse for alcoholic wear the intellectual batteries were being noisily recharged. The world of politics might have gone more smoothly without him, but at some human cost. I once took George to Bianchi's for lunch and he signed a copy of *In My Way* for Elena Salvoni, the head waitress. Perhaps this is why he achieved a mention in her memoirs, which is more than can be said of me.

Some months after *In My Way* was safely published – and the advance of £20,000 earned by a whisker as the result of a paperback reprint sale to Penguin – Liz Calder and I thought it would be pleasant to invite George and his wife Sophie to dinner. I offered our house in Kentish Town, and Liz was to bring her boyfriend, John Christopher (known as Jason) Spender, a nephew of the poet and working for the financial institution Slater, Walker, at that time one of the mightiest powers in the land. (Later I was to represent Jim Slater for an elegantly written book on investment; he described himself, simply, as Chm. Slater Walker Securities Ltd, 1964–75 in his *Who's Who* entry; and Walker had expunged Slater, Walker from his. Such is the pragmatic rewriting of history.)

Lady George-Brown, armed with a huge box of chocolates for my wife, arrived on time. On her own. George had been detained on business, she said. At the Lords. Minutes passed. Liz Calder and Jason Spender arrived. Half an hour went by. The small talk was becoming increasingly arduous, not least because I didn't feel that I could, in the presence of his wife, embark on George anecdotes. An hour passed. The meal, clearly, was becoming spoiled. My wife, slaving away in the kitchen while simultaneously trying to persuade our two babies to sleep, was growing increasingly moody: she thought George Brown an ass at the best of times. Sophie suggested I ring the Palace of Westminster. She told me that to do this you had to ring the Commons (listed in the telephone directory) and ask to be put through to the Lords (unlisted). To my surprise, it worked. I asked to speak to the

Lord George-Brown. I was asked my name. Whoever I spoke to returned after a while to say that Lord George-Brown had said to say that he was still tied up but that he'd be with us before too long. It didn't seem hopeful to those of us who knew him, which was all of us. Sophie suggested we began eating.

We had almost finished our soup when there was banging on the front door of an extravagance you normally associate with a mob in a Hollywood film about Robin Hood and his disgustingly merry men endeavouring to obtain admittance to Nottingham Castle. I hastened to the door, hoping the row wouldn't wake up the now sleeping children, and a splenetic, inebriated Lord George-Brown fell in, roaring and ranting in our hall for reasons I knew nothing of. I took him down to the dining-room, intro- duced him to my wife, whom he hadn't met before, and showed him his place, on the right of my wife. I doubt whether he'd have discovered the untenanted chair without guidance. He turned on everybody, glaring, lips puckered, then placed a hand on my wife's knee and said to her, slowly, leeringly and menacingly: 'It's a bit much. You invite me to dinner and then start eating before I arrive.'

Sophie tried to get him to behave, but she must have learned over the years that this was a lost war. He continued to roar and rant, and my wife gently asked him if he'd please lower his voice as otherwise he'd waken the babies and it had taken some time to get them off to sleep. With difficulty, George heaved himself to his feet, nearly pulling the oval table on top of him. 'First you invite me to dinner, and there's nothing to eat. Then you insult me. I'm leaving.' 'No,' said my wife, 'I'm leaving,' and she pro- ceeded to do so. George bumped down on to his chair, and the meal continued without her. He slurped his soup noisily, messily.

Half an hour later I found my wife in the Queen's Arms at the bottom of the street having a drink with a neighbour. 'You've got to come back,' I pleaded, furious and frustrated. 'Why?' she said, in her most stubborn and obtuse manner, which invariably brought out the prig in me. 'Because he used to be Foreign Sec- retary.' 'I don't care what he used to be,' she said. 'He certainly doesn't know how to behave today.'

I returned to the house on my own. Eventually she returned,

and soon afterwards Sophie suggested to George that they went home. I've no idea how late or early it was (it clearly wasn't that early: the evening had seemed to last for ever). I escorted them down our tiny street as George tried to remember where he'd parked his Daimler. Suddenly he swung round, pointed at me and bellowed like a villain in a melodrama: 'I've been warned about you.' Eventually he identified his car, or perhaps his wife did. He clambered in behind the wheel and somehow, heaven knows how, they drove off at, appropriately, funereal pace.

The next morning I left the house at the same time as the agreeable young man who lived almost exactly opposite and who was the local Tory Party agent. 'There was a man knocking on my door yesterday evening, asking for you. Hope he found you. Funny thing, he was a dead ringer for George Brown.'

I never heard from his lordship again. Not long after, he left his wife for another woman, and not too long after that he was dead. *In My Way* is dedicated 'For Sophie and the family who have made it possible and suffered so much because of it.' Yea, verily.

In later years, when a literary agent, I occasionally encountered David Owen in his capacity as husband to Deborah Owen, the American literary agent who contributed significantly to the success of the novelist Jeffrey Archer. George Brown first became Foreign Secretary at the age of fifty-two; David Owen, when appointed to the same job in 1977, was a mere stripling of thirty-nine. It is not for me to say whether the great office of state went to his head, but he always gave the impression of not suffering fools gladly, by which I mean we didn't have many significant talks together.

Once, in 1990 when Owen's vision of the SDP had come and gone, the committee of the Association of Authors' Agents was meeting of an evening in the Owens' kitchen in their handsome house by the Thames. Late at night, after hours of discussion about the net book agreement or some such scintillating subject, a saturnine figure appeared to enter the dark kitchen as if from the Thames, like a vision out of Dickens. 'Planning the revolution?' said Dr Death, as *Private Eye* refers to him. 'I'll leave you to it,' and he disappeared from the kitchen. It was a poignant moment as his revolution had clearly failed.

Years earlier, in 1978, when he was Foreign Secretary, my wife and I encountered him and Debbie at a preview of David Hare's 'socially committed' play *Plenty*. I have always been disappointed by plays of the Burke and Hare, body-snatcher lot, the David Hare/David Edgar/Howard Brenton generation, with the exception of the well-crafted work of Christopher Hampton. *Plenty* was no exception – journalism posing as drama or literature, an extended feature article with dialogue in place of perception or intellect or theatrical life and vigour. The night my wife and I saw the play at the National Theatre on the South Bank was hot, and afterwards we went on to the terrace of the theatre to have a quiet drink overlooking the Thames and the twinkling lights. The night air throbbed a bit as it always does there, and the river was blackly seductive.

David and Debbie Owen wandered along and sat down at the next table. Debbie, my wife and I chirruped away about the play. She, I vaguely recall, thought well of it; I had been bored. David Owen seemed irritated by the conversation, and spent most of the time looking morosely down at the Thames. I made some no doubt less than temperate criticism and the Secretary of State for Foreign and Commonwealth Affairs in Her Majesty's Labour Government snarled at me: 'If you don't realise that *Plenty* is a remarkable play then you don't know anything about the theatre,' and he turned his head away again, not to address another word to us. It was somehow made quite clear too that he disapproved of Debbie consorting with anyone who held such views.

# XIII

Interviewing writers is a curious, self-conscious business, for both interviewer and interviewee. It has become *de rigueur* these days, and the 'interview' is now more essential than the 'review', the sober appraisal of the work; as if the fact that it exists in book form is sufficient in itself, and its qualities, merits and distinguishing marks do not need to be assessed. What the writer has for breakfast; the extent to which he is (or isn't) a good father to his second family; or to which being an unmarried mother makes it more or less difficult to find time to write books (and, by the way, who do you think will win the World Cup, or the Booker?); these are all regarded as more crucial information, of more value to readers.

When I was conducting my series of longish interviews with leading playwrights for the *Transatlantic Review* in the latter half of the sixties, 'the interview' was a vehicle which enabled the playwright to say, seriously and at length, what he or she wanted to say about his or her craft. The exemplar, I suppose, was the scrupulous, even fastidious series of interviews undertaken for many years (and later collected in book form, as were the *Transatlantic Review*'s interviews) by the *Paris Review* which everyone, writers and readers, seems to regard as models of their kind. Writers, or so it is said, are encouraged to read and check their *Paris Review* interviews before they are set up in type to ensure that they faithfully represent, for posterity no doubt, what the author said, or even might like to have said. Yet it is as impossible for an interviewer to sound entirely neutral to an interviewee as it is for the eye of the camera not to select, organise and compose. Joe Orton relished being interviewed by a *literary* periodical of which he had not heard, and insisted upon donning a tie in front of the interviewer before the tape recorder was switched on: he wanted to *sound* properly dressed. Tom Stoppard seemed annoyed that I had thought the two-act original version of *Rosencrantz and Guildenstern Are Dead*, which I'd seen on the Fringe of the Edinburgh Festival in 1966 performed by the Oxford Theatre Group (with an ex-girlfriend of mine playing Gertrude), was sharper and even more brilliant than the extended three-act version which Kenneth Tynan corralled for the National Theatre at the Old Vic a year later. 'You're the victim of an illusion,' said Stoppard, later admitting that 'The *production* in London certainly went on a great deal longer because there was a great deal more of it.'

David Mercer was easy, in that socialist writers welcome any opportunity to sound off at length in print, and as primarily a television playwright he was gratified to be included in a series mainly devoted to stage playwrights. Mercer's plays, of course, were seen on television by millions more people than saw productions in the theatre. He was, in 1968, articulating received opinion about Beckett: 'Beckett is the incomparable master of the last fifty years and of the next fifty years probably. Beckett is the sort of Shakespeare of the twentieth century. One has only to think of Beckett to feel that there's nothing more to be said.' Indeed. John Hopkins rarely wrote stage plays, but his television plays were, like Mercer's, much admired. Hopkins, author of that exemplary television quartet of plays which I published at Penguin, *Talking to a Stranger*, was a precursor of Alan Ayckbourn in that the same domestic events are looked at from four different viewpoints in four different plays.

Arnold Wesker, as always, was perky and quirky, consumed with a Jewish conceit, a belief in himself and the quality of his plays, and a *joie de vivre* that was exhilarating. Wesker's first five or six plays were glorious, essential celebrations of humanity. If only he'd stopped there, but what is a writer to do? If his best comes first that is hardly his fault, although it may prove his tragedy.

The only playwright I didn't remotely warm to was Edward Bond. I was more than a little apprehensive as I arrived at the block of mansion flats in Willesden where Bond then lived, as the year before (1965) I'd published a letter in the *New Statesman* referring to the squeamish-quotient of Bond's second and most notorious play, *Saved*. Bond, agreeably enough by letter (he was not on the telephone, and confirmation of my interview had to be made by telegram), had agreed that I should interview him; and if he had noticed my letter he certainly didn't refer to it. It was unlikely that he'd associate it with his interlocutor from the *Transatlantic Review*. He, alone of all the playwrights I interviewed, insisted upon seeing proofs. The only change he made, I recall, was to a sentence in my preamble in which I wrote that he had 'tucked' two lumps of sugar into the saucer of my tea cup. 'You do not "tuck" lumps of sugar anywhere,' Bond wrote to me. He also seemed to have it in for the poor *Observer*. 'I read in the *Observer* recently,' I began, 'that you had spent years rewriting Chekhov. Presumably what they meant was writing imitation Chekhov?' I suppose it was quite rude for an opening question. Bond, who spoke volubly later, was fairly acerbic. 'I'm not responsible for what you read in the *Observer*. If you really read that it sounds a lot of nonsense to me.'

I wanted to do John Osborne, but he wrote me a charming and disarming postcard excusing himself. The point all too often neglected about someone who is perceived to be as boorish as Osborne is that, while being passionate about art and life, he can, conversely, be generous, enthusiastic and voluble. I do not begin to believe that he is a greater villain than smoother, more unctuous, easier people. Most of what he's written, including his two coruscating volumes of autobiography, indicates that Osborne is at heart an old pussycat, a sentimental Little Englander and even Empire Loyalist who feels, not liking to admit as much, that he has to fight it. Years later, when I was writing an article for *Tatler* on the National Theatre, Osborne kept sending me voluble postcards and letters criticising 'Dr Fu Man Chu', as he liked to refer to the Chinese-looking director of the National Theatre, Sir Peter Hall. I didn't think, when I wrote to Osborne and asked permission to quote, that he'd allow me to use any of his scatology, but he almost encouraged me to use anything and everything. It all added to the gaiety of the nation and not for the first time – *vide* Dean Swift and Monsieur Voltaire – made plain that the most biting and *constructive* criticism can be that which, at an oblique angle from 'reality', appears satirical rather than merely polemical and didactic. The latter invariably seems self-righteous, self-seeking, self-aggrandising. Throughout his professional and, it would seem, his private life, Osborne has, no doubt more aware of the fact than anyone else, gone around shooting himself in the foot. Indeed, it's astonishing he doesn't permanently hobble about on crutches.

Laurence Olivier essaying Archibald Rice in Osborne's melancholy masterpiece *The Entertainer* was one of the first major pleasures of my adolescence. The scene in which Archie's wife discovers that his father has eaten the cake she has baked for the return of her son from the army in Cyprus is one of the most heartbreaking episodes in world drama, on a par with anything by Chekhov and livelier than all of Sophocles, Euripides and Aristophanes. I had not, until seeing Olivier in *The Entertainer*, realised that a great actor *could* play parts such as Archie Rice with the same professionalism, conviction, truth and style he gave to the great classic roles. When I was younger and more snobbish in these matters, I thought it ridiculous that grown-up actors, serious actors, should waste their time and talent on anything but the dramatic heritage, as if the great plays of the world had arrived, shrink-wrapped, all at once. (Similarly, I despised people who read 'modern' novels. How could William Golding, Iris Murdoch and Angus Wilson be worth reading alongside Jane Austen, Balzac, Tolstoy? Of course I had not read them all, although I did read *Middlemarch* in one weekend sitting, the first weekend I was in London and knowing no one in 1962; or was that *Crime and Punishment*?)

In the very early sixties I glimpsed John Osborne on the stairs of the Royal Court Theatre in Sloane Square (the centre of the world to me) during the interval of a Sunday night production without decor. My cup ran over. He was talking to George Devine. My cup ran over twice. Then I saw him, very occasionally, in the bar of the Garrick, early of an evening in the eighties, before I set off to review a play. He always seemed to be on his own, looking a bit like an elegant Robinson Crusoe, and was prone to snap – perhaps 'peck' would be more accurate – if someone ventured to address him. Most of the Garrick barflies address one another by their first names, or by nicknames as if they are still at school. Amis is 'Kingsley' to everyone, or so it seems. Not so with Osborne. 'How are you today, Mr Osborne?' a voice would nervously enquire from the crowded window end of the bar; and Osborne's tight-lipped response, often with a cheroot jerked to his mouth, would make it plain as Punch that he didn't, thank you very much, desire to be drawn into a vacuous conversation.

On one such occasion I noticed he was wearing a tie similar to one I have, designed by the Scottish painter Craigie Aitchison to commemorate the bicentenary of the Royal Academy. On mine, a bird perches on a background of intense green; on Osborne's, the bird is seen against crimson. I remarked, casually and foolishly, to Eric Shorter, the theatre critic, then still in the employ of the *Daily Telegraph*, that Osborne was wearing my tie. Shorter, the mildest of men, asked Osborne what his tie represented. Osborne looked up from his tankard of champagne and gazed expressionlessly at Shorter for ever, or so it seemed, before pronouncing: 'It's my anti-theatre-critic tie.'

Once, in the mid-eighties, I signed up weeks ahead to spend Derby Day with the Garrick Club. Since I became a member I'd always had a mild desire to do the Derby, and with the Garrick. The day was cold and windy but not, I think, wet. Most of those on the Garrick open-topped bus were members who took a serious interest in horse racing, or at least in going to the races. We set off early, a breakfast of scrambled eggs and, for all I know, champagne having been served in the Club beforehand to the convivial early risers. The coach wended its way to Epsom Downs, and a lavish spread materialised at lunch time when it was in its place, among hundreds of others perched on Epsom Downs. Had I realised that it was almost impossible to see the race track and the horses from the top of the bus I doubt whether I'd have gone. It was like going to *Twelfth Night* and being unable to locate the actors.

There were not many Garrick 'celebrities' present that I recognised. Ian Wallace, the singer, was there, and seemed to enjoy himself, cocooned with friends. Osborne was there, wearing, I seem to recall, a striped seersucker suit. He normally sports black in town. He sat at the rear of the top of the coach, lying back as if on a *chaise-longue*, ministered to by his fifth wife, the sometime *Observer* second-string theatre critic, Helen Dawson, always most protective of him. He looked like a character out of Chekhov, less down on his luck than bored, irretrievably bored. I didn't see anyone dare speak to either Osborne. In fact, I think, the poor man was ill, but damned if he'd die.

The last time I saw him, again with his wife, he minced, then almost tumbled into Westminster Abbey, in black and twitching, flicking a stick, to attend Peggy Ashcroft's memorial service in November 1991. The second volume of his memoirs, *Almost a Gentleman*, had recently been published and stood high on the bestseller lists, largely because everyone was furious that, in a postscript, Osborne had severely castigated his fourth wife, the late Jill Bennett. This was less, I should think, because he grew, before the end of their marriage, unable to tolerate her than because he came to blame himself for having married her in the first place. Osborne's Webster-like spleen and ferocity over the grave of the poor suicide was distasteful to read, but the self-righteous criticism it provoked was unedifying too. He lists the names of his five wives in *Who's Who* like a roll-call, stretching out to the crack of doom.

# XIV

I could not have guessed it at the time, but fate decreed that one of my interviews with playwrights for the *Transatlantic Review* was to become a modest part of the theatrical archive or record. In 1967 I went with my Tiny Pal tape recorder to interview Joe Orton in the tiny flat he shared with his friend, Kenneth Halliwell, in Islington's Noel Road, facing the canal.

Orton's *Entertaining Mr Sloane* and *Loot* had recently both run in London to great critical acclaim. They were funny, macabre, stylish, highly wrought; like most of the best comedies, including those by the Ancient Greeks, a bit short for those who relish three hours in the West End, with or without interval drinks or ice cream. (The same, of course, may be said about the three-act version of *The Importance of Being Earnest*, which seems longer than it is because it has to be played with two intervals, or at least the sets have to be changed twice. The rarely performed four-act version, with Lady Brancaster in place of Lady Bracknell, is another matter.)

The *Transatlantic Review*, which Orton referred to as the *International Review*, was theoretically a quarterly but tended to emerge less frequently, as its proprietor and editor Joe McCrindle, a wealthy American with a monumentally low boredom threshold and houses all over the world, produced the magazine more or less by himself, with the aid (for prose) of the then unknown Heathcote Williams and (for poetry) of B. S. Johnson, fast becoming famous in English literary circles if not necessarily much beyond. I do not think McCrindle read poetry at all – his mind was, and I don't mean this pejoratively, singularly prosaic – and this allowed Johnson to indulge his taste for syllabics, a briefly fashionable, and easy, way of writing verse by counting syllables.

By the time my interview with Orton was published, the play-wright had been most foully murdered by his jealous lover. It was unfortunate that the contents page of *Transatlantic Review No. 24*, dated March 1967, stated that Orton was interviewed by one Giles Cooper, another fine if less famous playwright (most of his original work was done for radio, then a power in the theatrical land), who was also by then dead, having fallen out of a moving railway train. To this day I occasionally receive letters addressed to Giles Cooper.

Many of Orton's epigrammatic responses to my questions remain worth savouring today. Here are some extracts: '. . . I think this whole thing of commercial and subsidised theatre is ridiculous. There are only good plays and bad plays . . . When you're put on at one of the subsidised theatres, you do get an enormous snob audience. I think people like to feel they're being entertained and also being cultural at the same time . . . In actual fact, the "class" of my plays is going up all the time! *The Ruffian on the Stair* began by being pretty grotty and criminal; *Sloane* moved up slightly, since the characters were lower middle-class. (Lower middle-class nihilism, I was told.) *Loot* has moved up one rung more because it's now a woman who leaves £19,000 including her bonds and jewels. I'm sure you can – though I don't know that I can, yet – write about very upper-class people and make them as interesting as lower-class people.'

Then I asked him about taste. '. . . the kind of people who always go on about whether a thing is in good taste invariably have very bad taste. I think the English have the worst taste of any people on earth. No, I don't think there's such a thing as good taste and bad taste. Some things *offend* me, but they're rather odd things. For instance, those translations of Aristophanes by Dudley Fitts. [At the time repeatedly broadcast on the BBC Third Programme, the late lamented – at least by some of us – cultural channel.] They sicken me, but this is just *my* thing. They obviously don't offend a lot of people.'

We moved on to homosexuals, and the dear old *Observer*. 'Of course on this subject the English are forever striving to be great liberals. I notice that even the great champion of liberalism, the *Observer*, always refers to homosexuals as queers. They would never actually refer to coloured people as niggers. Even in quite serious articles they call people queers. If someone had written a play about West Indians the *Observer* would never say "So-and-so plays the nigger." That I think is interesting.'

Then the classics. 'I admire Voltaire. Aristophanes. I read him in prose translations. I prefer these because they're literal. You don't get anybody coming between you and the playwright. I'm very conscious of what's gone before. I like Lucian and the classical writers, and I suppose that's what gives my writing a difference, an old-fashioned classical education! Which I never received, but I gave myself one, reading them all in English, for I have so little Latin and less Greek.'

*Loot* seems to me probably the best constructed and most elegant classical English comedy since *The Importance of Being Earnest*. Orton said: 'I'd like to write a play as good as *The Importance of Being Earnest*.' Me: 'You admire Wilde?' Orton: 'I admire his work, not his life. It was an appalling life.' At that time two of Wilde's four comedies were receiving (crass) 'all star' revivals in London. I asked Orton if he saw any significance in this. 'No, I think that's the tail end of the reaction in the theatre which I hope we're finished with now. After the so-called dirty plays controversy the English have one of their periodic fits of morality, and I think we're seeing the end of it. We saw all those dreary Shaw revivals, and the dreary Wilde revivals, and I hope we've seen the end of it with *Staircase* and *Loot*! . . . I was quite serious saying in the programme that I'm a puritan. I'm not sure that the word puritan is right, but I think one can only write from that kind of standpoint.'

I asked Orton about his time in prison, and the reason why he was there. '. . . in actual fact I did not have a terrible time in prison. I had a wonderful time and wouldn't have missed it for the world. It's a curious society, a pyramid, and I suddenly saw how comforting it is to be in a pyramidical society, like Ancient Egypt must have been. I don't think you'd get any plays like, say, *Loot* from it, but certainly as far as living's concerned it's very comfortable. I wouldn't particularly like to do it indefinitely, but it was most interesting. I certainly have nothing against the police. They're a necessary evil.'

He went to prison because of 'libraries and library books. The thing that put me in a rage about librarians was that when I went to quite a big library in Islington and asked for Gibbon's *Decline and Fall of the Roman Empire* they told me they hadn't a copy of it. They could get it for me, but they hadn't one on their shelves. This didn't start it off but it was symptomatic of the whole thing. I was enraged that there were so many rubbishy novels and rubbishy books. It reminded me of the phrase in the Bible: "Of the making of books, there is no end", because there isn't. Libraries might as well not exist; they've got endless shelves for rubbish and hardly any space for good books ... you can always say when some things are rubbish and some things aren't. I can obviously say Gibbon isn't. He said a very funny thing about books: when the Arabs took Alexandria they used the contents of the library to provide fuel for the baths and Gibbon thought that probably the books were doing more good being so used than they were when being read.'

Not to put too fine a point upon it, Orton set about defacing library books, and did it with some style. 'I did things like pasting a picture of a female nude over a book of etiquette, over the picture of the author who, I think, was Lady Lewisham. I did other things, very strange things. There was the business when I got the biography of Sir Bernard Spilsbury and there was an illustration which said: "The remains discovered in the cellar at number 23 Rosedown Road". I pasted over the illustration, which was a very dreary one of a lot of earth, David's picture of Marat dead in his bath. It was in black and white. I left the original caption underneath, so that it really did look like what it said, "The remains discovered in the cellar at number 23 Rosedown Road". This picture of the corpse in the bath had quite an effect on people who opened the book.

'I used to write false blurbs on the inside of Gollancz books, because I discovered that Gollancz books had blank yellow flaps and I used to type false blurbs on the insides. My blurbs were mildly obscene. Even at the trial they said they were only *mildly* obscene. When I put the plastic covers back over the jackets you couldn't tell the blurbs weren't printed. I used to stand in corners after I'd smuggled the defaced books back into the library and then watch people read them. It was very funny, very interesting. There was a biography of Sybil Thorndike in which there was a picture of her locked up in a cell as Nurse Edith Cavell. I cut the caption from another picture and pasted it under the picture, so that it read: "During the war I received many strange requests". One of the interesting things at the trial was that the greatest outrage, the one for which I think I was sent to prison, was that I had stuck a monkey's face in the middle of a rose, on the cover of something called *Collins Book of Roses*. It was a very beautiful yellow rose. What I had done was held up as the depth of iniquity for which I should probably have been birched. They won't ever do that so they just sent me to prison for six months.'

John Lahr, who wrote vigorously about theatre for the New York literary (later literary *cum* soft porn) magazine *Evergreen Review*, must have read my interview with the late playwright, because he quoted from it in an appraisal of Orton which he contributed to the magazine in 1971. Later he wrote to me from New York to say that he'd been commissioned to write a biography of Orton. He was coming over to the UK to speak to people who had known Orton and could he meet me? I lent him my Tiny Pal tape and, as he told me some years later, he played it over hundreds of times to familiarise himself with the thirty-three-year-old Orton's genteel, camp Cockney accent laced with his native Leicester. I took him to lunch at Bianchi's, where – the object of the exercise – I introduced him to Elena Salvoni, who to all intents and purposes ran the place. It is only surprising that Elena Salvoni, played perhaps by Dame Maggie Smith, didn't make it into the celluloid version.

Elena and her husband, Aldo, live in a flat in Noel Road, and in the early sixties they befriended two young would-be theatricals who had just moved in, Halliwell (the better-known of the pair then, as an actor) and Orton. Even at the peak of his success, Orton did not invest in a telephone, and when his agent Margaret Ramsay or Hollywood called they would telephone Elena's number and she would knock on Orton's door.

Elena is certainly regarded as one of Soho's 'characters'. Her rise has, in a way, been remarkable. She has published a ghosted autobiography and was graced by Miss Christina Foyle with a literary luncheon at Grosvenor House. Most recently she has presided over L'Escargot restaurant (commonly known, naturally, as 'The Snail') in Greek Street, where most of her old customers from Bianchi's, including me, can no longer afford to eat. At the time of writing, L'Escargot is in receivership, although still functioning. Elena has been dismissed by the powers that be, and her friends are trying to raise money from grateful customers and others to set her up in her own place.

I don't want to sound toffee-nosed, but the cult of the landlord or *patron* is one I do not begin to fathom. Elena is an entirely agreeable, if surprisingly nosy, woman, yet I do not necessarily regard her as a soulmate. She, like any other restaurateur, is simply providing a service and should be grateful for your custom. The most outrageous example of a restaurateur getting above himself and even infiltrating his essence into his customers' meals was the late and appallingly rude Peter Langan, usually drunk. It is substantially the fault of food critics, desperate for something to write, that restaurateurs have been encouraged to see themselves as creative artists and thus think they can behave at least as badly as their customers do. I am not, I insist, making a snobbish point, more a practical one.

The last time I was taken to L'Escargot for lunch, in November 1991, I encountered Elena on my way back from the lavatory and she greeted me as effusively as ever, although I rarely go to the restaurant nowadays, and never if I am paying the bill. Elena always addresses me as 'Giles' when I'm on my own or with someone she knows, and as 'Mr Gordon' when I'm with someone unknown to her. This is obviously correct behaviour. I told her, apropos of nothing in particular, that Patricia Parkin, my companion, and I had just come from Dame Peggy Ashcroft's memorial service at Westminster Abbey, and that it was undoubtedly the theatrical occasion of the year. Elena, I thought, looked somewhat crestfallen. 'I didn't know Peggy's memorial was today,' she said, as guests, waiters and waitresses milled around her. 'I should have been there.' Nothing about the irresistible rise of Elena Salvoni would surprise me, but I hadn't known that she was, as it seemed from her remarks, an intimate of the great actress. Later it transpired that Elena had thought we were talking about Peggy Ramsay, the theatrical agent, who had died some months earlier.

Margaret Ramsay, who represented many of the better playwrights of our time, though not John Osborne and Harold Pinter, was all an agent should be and a bit more into the bargain. Friend, confidante, proselytiser and adviser to her clients, she as much as George Devine moulded the new drama, though for myself I wish she had left Edward Bond in obscurity. His linguistically numbing plays, not least *Saved*, in which a baby is stoned to death in its pram on stage, and *Early Morning*, in which Queen Victoria's body is eaten as a probably hungry audience looks on, are much admired in Germany. In the film of Orton's life, derived from John Lahr's biography, *Prick Up Your Ears*, Peggy Ramsay is played by Vanessa Redgrave. I met Peggy Ramsay only three or four times, but she was such a positive, outgoing character that I felt I knew her intimately. She exuded warmth, energy, commitment. When I reviewed for the *Spectator* a production of *Loot* in San Francisco I commented favourably on the set, which to my eyes and as memory served was a clever re-creation of Halliwell's and Orton's Noel Road flat, with a crucifix created from pictures cut out of magazines on the wall behind the bed. (In the preamble to my *Transatlantic Review* interview I had described the room as follows: 'His room has yellow walls and a red and grey ceiling. The walls are covered with innumerable colour pictures extracted from magazines: he has created a Christian cross by cutting out reproductions of icons, plus a gorilla. There is a poster for *Loot*, and one for *Seid nett zu Mr Sloane!* The room has two single beds, scores of records, a huge television set, some books, a pair of shoes under the bed. All very neat, very tidy.') Peggy Ramsay was incensed by my comments on the set, and wrote a furious letter to the editor of the *Spectator* saying that what I'd written was obviously rubbish as how could I know what Halliwell's and Orton's bedsitter looked like? She was also irritated that I gave the production a good review, as she said Americans could not play Orton any more than they could play Wilde or Shakespeare. She was certainly right about the Bard.

When I was dismissed from the *Spectator* in 1984 by the new editor, Charles Moore, and subsequent to a silly story (initiated by me) in the *Times* diary which quoted me as saying that I'd probably been dispatched because I'd never voted Conservative in my life, Peggy Ramsay telephoned me at my office. 'Darling,' she said, her voice crackling down the line, 'it's absolutely disgraceful. Your reviews are wonderful. Where would you like to take your column?' I modestly suggested the *Sunday Times*, although the Hungarian John Peter was working himself in there, following the bizarre and brief tenure of the poet and foreign correspondent James Fenton. 'Good. I'll see what I can do,' said Peggy, and slammed the telephone receiver down. I heard nothing further about this.

The last time I met her – although I saw her a few times afterwards, at first nights, or on railway platforms, always trailing blue-covered playscripts, their size seeming to dwarf her diminishing presence, her tiny, short-sighted, frail and ancient physique – was soon after I suggested to Nick Hern, then plays editor at Methuen, that I edit a modest volume to be called *Ortoniana*. It would comprise aphorisms from the plays, Orton's only published novel, *Head to Toe*, and other writings, and be similar to *Oscariana*, a successful Wilde concoction put together and published by Arthur L. Humphreys, manager of Hatchard's of 187 Piccadilly, W, in M.D.CCCC.X. (I quote the title page) and later lover of Mrs Wilde. Hern was sufficiently taken by the idea to pay me £100 on account. He spoke to Peggy, who was Orton's literary executor and thus controller of his copyrights, and she suggested lunch at a rather lush restaurant in St Martin's Lane, just down the road from her offices in Goodwin's Court, behind the Garrick Club. She invited the etiolated painter Patrick Proctor as well. He had known Orton, and provided the drawings for Anthony Blond's original 1971 edition of *Head to Toe* ('Worthy of Swift' according to Auberon Waugh) and had drawn the playwright naked but for his socks, as a horizontal gatefold, for the title pages of *Prick Up Your Ears*. Either she or Hern had had the idea that Proctor might illustrate *Ortoniana*.

The lunch was hilarious. I remember drinking more than talking, and listening to Peggy and Proctor reminiscing about Orton. It was all exceedingly jolly, with Peggy insisting that Joe was not *nearly* as good a playwright as people thought, and had he not been bludgeoned to death any subsequent plays he might have written would, darling, have been disasters, and why on earth did I want to do the book and Nick to publish it? Suddenly, having hastily summoned the bill, which cannot have been modest, she arose and, more or less legless, the three of us followed her back up St Martin's Lane and lurched into Goodwin's Court. I can see us now: the diminutive, grey-stockinged Peggy Ramsay; the skinny, gangling Proctor, well over six feet, bending down all the while to hear what Peggy was saying, as if he were a drawing by Mervyn Peake; and squattish, plumpish Hern and me collapsing behind, much the worse for alcohol and Orton. Peggy was the only one of us who climbed the steep, ladder-like flight of stairs to her office without even touching the handrails, let alone being supported by them. The book, which still seems a good idea, came to naught through no one's fault but mine. I returned Methuen's £100 the day before I received a letter from Hern, the hunter, saying that he was resigning from Methuen to found his own theatre books list, the fortunes of which have since been chequered.

Methuen came, reasonably enough, to be regarded as Orton's publishers. Peggy Ramsay was never much interested in the publication of plays, although it was almost big business in the sixties, the heyday of what was grandly thought of as the New English Drama. During my eighteen months with Penguin, I signed up thirty-odd plays. One of these was *Loot*, which I shouldn't have been allowed to publish as Peggy had already contracted it to Geoffrey Strachan at Methuen. She may have thought it was Methuen's option title, and in a sense it was, in that Methuen had published in paperback – only in paperback – *Entertaining Mr Sloane*. But so, confusingly, had Penguin, in *New English Dramatists 8*, having acquired the paperback rights from Hamish Hamilton who first published the play in hardback.

The truth was that Peggy said yes to any publisher who wanted to publish her clients' plays, a healthy attitude – at least in terms of enthusiasm for and commitment to her authors – and no doubt she vaguely imagined that, as in the world of the theatre, most 'productions' wouldn't get off the ground. But it is infinitely less expensive to publish a book than to mount a theatrical production.

Maybe she was over-excited because Orton had dedicated the play 'To Peggy', and she wanted everybody to read it. She couldn't quite understand why Geoffrey Strachan and I both felt a little hurt, even compromised, he in particular. The copyright line in Penguin *New English Dramatists 13*, where *Loot* is concerned, reads 'First published by Methuen, 1967; published in Penguin Books, 1968; copyright © the Administrators of the Estate of Joe Orton deceased, 1968.'

In connection with publication, I accompanied Charles Marowitz, the swashbuckling if somewhat seedy and subversive American director of *Loot*'s first London production (Peter Wood's earlier production having died on the road in Wimbledon – game, set and match to the watch committees and philistines who objected to the language as much as to the coffin and false teeth on stage – in spite of Kenneth Williams starring as Truscott of the Yard) to see the Lord Chamberlain, or rather the Lord Chamberlain's man. In the sixties, plays still had to be vetted by the Lord Chamberlain, Lord Cobbold. His office was in St James's Palace, where I was, years later, regularly to visit a succession of the Prince of Wales's men, and I vaguely remember a musty room full of scripts in manilla envelopes. The Lord Chamberlain's Comptroller of Plays was, I think, a military gentleman. You'd have thought therefore that he would have been at home with rude language and sometimes less than tasteful activities, but real life was one matter, art or entertainment another. The Comptroller, or the Comptroller's man (how many censors were there with that filthy new English drama spewing all over the place like a leaking sewer?) would read out a list of rude words with page references, and Marowitz would agree that, say, 'bum' should go and be replaced by 'bottom', on condition that 'penis' could stay. ('Willie' was retained for W. Somerset Maugham.) And so the horse-trading continued. It wasn't helped by Marowitz invariably misremembering Lord Cobbold's name. 'Tell Lord Cobblers . . .' he would say, and the Comptroller or the Comptroller's man would sigh, having long since ceased to correct Marowitz.

The published text of *Loot*, in both its Methuen and its Penguin versions, contains what is, to my mind, one of the funniest pages in English literature. It is described, improbably, as an 'author's note' and I quote it in full:

The Lord Chamberlain grants a licence to the play subject to the following conditions:

(I) The corpse is inanimate and not played by an actress.

(II) On page 77 the casket is wiped with a handkerchief. The Lord Chamberlain is particularly anxious that no stain shall appear on the handkerchief.

The following alterations to the text are required:

### Act One

Page 32. 'Run by a woman who was connected with the Royal Family one time.' For 'Royal Family' substitute 'Empire Loyalists'.

Page 32. 'Under the picture of the Sacred Heart.' For 'Sacred Heart' substitute 'Infant Samuel'.

Page 43. 'While Jesus pointed to his Sacred Heart, you pointed to yours. I never point. It's rude' must be cut.

Page 45. For 'Consummatum Est' substitute 'Kingdom Come'.

Page 54. For 'buggery' substitute 'beggary'.

### Act Two

Page 77. 'Run by three Pakistanis aged between ten and fifteen. They do it for sweets. Part of their religion.' For 'Pakistanis' substitute 'kids'. 'Part of their religion' must be cut.

Page 82. For 'fucking' substitute 'bleeding'.

That part of the Lord Chamberlain's job which was apparently concerned with seeing that plays were fit for consumption only by morons was abolished in 1968. It might be observed that the quality of playscripts has not on the whole improved since then, even the work of Osborne, J., a playwright still sadly lacking a knighthood.

# XV

To me, Richard Ingrams and Auberon Waugh in their different ways are the best journalists and the most influential (quite a different consideration) of the last two decades in this country. The journal of record of the period has not been *The Times*, which when it deposed classified advertisements from its front page began to relinquish its far from brief authority; nor, sadly, the essential *Independent*, too solemn and lacking in flair; nor the *Daily Mirror*, always less of a *newspaper* than its adherents pretended, even before its rape by Captain Maxwell; nor, even, the *Spectator*, to which I am addicted, a self-reflecting gilded lily. It was – and is still, though to a lesser extent – *Private Eye*, which recorded, fortnight in and fortnight out, the transformation of British society and commented upon it. Its uncomplicated, vilely printed balance of news, gossip and jokes presented more pungently and accurately than any other sheet the underbelly of the mangy lion and the castrated unicorn, what was really happening. It could be seethingly cruel but, like Hamlet to his mother, was cruel to be kind. If it caused the children of certain people in the public eye to come crying home from school, for which Clive James condemned it, those people should have thought twice before behaving disreputably; and if they didn't realise they were behaving reprehensibly, that was worse. Words and phrases minted in the inky pages of the *Eye* insinuated themselves into everyday usage. When did the *Guardian* or the *Daily Telegraph* mint language? This is a creative task and *Private Eye* undertook it, if sometimes surreally, with élan. Throughout most of this period the *Eye*'s editor, moralist, philosopher and presiding genius was Richard Ingrams, never called Dick, Dickie or Rick, whose name illogically suggests to me that he's descended from the Reverend R. H. Barham, the author of *The Ingoldsby Legends*, that glorious allegorical cornucopia of poems about Victorian society, a slightly up-market precursor of *Private Eye*, 'The Jackdaw of Rheims' being the best-known single poem in the compilation.

Ingrams' style, in person, is deceptive; or perhaps it isn't. At the fortnightly *Eye* lunches at the Coach and Horses pub in Soho he sits these days at the centre of one side of the board with his successor as editor, Ian Hislop, at the head of the table. Ingrams says little as the guests stand around the sterile room being introduced, and most of them drinking mineral water, or as they sit down and begin eating. He listens, although he appears abstracted, his mind elsewhere. As the meal progresses, and subject to how informative the guests – journalists from national newspapers, politicians, television people, publishers – sitting beside and opposite him are, a modest-sized notebook, indeed a tiny notebook, will have found its way on to the table in front of him without having been seen to emerge from a pocket. Quite unostentatiously Ingrams, jackdaw of morality, will be taking notes. He will cover two or three pages by the time lunch ends, when MPs begin to drift back to Westminster, publishers to their offices, television people to their studios, journalists to what these days passes for Fleet Street, the *Eye* staffers back to their glasshouse in Carlisle Street.

Ingrams, born in 1937, always wears scruffy, moss green jackets (I'm assuming, probably incorrectly, that he possesses more than one) and crumpled flannels. The jacket looks as if it has been for many years a collector of lichen. If the *Guinness Book of Records* listed the world's most insistent public nose-picker Ingrams would surely be in a class of his own. Yet women – almost without exception, and especially if they are young and attractive – find him charming and romantic. I suspect it's a case of the father figure as romantic lead. The staff of the fortnightly magazine of which he is currently editor, embarrassingly (not that he seems embarrassed) named *The Oldie*, all appear to be female and aged about seventeen.

Ingrams should never have been appointed television critic of the *Spectator*, which he was for many years, as he sensibly despises the triviality of the medium and more than once contrived to write his column without evidently having watched any of that week's programmes. On the other hand, his column in the *Observer*, where he reveals himself regularly as an astute commentator on the previous week, is one of two reasons for reading the paper, the other being Alan Watkins' elegantly dogmatic and educative political commentary. The reason why so many people were at first surprised and impressed by Ingrams' musings and agitations in the *Observer* was that most of us had not known if he could do it, given that the majority of the stories in the *Eye* are not by-lined, and the rest are mainly pseudonymous. Ingrams gave up his *Observer* column, where he was replaced by the lightweight and irritating Simon Hoggart; but Hoggart soon departed to become the paper's political correspondent and Ingrams returned.

In the seventies, Sir James Goldsmith issued more than sixty libel writs against the *Eye* and thirty-seven of its distributors (not including W. H. Smith, because it was only later that WHS decided it could afford to sell the satirical fortnightly). At the same time Goldsmith applied to the High Court to bring an action for criminal libel against the *Eye*, the first time for more than thirty years that the law had been invoked against a paper .

In 1973 Ingrams asked me (and thus I became his literary agent) if I could find a publisher for *Goldenballs*, his account of *Private Eye*'s and his long-running feud with Sir James Goldsmith which resulted in the one-time grocer being awarded what no doubt were referred to in court as exemplary damages. The manuscript was informative and funny, and of course cocked a snook or twenty at the Establishment. André Deutsch distributed and up to a point published the magazine's books (although the *Eye* always carried the financial can), but I decided not to approach the Hungarian publisher as I thought he wouldn't offer a decent advance for what I regarded as a hugely saleable book. Publisher after publisher initially expressed enthusiasm, then mumbled an excuse for wriggling away. This is often what happens when an editor shows a manuscript to a sales manager, or a finance director, or above all a lawyer. Publishers publish what they're allowed to publish.

In each case the manuscript was apologetically returned. It looked as if Geoffrey Strachan of Methuen, the bearded sage who published Orton and Bond and saw the joke in Adrian Mole, was going to take the plunge – until Richard Ingrams and I were summoned to a meeting at the offices of solicitors Rubinstein Callingham, as they may or may not have been called then: the names of solicitors' firms change more frequently even than those of publishing houses. Michael Rubinstein, regarded at the time as book publishing's top libel lawyer, had read the manuscript for Methuen (and possibly for a number of other publishers beforehand) and wanted to make a few comments. We met at his Gray's Inn offices together with two or three greyish members of the Methuen board, or possibly of an even higher board, that of the unimaginatively named Associated Book Publishers, the holding group.

The meeting was friendly enough but, I realised from the beginning, destined to be abortive. Rubinstein in earlier years had been the *Eye*'s solicitor, but he yielded the position because he felt the paper usually disregarded his advice, which no doubt was true. More recently he had featured in its pages as 'the world's worst solicitor', by which Rubinstein – a thoroughly amiable man who regularly wins fivers or book tokens by submitting ridiculous cuttings from the press to the 'This England' column in the *New Statesman and Society* (as we have to try to remember to call the old *Staggers*) – seems amused enough, though being sensitive he must find the appellation hurtful.

'Very nice to see you again, Richard,' Rubinstein beamed at the beginning of the meeting. Ingrams, not given to small talk, smiled happily and nodded his head a little. 'The only trouble,' went on Rubinstein, 'is that you've libelled twelve individuals in this book.' 'I expect they're all your clients, Michael,' said Ingrams. Rubinstein, in the way lawyers can quickly adopt, looked worldweary, rather like a vicar confronted with a reluctant parishioner. 'That has nothing to do with it, Richard,' he said; he can be pretty severe on behalf of his client. (Years later I encountered Michael Rubinstein in the street, and made a light-hearted but neither improper nor disreputable remark about a legal matter which pertained at the time between us. 'Your client should take this matter more seriously, Giles,' he replied. The matter was trivial and his client rather touchy, but as soon as lawyers are expensively wheeled in it is necessary that they put aside their sense of objectivity and that the most fatuous and trivial of matters are 'taken seriously'.)

*Goldenballs*, with most or all of Michael Rubinstein's clients still featuring in the text, was published in 1979 by *Private Eye* 'in association with André Deutsch'. Barry Fantoni, painter, cartoonist and *Eye* contributor, provided a very fine jacket design, portraying a libel writ and a jar of Marmite, and the book sold many copies. The subsequent paperback, ironically, was published by Methuen.

If you were invited to the *Eye*'s Christmas party – a fairly maudlin annual event at which Ingrams, usually wearing a tissue-paper crown from a cracker, would play carols at a piano for hours with the likes of Miles Kington, Auberon Waugh and Alexander Chancellor joining in – you often would, without even trying, discover the identity of various of the contributors. Some years back an MP, eager to reveal his pseudonymous *Private Eye* identity, sidled up to me and said, 'Happy Christmas. Who are you? I'm "Old Muckspreader" ' (the writer of the farming column).

Much sanctimonious pomposity is emitted by journalists and the custodians of the press about research, the checking of facts, the reliability of sources and so on, and indeed our discriminatory libel laws make this posturing necessary. Nevertheless, the protestations of journalists are frequently a self-serving attempt to justify their vulgar activity. Ingrams – as does Hislop to a lesser degree (he being rightly curmudgeonly at providing handouts for egregious litigants) – tends to trust his sources, having satisfied himself down the years that the chap's heart is in the correct place and that, on the whole, he gets his stories right. This is why a story in the *Eye*, even if it is incorrect in detail, in a fact or two, is rarely wrong in tone, in the stance adopted. The pompous are deflated, the baddies named. Don't come back, Cap'n Bob, nothing is forgiven.

Ingrams shares with me a passion for collecting second-hand books. We occasionally encounter one another, snout to snout, bending over the same tray outside the window of a second-hand bookshop. I have sometimes sent him catalogue entries for books which I've thought would interest him. I was pleased to be able to tip him off about a first edition of Cobbett's *Rural Rides*, a work which he had edited and which I knew to be one of his favourite books. He did not possess a first edition, and first editions are crucially important to obsessive collectors. Being secretive by nature as he is (or maybe it's because I didn't go to Shrewsbury or Oxford with him), he didn't think to tell me whether he acquired the copy.

I remember with particular pleasure *Private Eye*'s twenty-fifth birthday luncheon party in 1986 at the Grand Hotel, Brighton. The *Eye* had commandeered a whole train to convey guests from Victoria station to the raffish Sussex coastal resort. I sat in a Pullman carriage next to Tariq Ali, prince and socialist, as the train pulled out of Victoria and champagne was served.

Why do I seem to remember that we talked about cricket? – because I don't think we can have done. No one ever talks to me about cricket unless I raise the subject. Why should my friends and acquaintances assume that I'm not interested in cricket? We were bussed from Brighton station down the hill of the Regency resort to the Grand Hotel. I happened to step out of the coach alongside Auberon Waugh, who looked up admiringly at the hotel's wedding-cake façade. The Grand had just reopened – the *Eye* celebratory lunch was one of the first events subsequent to reopening – after being refurbished, repaired and generally patched up after the IRA explosion which was intended to demolish the Prime Minister and her Cabinet. Bron commented: 'The last time I looked up there, Mrs Thatcher, the Tebbits, and her Cabinet were mostly hurtling down.'

Germaine Greer ('Rose Blight') and Jeffrey Bernard ('Captain Mad'), both *Eye* columnists, were there, but I cannot recall seeing 'Old Muckspreader'. Larry Adler, someone I've never seen the point of, played the mouth organ interminably, and Peter Cook gave his usual rendition in a raincoat. At lunch I sat next to a delightful elderly man, George Adamson, who illustrated in volume form (but not in the *Eye* itself) the early years of 'Dear Bill', the collected letters of Denis Thatcher, assumed to be addressed to his friend Sir William Deedes, one-time politician and later editor of the *Daily Torygraph*. In more recent years, I was to appear in the *Eye*'s continuing saga pertaining to the fortunes of the Waleses' marriage, 'Heir of Sorrows', as Edinburgh-born Sir Gordon Giles, unctuous and sycophantic literary agent to Prince Charles.

The lunch, or rather the speeches, seemed to go on and on. Brighton's second-hand bookshops are, or were, among the best in the country, and as soon as I could decently escape I hurried out of the Grand, along the sea front (there were still two glorious piers then, and barber's pole Brighton rock everywhere you looked), then up the Lanes. I kept encountering Miles Kington and cartoonist Michael Heath, fellow refugees from the lunch and enthusiastic book snatchers. I bought a first edition of Douglas Jerrold's *London* with Doré's electrifying drawings, and a first (one of one thousand copies but *not* in the original pink cloth) of *An Ideal Husband*. My day was made when, checking my cheque against my bank card, the bookseller said: 'It's a long time since you've published a novel, Mr Gordon.' This close encounter of the flattering kind was almost sufficient to persuade me to write another.

I do not know how he did it, I do not know how he got there, but Ingrams was raking the shelves by the time I reached the first shop I entered, and I know he'd been at the Grand when I left. Or had he? Like the Ghost of Hamlet's father, 'Tis here; 'Tis here; 'Tis gone. He is an elusive man, oddly, Englishly, difficult to pin down.

Less to say about Auberon Waugh. The surname, of course, is Scots, which in their mincing way the English, including custodians of the name, cannot be bothered to pronounce as it should be pronounced. The Scots, dramatically, pronounce it Woch, with the emphasis on the last syllable, as if rinsing their throats. I have never been his agent. Being essentially a traditionalist, he uses his father Evelyn's agents, A. D. Peters (later to amalgamate and call themselves Peters, Fraser & Dunlop when times became harder for literary agents). Whenever I meet Waugh, although he is always polite enough, I feel he is a bit wary, as if he does not quite know how to place me: I didn't attend Downside or Oxford, nor is my father the most brilliant novelist the world has known.

I was, though, utterly beguiled by his diary in *Private Eye* which, blending politics with surrealism (or perhaps, more precisely, surrealism with politics) and stirring in lashings of gossip and innuendo, created a mix from which the reader didn't invariably recognise events as reported in the newspapers during the previous fortnight, but whose tone, nuance and humour were exemplary. I trusted, as did tens of thousands of others, the stance and its veracity. It had more to do, if you like, with the eccentric Scots-Kentish Town poet Ivor Cutler, *An Evening of British Rubbish* (one of the great theatrical anarchic events of the sixties) and *Beyond the Fringe* than with Alan Brien's *Sunday Times* diary.

Bron, as he doesn't seem to mind anyone calling him, is obsessed with his father's novels – a very Achilles heel – which are good, but not that good. By absolute standards, Evelyn Waugh cannot be considered a great novelist; his terms of reference are too narrow, his uncompassionate view of the world too restricted. It is sad that Bron feels inferior to his father as a writer (although, admittedly, the son's *novels* are not in his father's league) and that so many mean-spirited individuals choose to put him down by suggesting that his utterances are published only because he is Evelyn's boy. Quite untrue. No journalist has seen our times, the muckiness and divisiveness of our politicians, more accurately, or expressed himself more trenchantly.

Being his father's son persuaded Bron in his twenties to become a novelist, no doubt with the intent of being a great one. The five he wrote and published, and in this they are like most novels, failed to change either the world or the course of literature, and I suspect Bron will never altogether become reconciled to the fact. Thereafter he fancied himself as a fiction reviewer, and for seven years (1973-80) tended to demolish, like a trencherman with a gargantuan plate of roast beef and three veg, a novel a week and at generous length in the *Evening Standard*. Occasionally he'd go over the top and lavish fulsome eulogy upon a book, but it was never, I think, one by an American, even though during the seventies they were thought to be writing the things better than we were (certainly more earnestly). He later reviewed fiction elsewhere, including the *Daily Mail*, but his real influence was at the *Standard*. No regular critical appraiser of fiction has influenced readers since, and consequently the art and craft of fiction has been sold short.

I was writing and publishing novels while Bron held sway at the *Standard*. The PEN Club invited the two of us to share a platform on which I would speak about what it was like to spend a year (or however long) agonising over a novel, wrestling with all those words, and what it felt like to have your baby peremptorily exposed in the public prints (if you were lucky) by reviewers. Bron would respond by speaking about how awful most new fiction was, and the agonies of the reviewer's life. It may surprise readers to learn that in the seventies I was regarded as quite a promising novelist, of the 'experimental' kind, at a time when people were interested in 'the novel'; and, for some, 'the experimental novel' was regarded as 'the way forward'. Hindsight proves them wrong. Not excluding the outmoded genre of science fiction, there is no 'way forward' for 'the novel'. Anyway, my novels tended to receive respectable reviews and puffs from my friends and those I admired, and were increasingly hysterically condemned by those I didn't know, in particular by Martin Amis, who was making his name as a smart alec.

I'm happy to say that I managed six novels, all long out of print and occasionally offered at absurdly inflated prices by second-hand booksellers, particularly in the States, where I'm sometimes described as 'this important British writer'. Bron only managed five. When he published his fifth, in 1971, he proclaimed that he'd deprive English literature of any more of his fiction until Public Lending Right was enacted. When it was enacted he continued to deprive English literature of his fiction. Bron's novels are, in every sense, thoroughly conventional. Mine, or so *I* thought, were advanced, intense and highly intellectual; or if not 'intellectual', significant cultural artefacts. Why otherwise would Valentine Cunningham, an English don no less, write in the *Times Literary Supplement* when reviewing one of my books: 'There is even a case to be made for Giles Gordon being the only true inheritor of the late B. S. Johnson's mantle as one of the serious anglicizers of French modes'? I'm not sure about that 'even', but I was, for a while, persuaded 'even' if few others were. Am I being too modest? Certainly not. It is not in my nature. I never see the point of modesty. It doesn't get anyone anywhere. My children, on the other hand, invariably regarded my novels as entirely autobiographical. Families usually do, not choosing to understand that there is a difference between fiction and non-fiction. Possibly they are correct, but this cannot be conceded by novelists as otherwise they would have to regard themselves as purveyors of non-fiction. There is, at least, a paradox in that the act of writing fiction is a non-fiction pursuit.

In truth, I wrote two distinct kinds of novel, of which *About a Marriage* (1972) – its first draft written in a week in a friend's cottage somewhere in England – was the only wholly autobiographical one, and the only one which did at all well at the box-office. It was serialised in three successive monthly episodes in the trendy young women's magazine *Honey*, went into a reprint in its original Allison & Busby hardback edition, was bought by the slightly risqué New York publisher Stein & Day (who presumably failed to realise the book was wholly ironical, since the American jacket was a chaste white with silver italic lettering, as if the book were a marriage manual) and reprinted by Penguin with a fairly louche cover showing bits of a naked couple's bodies: both a navel and a female nipple are prominent on the front. Second-hand copies of the Penguin, if you can find them, tend to sell for £1. I buy them up whenever I see them in case no one else does. Sheer nostalgia rather than vanity, of course.

Bron, then as now, lived in his parents' old home, Combe Florey in Somerset and I thought it would be a useful thing – I had no ulterior motive – for him and me to meet for lunch before the PEN event so that we could discuss not what each of us might say but how the evening might be structured. He replied to my letter, saying that he thought this was quite unnecessary but if I'd agree to pay for the lunch he'd be prepared to turn up. I thought this was rich as, in any case, it was the reviewer who made his living by the grace of the novelist; it should also have occurred to me, especially as editorial director of Gollancz, that in the matter of money it was thanks to the publisher that the novelist was able to indulge his or her art in public. On the other hand, if authors didn't produce publishable books what would publishers do for a living? Or reviewers? Perhaps it was appropriate that I paid for lunch.

I booked a table at my then favourite restaurant, Bianchi's in

Frith Street, upstairs. There was a Bianchi's downstairs, but it was said that the only people who lunched there were the Mafia. Certainly they tended to speak Italian or American. Upstairs was presided over by Elena. At one o'clock, Bron, whom I hadn't previously met, and I sat down at the coveted corner table – out of sight of other customers and thus a favourite table of lovers or would-be lovers. Not that Bron and I had that in common. I cannot recall a word of what passed between us but it was all most amicable. I do remember that the day of the week was a Tuesday, and I further remember that my latest novel had been published two or three weeks before, to the usual mix of one or two favourable reviews and more of the other kind. I also recall – and at the time it was quite a relief – that Auberon Waugh hadn't chose to review my novel in the *Standard*.

We met again that evening at the dowdy and precarious-seeming PEN Club in Glebe Place, Chelsea, to confront a surprisingly large audience. Even then Waugh was a figure the literati loved to hate, or hated to love, but I was astonished that so many middle-aged, *mittel* European *émigrés* (the backbone of PEN meetings) found him such a draw. He was asked to speak first and began, and almost ended, by reading aloud every word of his 1,000-word review in that day's *Standard*, the paper's book page in those days appearing on a Tuesday. The review was of my novel, and it was appalling. To call it a hatchet job would be to damn with faint praise. I had to sit there, sinking lower and lower into my seat, trying to disappear through the platform, as sentences of insult and sarcasm reeled out. By the time Waugh had finished, I felt utterly numb, as if traumatised by a road accident.

I cannot recall a word of what I said in response. Maybe I didn't manage one, let alone an 'entertaining' speech. I do remember, though, that I sensed a huge surge of sympathy for me, empathy even, from the writers in the room; and PEN members, almost by definition ('PEN' stands for Poets, Playwrights, Editors, Essayists, Novelists'), are concerned creatively with writing. I began to feel a bit sorry for Bron. No doubt he could easily live with it, but he had definitely miscalculated the effect of his words on this particular audience.

What is inexplicable to me is that I hadn't, sometime during the busy day, looked at the *Standard*, even before Waugh and I had met for lunch – the evening paper was always on sale then by about 11 a.m. – to see if Bron had reviewed my book. I remember looking on the previous two or three Tuesdays and being disappointed (writers are gluttons for chastisement). Obviously he was holding back his notice so that he could have fun with it at PEN. The nearest I ever came to getting my own back was when the literary editor of the *Spectator*, Christopher Hudson, asked a number of novelists who had been savaged by Bron to review his latest (and, as it transpired, valedictory) novel, *A Bed of Flowers*. I wasn't, of course, greatly taken with it. I concluded, echoing Jaques in *As You Like It*, that Mr Waugh's novel came 'sans wit, sans wisdom, sans (almost) everything'.

Bron reviewed the future Nobel Prize winner, Saul Bellow's *Humboldt's Gift*, in the *Standard* on its British publication in 1975. He ended his disdainful notice by saying something like 'The novel is so appalling that I've tossed it into the wastepaper basket.' Like most British reviewers, he could never come to terms with the fact that, almost to a man and certainly to a woman, American novelists lack a sense of humour. Scott Fitzgerald is almost the only exception, and he's hardly a laugh a sentence. You don't read Melville, Henry James, Faulkner, Hemingway, Henry Miller, Norman Mailer, Joan Didion, Don DeLillo, Harold Brodkey for the *jokes*, and without some modicum of humour the American or any other novel is a fairly formidable object.

I couldn't resist writing to Bron, who being a gentleman is a most punctilious correspondent and invariably replies, saying that I didn't believe he'd 'trashed' his review copy of *Humboldt's Gift*, and although I had no intention of purchasing a copy of Bellow's masterpiece I found it hard to believe it was quite as enervating as he said it was, and would he be inclined to present me with his copy so that I could make up my own mind? He replied, on the Combe Florey letterhead with its crisp engraving of the house occupying at least a third of the notepaper, indicating that if I were to send him sufficient postage stamps he'd endeavour to retrieve the product from the wastepaper basket. I did so and the novel duly materialised. If anything, I found it harder going than Waugh had done. Tucked between its pages was the Alison Press and Secker & Warburg review slip. Written on it in ink were dozens of page references and notes in Bron's small neat hand. I was gratified and amused to sell the book with its 'unique' review slip 'in Auberon Waugh's holograph' to a classy second-hand bookseller for a considerable sum when particularly short of cash in 1991.

# XVI

While writing about Ingrams, Waugh and *Private Eye*, let me briefly praise cartoonists in general and the *Eye* illustrators in particular. One of Ingrams' gifts as editor was to select and print in each issue quite the funniest and sometimes (though usually that accolade went to the *Spectator*) the best drawn cartoons published in the British press. They were not so much 'political cartoons' of the grandiose, heavyweight kind which embellish the leader pages of the dailies, although there were some of those, ferociously limned by Scarfe or Steadman. Rather they were allusive comments on our lives and times, visual equivalents, if you like, of *Three Men in a Boat* or *The Diary of a Nobody*. The best make you laugh *intelligently*, and I am flattering myself and you that it is a better thing to laugh intelligently than to laugh stupidly.

It is a fact that most cartoonists and artists (I exclude Goya) are gentler, nicer, if usually more melancholic individuals than most writers. Cartoonists are, though, in themselves, sometimes exceedingly gloomy. Few people I've known are naturally more morose than the witty Mel Calman, whose drawings are instantly recognisable because he's the one who can't, or who has made it his stock-in-trade not to, draw faces. I suspect he regards faces as both irrelevant and misleading. He who in public life smiles is frequently a villain, especially if a press photographer or television camera is in the vicinity.

The thoroughly likeable Calman, in his lugubrious way, tells a story – funnier because he tells it deadpan, tells it Jewish – of how he was introduced at a *Radio Times* party to Barry Fantoni, another cartoonist, famous in those days – the early sixties, probably – when Fantoni was regarded as a leading 'pop' artist and exhibited a notorious painting at the Royal Academy of HRH the Duke of Edinburgh in his underpants. After semi-coherent introductions had been made, Fantoni (born 1940) slid round the group to whom he had been introduced and stopped at Calman (born 1931). (What Calman, least celebratory of men, was doing at a party is another matter.) 'Did I hear that your name was Calman?' said Fantoni. Calman nodded. 'The cartoonist?' persisted Fantoni. Calman nodded again. 'I must tell you that your work is boring,' said his interlocutor. 'The drawing is boring. Why is it so boring?' Calman's visage, as befitted one who draws no faces, registered not a flicker of emotion. Before making his excuses and moving away, Calman mumbled, 'I try to deliver the drawing on time.'

Barry Ernest Fantoni was at Camberwell School of Arts and Crafts with my first wife, and as a result I met him and he asked if I would be his literary agent. He and Ingrams write the E.J. Thribb encomium to a deceased famous person which appears in each issue of the *Eye* (invariably beginning: 'So farewell then . . .') and it was a pleasure to negotiate a contract with Deutsch for the *Selected Poems of E. J. Thribb*, a slim volume which was subversively got up to look as if young Thribb was a Faber and Faber poet, a new Auden perhaps, or an Eliot. (Fantoni's delectable red-haired wife, Tessa Riedy, had been Christopher MacLehose's secretary at the *Scotsman* when MacLehose dispensed with my services. Tessa Fantoni is now a talented bookbinder and repairer.) For many years Fantoni had helped select the cartoons at *Private Eye* (I don't believe he ever used a drawing by Calman) but he wanted to write fiction too. Nothing if not ambitious and supremely self-confident (and also, it has to be said, hugely talented as a draughtsman: he once gave me a ravishing little drawing of the Venice skyline, seen from the lagoon), he thought he could pen a successful series of thrillers. The Trojan War must have seemed a mere interlude compared with the effort and commitment Fantoni devoted to his Mike Dime books, vague homage to and pastiche of Dashiell Hammett. Sadly, Fantoni decided when the world took little notice of either Thribb or his thrillers that the future lay with Chinese horoscopes. 'We get on so well together, Giles, because we're both monkeys,' he explained to me. Thereafter the world and his wife's every move was explained entirely in terms of Chinese birth signs, even though not everyone was Chinese, a point which seemed to elude Fantoni. 'Of course he'd behave that way,' the Cockney Italian would explain. 'He's a snake, isn't he?' (Or a rooster. Or a buffalo. Or a whatever.)

At first it was all quite a jape and made a welcome change from those unmesmerising horoscopes which appear in so many papers and magazines. One of my cardinal rules in assessing at a first or early meeting with someone whether I'll get on with them in the long term is whether or not they say: 'What's your birth sign?' If you respond that you cannot remember, they don't believe you. If you confess that you're a Gemini they tend to respond inanely that your relationship with them is preordained. Either way, the relationship is doomed.

Barry Fantoni wrote a book about Chinese horoscopes (called, you guessed, *Barry Fantoni's Chinese Horoscopes* (1985)) and then, even more embarrassingly, in 1988 *The Royal Family's Chinese Horoscopes*, which may or may not account for the marital problems, as I write, of certain members of that family. The first *Chinese Horoscopes* went into a revised edition, which corrected the error in the first that Muhammad Ali was a famous horse; by 1986 he'd become a famous snake. Either way he was eventually beaten.

During this time Fantoni also had a radio series on – yes, you're right – Chinese horoscopes. People would phone in and Barry would describe their traits entirely in terms of whether they were goats or rats or tigers, or another animal. At all hours of the day and night my teenage daughter, with a constant ear to LBC, would shout out, 'Dad, Barry Fantoni's on the radio talking about Chinese horoscopes.' It became too much for me, especially as Fantoni's belief seemed absolute.

To my surprise, since I assumed he'd be relieved as I was doing nothing positive for his 'career', burgeoning or otherwise, he seemed thoroughly put out when I tentatively suggested we terminate our professional relationship. Another characteristic of Barry's was to end conversations by saying 'God bless', which smug sentiment invariably set my teeth on edge. For years afterwards Richard Ingrams used to introduce me to people as the only man who'd had the courage to sack Barry Fantoni.

I do not think I could ever fathom the cartoonist's mind. Michael Heath, who is a one-man industry, draws dozens of cartoons in a week, or probably in a day, and you sometimes have the impression from the national press that he appears in every issue of every paper and journal. Yet whenever I meet him – and I encounter him quite often as he is the *Spectator*'s picture editor and his office is in the same street as mine – never does he voice an opinion or remotely indicate what he is thinking. It is as if he is a blank sheet of paper. Yet his views, as conveyed by his cartoons, on what is happening in our society, at the deepest and the most trivial levels, are as astute, individualised and stylish as those of any garrulously opinionated wordsmith. I have over the years bought a number of pieces of original art work from cartoonists. As a generalisation, the younger and less established the draughtsman, the more you are charged. The exception, in my experience, is William Rushton, whose originals may set you back almost as much as a modest Rembrandt. Michael Heath, without exhibiting much enthusiasm, will sell you any drawing for a bottle or two of whisky, but he has to nominate the brand. When Peter Ackroyd's mammoth biography of Dickens was published in 1990, Heath drew for the *Spectator* a cartoon of two typical American tourists in London, with the caption: 'We've seen Dickens' house; we now want to see Peter Ackroyd's house.' The *Spectator* is at 56 Doughty Street, our offices are at 43 Doughty Street, and Dickens' house is at number 48.

Around the time Ackroyd's biography was published the *Standard* invited him to feature in a series on 'second homes', Ackroyd having recently acquired a house near Barnstaple in Devon, with a large swimming pool, in spite of the fact that he does not swim. Heath remarked to me wrily that his original caption had read: 'We've seen Dickens' house; we now want to see Peter Ackroyd's houses.' I bought the original, with the caption as printed. A few days later some Americans pressed the buzzer at our office door and were admitted. I happened to be in the reception area at the time. 'Is this Dickens' house?' one of their number drawled, and it was all I could do to resist responding, 'No, but it's his biographer's agent's house.'

Cartoonists rarely attend *Private Eye* lunches. Fantoni never went, perhaps because the fare wasn't to his taste. When Ingrams was editor, the lunches provided by the Coach and Horses' landlord, Walter Matthau look-alike Norman Balon (who, like Elena Salvoni, had his memoirs ghosted though he wasn't graced with a Foyle's luncheon), were, appropriately, plain or vile, according to taste. They invariably comprised overdone steak and fat chips and a school pudding (perhaps Fantoni resisted lunch because he hadn't attended public school), and if you were reckless enough to ask for cheese instead Norman would provide it but with muttering, scurrilous resentment. It has to be recorded that when Hislop became editor the quality of the lunches improved.

# XVII

As someone who barely passed an exam at school let alone undertook so-called further education, I've twice done stints of 'teaching' American students in London to write. The notion is, of course, preposterous – not that Americans should be able to write, but that by 'teaching' teenyboppers how to swing a tolerable sentence one could enable them to do so. But Americans take all this most seriously back home, and when I was made the offer in 1971 to teach a creative writing course for the Tufts University program at the Reynolds Hotel, off Gloucester Road, I grasped the nettle instantly. Not having had a life as an undergraduate, I felt, having passed my thirtieth year, that I'd missed out on something essential to the flowering of my intellect.

I taught my creative writing course for ninety minutes at lunchtime on Tuesdays and Thursdays at the Reynolds Hotel, where the Tufts students lived and were taught. They were a delightful crowd, the girls more often than not pretty in a blonde, bobbysoxed American way. Why they might, any of them, have succeeded as Great Writers was because they believed that by dedication, by striving to write more and better, they could become the real thing, that writing was more to do with application than genius. It was all quite humbling, utterly uncynical. It was rewarding for me because they demanded the most searching if not necessarily the most rigorous analysis which all too often their flimsy three-or four-page misspelt and surreally punctuated stories could not usually command.

I taught the Tufts course for five years. The stipend was particularly welcome because we were paid at US university rates. The course was run by a languid and rather louche BBC radio drama director named Anthony Cornish, who treated the faculty and students as if they were appearing in some community drama and he was gently choreographing a chorus of cretins.

Best of all were those lunchtimes when, escaping from my office at Gollancz and thundering backwards and forwards along the Piccadilly line, I didn't have to pronounce on some technical aspect of writing ('How can you make the semi-colon pay dividends for *you*?') but simply introduced a guest speaker. One of the features of the London program was that Tufts would pay handsomely – £20, I seem to recall, was the going rate – to practitioners in the area of each course to chat to the students about their subjects. Most years I persuaded the same writers to address my students: the poet Dannie Abse, the playwrights David Edgar (bearded) and Christopher Hampton (long-haired), the novelist Barry Unsworth, the biographer Michael Holroyd. This last twice tried out major pieces on my students, but I'm far from sure they were cognisant of the privilege.

I didn't have more than a token poet (not that Dannie Abse, who should have been the first Welsh Jewish Poet Laureate when Ted Hughes landed the job was in any sense that) because assorted poets were invited to address George MacBeth's class on poetry. Nor did I have a representative Anglo-Saxon: they all went, presumably, to Kevin Crossley-Holland's class. Crossley-Holland was, to the amusement of the rest of us, the most successful drummer-up of students. (And we weren't all nobodies: the venerable E. Martin Browne, who directed the original Canterbury Cathedral production of *Murder in the Cathedral* – Eliot, not Agatha Christie – as well as some of Eliot's later plays, conducted a course on modern verse drama, a lost cause if ever there was one.) Thanks to the boyish disingenuousness, hairy cheeks and stooped back of Crossley-Holland, each year all the new recruits were eager to study Anglo-Saxon, that essential academic subject.

Some of my students were rather good, the girls usually more talented than the boys, though the boys on the whole tried harder. One of my students is now in a senior position at a leading New York publishing house; another is married to the co-proprietor of the Caprice and Ivy restaurants in London. Do I get a discount when I try to book a table at the Ivy? Do I even get a table?

A few years later I was asked to conduct a course in dramatic criticism for another American university, Hollins College's London program. This, in a way, was harder work because more precise in its requirements. Most of the students were majoring in drama, whereas at Tufts they were mainly English majors (some of them might have been more accomplished as drum majorettes). The Hollins course essentially consisted of going to see plays in London and writing critiques of them. So popular was this class that it was divided into two, one taken by David Roper, then the *Daily Express* theatre critic, who thought it educative for his students to see farces and light comedies. I endeavoured to send my students to the heavies, the RSC and the National.

These students got to meet the odd professional too. John Caird, associate director of the RSC and co-director of *Les Misérables* with Trevor Nunn, came with the prompt book for his 1983 RSC production of *Twelfth Night* and talked didactically and illuminatingly about how and why he directed the comedy as he did; really strong textual stuff. Ex-RSC actor David Buck, soon to die of cancer, who at the time was appearing in the West End in his own one-man adaptation of Robert Nye's great novel *Falstaff*, arrived with make-up and costume and for an hour, all the while talking energetically about the part and his interpretation, applied his make-up so that by the end of the class the cherubic-faced actor (well, something of the sort) had become Prince Hal's hirsute drinking companion: his was the face of Falstaff. US university programs, inevitably spelt thus, were at the time something of a growth industry in London, and they provided stimulating work and attractive pay to many peripatetic Britons. The architectural historian Gavin Stamp, later to discover the glories of Glasgow, taught at Hollins, and so did Peggy Reynolds, recently disclosed by Jeanette Winterson as her lover. I was always attracted to her little lace-up boots.

My only other experience of academe was one I did not enjoy at all, and I can't for the life of me remember how or why I ended up doing it. I don't think I applied for it. In 1974 I was appointed the grandly named C. Day Lewis Fellow in Writing at King's College, London. The previous year the relentlessly 'experimental' novelist Eva Figes, much more serious about literature than I was, had held the Fellowship, but at University College, London. At the time 'experimental' novelists were all the rage in certain quarters, and there were only a few of us who were, rightly or wrongly, regarded as such. I suspect that the more staid King's literature department didn't want to fall behind University College, where Karl Miller ruled as professor and his staff included the novelists Dan Jacobson and A. S. Byatt. King's could only really compete with David Nokes, who in 1991 was to acquire a smidgen of creative fame when he co-adapted Samuel Richardson's enormous and intractable novel *Clarissa* for television, in three parts: who would need to attempt to read the book again? Otherwise the dons were all heavy academics, mostly very heavy. There was an excitable, bearded lecturer named Richard Proudfoot, who enjoyed Shakespeare and was responsible for assisting the students to mount productions of the plays. Roger Sharrock, one of the two professors of English and the one who had rooted for the Fellowship to be held at King's – although whether he wanted me I do not know – was a learned Bunyan scholar. The other professor, whom I don't recall meeting, was a Chaucer man. They are both long since dead. Little wonder I did not feel at home, though Sharrock could not have been more helpful and sympathetic. He was inclined to invite me into his room around the middle of the afternoon and quietly (he was a soft-spoken man) dispense sherry, a drink I have always detested and only associate with universities and Church of Scotland ministers. I think the problem was that I was regarded by the rest of the staff as Sharrock's creature. I was particularly resented, as he admitted to my face when I confronted him, by the somewhat glib American Beat writing authority Eric Mottram, who was popular with the students who were interested in contemporary writing, and who had, when the Fellowship was discussed in the department, rooted for a writer other than me. I think it was one Bob Cobbing, a 'sound' poet, whatever that means, or meant.

Sharrock tentatively suggested that I give a series of lectures, as if to justify my position. I proposed, and he readily accepted, that I discuss the recent English novel in terms of the writers who had been undergraduates at King's, of whom there were quite a few, including Maureen Duffy, Susan Hill, and B. S. Johnson. I couldn't understand why only four or five students turned up each week.

The answer, apparently, was that my lectures took place at precisely the same hour as a series of Mottram's which the students had to attend in order to qualify for their degrees. Whether this timing was due to Sharrock's inefficiency or Mottram's mischievousness I shall, presumably, never learn.

Soon after my arrival I was invited to meet the principal of King's College, General Sir John Hackett, victor of most battles since Agincourt. We took sherry together and exchanged a few pleasantries. I've no idea if he knew why I was there, or whether he thought I was a mathematician, astrologer, divine or whatever. Perhaps it was because of Hackett's presence at King's that the department of war studies seemed to thrive.

I was given a room, so small that it seemed to consist of nothing but two brick walls, a door and a window looking out on to Betjeman's favourite church in the Strand. For two terms, the length of the Fellowship, I spent a couple of days a week in my room, waiting for undergraduates, graduates too, if they were so inclined, or members of the staff, to visit me – hardly Mahomet – to discuss writing, whether by Cecil Day Lewis, themselves, myself, or anyone else. Only one came more than once, and he came regularly. He put in an appearance almost every day I was there, and I charted his visits in the journal I began out of boredom to keep. He unnerved me more than a little and I found him unpleasant, though sullenly, angrily intelligent. He never seemed to do any writing, or none that he showed me. He was forever trying to persuade me to have a drink with him in the pub near the College in the Strand. He was half Pakistani, brought up in South London, and claimed (I don't know why I was sceptical, but he had an air of untrustworthiness about him) to know the short-story writer and novelist Francis King. King had encouraged him, he suggested a bit ominously. I clearly wasn't encouraging him. I considered the young man, wearing jeans and a leather jacket, menacing. Perhaps he was just young and lonely, but I objected to his angry patronage.

When I wasn't writing my journal in my antiseptic little room, I was striving to write a novel, and I see that in the prelims to *100 Scenes from Married Life* I thank the Arts Council for the C. Day Lewis Fellowship which enabled me to finish the book.

I must have read more than I remember of the work of my insistent visitor, because he told me years later when we encountered one another at the Hampstead Theatre one evening, that it was entirely my fault that he'd given up writing prose and novels and taken to writing dialogue. I'd told him, he maintained, that his prose was so appalling that he'd never make a novelist. I was at the theatre that evening to review *Birds of Passage*, an intelligent first play which in a pleasing way paid homage to *The Cherry Orchard*, and which received one of its best reviews in my *Spectator* column. My importunate friend was there because he'd written the play. His name was Hanif Kureishi, and he was shortly to achieve wide acclaim for his sparkling film, *My Beautiful Laundrette*. In 1990 he published his first novel and there wasn't much wrong with the prose. David Hughes and I had been so taken by the first chapter of the novel, *The Buddha of Suburbia*, which was initially published as a short story, that we included it in *Best Short Stories* 1988.

Perhaps I'm just not very good with writers from the Indian sub-continent. In 1970, Liz Calder, then Gollancz's publicity manager, had left her husband in Derby (said to be the wife-swapping capital of England at the time), where they had been living, and was lodging in London with a friend of hers, Clarissa Luard, and her Indian husband. One evening Liz took me to their house for a meal and I met the husband, who informed me that, although he worked in an advertising agency, he was a serious writer and would soon be able to show me his first novel, which he trusted Gollancz would publish. There was undoubtedly a feeling in the air that the book would be worth waiting for. Again, the author, who had been educated at Rugby and at King's College, Cambridge, did not exude the traditional lashings of British diffidence and false modesty. When, a few months later, he submitted his manuscript to Gollancz I found it uncompelling. It was science fiction, a genre by which I'm generally not stimulated (although, as an erstwhile contributor to *New Worlds*, my old stories pop up occasionally in science fiction anthologies of the 'new wave'). I sent the fairly hermetic manuscript back to its deviser with a polite rejection letter and thought no more of it.

I was succeeded as editorial director by Kevin Crossley-Holland, who found Livia Gollancz even more exhausting than I had done and who resigned in 1977 to become a full-time freelance writer, recycling Anglo-Saxon literature, writing his own quiet poetry and lecturing. He was succeeded by Liz Calder. Gollancz announced a science fiction prize and the winning book was the novel I'd turned down, *Grimus*, which was published in 1975. I think the book did modestly, but its successor, published by Liz when she was at Cape, won the Booker Prize. This was *Midnight's Children*, and the author, of course, was Salman Rushdie, who has had his troubles since.

A few weeks before the poor man had to disappear into internal exile as a result of the terrible *fatwa* pronounced against him by the Ayatollah Khomeini, I met him at a party and congratulated him on the story, 'Good Advice is Rarer than Rubies', which David and I had selected for the same issue of *Best Short Stories* as Kureishi's 'Buddha of Suburbia'. I commented on how much I had enjoyed his new, plain style, which reminded me in its freshness of the delicious elderly Indian novelist R. K. Narayan. We had found the story in a recent issue of the *New Yorker*. Rushdie told me, a little sardonically, that it was one of the first stories he'd ever written and it had been rejected by everyone, including the *New Yorker* at the time. Ouch.

I have probably edited too many books, but I must mention another here, *Shakespeare Stories*, published in 1982 by Christopher Sinclair-Stevenson at Hamish Hamilton, with a colourful jacket and black and white drawings by Robin Jacques. I asked a number of writers to take any aspect of Shakespeare that appealed to them and to see how, in fictional terms, the inspiration flowed. The result, I think, is a remarkably intelligent and stimulating book which was quickly remaindered and never went into paperback. Salman Rushdie delivered a stunning piece on Yorick's skull, homage both to the Bard and to the sage of Coxwold and father of the English picaresque novel, Laurence Sterne. Angela Carter provided an overture and incidental music to *A Midsummer Night's Dream*, Kingsley Amis took Macbeth to Rome to see the Pope, Gabriel Josipovici looked at Malvolio anew, William Boyd updated the Forest of Arden. Best of all, perhaps, J. L. Carr recorded the terrible conclusion to the life of Francis Feeble, the woman's tailor, one of Falstaff's recruits.

It was essential that novelists such as Rushdie, Kureishi, Ben Okri, Timothy Mo and Kazuo Ishiguro should have broken through and made their mark on the contemporary 'English' novel, because an art which had reached its peak by the end of the nineteenth century was by the mid-twentieth century in danger of expiring as it contemplated its increasingly self-regarding navel. The British novel (I exclude the Irish, which is a much more robust and vibrant affair) was stifling itself with lack of air, scope and vision. In the sixties, to those of us wrestling with trying to do something different – yes, almost for the sake of being different – the fiction which was at the time highly regarded seemed so much fluff on the navel of both life and letters. Kingsley Amis, John Wain, John Braine, Malcolm Bradbury may have seemed shocking, even revolutionary a few years earlier, but they and Margaret Drabble, who had a towering reputation and readership, and countless others of the then acceptable faces of faction enraged us. Could the novel again not be more than social chit-chat, and sub-sociology, however decently executed?

I was particularly drawn to B. S. Johnson (born 1933) who, when I knew him, looked a bit like an upended elephant without its trunk and who always seemed to be sweating profusely, whatever the weather. Why he seemed *so* big I do not know. He was an uneasy man to be with, to know, especially I suspect if you disliked soccer as much as I did and didn't enjoy sitting (or standing) in pubs drinking endless pints of beer. He was disconcerting in seeming to have no sense of humour whatsoever – though on occasion he would strike up manic laughter – while writing some of the funniest books of our time. His first two picaresque novels, *Travelling People* (1963) and *Albert Angelo* (1964), are hilarious neo-Fielding epics of young men trying to find their way and make good in the modern world. They lack the easy, self-satisfied, moralising of Amis Sr, Braine & Co.

Bryan Johnson was a working-class lad who had the singular fortune to marry a beautiful middle-class girl, Virginia Kimpton, who had knees that I lusted after. He was extremely aggressive, and quarrelled readily, unnecessarily with those who wished him well as much as with those who couldn't have given a hoot. His working-class chip could hardly have been more blatant. He quarrelled particularly with publishers and the so-called literary establishment. He moved from gentlemanly lethargic Constable after his first two novels to Secker & Warburg, where the affable David Farrer, the best editor (as opposed to publisher) in London, offered him a three-year contract in return for two novels with the advance to be paid as a monthly salary. This was, in 1965, quite revolutionary. Johnson was able to give up his teaching job and concentrate upon his books, additional income coming from his weekly soccer reports for the *Observer*. *Trawl* (1966) was a Beckettian monologue about deep-sea fishing. *The Unfortunates* (1969) soon became famous – infamous rather – for being the novel in a box. It was published jointly by Secker and Johnson's paperback publishers, Panther, because if a book isn't in its first edition bound between hard covers it is difficult to envisage how a reprint could appear in paperback when it couldn't be bound in paper covers.

Thus the finished book bears a note on the inside of the box: 'This novel has twenty-seven sections, temporarily held together by a removable wrapper. Apart from the first and last sections (which are marked as such) the other twenty-five sections are intended to be read in random order. If readers prefer not to accept the random order in which they receive the novel, then they may re-arrange the sections into any other random order before reading.' Thanks, Bryan.

The idea behind the novel was, of course, to try to simulate the randomness of life, and it was in its way a brave effort. I had attempted something similar about the same time but failed even to find a publisher: a novel in fifty-two pages, the same number of pages as cards in a pack. There were four different 'stories', four different strands, each loosely representing a suit in a card game. Each page had four paragraphs, each paragraph beginning with a capital letter and ending with a full point. There was also a joker, a fifty-third page which could take you anywhere and destroy the intellectual or human structure that in your random reading you'd built up in your head.

Such efforts, for better or for worse, were an attempt to kick fresh life into the novel, to relate it in some degree to aesthetics, to typography and graphic design. To remove it from the fashionable sociology courses of the new universities, where greyness seemed to rule. Johnson was deeply concerned as to the look of his books, and each one in its different way is a modest visual treat. *The Unfortunates* was, inevitably, a financial disaster and for a previously unforeseen reason. The large majority of 'literary' novels in the sixties and seventies were sold to public libraries, and libraries could not apparently devise a way of coping with a book from which borrowers (though why should they have been so minded?) could so easily have purloined a section or two and kept the pages at home as a souvenir. Admittedly Joe Orton might have had fun had he been let loose with a copy. The novel today, when it infrequently comes up, fetches a hefty price in the second-hand market, presumably because there are so few perfect or even complete copies around and because most of the edition was pulped, or perhaps simply crushed.

Johnson's next two novels, to the surprise of almost everyone at the time, were published by the urbane and gentlemanly Philip Ziegler at Collins, neither a house nor an editor then associated (any more than now) with serious fiction, outwith the subsidiary imprint Harvill Press. *House Mother Normal* (1971), set in an old people's home, devotes precisely the same number of pages to tracing a day in the lives of eight inmates, after which the same space is granted to the house mother, who tries to explain all. *Christie Malry's Own Double-Entry* (1973) is probably Johnson's funniest book, the protagonist, a junior bank clerk, treating his life as if it is double-entry bookkeeping. His final, unfinished novel, *See the Old Lady Decently* (1975), was published by Charles Clark at Hutchinson, the head ephor at the Edinburgh Academy who had presided over the ephors' court which had administered punishment to my posterior all those years before.

Charles Clark had read law and qualified as a barrister, eating paper and drinking ink or whatever it is that they do at the dinners of which they have to partake. He clearly thought this ridiculous because he soon changed professions, becoming a publisher, setting up and brilliantly running Penguin Education. When the antediluvian figure of Sir Robert Lusty (he was, bizarrely, knighted for being deputy chairman of the governors of the BBC, not for services to literature) was put out to grass in 1972, Clark became managing director of the Hutchinson Publishing Group. He was keen to learn about general publishing, and was sensible (or foolish) enough to seek my advice. Perhaps as a result he became inspired by the idea of publishing the liveliest novelists around, and thus (irony intended) immediately signed up Bryan Johnson and me. My 1974 novel *Girl with Red Hair* is, according to the blurb, 'more than a mystery novel, it is a mysterious one'. Perhaps that is why it ends with an index which includes the names of Allison, Clive (who published my first three books at Allison & Busby); Amin, President; Freud, Sigmund; Glyn Mills (my bank at the time); Hockney, David (the reproduction of one of whose etchings adorns the jacket of a later novel); Rohmer, Eric (the director of the captivating *Claire's Knee*); and Sassoon, Vidal (a hairdresser).

Hutchinson, like Collins not a house noted for its highbrow fiction, generously espoused the work of Bryan Johnson and myself, our books being edited by Tony Whittome, who preceded Clark from Penguin, where he had been deputy chief blurb writer. Clark and Whittome signed up collections of stories by both me and Bryan, and in a moment of extravagant optimism an anthology of new 'experimental writing' to be co-edited by us. In the introduction to his collection of stories (or, rather, 'shorter prose which he wishes to keep in print'), *Aren't You Rather Young to be Writing Your Memoirs?* (1973), Johnson set out his list of contemporary writers 'who are writing as though it mattered, as though they meant it, as though they meant it to matter ... Samuel Beckett (of course), John Berger, Christine Brooke-Rose, Brigid Brophy, Anthony Burgess, Alan Burns, Angela Carter, Eva Figes, Giles Gordon, Wilson Harris, Rayner Heppenstall, even hasty, muddled Robert Nye, Ann Quin, Penelope Shuttle, Alan Sillitoe (for his last book only, *Raw Material* indeed), Stefan Themerson, and (coming) John Wheway (stand by): and if only Heathcote Williams would write a novel ...' Tough on the generous and hugely talented Robert Nye, and poor Alan Sillitoe. If John Wheway came I missed him, and Heathcote Williams has gone on to write bestselling poems about whales and elephants. You can't win 'em all.

Our anthology was to be different in kind and tone from the usual run of realist fiction approved by the literary editors of the time. It cannot be stressed how much more influence the books pages of the (far fewer than now) quality papers had then than they do now; especially, as Jimmy Porter called them, the posh Sundays. People bought books as a result of reviews, talked about them, and not only in Hampstead.

In 1968 Karl Miller edited as part of a Penguin series on contemporary writing in different languages and countries of the world (it was and remains an invigorating and instructive series) one entitled *Writing in England Today*. Of course it contained substantially the same old roster of acceptable names. Bryan and I wanted to provide an antidote, a counterblast to that admittedly influential anthology, something which would get an argument going. Why must contemporary writing be all about beery neo-realism, Amis and chips, with a bit of colourful travel writing thrown in?

The day Charles Clark telephoned me to confirm that Hutchinson would commission our anthology – published in 1975 under the title *Beyond the Words: Eleven Writers in Search of a New Fiction* – I telephoned Bryan to inform him. The phone seemed to be permanently engaged. It wasn't until the following day that I was told he had killed himself a few hours before I began ringing. Charles Clark, absolutely against my inclination at the time, persuaded me to edit the book on my own. Not all the authors I invited to contribute would necessarily have been in a volume co-edited by Bryan and me. Indeed, I doubt whether we could have agreed on a mutually acceptable list.

I set out my ambitious objectives, my credo, in an introduction:

I would tentatively suggest that this book be considered as an antidote to Karl Miller's Penguin, *Writing in England Today*. Of Professor Miller's authors, only Anthony Burgess appears in the present compilation. Incidentally, all the work in Professor Miller's anthology had been published previously. The book was influential, partly because it was published in paperback, partly because of Professor Miller's authority, particularly perhaps because it was the only major anthology of the last fifteen years purporting to be 'representative' of contemporary writing in the British Commonwealth. In fact, the book was not merely idiosyncratic, it was perverse. It omitted any writer whose abilities and inclinations were remotely divorced from the, so-called, realistic; or, rather, any such individual piece of writing. Even Scotsmen (and certainly I include Karl Miller and myself as such) should have faith in the imaginative powers of the writer, of his visionary impulse. Where has 'being realistic' got the present decade? Where has 'social realism' got this century?

Goodness me. The book was a hefty tome, colossal and disorganised in manuscript, of which I was and am inordinately proud. It was dedicated to the memories of B. S. Johnson (1933-1973) and Ann Quin (1936-1973), a young novelist of some little achievement (her novel *Berg* promised riches to come) who had drowned herself or been drowned at Brighton. The eleven writers in search apparently of a new fiction (why not eleven new fictions?) and in alphabetical order were Anthony Burgess, Alan Burns, Elspeth Davie, Eva Figes, myself, Bryan, Gabriel Josipovici, Robert Nye (who, judging by his photograph on the front cover, should have been in search of a new photographer, or possibly a new hairdresser), David Plante, Ann Quin and Maggie Ross.

Burgess was there as a kind of father figure. Bizarrely, he chose to contribute some chapters from a children's book. Each writer set out his stall, his or her credo, and there followed new and previously unpublished work by each of them. I contributed two stories, the first of which was about Bryan's funeral. (And if that isn't social realism . . .) Michael Bakewell, Bryan's loyal agent, supplied part of the screenplay for a film the writer had been making, commissioned by Harlech Television, poignantly entitled 'Fat Man on a Beach'.

The anthology was given for review to some heavy critical guns. Christopher Ricks was quite annoyed by it in the *Sunday Times*. I remember being telephoned by a friend at my office on a Friday morning to be told that Martin Amis, then more coming than up, had reviewed it in the still widely read and influential *New Statesman*. I slipped out to buy a copy in the Tottenham Court

Road. Leafing through the pages to find the review on my way back to the office, I was elated to see that he'd devoted a page and a column (I think it was) to discussing *Beyond the Words* and *Farewell, Fond Dreams*, my own second collection of stories, published by Hutchinson on the same day. Martin Amis was not then the revered figure he is now taken to be. He was still snarlingly, lip-curlingly keen to prove that he wasn't merely Kingsley's son, practising the same craft in the same furrows. As I began to read his review, in the blinding sunlight, I realised that Amis *fils* had undertaken a hatchet job of voluble pretensions. He loathed and detested everything about the anthology, and as I recall didn't have much to say in favour of my own book either.

Bad reviews are never fun to receive. Even if you have little respect for the reviewer, they are an assault on your identity, your talent (such as it is, but it is all that you have) and your artistic ego. It doesn't occur to you at the time – how could it? – that a review of a book that has clearly driven a critic berserk is infinitely more reassuring, even life-enhancing, than one that exudes boredom, blandness and indifference. Reading Martin Amis's was, at the time, akin to drinking hemlock. I nearly passed out on the street with alarm.

I have only met him once, two or three years later when we were participating in a debate at Durham University Union. He and I, it will not surprise you to learn, were on opposite sides of the motion. I was dreading meeting him, but he was civil enough in his somewhat suburban way. He had that same month been featured in some glossy magazine as Britain's most eligible bachelor, or something of the sort; and the undergraduates, especially the women, seemed more excited by this than by anything Amis had to say. I was seconding the motion, Stan Barstow proposing it. When I arrived, I was asked by the secretary of the Union if I'd heard of Barstow. 'He's a Northern writer, you know.' Given this youthful, supercilious patronage of the author of *A Kind of Loving* and other truthful books I suspect that Barstow was a last-minute substitute for some flash metropolitan scribe who had pulled out. When Barstow arrived, from nearby Ossett, he was asked, so he told me later that evening, if he knew me. He was too tactful to tell me how *I* was described, and I too anxious to ask him. ' "Do I know Giles?" I said to the lass. "Look here, young lady, I only agreed to do this because Giles was coming." '

Stan Barstow, one of nature's gentlemen, was the first writer I ever interviewed, in the sixties, for my column in the *Scotsman*. The £10 I received for the column each week helped to pay the rent of my bedsitter in Ridgmount Gardens, Bloomsbury, and allowed me to have Sunday lunch at Jimmy's wonderful Greek restaurant in a basement in Soho, where I spotted famous people like Willie Rushton. By which I do not mean to imply that Jimmy's was expensive. It wasn't, but the helpings of moussaka, stuffed vine leaves and afelia were the best value in Bohemian London at the time. The meal was always accompanied by a doorstep of bread. The second author I interviewed for the *Scotsman*, William Trevor, I took to Jimmy's. He told me years later how alarmed he'd been when I'd seized my chunk of bread and thrust it under a wobbling table leg, but how impressed that the table wobbled no more.

Bryan Johnson, who was the archetypal professional writer in the most discriminating way, had published, in addition to his seven novels, a collection of stories, *Statement Against Corpses* (1964) (superb title) with the Pakistani poet Zulfikar Ghose, two collections of poems, plays and film scripts. The titles of the volumes of poems were – wait for it – *Poems* and *Poems II*. Very Bryan that. He was most down to earth about his poetry. Let the work speak for itself, which it does, beautifully. It is, like Robert Nye's poetry, the real McCoy, translucent as a glass of water.

By the end of his career (he died aged forty), he had, I think, won the grudging respect of the literary establishment, and he was accorded major review coverage. Auberon Waugh, who might have been expected to mock B. S. Johnson, wrote in the *New Statesman* on 23 November 1973:

Last week there appeared what I thought an extremely promis-ing first novel, if I may be allowed to differ from the *New Statesman*'s reviewer on the point, by a young man called Martin Amis, whom [like Johnson] I have also never met. He used many of the comic devices pioneered and developed by B. S. Johnson. Perhaps Amis had never heard of Johnson, let alone read him. It does not matter. All cultures possess their own impetus, their art forms absorbing whatever is put into them with or without the awareness of individual artists. My point is that he has contributed something to the main stream of English writing, and that must remain his achievement. But it is a terrible shame he is dead.

Waugh getting it right again. Johnson was like a raging bull, a whale out of water, ultimately floundering fatally in the slightly cynical, very superior, oh so sophisticated literary world of London. Most working-class writers manage to come to terms with the act of writing, creeping up into the middle classes without necessarily changing their colours: Stan Barstow, Keith Waterhouse and John Wain are still, I think, essentially the men they were. They have learned – whether easily or with difficulty I neither know nor would presume to guess – to cope. Bryan couldn't, or wouldn't. He refused to accept, to absorb, the compromises, the selling out.

When he spoke each year (sorry, semester) to my Tufts students at the Reynolds Hotel he was nothing short of magnificent. It was as if his life depended upon his performance. There was no cynicism, no suggestion of this being an easy payday. Afterwards, once, we had a pizza together. He insisted upon paying (he was not remotely a rich man, and his wife stayed at home bringing up their two sons) because, he said, I'd provided him with work and he felt he'd been adequately remunerated for his talk. He had a tiny, little voice, sawn-off Cockney. There was no attempt to refine it, to slither into gentility. You had to concentrate hard to hear him, another strange contradiction in a man of contradictions. He was a puritan, at heart a simple soul. That was his tragedy. He had to see literature, as one who created some of the stuff (and he knew he did), as something which could be corralled, disciplined, made perfect. He believed that a novel (as well as a short story or a poem) could with striving, craft and artistry, be got right, and not just be an approximation to what had at first been envisaged.

He resisted, at least in his later work, the messiness of fiction, the loose ends, the lack of explanations, the trite conclusions.

Everything was tied up. 'Telling tales is telling lies,' he endlessly asserted. To which the answer, surely, has to be: Well, yes. And: Well, no. Even a child 'telling tales' on someone is telling the truth, the truth as he or she sees it. Subjective rather than objective truth but still the truth. Maybe it's socially unacceptable to 'tell tales' in that way, but it isn't telling lies. Bryan would eschew the 'Once upon a time' approach, the invention or rehearsing of a story, the spinning of a dextrous verbal web with fictional ante-cedents. In doing that he surely cut himself off from an essential part of the novelist's armoury and palette. He believed he looked truth in the eye and wrote about life, albeit as fiction not as fact, both as he saw it and as it was, as if the two approaches were synonymous, the subjective objective. He became, as the 'experi-mental' writer has to become, schematic if not didactic. *House Mother Normal*, for instance, is more of an interesting idea for a novel, as opposed to a film, looking at the lives of each of the characters, all in precisely the same way. None of them is allowed to be more or for that matter less interesting than the others. Ultimately it is too pat, too neat, closer to working with graph paper than the product of a fertile imagination.

The paradox was that Johnson did, when he would allow himself to do so, tell tales splendidly; and he wrote at all times a delight-fully cool, classical English, closer to that of Old Etonion Orwell than to his revered 'Sam' Beckett. Had he had a sense of humour as a man, as opposed to as an artist, he could, as Auberon Waugh understood, have become as successful a comic novelist as any. Maybe it is a contradiction in terms to expect 'experimental' novel-ists, at least when being 'experimental', to possess or apply a sense of humour to their material. It is, I have to admit sadly, a fact that the 'experimental' novelists of the 1970s, except of course myself, utterly lacked a sense of humour, whichever way that is construed or interpreted. Why it should be that you cannot labour away at creating 'experimental' fiction with a sense of humour I do not know, but it seems that to be 'experimental' is to be humourless. Here endeth this particular lesson.

Whether I succeeded to any extent with my 'experimental' stuff I do not know, nor is it for me to say. It should be realised though that with the exception of the very, very humourless it is not the writers themselves who slap on labels saying 'I am an experimental writer' but the critics, and it is usually meant disparagingly. No one has met the child who, when asked what he or she wants to be when grown up, replies 'an experimental writer'. Every writer of achievement is an experimental writer, but he or she is only successful if the experiment is not intrusive. The engine room, the mechanics, should not be brought before the reader's gaze.

Eventually life for Bryan Johnson became just too much. He cared too greatly. Beneath the bulk he was more sensitive than most, more easily hurt, and there were difficulties with his marriage. He wanted to get away from the mess of everything. One Saturday afternoon in October 1973 as the light was beginning to go I answered a ring at our front door bell. Bryan was standing there. His short, light-coloured, cropped hair seemed to stand on end, and somehow it gleamed. His clothes were smeared darkly, and there were black oil stains on his large hands and on his face. Sweat, even more than usual, was pouring off him. There was no greeting, no explanation, only a request to use our phone. His fucking car had broken down in Camden Town. The vehicle, it soon transpired, could not be repaired that evening. We invited Bryan to stay the night. Why he couldn't go home to Islington I cannot remember, though presumably it was more to do with the state of his marriage than the state of his car. He telephoned Virginia and told her where he was and that he was spending the night with us.

He had some food with us and our young children. Over the kitchen table, after the children had gone to bed, Bryan talked of suicide, of how he couldn't cope, couldn't go on; over and over again. I hope we were sympathetic. In the morning, he came down to breakfast, heavily; but he was always heavy. I can see him now, sitting at our oval oak dining-room table (bought for £8 from Tutte Lemkow, the dancer, who was married to Mai Zetterling before Mai married David Hughes, and who spoke English with a drawl more English than the upper classes) like a plasticine version of Rodin's *Thinker*, elbow crushed on to the table surface, face almost buried in the palm of a hand, motionless, lost. 'Why's that man asleep at the table?' asked my son Gareth, aged three, in a loud, hoarse voice. Bryan soon departed, heading for Camden

Town to meet the mechanic who was to repair his car. I remember that, as soon as he'd left, my wife and I said, matter-of-factly, that those who talked about suicide usually didn't commit it.

Three weeks later Bryan cut his wrists, Roman-fashion, in the bath at his flat in Dagmar Terrace. His body was identified by a writer friend, Barry Cole.

# XVIII

On the whole, writers should write and readers should read. It may be argued that in our bardic tradition, long before Caxton set up his printing press in the precincts of Westminster Abbey over five hundred years ago, would-be readers, who mostly couldn't read, would gather round and listen, mouths open, to a storyteller. Which is true but says little, if anything, about today. We have printed books by the million, and printed books are devised mainly for people to read quietly in their own chairs in their own private 'space', as contemporary jargon would have it. Most novelists, to a certain degree the inheritors of the storyteller's mantle, write in solitude to be read in solitude, hence, if the work is good, the subtlety and exactitude of the prose, its precision. Which is not, I realise, to say that the occasional novelist – Dickens leaps to mind – isn't a dab hand at recitation. Yet as a general rule, books which read well aloud aren't major books, don't have staying, discriminatory power, and cannot bear being read repeatedly, as the masterpieces of prose fiction can.

The same, I'm afraid, applies to poetry. Poetry readings have in the Western world been terribly fashionable since in 1965 the whimsical neo-Blakean Michael Horowitz (Horrid-wits to all his friends, and some not his friends) hired the Albert Hall in London and filled it with assorted poets including Adrian Mitchell, Allen Ginsberg and other Americans, and available Russians. This 'event' marked the beginning of a return to public poetry, where a poet was regarded as successful, or not, subject to his popularity at public readings. Because, for obvious reasons (not least the length of the work), poets were a greater attraction as public orators than prose writers, it was around this time that the sale of poetry in volume form began to rise and that of novels to fall. 'Punters' craved to have their slim volumes autographed by those they had heard reading, as if the poets were film stars or leading classical actors, even if they had no particular intention of looking at the books again. Contrary to popular book trade mythology or prejudice, the rise in the sale of poetry and the fall in the sale of 'literary' fiction had little to do with the binding in which the work came – poetry began to be published in paperback whereas novels were still first brought out in hardback – or price: poetry by the page, even in paperback, was infinitely more expensive than prose; and it wasn't usually (though who could prove that?) that the words, the lines, were *better*. Two publishers, Quartet and Wildwood House, in the early seventies published some novels as paperback originals (as opposed to hardback) but they were not a success. Conservative literary editors tended not to review them.

I was not invited to do a second Arts Council writers' tour, which I was sorry about, and after some years the admirable scheme was abandoned. 'New initiatives' were called for by 'new people'. Only in Britain would a scheme as efficient, as cheap to administer and as much enjoyed by everybody concerned as the Arts Council writers' tours be abandoned. I did sup once or twice at the table of the British Council, which is a much more hard-working and less glamorous organisation, taking British *kultur* abroad, whereas the Arts Council purveys culture at home. There is, inevitably, more than an element of patronage about it, of Lady Bountiful dispensing largesse in the missionary position.

In 1989 I compiled for the British Council a bibliography, *The Twentieth-Century Short Story in English*, which took infinitely longer to put together than I thought it would (short story? short bibliography? don't you believe it). I was not responsible for the title, which would surely lead you to assume that the bibliography would be dominated by Americans. None is represented. Patricia Highsmith, Sylvia Plath and Paul Theroux are thus omitted, but Henry James is there because he acquired British nationality in later years. Highsmith and Theroux know what they have to do to appear in the second, revised edition of my bibliography, if there ever is one. The compilation of this list is the nearest I will get, I imagine, to doing work of a 'scholarly' or 'academic' nature, although all I did, really, for days and days on end, was sit in libraries and look up lists and copy things down.

More romantically, I was sent in 1988 to Istanbul as one of two British delegates each of whom had to deliver a couple of papers at the XIXth All-Turkey seminar of teachers of English at Bogazici University. Every year the British Council dispatched two likely lads, one a lively don, the other a 'writer' or more maverick figure. The previous two years the British speakers had included Jeremy Treglown and A. N. Wilson, later and modestly to be a biographer of Jesus, whose subject was humour. The Turkish academics had anticipated a witty analysis of, say, Swift or Wodehouse (if not Surtees) – they are all terribly well read – and were a bit bemused to be regaled by Wilson about *Private Eye*, which none of them had seen or knew anything about. Twelve months later, they were still bewildered and kept asking me if I could *explain Private Eye*'s humour. I couldn't. My travelling and lecturing companion was John Carey, Merton Professor of English Literature at Oxford, who doubles, or slums, as principal book reviewer of the *Sunday Times*. I was not looking forward to meeting Carey, if only because I might be shown up as a sham. What, indeed, were my credentials for lecturing the late Ottoman Empire on English literature? Carey, who didn't wear a three-piece tweed suit and brogues, couldn't have been more of a surprise, or more agreeable. He was clearly a working-class lad, with a private passion for bees and bee-keeping, who had made it in academe. Although he established his reputation with books on Milton and Donne, he prefers his contemporary writers down to earth, and I tend to prefer mine highfalutin: when High Art is available why settle for low art?

My first subject was the English theatre from *Look Back in Anger* to the present, which seemed to go down well – that is, heads were lowered most of the time and endless note-taking indulged in – probably because hardly anyone at the conference had seen any of the plays. The second was the English novel since *Lucky Jim*, which was less of a success, perhaps because I talked mainly about my own clients, who have to be the best novelists, including Peter Ackroyd, Robert Nye, Barry Unsworth, Michael Moorcock, Allan Massie and Fay Weldon. One Turkish academic was terribly excited that I had *met* Fay Weldon, as her own talk, to be given the next day, was on 'The Metafiction of Fay Weldon'. The paper on Fay Weldon's metafiction seemed interminable, and to make things worse the Turkish academic delivering it had a heavy accent. She ploughed her way through novel after novel. After she'd discussed six or seven, Carey, sitting next to me in the front row of the hall, asked me out of the side of his mouth how many more books had to be covered. I counted up. 'Five,' I whispered back. Ten minutes later I was obliged to put in a correction. 'She skipped two. She's gone back to them now. Six to go.' Come back David Lodge, all (or much) is forgiven. It transpired that they were universally into metafiction. Other lectures – and they all went on infinitely longer than Carey and I, who stuck religiously to the fifty minutes we'd been allotted – were on the metafiction of John Fowles, William Golding and Iris Murdoch. The Merton Professor of English Literature confessed to me at the beginning of the proceedings that he had no idea what metafiction was, and by the end of the conference he confided that he still didn't understand. Presumably someone else teaches metafiction at Oxford.

Carey's papers were on Philip Larkin and Ted Hughes, two poets whom he admires only just this side of idolatry. He spoke warmly, richly, on Hughes' animal poems and the imagery therein, in an easy and friendly way which must almost have disarmed the Turks. This was nothing, though, on his paper on Larkin, to me probably the most overrated of post-Second World War English poets. It's not that Larkin is *bad* – he's nothing as grand as that – but that he's so deliberately, cunningly mediocre, so petty bourgeois and uninspirational in poetic stance. You feel (well, I do) diminished by reading him, that there is less to life than you thought there was. His mentor John Betjeman, a craftsman of the old school, at least seems to be sending himself up most of the time, and has a sense of rhythm; Larkin is sending himself down. Carey's paper was magnificent.He built, gentle unpretentious sentence by gentle unpretentious sentence, a case for Larkin being a very considerable poet indeed. He talked about Larkin's roots, and how a reading of the poems was enhanced by knowing intimately the area in the north of England whence Larkin came. He drew out the humanity, the compassion, even the gentle fun-poking (if not rib-tickling) in Larkin's work. If Larkin had been a religious leader I'd have signed up immediately, taken the pledge. Apart from Roy Foster on Yeats, it was the best lecture I've heard on a poet.

Carey, from East Sheen and Richmond grammar school, affected a black leather blouson as he and I went for a stroll one afternoon when we escaped from the metafiction (we were expected to be present at all the papers) into Istanbul itself. As we walked towards a particular mosque, we were picked up by an increasingly menacing young Turk who wanted us to take him back to England. We couldn't shake him off. He seemed put out only when we explained to him that John lived in Oxford and I lived in London. I think he wanted to be our houseboy. But he still followed us, threateningly. We were uneasy as more and more fearsome-looking young Turks surrounded us, like – homage to Carey's bee-keeping passion – bees round a honey pot. Eventually we reached the Qtar Mosque, took off our shoes and entered the awesome building. I said nothing to Carey but was certain that when we came out our menacing friend would either have disappeared with our footwear or done something lingering to it. I couldn't imagine what the latter might be, but definitely something that would call for an investigation by Hercule Poirot, preferably played by Peter Ustinov. Of course our shoes were fine but, on the way back, it was quite some time before we were able to throw the youth off our track.

Carey had shown me some bowls he'd purchased in the covered market a day or two before. They were simple and beautiful, painted in traditional blue, white and red Turkish designs. I complimented him on his purchase and he offered to take me to the stall, if he could find it in that frenetic, exotic Arabian Nights bazaar. We found the stall, or it may have been a similar one selling the same goods, and I began bartering for soup bowls. I acquired half a dozen for a price considerably less than he had paid. (None of which matters as he'd paid about £2 a bowl.) '*That's* why you're a literary agent,' he said, oddly impressed at my transaction. 'And that's why *you're* a professor of English,' I responded.

A year or two later, the British Council sent me, on my own, to Positano to give a talk – an amalgam of my two papers at Istanbul – to a grand and bustling conference of teachers of English. It was not a success. I took a taxi from Naples, the taxi driver having indicated a certain price and mileage. After nearly an hour of cruising the meandering coast road around the Bay of Naples, I realised either that he'd intended to con me from the beginning, or to be more charitable, that I'd failed to interpret his Italian adequately. As I'd run out of money, he gallantly deposited me on a sweltering hot road, miles, it transpired, from anywhere. I failed to hitch a lift, and eventually had to walk through a three-mile-long and highly dangerous tunnel before reaching the nearest railway station.

When I arrived at Positano, no one seemed interested either in my tedious account of my unfortunate journey or in my talk, which took place in a handsome, recently built auditorium that was defiantly 'state of the art' and must have seated twelve hundred people. I was introduced by someone who was not the person I was told was going to introduce me, and his potted biography of me must have been of some other speaker. I should say that during the fifty minutes or so during which I spoke three or four hundred people left the auditorium, most of them noisily and in twos and threes and fours, and two or three hundred came in. How many arrived, listened for a few minutes, then departed I do not know.

The British Council encourages those it sends abroad to compile reports on their experiences when they return home. I gave the Positano conference the thumbs down, which is why, I feel sure, I haven't been asked to wave the flag for the Council again.

# XIX

One of the great causes of my lifetime – and I was honoured to be peripherally associated with it – was the battle to establish Public Lending Right; and battle it was. Although various people were credited with planning strategy and being in the front line, the establishment of PLR was significantly and almost entirely due to the indefatigable, selfless efforts of, first, Brigid Brophy – who was handed the torch by her father, John Brophy – and soon after of Brigid Brophy *and* Maureen Duffy. I set this out as I do because there is a tendency these days – and I mean no dishonour to Maureen Duffy, as she knows – to assume, with Brigid Brophy for so many tragic years locked in the hell of multiple sclerosis and doomed to non-life in a nursing-home bed in Louth, Lincolnshire, to give the principal credit to Duffy. The two novelists fertilised and gave strength to each other, and their own 'careers' as novelists suffered.

It was, as I say, the prolific author John Brophy, aided and possibly distracted by A. P. (later Sir Alan) Herbert, who started the cry for PLR, for writers to be paid a pittance (Brophy's shilling, as it was known) each time their books were borrowed from the UK's public library system. At the beginning of the seventies, the Arts Council's Working Party on PLR set up a sub-committee to investigate how in practice PLR might operate. This sub-committee comprised Michael Gilbert, thriller writer and, at times, solicitor to the Society of Authors; Graham C. Greene, publisher, of Jonathan Cape, and a very political animal; the well-intentioned but somewhat misguided Victor Bonham-Carter of the Society of Authors; and Ronald Barker, the dyspeptic secretary of the Publishers' Association. The sub-committee, in its lack of wisdom, decreed that the fairest basis for PLR payments would be a royalty calculated as a percentage of the published price of each book supplied to public libraries during the year. This was clearly nonsense, if only because authors of the more expensive titles would garner most of the loot. Also, it had nothing to do with equity, since authors should be rewarded each time their books were *borrowed* by readers from public libraries. To add real insult to injury, the working party, which of course did not contain one full-time author, declared that authors should receive 75 per cent of the government handout, publishers 25 per cent.

It was as a result of this kind of bureaucratic insensitivity that Brigid Brophy and Maureen Duffy realised that some serious thinking and lobbying needed to be done, and urgently. With novelist and short-story writer Francis King, novelist Lettice Cooper and Sir Michael Levey, eminent art historian and director of the National Gallery as well as Brigid Brophy's husband, they formed the Writers' Action Group. WAG started as it ended, a modest but restlessly energetic body which most writers who weren't remotely stuffy joined. Even Kingsley Amis was a member, as well as ex-librarians Angus Wilson and John Braine. Operations were conducted from the Leveys' flat in Old Brompton Road, and amazingly detailed monthly newsletters were posted to members. Written by Brophy and Duffy, these newsletters were remarkable for the quantity and fascination of the information conveyed as well as for the number of words, perhaps 1,000 typed on each side of a foolscap sheet with 'stop press' news typed in the margins. In reading these wonderfully entertaining documents, which some publisher should print in book form, your eyesight suffered cruelly, but your heart and mind and sense of justice were stirred.

Parliament was lobbied throughout the seventies, and there was a tremendous demonstration in 1975 in Belgrave Square, outside the Office of Arts and Libraries, in which was lodged the Minister for the Arts, Hugh Jenkins. (He later became Lord Jenkins of Putney, not to be confused with Lord Jenkins of Hillhead. Both Jenkinses lost their parliamentary seats in, respectively, Putney and Hillhead, and thus it is perhaps odd that they chose to commemorate their pasts when they were translated to the Upper House; but that is the way of politicians.) The demonstration, which brought the press out in droves and the police on horses, was led by such worthies, if not all members of the great and the good, as Lord Willis of Chislehurst (otherwise known as Ted Willis, one-time contributor to the much-revered television series *Z Cars*, and a luminary of the Writers' Guild, the more down-market rival to the Society of Authors), Jacquetta Hawkes, Lady Antonia Fraser, Elizabeth Jane Howard and her then husband, Kingsley Amis. The Minister appeared on his balcony and was astonished to be booed. He promised, as politicians do, that he would see what could be done. Parliament and the world knew that writers meant business.

If it hadn't been for the twitchings of so many bureaucratic librarians and their official body, the Library Association – which, while approving of inanimate books, tends to disapprove of ani-mate authors – I suspect PLR would have been on the statute book years before. Public librarians, at first almost to a man and woman, thought it an abuse of ratepayers' money to recompense authors for books which they, public librarians and thus civil servants, had already paid good money for. Both WAG and, to be fair, the Labour Government had made it plain that there was no question of ratepayers coughing up more cash to bolster authors' income. The money would come, if it came at all, from central funds, not from local government. None the less, the Library Association continued to think that there was somehow bound to be less money available for its 'authorities' to purchase books. The writers' case was that once one copy of a book had been sold to a public library it could be loaned out one hundred times and the author would never receive more than the royalty on the single copy. Were the price of the book £15 and the author receiving the conventional 10 per cent of the published price, he or she would be compensated to the tune of £1.50 in return for giving hundreds of hours of creative pleasure to countless readers. (In addition, and this was never spoken of, public libraries were entitled to a 10 per cent discount from the booksellers from whom they were obliged to purchase their books as opposed to direct from publishers. This was a reasonable device to try to prop up the retail bookselling trade. Thus, if you as an individual were to purchase a novel by, say, Brigid Brophy for your own edification you would be paying more for it than the public library which might loan it out one hundred times. Was this fair, or what?)

The Society of Authors, which twenty years ago was an infinitely more cautious and conservative body than it is today (which is not to suggest that it has become a hotbed of militants), declined, in a serious and committed way, to join WAG in fighting for PLR. Brigid Brophy and Maureen Duffy therefore decided, with typical chutzpah and rather cleverly, that to all intents and purposes WAG should take over the Society of Authors. The Society's affairs were, and are, nominally run by an elected committee of management of twelve authors. In fact it was run then by a secretariat of three paid executives, not themselves authors and one a part-time publisher. Each year four members of the committee retired and four new members were elected. 'Elected' was hardly the word, as the secretariat would propose four writers that they assumed they'd be able to get on with – that is, the committee would leave them alone to implement 'policy' – and no one would demur. Brophy and Duffy decided to persuade four WAG members to be nominated for the following year's Society of Authors committee of management alongside the nominees of the Society, so forcing a postal ballot of members. Thus it came about that, in 1973, Brigid Brophy, Maureen Duffy, B. S. Johnson and – truly screaming and shouting and trying to say no – little me put our heads above the barricades. I was easily the least well known and thought my nomination was a waste of a valuable place. But Brigid Brophy in particular was firm about it and I did my duty.

To my astonishment, I returned from holiday that summer to find that I alone of the WAG members had been elected. Brophy and Duffy had understood that, because I was better known as a publisher than as a novelist, the old dears of the Society would have regarded me as a safer bet than the other three, who might have caused disturbances and rows. It has to be remembered that the vast majority of members of the Society were not full-time writers living off their earned income, or income earned from books, and publishers were gentlemen whereas writers who contested places on the committee clearly weren't. The result of the ballot, in short, was disgraceful and I attended my first meeting of the committee in a right old state of nerves.

Michael Holroyd was the new chairman of the committee of management, and he could not have been more welcoming. His memory of events differs somewhat from mine, however, so perhaps there was more going on beneath the Society's bland surface than met my naive eye. I thought the idea was that I'd quietly blend into the mothers' meeting atmosphere of the Society and everybody could forget about nasty, rude WAG and even PLR, and leave Victor Bonham-Carter (the Society's 'expert' on the subject) and sympathetic publishers to work it out. I did my best to keep the WAG end up, taking detailed briefings from Brophy and Duffy before each meeting of the committee. To my relief, I was joined, after a year by Lettice Cooper and Francis King, and in the third year by Brigid and Maureen. By then there was a majority of WAG members on the Society's committee and thus we were able to lobby Parliament both strenuously and with authority.

In parallel with this, Brigid and Maureen had persuaded the Writers' Guild, which essentially looked after the interests of television and screen writers, to admit book authors to membership. As soon as my years on the Society of Authors committee were over (Antonia Fraser had succeeded Michael Holroyd as chairperson), I, like many if not most WAG members, resigned from the Society and joined the Guild, which was a bit like leaving the SDP to join Labour. This was, of course, expediency, exclusively to try to see PLR enacted by Parliament.

It is an odd fact that most playwrights and writers of film and television screenplays, however brilliant with dialogue, are hopeless when it comes to sentences, and give up the struggle altogether where subordinate clauses are invoked. If you make your living – and unlike most members of the Society, Guild members did make their living, in those distant days, from their typewriters – by writing dialogue to be spoken, particularly for soap operas, you needn't be concerned much with such arcane matters. Guild members tended to wear jeans, leather jackets and anoraks, whereas Society members sported old tweed jackets with leather patches, or if they were female, which most were, comfortable woollen garments and lengthy skirts. If you think I am making a social point (but not, I hope a snobbish one, though many confuse the two) you would be right. Some of the more committed book writers remained active with the Guild after PLR was obtained, notably Maureen Duffy, who became president or some such undemocratic title, but most of us sloped back to the Society which, under its new and quietly determined barrister secretary, Mark Le Fanu, readily reabsorbed us. It is fervently to be hoped that the Society of Authors and the Writers' Guild will soon amalgamate. Although the Guild, true to its origins, is affiliated with the TUC and the Society is not, writers will only be represented properly when they are represented by one authoritative body, both the anoraks and the cardigans.

When the PLR registrar's advisory committee was set up in 1986 I became a member. I was the nominee of the Association of Authors' Agents. It was the most agreeable and useful committee I have sat on, largely due to the amiability and common sense of the registrar, John Sumsion, who was previously employed not in the book trade but by the boot and shoe industry. His private passion was singing, though, perhaps mercifully, he didn't indulge during committee meetings. Sumsion had no axe to grind other than to see that the PLR Act was interpreted as Parliament intended it to be, and to see that in practice it worked. This was only achieved because both authors and publishers trusted him and his intentions, an extraordinary feat on his part, given the natural antagonism between authors, publishers and librarians. In the early years there were one or two difficult local authority representatives on the committee, particularly a humourless young man with red hair who should go far in local government because he seemed to be against anything if it meant spending money. Even the librarians were affable and, unlike so many of their breed, seemed genuinely to approve of, or at least accept, the principle of PLR, of authors being paid for the public borrowing, if not always necessarily reading, of their books.

Shirley Hughes, the joyous and cuddly-looking children's author and illustrator, was a member of the committee and spent the entire three hours or so of meetings – while not missing a word of what was said and on occasion passionately joining in – drawing faces, usually starting with those of us sitting round the table in the drab offices of the Department of Education and

Science in Waterloo where we usually met of a wet afternoon. No one seemed to have the courage, though, to ask Shirley if they could purchase their sketch.

The funniest man on the committee was the representative of the Publishers' Association, Peter Phelan. He had, as assistant secretary, served the PA well for many years, but must have been regarded as too witty and undoctrinaire to become secretary. He was much brighter than most publishers, and certainly more adept and eloquent with the English language, and that might have been an embarrassment. He had another life as a stalwart member of the amateur acting profession (and in Peter's case that would not be a contradiction in terms). Unlike John Sumsion with his singing, Phelan occasionally had to be stopped from offering recitations at meetings. He and I, years before when the world was young, had shared a passion for the same girl, who ended up as a publisher's rep and married a famous author, but that is another story, possibly for another book.

The PLR committee met four times a year, three times in the ghastly Department, once at the PLR offices at Stockton-on-Tees where we witnessed the operation in action. We were, on these privileged occasions, permitted to view on the computer any author's PLR figures on condition that we instantly forgot them. I kept being shown my own, which grew worse every year, mainly I hope because I had not published a book for some years.

The only, and probably inevitable, drawback in the PLR scheme is that to those that have shall be given, and to those that haven't, not. The most successful author – year in, year out – is Catherine Cookson, who averages over thirty titles in the top one hundred books borrowed from Britain's public libraries. This is an astonishing achievement. No doubt the likes of Jeffrey Archer, John le Carré and Dick Francis would achieve as many borrowings if they had published as many books as Mrs Cookson. The maximum sum which any one author could receive in a twelve-month period was £5,000, raised to £6,000 in 1989. Mrs Cookson gives hers to charity and for all I know Lord Archer gives his to swell the coffins of the Tory Party, but it is desperately frustrating that poets and other 'serious' literary writers are borrowed less, in comparison with the bestselling popular novelists, than some people had assumed when PLR was but a determined idea in Brigid Brophy's incredible mind and it is a particular sadness to me that Brigid gleans but a pittance each year.

From the Victorian age, public libraries were one of this country's glories, one of our greatest achievements: free education for all; and certainly implicit in the word 'education' was entertainment. It is only with the all-pervading influence of television that entertainment has become virtually synonymous with enervation. Public libraries are being starved of funds to buy new books, and as a direct result publishers are having to cut back drastically on what they publish, which isn't necessarily a bad thing. For years, far, far too many indifferent books have been brought out. The risk in cutting substantially the number of titles published is that the indifferent books will be the ones to stay, while the original and 'difficult' ones will go. Until the mid-eighties, for instance, Gollancz was selling the most substantial part of its output of thrillers and science fiction to the public libraries, and as a result the firm could afford to continue publishing thrillers and science fiction, but also more adventurous books, less assured sellers.

A writer who did not live to reap the benefits of PLR was Philip Mackie. In the late fifties, André Deutsch published his first novel, *Marching through Georgia*. It was not, I think, too much of a success. Little matter, except perhaps to Deutsch, as Mackie went on to become just about Britain's most successful writer for television, scripting series (*The Caesars; I, Claudius; Napoleon in Love*) and single plays. He also had a string of West End successes. He was a prolific writer, as professional as they come. He lived in William Morris's Kelmscott Manor in Gloucestershire too, which shows what taste he had. When he was at the height of his success, he encountered little André Deutsch at a party. 'Philip Mackie,' said Deutsch when they were introduced. 'Your name is familiar. Now, why is it familiar?' 'You once published a novel of mine,' said Philip, who had a dry, modest, self-deprecatory way with him. 'I remember,' said Deutsch, who remained an independent publisher for as long as he did because he never took his eye off the balance sheet. 'I know it wasn't particularly successful, but why did you never write anything else?' There is a serious point there as well as a joke at André

Deutsch's expense. Publishers can think only in terms of books, and preferably books published by themselves. Any other form of writing is an irrelevance. This, sadly, is why so many books published are of little interest to a larger readership. There is, as Coriolanus was forced to notice, a world elsewhere.

# XX

I used to have a tremendously soft spot for Lady Antonia Fraser. I think a lot of us did in the sixties and seventies. She was beautiful, in the way of an English rose (although her father is Irish).

In 1975 she invited me out to lunch, and we went to Bianchi's. She had been asked by Canongate, a young Edinburgh publishing house set up by a friend of hers, to edit a personal selection of *Scottish Love Poems* and she wanted me to suggest possible contributors. She had asked the poet and translator James Michie the same question, and I'm sure Michie was much more helpful to her than I was. James posed very much as a man of the world, and liked to give the impression that he had as great an understanding of and feeling for women as he had for poetry, which was considerable. Maybe he did, but he married a few times, admittedly always most attractive women. I've never been certain whether the man who genuinely understands about women is the man who stays happily married to the same one, or the one who swans about, Casanova or Don Giovanni fashion, plucking feathers everywhere.

I take full credit for persuading Antonia to write her first ever prose fiction, a ghost story about cigarette butts being left in the ashtray of an otherwise untenanted car which I commissioned for *Prevailing Spirits*, a collection of new Scottish ghost stories published by Hamish Hamilton in 1976, the other authors including George Mackay Brown, Fred Urquhart, Iain Crichton Smith and Dorothy K. Haynes. I think Antonia's story was commissioned at the same lunch.

I particularly remember the occasion, however, because she mentioned the name of a playwright she'd recently met, somehow suggesting that playwrights were not a species which tended to swim into her orbit. She asked me what I thought of his plays. Pinter was the name. Luckily I revered them. She was to marry him in 1980. Another story which went the rounds was that when Pinter travelled to Brighton, I think it was, to tell his parents that, subsequent to the break-up of his marriage to the actress Vivien Merchant, he was to marry Lady Antonia, his parents' only expression of concern, according to the tale as told, was that their Jewish son would have to become a Roman Catholic.

Antonia Fraser has, since the deserved success of her biography of Mary Queen of Scots (1969), become one of the literary great and the good, as has Michael Holroyd since his success with the first volume of his biography of Lytton Strachey (1967). I remember he came to dinner in the late sixties. Diana Crawfurd, my own agent at the time (but slightly more successful with the likes of David Frost and John Wells), was also present. What I remember of the evening is Holroyd saying hardly a word. He listened to everything, and probably returned home to bed and wrote a full account of the evening on the backs of envelopes. It was only when, the morning after the night before, I realised that Holroyd, most genial and sympathetic of writers, had said hardly a word that I understood why he was, essentially, a biographer. You can only with difficulty stop novelists from talking. Nowadays, though, it is hard to get a word in when Michael is in the room. He is wonderful company.

John Gielgud, without doubt, was exceedingly famous – in the way that 'stage' actors were then, but aren't now – in the fifties and the sixties. It was right that he was, for he'd done the state of the theatre, the Old Vic in particular, some service. In 1935 he and Laurence Olivier alternated Romeo and Mercutio (Peggy Ashcroft was less ambitiously stuck with Juliet) and their performances were regarded as sensational, as if England and Australia had tied in a test match. Gielgud and Olivier, un-English names both, were acclaimed, by those who like to acclaim, as respectively the soul and body of English classical acting. Later other actors, aspiring to the thrones of these 'verray parfit' theatrical monarchs, were nonchalantly to essay on successive nights different roles in the same play: Richard Burton and John Neville did Othello and Iago (or am I romantically imagining that? I cannot find it in the record books), and in 1973, at Stratford and in London, Ian Richardson and Richard Pasco swapped Richard II and Bolingbroke finely, with Pasco surprisingly more impressive as Richard, and Richardson as Bolingbroke.

The sad thing about young actresses, as presumably they agree, is that, unlike the fallen of the two world wars whose memories we guiltily contemplate for a moment or two each Armistice Day, they grow older, and playwrights have written too few great roles for them. Gielgud's child-bride Juliets – with the exception of Peggy Ashcroft, who, now that she is dead, will never grow old – have faded and fallen. Yet although Gielgud, aged eighty-eight as I write, will presumably never, at least on the boards, attempt Romeo again, those of us too young to have seen him in the role can imagine the bald old Magus, the distinguished self-deprecating buffoon of so many Hollywood character roles, as the young lover of Verona. (I was distraught, as a teenager, to find that Juliet's so-called tomb – '*Tomba di Giulietta*' – in fair Verona was used by visitors as a giant ashtray.) And the voice, down the decades, Gielgud's unique, champagne fluted instrument, will not have changed that much. But his Juliet will have descended long since into the part of the Nurse, if she hasn't dissolved into great-grandmotherhood and senility. (The Nurse of the 1935 production, Edith Evans, has presumably ascended.)

I haven't seen Gielgud's legs naked (except in the 1952 black and white film of *Julius Caesar*, where he was an angry, virile Cassius with James Mason a mellow Brutus and Marlon Brando putting in a moody, far from disgraceful performance as Mark Antony) although I have, I suppose, seen him in doublet and hose. I have seen Olivier's legs unclothed, in *Coriolanus*, when the legs alone of the fifty-two-year-old maestro must have frightened the Volscians. Yet Olivier had soul as well as body, and Gielgud body as well as soul. Gielgud's final Prospero was a very corporeal presence, tetchily roused to wrath, a furious communication of his fairly fragile human frame, almost flying apart on the National Theatre's Olivier stage, a mass in movement, costumed as surrogate Dr Dee.

Is it 'the critics' (and more of *them* later) or the public, individually and collectively, who decree that the one great actor is spiri-

tual, the other physical? It is, surely, as much to do with precon-
ceptions as anything else. You go to see an actor in a particular
part and your expectations are, to some extent, based on what
you last saw him in, how he performed then. If the actor has a
history and you, as a member of the audience, have partaken of
it, you cannot on subsequent occasions come fresh to his performance without prejudice, without expectation.

If you saw Antony Sher's Richard III you would expect his
Arturo Ui to be similar in kind; and it was, but less so. It even
included a parody of his bottled spider, a laugh for the initiated.
'Less so' because the bunch-backed toad of 1984 was a thrilling
miscreation, the first to escape wholly from the spider's web of
Olivier's Dick the Turd (1944). Also because the performance was
unexpected. When Sher plunged on to the Stratford stage pursued
by his crutches, Shakespearian acting – at the Royal Shakespeare
Company, at the National Theatre, and, frankly, everywhere else
in the land – was in the doldrums, although it didn't suit those with
vested interests to say so. These included the theatrical industry in
all its manifestations, the critics – and not least theatregoers paying
for their tickets (plus VAT), who didn't want to hear that the
previous generation of actors and actresses was superior to the
one they were watching, *because* (a) they had paid for their seats
and did not, understandably, feel inclined to admit that they hadn't
had value for money, although privately they might have been
disappointed, and (b), having handed over their cash or wielded
their flexible credit cards, they just wanted to have a good time.

I remember in my teens being terribly shocked by the underrated Scots lyric poet George Bruce, who made his living as a
dogmatic BBC Radio producer and critic, voicing the opinion
that as an 'objective' critic you couldn't or shouldn't enjoy a
performance; that you had a responsibility to withhold a personal,
emotional response in order to assess the work – play, film, concert, book, exhibition of paintings (he was specifically talking
about film) – objectively, as if there were some sort of 'correct'
response. This striving after objective correlative might have made
Bruce an intelligent critic in objective terms, but who wants or
needs so-called objective criticism, any more than, if they have an
aesthetic response to art, they want or need Marxist criticism? The

essence of good criticism is an informed, discriminating, enthusiastic (but not necessarily favourable) commitment to the work and an engagement with it.

Maybe Bruce had a point. Most theatre critics, film critics too, being essentially enthusiasts for their art form, prefer to rave rather than to condemn, to praise rather than to censure; yet, paradoxically, the mightier their expectations, the more they are likely to be disappointed. However, this philosophy cannot be carried too far or it would begin to suggest that Milton Shulman, the recently retired theatre critic of London's *Evening Standard* and arguably the dullest theatre critic in the history of the world, was a paragon. But more of Shulman anon; back to Gielgud.

He was famous in the fifties and the sixties, as I have said, for acting on stage. He was also notorious in many quarters, for having been involved in a homosexual scandal, something to do with a public lavatory. To my mother, before the scandal, Gielgud was the greatest actor of them all. She never took to Larry, finding him a bit coarse, a bit vulgar, besides which there was that business with Vivien Leigh. My mother thought Larry shouldn't have played the seedy Archie Rice if he was a tiptop classical actor, and if he hadn't been vulgar and crude he wouldn't have done, would he? (She was probably right there.) My father, whenever the subject came up, reminded her how much she'd *enjoyed* Olivier in *The Entertainer*, which visited the King's Theatre, Edinburgh, for a week after it had completed its run in London. At this point she always smiled, a little sadly, a little moistly, and admitted that it had been funny, that she had had a good time, but he shouldn't have done it, Olivier, not in that disgusting play by that unpleasant and bad-tempered John Osborne, when he could have been doing Shakespeare, or at a pinch Ibsen or Chekhov. Those were her three playwrights, with the Russian very much third as he didn't tell much of a story.

When Gielgud was branded, or whatever bourgeois opinion did to homosexuals in those days, in my mother's eyes he'd fallen, like Icarus, from grace. Not only would she not go to see him any more, his name was banned from being mentioned in the house. Nor could I discover what he'd done to be undone, what could merit this instant, terminal banishment. I didn't like to ask anyone at school, in case I'd be associated, somehow, with the disease, or whatever the problem was. Could I catch it, or be tainted with it, simply by mentioning it, even thinking about it, the lust that dare not squeak its name? My parents' belief, sincerely held, was that it was better for all of us not to know about these things. They were matters which, simply, were not relevant to their lives and wouldn't be to those of my brother, my sister and me. Thus was a great actor consigned to darkness, but to me Gielgud's mysterious power had become all the more mesmerising.

In 1955, when I was fifteen, the Shakespeare Memorial Theatre Company was to visit Edinburgh for a week. (I have never understood, really, why single weeks tended to be meted out to the so-called provinces, whether the production was of Shakespeare, or of *The Brass Butterfly* – I walked out of William Golding's play, grandly thinking it frivolous – or of *The Reluctant Debutante*, or *The Amorous Prawn*, a title I delightedly appreciated. I understand the simplistic economic argument, that theatres are conveniently rented for a week, but beyond that it seems arbitrary.) The production, by George Devine, with sets and costumes by the Japanese sculptor Isamu Noguchi – who, being foreign and thus difficult to get to grips with, was invariably named on posters and programmes and in reviews as simply Noguchi – was of *King Lear*, or *Lear* as everyone called it in those days, before Edward Bond modestly purloined that title for his updated eye-gouger. The production, at Stratford, had been wittily clept 'The portable WC *Lear*'. This had less to do, it should be stated, with Sir John's reputed investigations of public lavatories than with Noguchi's sets and costumes, which seemed to consist of gaping holes, of material not there, of bodies being exposed. The sets, which slid around creakily on rails and castors as sets regularly do today but didn't then, resembled not so much Lear's Britain as the cheese counter of a traditional family grocer's invaded and savaged by regiments of mice.

I had booked myself a seat for the mid-week matinée in the Upper Circle of the King's Theatre, miles away from the stage, yet it never occurred to me in those early heady days of theatre-going, when I couldn't afford anything better, to sit nearer the stage. Indeed, so in natural thrall was I to the gods' eye view that more than once I recall opining that I couldn't understand why anyone, whatever their bank balance, sat other than in the gods, because for sixpence you could hear and see everything more clearly than in the dress circle or stalls, where the actors seemed to be talking more loudly than necessary and, if you were too close, you couldn't relish the complete stage picture as devised by the director. It was all too easy to be snobbish and ridiculous in Edinburgh in the fifties and not to realise it if your parents were sufficiently well-heeled to send you to one of the classier public schools. Besides which, my parents had on occasion taken me to the theatre and, of course, we sat in the stalls or dress circle.

It was virtually impossible, at the Edinburgh Academy, to be excused games practice (although it was even more improbable that you'd be excused Combined Cadet Force training after school at ten past three every Monday). I think the matinée of *King Lear* commenced at 5 p.m., although that is unlikely, given the length of the play and the fact that the evening's performance must have commenced not later than 7.30. I don't remember the games practice, but I do remember arriving at the King's Theatre, covered in mud, clutching my rugby gear – blue and white striped jersey, navy-blue shorts, football boots – and some books for homework and realising that, owing to the meandering tardiness of the 23 tram from Inverleith to Tolcross (or was it a 23 bus by 1955?), I'd missed the opening lines, possibly the opening scene (I didn't know the play) and thus the entrance of John Gielgud.

I was lighted into my seat by an usherette's torch and staggered and plunged along the row, disrupting people's concentration. To this day I can recall an incredible din from the stage, of raised voices and shouting, musical instruments (were they the statutory sennets and braying of trumpets and kettledrums, or did Mr Noguchi provide tinkling Japanese music?), and actors whose names I already knew lurching around the stage in coloured rags with the great Gielgud, identified only by his voice, dragging about with him what resembled Autolycus's antique shop, or the left-overs, the rest having been consumed by howling beasts. Even amidst the din, the cacophony, the jangling row, the lyrical precision of the actor's woodwind rose and soared and floated above the brouhaha, the chaos of his disintegrating abstract or at least abstracted kingdom.

Then, in what seemed the only still moment of the production, my rugby boots – first one, then the other – fell off my lap where for some reason I was harbouring them and seemed to detonate throughout the theatre. The noise echoed and echoed in my head, for hours, days, weeks, and I felt that, even in the uncomforting dark, everyone was peering round at me, staring and – who knows? – this had all something to do with poor Gielgud's homosexuality, which by then I could sketchily fathom. The distant stage had become a still, silent world, the actors but mouthing the words, the sound switched off, as my rugger boots crashed and crashed again, echoing, echoing, and re-echoing.

That, from afar, was my first encounter with Gielgud. On another occasion, some years later (I was visiting Edinburgh at the time, by then living in London), I passed him in Princes Street. He was, needless to remark, neither naked nor swathed in theatrical apparel, whether devised by Noguchi or someone with more conventional visual tastes. He wore, as it might be said of a member of the services when not on parade, mufti. I searched his face for meaning, for a clue. He looked ordinary and unassuming, not like an actor – whatever an actor looks like – which was deeply disappointing.

Once, later again, I accosted him in the street. I was returning to my office in Henrietta Street, Covent Garden, after what must have been a convivial lunch when, crossing the road to Moss Bros from Garrick Street, I saw Gielgud pattering along towards me in the direction of the Garrick Club. 'Sir John,' I declaimed delightedly, then realised that as I'd uttered my recognition of him aloud I'd have to follow it up, justify the greeting. He looked slightly alarmed, as well he might, as if to say: 'Do I know this fellow?' He stopped, I stopped. My mind raced to find something both coherent and relevant to say. I had it. A few weeks before he'd given an enthusiastic review in the *New Statesman* to a delightful book I'd published at Gollancz, *Pulling Faces for a Living*, a volume of memoirs of, mainly, other actors by James Dale (not to be confused with the younger actor, Jim Dale), who had played Pistol in *Henry V* at Stratford in 1916 and, after the war, Tybalt and Brutus, but in later years was best known for the playing of his namesake, Dr Jim Dale, in BBC Radio's uncompulsive *Mrs Dale's Diary*. I patronisingly thanked Gielgud for his review, and he looked blank. He frowned slightly, as if trying to recall it; then his face lit up. 'Ah, yes,' he said, the voice soaring. 'I gave it to Ralph Richardson. He adored it.' I replied that I was glad of that, then made a number of comments about the book. Gielgud responded to everything I said with 'That's just what Ralph said,' so much so that I wondered if his fellow actor had written the review and had purloined Gielgud's byline. At this time the two knights were a famous double-act, appearing together most notably in David Storey's *Home* and Harold Pinter's *No Man's Land* and in, it seemed, innumerable newspaper interviews. The genre of the Gielgud/Richardson interview, for so it appeared, was devised by a lugubriously dyspeptic *Observer* journalist named John Heilpern, who later had the idea of writing a joint biography of Sir John and Sir Ralph. As his then agent I agreed terms with a publisher and all looked set fair until Sir Ralph (or was it Sir John?) said that he'd only assist with the book, which was substantially to consist of a dozen or so interviews, if the interviewing sessions could take place over twelve lunches at restaurants of his choice. The cost of the lunches would quite likely have amounted to more than the advance Heilpern was to be paid. No more was heard of the book, or much more in the UK of Heilpern, who went to seek his fortune in New York. In 1977 Heilpern had published *Conference of the Birds*, a magnificently dry account of Peter Brook and his travelling troupe taking theatre to African villages. It didn't seem at all pretentious at the time.

Eventually Gielgud felt my audience with him had gone on for long enough. 'Very nice to see you,' he said, nodded by way of farewell, and pattered on along Garrick Street, no doubt into the Club. Later, when I became a member of the Garrick, as we nine hundred members invariably refer to it, I was told a vintage Gielgud story, though others attribute it elsewhere, perhaps to Sir Henry Irving (unlikely for at least two reasons). A member one day went into the lavatories at the Club, which had recently been refurbished. Standing there, confronting the spanking new urinals, he looked up and observed that the member standing next to him was Gielgud. 'Good morning, Sir John,' said the sycophantic member. 'How do you find the new urinals?' 'Ah,' said Gielgud, elegiacally, 'the new urinals are perfectly splendid. The trouble is that the cocks are as old as they always were.'

In 1979, two BBC television producers, John Miller and John Powell, persuaded Gielgud to record a series of programmes for radio on his life and acting, and they edited the scripts for publication in 'popular' book form by, somewhat improbably, Sidgwick & Jackson, under the title of *An Actor in His Time*. It wasn't a bad book, if you took it for what it was, but given that Gielgud is, as a writer, a fastidious stylist and an elegant raconteur – his anecdotes ('I remember when my second cousin William Shakespeare was rehearsing *Hamlet* at the Globe . . .') always contributing to some theatrical point, a lesson in technique or experience – the heavily illustrated package was pedestrian.

An advertisement in the *Evening Standard* a few weeks before Christmas disclosed that Sir John would be signing copies the following day at Hatchard's in Piccadilly. I solicited orders from colleagues at our literary agency, purchased six copies of the book and joined the queue which wound around the bookshop at lunchtime. Gielgud sat at a table, signing away, like Father Christmas reluctantly bestowing largesse. I thought of Coriolanus in the market-place, persuaded to show his wounds. Eventually it was my turn to come face to face with Gielgud. He gave me a weary, cautious smile, not unfriendly but certainly unfamiliar: mercifully, he wasn't a 'star' who bestowed gushing, synthetic benevolence upon strangers; he wore the gown of humility unforthcomingly. No doubt agent or publisher had insisted he sit in the market place and hawk his wares, albeit warily. He started to sign the books, held open for him by an assistant, 'John Gielgud, 1979'. There was no attempt to inscribe copies 'For darling Lollipop with Christmas love from Johnnie G', that kind of odious, obsequious practice in which lesser actors and greater 'personalities' indulge. No admirer of Gielgud would, in any case, have deigned to ask for a personal message of this sort, or to indulge in banter: 'Thought you were good as Benedick, Sir John; very good as Benedick'. 'Oh how kind of you' – and an aloof, cutting, wintery smile. How he'd have stormed back to his flat, humiliated, spluttering.

As he neared the end of signing my pile of books, I whipped my left hand out from under my raincoat to reveal my long-treasured green cloth-bound (since the book had been in my possession it has lacked a dust wrapper) copy of *Early Stages*, his magical and gracefully written first book, published by Macmillan in 1939. 'Sir John,' quoth I, self-consciously, 'would you do me the honour of signing my copy of *Early Stages*?' Gielgud's face lit up. A wide, unguarded smile spread across his aristocratic features. 'Oh, that's a *much* better book than this,' he said somewhat too loudly, causing a couple of besuited executives from the publishers to move forward, and an assistant from the bookshop to admonish me for producing a book I hadn't purchased there and then. By implication, Sir John was included in the dressing-down; he shouldn't have been conspiring with me. He closed the book, handed it back to me with a little courteous inflection of his head. I mumbled my thanks and fled into the snow. The title page, like the others, was simply inscribed with his name, and the date. I had, in truth and cockily, hoped for something more.

I did think apotheosis had been achieved some years later when, leaving the Garrick one day in the company of a fellow member, I heard the unmistakable voice immediately behind me. 'Goodbye, Giles.' Tongues of angels could not have sounded sweeter. (All right, I'd probably had a good lunch.) After all these years, I thought, of watching him from afar, from seats in the gods and the stalls. After all that, he knows who I am and chooses to address me by my Christian name. Should I, familiarly, return the greeting, or farewell, 'Cheerio, John'? Of course I couldn't. Not even, showing proper deference, 'Good afternoon to you, Sir John.' All this, as we tumbled down the stairs of the Club, in the twinkling of an eye. The member beside me turned his head. 'Goodbye, John,' he said. The member was Giles Playfair, a writer on matters penal and theatrical, whose father, Nigel Playfair, had in 1930 directed Gielgud as John Worthing in a landmark production of *The Importance of Being Earnest* at the Lyric Theatre, Hammersmith.

If you're called John, presumably you're used to the arbitrary and regular utterance of your name. The same might apply to Sir John, as that seems to be the title of half those in *Who's Who*. It's rare that I encounter another Giles, though I once came face to face with a Giles Gordon at the *Spectator*'s summer party. I think he was a solicitor, and he was quite annoyed, he told me, at being taken for the author of my rather seedy novels. Neither of us, of course, could believe that there was another Giles Gordon, which may explain why I frequently receive letters addressed to Gordon Giles, and even friends sometimes write to me as 'Dear Gordon'. Perhaps I have done something to incur their formality.

I have seen Gielgud a few times in recent years, sometimes darting up and down Charing Cross Road, ramrod straight and moving like a minnow through crowded waters. Once or twice I've observed him eating lunch at the Garrick, the only member who somehow is justified in sitting at the head of the long table. Not many have dared to usurp his unacknowledged place, but I have seen Sir Kingsley Amis holding court there, and Sir Peregrine Worsthorne, though neither, come to think of it, until after he became a knight. Gielgud reduced me to tears at the Westminster Abbey memorial service for Ralph Richardson in November 1983, reading from *Pilgrim's Progress* (Mr Valiant-for-truth), and just failed to do so in November 1991 at Peggy Ashcroft's, mainly because he'd been preceded by Donald Sinden, humming and hawing his way through the great speech in *Henry VI, Part III*, in which Queen Margaret humiliates the Duke of York. Prior to this we'd had the grandest theatrical performance in years, with addresses from Harold Pinter and Sir Peter Hall, and readings by Janet Suzman, Geraldine James, Dame Judi Dench, Ben Kingsley, Paul Scofield, Willard White and Ian Holm. The proceedings concluded with Sir John Gielgud, CH, reading first from *Antony and Cleopatra*:

> So, fare thee well.
> Now boast thee, death, in thy possession lies
> A lass unparallel'd.

and then, inevitably and irrevocably, from *The Tempest*:

> Our revels now are ended.

Gielgud read **Prospero**'s elegy at Laurence Olivier's memorial service, and at **Peggy Ashcroft**'s. Surely the organisers of his, if he proves not immortal, will not be so crass as to include it, for who could remotely begin to compete with the Master's blood-curdling, bowel-dissolving, lyrical gravitas? Perhaps Paul Scofield could, but the lines, the part in our time, are Gielgud's. They who do not thrill to the mellow music of that voice or who have not witnessed his high style have not experienced at its most incomparable the art of classical English acting.

Acting, at least classical acting, is intrinsically about the voice, the speaking and projection of the lines for their essential sense and meaning. The rest follows. Radio, contrary to the protestations of its adherents and somewhat paradoxically, is rarely an adequate substitute for the stage. The oral music of the spheres is not conjured on the air: you are too aware of the limits of the medium, the inadequacies of the human voice in exposed isolation, and the absurdity of the 'props'. Even more – the qualifications of art, the frustrations of life – are television and film remote from the experience of participating in a 'live' performance – *Richard III* is happening *now*, as you observe it – because the technique of acting to camera and celluloid is different from acting to a live audience. The whole thing is insulated, hermetic, behind glass.

I would construe it thus: there are certain actors, and they tend to be the 'leaders' of their profession as genius will out – Gielgud, Olivier, Michael Redgrave, Ian Richardson, Alan Howard, Ralph Richardson, Peggy Ashcroft, Judi Dench, Vanessa Redgrave, Ian McKellen – whose very voices thrillingly define and transform the world when the bodies that are custodians to the voices step out from the wings and on to the stage. The voices – and how different in kind they are but with the same quality as unique instruments – do things with words, make sounds, that raise the lines, their sense and meaning, to a higher level than we had thought possible. We can try to analyse why, say, McKellen's Hamlet is superior to, say, Roger Rees's (unmemorably milk and water), but all we are doing, in truth, is describing, reporting what we observe taking place on stage with as much wit or intellect as we possess. Everything else is extrapolation, wish-fulfilment, our interpretation.

It is analogous to analysing why Eliot's poetry is superior to, for instance, the nostalgic, sub-Yeatsian verse of Seamus Heaney, or the almost anti-art, snook-cocking Pooterish lines of Philip Larkin.

Why should our football-dribbling working-class (or pseudo-working-class) high priests of 'culture' who extol the, presumably, therapeutic virtues of easy art – social realism in general, L. S. Lowry's paintings, David Edgar's stage adaptations of Dickens and Robert Louis Stevenson, Pat Barker's novels in particular – be so highly regarded as chroniclers of the times? You'd think they'd be relieved to transcend their roots (not you, Arnold Wesker, or Alex Haley) and aspire to more imaginative matters, but even the further educated working-class animal, unless he or she deviates from the sexual norm, and even sometimes then, remains a stubbornly conservative beast. So conservative that he or she is likely once more to vote Labour with Mrs Thatcher gone, which nowadays means conservatism with a capital C; N for nostalgia and M for memories of jam butties and piss-like beer. Added to this is usually a sense of guilt at having escaped from or transcended lower-class origins.

It is right and invigorating that you should have to work at art, be educated – by experiencing it, concentrating upon it, throwing yourself in the deep but not necessarily pretentious end – to derive most from it. Brigid Brophy once purred down the telephone at me: 'I always forget, Giles, you actually enjoy Shakespeare in performance.' It may indeed be a shortcoming in me, an admission of inadequacy, but I derive more from a dull or indifferent performance of Shakespeare than from sitting in my study (oh that I had one; there is no quiet room when you live with children). Or at least that used to be so. Being a professional theatre critic for five years or more has deadened my response to the duffest Shakespeare, and few playwrights are more regularly done so badly as Shakespeare. Even so, I cannot regard one of his plays as simply a dramatic poem best consumed off the page. His way with words is remarkable. It hardly needs me to ascend from the cellarage to confide that. His ability to characterise through his verse is second to none.

Thus when you've read *Othello* you've a pretty accurate idea of what Othello and Iago are like – the one noble and gullible, the other ignoble and malevolent – and Desdemona too: she's a thinner, less developed character, catalyst to the protagonists – Iago the knowing, Othello the unknowing. You see how Shakespeare, four hundred years and many cultures ago, saw them. And yet Gielgud's puzzled, proudly broken Moor was as different from Olivier's rose-sniffing, barefoot romantic as Michael Gambon's burly, fruity warrior was from Donald Sinden's haughty, self-confident colonialist. Plays, particularly the greatest, are written (with a few exotic exceptions, such as *Peer Gynt*) to be performed by flesh and blood, and the playwright, if he has any sense, realises that actors and actresses bring much to his lines. With new plays, those that haven't stood the test of revivals, if the actor is accomplished and yet is able to make little of his part it is likely that there isn't much to be made of it, that the play is not built to last. Which is why, ultimately and inevitably, the best and most ambitious actors and actresses can only fully exercise their talents exploring the classics.

Conversely, those who keep away from the classics probably do well to avoid them. Occasionally, especially these days when the art of speaking Shakespearian verse has largely been lost, and the tradition has failed to be passed down, or picked up, a good actor who isn't by experience or inclination a classicist will have a go and disappoint. John Thaw's Cardinal Wolsey opposite Richard Griffiths's Henry VIII and Gemma Jones's Katherine of Aragon at Stratford in 1983 was a case in point. We do not possess a more brilliant or subtle television actor, but Thaw completely lacked the theatrical personality (which is not snidely to suggest that he lacks real personality) to puff out the butcher's son from Ipswich making it at court and in Rome. Conversely, Donald Sinden (Stratford's 1969 Bluff King Hal) always comes across ridiculously on the box, as if he would burst its cerements: he cannot contain himself, scale himself down.

I watched Thaw walking along a street in Stratford the year he essayed the right-hand henchman of the king with six wives (and Sir Toby Belch, knight at first without a wife). His reticent, almost reluctant facial gestures, his economy with his limbs even when out walking, no doubt his acquiring of a morning paper at W. H. Smith, were all of a piece with his detailed, meticulous, naturalistic acting. Whereas to watch Sinden descending upon pavements of the Warwickshire market town was like observing a royal progress, and his acquisition of a newspaper must have resembled the purchase of a particularly luscious virgin in the market-place of Baghdad when the Arabian Nights were in full swing.

What makes a great actor is not simply (or far from simply) what Kenneth Peacock Tynan memorably defined as High Definition Performance (HDP), although it is a most useful epithet. To it should be added, or embraced within it, the actor's character, his or her instinctive intelligence, and how it is brought to bear on the role being portrayed; his or her musical way with words, the athletics of the voice. All actors, by definition, bring a part of themselves to their performances. The duller, even the most 'competent' ones, tend to reveal that those particular emperors possess few clothes. Most roles are enhanced by being assumed by fine actors. Only Brecht's sullen tracts, attitudinising political pamphlets of tedious didacticism, are somehow diminished by being strongly cast: all actors have to be equal, and none more equal than others. That's what the perfect society should be like. As told by Bertolt.

There is another problem about acting which is sometimes mentioned, but usually only to be dismissed as there's little, if anything, to be done about it. There are supposed to be (who does the supposing, do you suppose?) two kinds of actors. There are those who always give the same performance – that is, play themselves, or a large part of themselves with a smidgen of artistic, as opposed to facial, greasepaint – and there are those who every night give a different performance: that is, those you wouldn't identify if you didn't know from the programme that X is playing Y.

In truth, this polarisation of actors is a flattering unction. The actors you do not recognise, unless you are a professional theatregoer or visit the theatre frequently, tend to be actors who lack, yes, charisma. I have never, for instance, understood the appeal of Edward Petherbridge, a wan and wry chameleon-like performer who invariably seems intellectually etiolated. I always have to consult my programme, usually a near-impossible feat in the dark, to have it revealed that it is Petherbridge on stage. It isn't that he's a particularly subtle actor (for is not that almost a contradiction in terms?), or a master of disguises. Nor is it that he has so buried himself in his parts that the characters portrayed have consumed the actor. He may, for all I know, be the most delightful, witty, stimulating of human companions in private life, but as an actor I find him awesomely dull. (I take Edward Petherbridge only as an example, because theatrically minded readers may recognise his name and have seen, if not necessarily remembered, his work. I could have named scores of others, including most present members of the Royal Shakespeare Company and the National Theatre.)

My mother, connoisseur of Gielgud, held it against Olivier that he was always recognisable, always showing off, as if acting isn't dangerously about showing off, escaping from yourself and becoming, at least in part and for a space of time, another. Olivier may have devised a different make-up, a different bodily contortion and series of physical attributes, a different voice (Captain Brazen, Strindberg's Father, James Tyrone in *Long Day's Journey into Night*, Othello could hardly have been taken by the same actor) yet he was always Olivier, a little touch of Larry in the night. Of course he was, I'd shriek at my mother. You are proclaiming, whether you admire it or not, the versatility of a great actor, a man whose living, his life, is endowed by, conveyed utterly in, his acting.

But Gielgud, she used to say, and go dewy-eyed. Gielgud is always different. Gielgud is the servant of his craft, the ambassador of his art. He immerses himself in his roles, becomes them in the opposite way to Olivier, puts himself at the service of play, production and cast. Yet, of course, she'd concede that the Gielgud voice, most insinuating of instruments, invariably identified him, lent distinction and humanity to the actor: however characterised, his John Worthing, his Cassius, his Lear emanated from a single essence, one man.

However playwrights may protest, directors too, and designers, audiences go to the theatre to witness performers in action in much the same way as they troop to sporting events. Great acting seems to me in many ways analagous to boxing at the highest, world championship level (yes, I know boxing's for real and acting's pretending), whereas mediocre acting is something akin to the majority of fights. Actors may (or may not; they may simply be trying to earn a living) be pitting themselves against the gods. At least we audiences like to feel that. Lear may ('O let me not be mad, not mad, sweet Heaven') unwittingly be taking on the elements, thunder sheets and other sound effects as well, but his real contest is with the evening's spectators. Actor versus audience. It isn't, any more than it is with punters at a prize fight, that the audience wants actor or fighter to lose, but that it thrills to see the performer – actor or boxer – pushed to extremities. For audiences, sado-masochistic to some unexplored degree, identify with the protagonists whom they have paid to see in action: there, but for the grace of God . . .

When the actor (or fighter, if the audience is backing him) fails, the audience is appalled, saddened, and identifies. Thus the fall of Icarus is one of the most potent Western myths. (Myths? Tell that to W. H. Auden.) As members of audiences, we identify more readily with failure than with success. Oddly, as most of us were once young, we do not identify with Juliet and Romeo when they are in love; we identify with them in death, while reflecting that they were pretty silly to have let events career so out of control. We identify with Nora when she is having such a miserable time in her husband's doll's house, not when she slams the door and departs, inventing the future in her own image. We identify, above all, with so many of Chekhov's characters because they are terminally, magnetically wedded to failure. That is their tragedy, our triumph; or vice versa. They make us seem good. Our lives cannot always be as unsatisfactory, as uninvigorating as theirs. Similarly, a boxer is not so much fighting any old opponent as drawing more out of himself when fighting at the highest level: the risk of failure, of losing, is more considerable, more dangerous. The RSC and the National are at their best when their productions are strongly cast, when the leading parts are played by actors of weight. The director Michael Rudman has opined that 60 per cent of a successful production can usually be put down to getting the casting right. To a considerable extent, Peter Hall's early Stratford productions – his autumnal, near perfect *Twelfth Night* (1958), his sandpit *Troilus and Cressida* (1960), *The Wars of the Roses*

(1963) – were as glorious and life-enhancing as they were because the ensemble acting was impeccable; they weren't a case of a star, or even a handful of stars, and a phalanx of extras.

One of the worst evenings I have spent at a playhouse – and I must have spent thousands of evenings watching plays – was at the press night, as first nights self-servingly came to be called in the late seventies, of the RSC's revival at the Barbican in 1984 of *The Happiest Days of Your Life*. It was a routine production of a third-rate comedy which the RSC should not have embarked upon. It was presumably an attempt to cash in at the box-office. One of the leading actors, early on, began to lose touch with his lines. As the evening wore on (and wear and tear were the order of the night) he lost more and more of his lines. It was agony to watch, and the embarrassment in the auditorium, the identification with the increasingly troubled actor, was palpable. The referee, you felt, should have stopped the unequal contest. (The fact that the lines weren't worth remembering is another matter but not the issue.) The performance became increasingly painful, terrifying to have to observe. Instinctively you tensed yourself for the actor's next dry and for the prompter's words, which everyone in the theatre seemed to pick up with the exception of the actor in question. (This was especially cruel because, as we all discovered that evening, the prompter's voice, like Jehovah's, at the computer-ised Barbican – what a disagreeable venue it is – comes booming down from the roof, snarling mockingly from above the pro-scenium – if the theatre has one – hurling Zeus's thunderbolts to recalcitrant thespians.) Everyone in the audience identified with the actor's plight. It was a huge relief when the final curtain came down, or rather went half way up and came half way down as it modishly does at the Barbican, and everyone could go home. The actor, Paul Greenwood, is an excellent performer who, to the best of my knowledge, had not suffered from loss of memory previously, and has not been subsequently affected by his ghastly evening.

At a party in 1991 given in London by the Edinburgh imprint Mainstream to celebrate publication of Harry Chapman's first novel, *Spanish Drums*, I was introduced to a corpulent Lindsay Anderson, who immediately asked if I was middle-class. I told him that I was, and he responded that this then was my misfortune. I professed, not at all defensively, that there was nothing I could do, or indeed wanted to do, about it. It was a fact of my life and other matters were of more concern. (Anderson, who hasn't resisted gracing the pages of *Who's Who*, was educated at Cheltenham College, then Oxford; his parents are revealed as Major-General A. V. Anderson and Estelle Bell Sleigh. This most socialist of directors is an irretrievably upper-class Scot.)

When I asked him if he blamed the Prince of Wales for being a member of the aristocracy he became quite petulant. The revered film director had suggested I change my class, and I enquired, all logic, if he'd have asked the same question of the Prince. He seemed a sad old dinosaur, still in his late sixties judging people by their backgrounds rather than their views or what they had or hadn't achieved. It is precisely because of this kind of attitude – the ingrained prejudices of the British intelligentsia – that we are unlikely to have in the foreseeable future a government representing intelligent radical views.

Yet, in the sixties and seventies, Lindsay Anderson was, rightly, such an influence on younger film-makers and people in the theatre. I did goad him, though, by saying that I thought his production of *Julius Caesar* in 1964 was the worst of the play I'd seen, treating it entirely in class terms rather than as the great political power game it is between two or even three groups of equally privileged men on the make. In Anderson's production the tribunes of the people, two minor characters who act as *dei ex machina*, were lent more influence than the mighty Julius.

# XXI

Once writers are accorded some degree of success, they tend to adopt, for reasons of self-preservation, the patina of achievement and confidence, the mantle of invulnerability. Readers need to be assured that their writers are confident and secure in what they are doing, whereas the writers, unless they are total self-deceivers, have no judgement as to the quality of their work. But this ability to look and play the part is something some of the more highly favoured writers of today are adept at carrying off. No names, no libel writs.

I thought, wrongly, that the life of a literary agent would be more relaxing, less frenetic, than that of a publisher. In both occupations, the difficulty is finding the time to read, and to read properly, thoroughly. It cannot be done during office hours, because you are always on the telephone or 'in a meeting'. Thus it has to be undertaken in the evenings and at weekends. There are no forty-hour weeks for anyone in the book trade, publisher or agent.

Publishers like to delude themselves that their interests are identical with those of the authors they publish; which, if it were true, would surely result in authors being paid as much as booksellers. As it is, most authors receive but 10 per cent of the retail price of a hardback, 7½ per cent of a paperback. Booksellers receive a percentage in excess of one third of the retail price. Yes, I understand that booksellers have overheads of a kind which authors do not, but booksellers at any one time have thousands of titles to sell, and authors usually only have one. Of course it doesn't all come down to money, and some favoured authors receive lavish advance payments to enable them to live in the style to which they delude themselves they are entitled while they're wrestling with their self-inflicted masterpieces.

Publishers have to believe that they are in partnership with authors, and so they should be. The difficulty with the concept is that it is the author who manufactures the product, the staple diet, the words that are the book, off which the publisher and his or her staff live. However 'creative' the publisher – and some are very creative – however much he or she assists the author, the author is and remains the creator, even if the idea for the book emanates from the publisher, even if the publisher's suggestions and editorial work are crucial and radically improve the text. It was easier for authors and publishers to seem to be partners when publishers owned and ran their own establishments. Now they mostly do not, and those who do, almost without exception, are undercapitalised. Thus they cannot, in empirical terms, treat the author as a favoured citizen. Hence (and here lies the point) the irresistible rise of the literary agent which, quite by coincidence, coincided more or less with my joining the ranks of agents in 1972.

It is generally assumed that, with the world in recession, the days of 'powerful' agents are over, but I do not believe this for a moment, although indiscriminate gargantuan advances may be a thing of the past, and that is no bad thing. Authors need agents as buffers between themselves and publishers, so that when money has to be discussed they do not have to behave as tradesmen doffing their caps, touching their forelocks, to those gracious enough to employ them. When a publisher says to an author, if no agent is involved: 'I thought I'd offer you an advance of £2,000. Will that be all right?' the author, authors being docile, even servile when it comes to such matters, is almost bound to reply: 'Thank you. I'm sure that's fine,' when he'd actually been hoping for five times the sum. Publishers have difficulty in understanding the psychology involved, and agents take the stick. That's fine. That's what they are for, and how they earn their 10 per cent. Some now are taking 15 or even 20 per cent.

Publishers – which, in truth, is to say editors – used to stay with the same imprint for many years, if not for a lifetime. Nowadays few do. If they are any good, they will be spirited from job to job until, probably, they are in their forties, when they will settle down. This provides little security for their authors. I represent one writer who has had four books published by the same editor but at four different publishing houses. This is madness, and obviously the author will never have a collected edition of his works, not that many writers do so any more. (H. G. Wells was almost the first major author not to have a collected edition, because he hopped from publishing house to publishing house; those who stayed put tended to have one.) And so the agent has in many cases become, *de facto*, the rock-like component in the author's life, the father figure.

It is much more fun, and more rewarding, to represent 'successful' authors than writers in whom you believe but no one else seems to, and who hardly provide a living wage. (Yes, I do understand that no one owes an author a living and that there are infinitely too many books published, some 78,835 new titles in 1992, an alarming 16.44 per cent rise on the number of titles published the previous year.) I'm constantly amazed at how well professional authors behave, who toil away at their manuscripts and whose books don't sell. They are modest to a fault. Well, some of them.

It's invidious to pick one, but of the eighty-odd authors I represent Fay Weldon is probably my favourite. I would follow her to the Promised Land. I would die for her. She has the energy of a regiment, and I have not encountered a sharper, more wide-ranging mind. Her intellect, which is worn ever so lightly, is formidable. She is compassionate in her defence of human rights, and tireless in her practical assistance for and encouragement of new authors. There is not an iota of jealousy or envy in her make-up. 'I've always felt guilty about Salman Rushdie since we failed to give him the Booker Prize,' she once said to me. She was the chairperson of the judges in 1983 when it looked as if Rushdie might be the first novelist to win the coveted prize for a second time. In fact it was awarded, on Fay's casting vote, to the South African writer Professor J. M. Coetzee for *Life and Times of Michael K*, which novel Fay obviously believed to be the best. Since Rushdie has had his troubles, no one has been more helpful to him than Weldon in attempting to sustain him and keep his spirits up.

In 1989 she was awarded the prestigious *Los Angeles Times* Prize for the best novel of the year for, ironically, one of her slightest and shortest books, *Heart of the Country*. (Coincidentally, Coetzee's first novel was called *In the Heart of the Country*.) Previous winners of the international award were Gabriel García Márquez, Margaret Atwood, Milan Kundera, Louise Erdich and Thomas Keneally. The prize was $1,000 plus a free trip to California for the winner and a chosen companion, who were put up for the best part of a week at a decent hotel in downtown Los Angeles. Fay's husband didn't want to go, and thus she decided not to fly over to receive her cheque. 'I'd go if you asked me,' I said, never having been to Hollywood or Los Angeles, only to San Francisco where, some years before, my sister and her family lived at Laguna Beach. Fay seemed surprised but she asked me and, reader, I accepted. We flew luxury class, the *crème de la crème*. You sit, along with perhaps a dozen other people, at the front of the plane in infinite comfort: deep-pile carpets, armchairs that swivel, acres of space around you. You are given useful gifts (and useless ones), the champagne flows. We travelled on the same flight as the actor who plays the Incredible Hulk (instantly recognisable), and his incredible girlfriend or wife.

On the day of the prize-giving ceremony, Fay had her hair done in the morning, while I went walkabout in downtown Los Angeles and felt invigorated. The only way to see and try to become familiar with cities is on foot. When I mentioned this after my peregrinations everybody seemed appalled: I could have been raped, mugged, assassinated, and not only because I was wearing a white linen suit and might have been mistaken for Tom Wolfe, which hilariously once I was at a party in London when wearing the same suit. In fact, many people I passed on my walk seemed to be smiling at me. Ah, I was told, that was because no one, but no one, went strolling about downtown Los Angeles. When I remarked that, in any case, I didn't drive, this was regarded as an irrelevance rather than a sign of insanity. I could have hired an automobile.

The evening was a grand affair, and had a class and style which none of the UK literary awards ceremonies has. First there were the presentations to the winners in various categories. They went on for hours, but they were happy hours, with speeches of substance made in an elegant and comfortable theatre. Then there was a dinner back at the *LA Times* for the winners, their partners and the top brass of the newspaper plus a sprinkling of Los Angeles literary worthies. Fay, whose genius is to surprise, astonished everybody present, probably including herself, by standing up near the end of the meal and thanking Jack Miles, the paper's literary editor, and everyone else for the prize and saying what a terrific time she had had and was going on having. This was the tenth year of the awards and, apparently, no one had made such a gesture before.

It must have been 2 a.m. when she and I took the lift up to our bedrooms. We alighted on the eighteenth floor, agreeing to meet for breakfast at 8 a.m. For me it had been a long, exhausting day doing nothing. For Fay it had been hard work, and she'd been on display.

When I went down to breakfast, bleary-eyed, Fay was sitting there drinking orange juice and reading the paper. 'What have you been doing since we parted last night?' she asked. I gave her a tired look. 'I've been writing my new novel,' she said, squeakily, with the excitement of a little girl, an eagerness and a commitment which I think are necessary to maintain if you are to write novels as engaging and provocative as Fay's. She'd scribbled six or eight pages in the previous hour or two, faxed them to Jane, her secretary in London, and would receive them back later in the day immaculately typed. She'd revise those pages, then write the next. On the flight back to Heathrow, we hardly spoke. It was night but Fay spent most of the time working on her novel.

In the early eighties it occurred to me that it would be interesting to see whether any magazine – any writer for that matter – could publish a serial novel today, as Dickens and many other Victorian writers had done, designing their work for publication in monthly episodes in periodicals. At lunch one day I raised with Fay the idea that she might consider writing a serial novel, in *weekly* parts. She immediately responded enthusiastically, and the editors of *Woman* magazine needed little persuasion to commission the story. Fay wrote the first ten episodes of *The Hearts and Lives of Men* starting with 5,000 words for week one, followed by three or four weeks of 3,000 words, settling down to 1,000 words per week – and a prefatory note to the first episode, when it was published, invited readers to write to the author about the serial, saying what they thought, which characters they liked, which they hated, who should be advanced and developed, who diminished or even killed off. The idea was that Fay would not write any episodes subsequent to the first ten until she'd received some feedback.

In a sense, the serial could run for ever. More practically, it was scheduled for a year. Surprisingly (surely), the response of readers was virtually non-existent, as if readers were embarrassed in this way, being invited almost to collaborate as, to some degree, co-authors. They were readers, Fay was a writer. How could they involve themselves in the creative process? Perhaps if the readers of the papers which published Dickens' novels in serial form had been asked how they thought events might progress they, too, might have walked away. As it was, *The Hearts and Lives of Men* in its serial version was enormous fun, with built-in homage to *Little Dorrit*. The serialisation continued for thirty-eight weeks. Given that the majority of the episodes were only 1,000 words – that is, a magazine page, allowing space for a picture – the ingenuity that Fay displayed in keeping the story moving and not losing sight of characters for too long was exemplary. For the novel derived from the serial, she reordered some of the episodes and expanded the chapters, the result being her longest and commercially most successful book to date. It was also, no doubt, her most 'down-market' and 'popular' novel, in that plot and character in the nineteenth-century sense were paramount.

Every agent, every publisher needs the odd break, the book that does unexpectedly, exceptionally well. Janet Fillingham, who ran the film and television side of our agency for many years, took on as her first client a promising young(ish) working-class playwright from Leicester, Sue Townsend, who wrote quirky plays for fringe theatres. She still writes quirky plays for fringe theatres. The National Theatre commissioned a play from her, but, as with the majority of plays it commissions, it didn't find its way on to any of the National's stages.

In the early eighties, Sue wrote a few scruffy pages (although she is a hugely sophisticated and widely read reader, she cannot for the life of her punctuate or spell) about a lad called Nigel Mole. Whether she had read the Nigel Molesworth books I do not know. Janet Fillingham sent the pages, a stroke of near-genius on her part, to John Tydeman, in those days merely a BBC Radio Drama producer, now the august and Garrick-tied head of Radio Drama. Tydeman was much amused but urged that Nigel should have his name changed by deed poll. The boy took the hint and re-emerged as Adrian Mole. The story or sketch was broadcast, and repeated, and Tydeman asked for more. Sue provided. Listeners loved it. I thought there might, just might, be a book in it and some of the early scripts were submitted to my old theatre-going friend Geoffrey Strachan at Methuen.

Strachan, nowadays grizzled and somewhat bent from the strains of conscientiously looking after his authors, a Santa Claus among publishers, immediately saw the point in Adrian Mole and encouraged Sue to finish the book. *The Secret Diary of Adrian Mole, Aged 13¾* was published on 7 October 1982 and seemed destined to remain a secret. Nobody reviewed it, hardly anybody bought it. Then John Tydeman arranged for the radio readings to be repeated, as they'd been so much enjoyed, and the whispering, word-of-mouth campaign began. It is especially word-of-mouth, the recommendation of happy readers, which sells books, much more than publicity stunts or advertising campaigns, let alone the fashionable 'dump bins' and expensive campaigns of the late eighties and early nineties.

Radio wins readers too. People who listen to radio, and books broadcast, borrow or buy those books, and read them. 'Viewers' of television, who might more accurately be clept 'voyeurs', may be persuaded to buy the novel of a classic serial but it probably remains on their shelves unread. Such was the success of the first two Mole books on radio (the second was *The Growing Pains of Adrian Mole*, 1984) and the continuous raving of readers that together they were the most commercially successful books of the eighties, selling many more copies than any two books by any other writers, including he who was destined to become Lord Archer of Weston-super-Mare.

Townsend is a classic if rare case of an ultra-successful author not spoiled by success, the exception that proves no rule. She's definitely a millionairess, but then so are many these days who, understandably, are loath to admit it. She is prodigal with her cash, giving most of it away. During the miners' strike in 1984/85 she invited a number of picketing miners to stay at her house in Leicester. They complained that none of the newspapers, not one, supported their campaign. Sue pointed out that the *Guardian* did, and they looked uneasy, bewildered. She indicated that day's issue in front of them. They continued to shake their heads, and didn't attempt to pick it up and read it. They didn't know about the *Guardian*. Their prejudices were their prejudices, their ignorance their strength. Without it, how could they have followed King Arthur Scargill?

In the UK, the Mole books were regarded as funny. Adrian is an adolescent with spots and growing pangs and a love for Pandora, the girl next door, and millions of people readily identified with him. The books also led to a spate of imitations: if we cannot write a novel in joined writing and with paragraphs, at least we can write a diary better than that semi-literate housewife in Leicester, was the general feeling. Once, Sue was in hospital for an operation. A name tag was attached to her arm as is *de rigueur*, so that, baby or adult, you aren't inadvertently swapped or don't have the wrong part of your body sawn off. After the operation, she came to in bed. A nurse examined her, then checked her name tag. 'Funny,' she said, 'two of you in Leicester.' Sue looked bemused. The nurse went on: 'You've got the same name as that awful woman who writes those frightful books.' Sue didn't own up to authorship, but she constantly told the story against herself.

The first book was reviewed nowhere, the second everywhere, and on the whole by big literary guns. Only in the USA, where they were reviewed with high seriousness as the first substantial criticism of Thatcher and Thatcherism, did the books not sell. They were translated into over thirty languages and struck a chord everywhere except in the po-faced States. The second time Mole was published in America, the first two books in one volume, I suggested the addition of a glossary, explaining, for instance, what a Thatcher was, but it made no difference. Mole went down a treat in the USSR, and Sue Townsend, creator of Adrian but no mole, became addicted to Moscow if not Aeroflot. And she once sent me a postcard from Tokyo airport: 'I've been sitting in Tokyo airport for hours. The Japanese gentleman sitting opposite me has been reading *Adrian Mole* in Japanese [how did she know, how could she tell?] from beginning to end, or rather from end to beginning. Not once has a smile crossed his inscrutable face.'

Her latest novel, *The Queen and I*, is as funny, as original as the Mole books, and deposits our beloved Queen and her extended family on a housing estate in the Midlands and reports on how they cope, and how the housing estate manages with the Windsors in its midst. The novel was written before the antics and *angst* of some of the younger Royals came to the attention of Andrew Morton and the tabloids, but *The Queen and I* – Orwell laced with Waugh and dollops of Wodehouse (though actually, like all original authors, Sue Townsend is *sui generis*) – unlike any other 'Royal' book, reveals an understanding of the symbiotic relationship between our Royal Family and ourselves. It cannot help declaring its affection as well as its anger, and for this reason, as well as because it is by the author of the Mole books, it commanded the bestseller lists for weeks.

Peter Ackroyd, born in 1949, and thus to me something of a stripling, is probably the most brilliant writer of his rather clever generation. He is like a man driven, by demons, to work, and I sometimes fear he will burn himself out. But I think not. He has far too much to say, is utterly fascinated by time, in the Eliotian sense, of the past and repetition, the encrustation of history on the so-called present. He is also, which tends to surprise those who don't know him, immensely funny and possibly – the sports journalist and novelist Brian Glanville and playwright and novelist Ronald Harwood apart – the best mimic in London. Christopher Sinclair-Stevenson has been quoted as saying that if he were permitted only one more lunch on earth he would want it to be with Ackroyd as he'd make him laugh so much. But not *everyone* finds Peter that funny. He and I share a dentist, Lester Kaplan. Once, when I was in his chair in Harley Street, my mouth stuffed with the drill and other devices of his trade, he asked – the way dentists do when they know you cannot answer sensibly – whether I'd seen Peter recently. I replied as best as I could, at the risk of being lacerated, and found myself ludicrously expounding upon Ackroyd's sense of humour. 'I don't find him funny when he's sitting here,' said Kaplan. 'In fact, I don't find Peter at all funny. There are no jokes.' I wonder who all these courageous and witty fellows are who quip in the surgery and have their dentists split their sides laughing?

Peter always works on two books simultaneously, in the morning his non-fiction book of the moment, in the afternoon his novel; and in the evening, as likely as not, he'll be reading or writing his literary journalism, his latest review for *The Times*, whose chief reviewer he is. This, he insists, is a permanent, seven-day-a-week regime, except on the rare occasions when he slips away on holiday (where, of course, he works) or to have a meal with Sinclair-Stevenson. (The latter's latest title, in the whirligig of publishing, is editor-at-large at Reed Consumer Books. His colleagues all know him as editor-at-lunch, which is his forte.)

His dog is called Dickens (but Ackroyd's enormous biography of that name is not about the dog, unlike *Flush*, Virginia Woolf's biography of a dog) and begins to bark ruthlessly if you engage Peter for too long on the telephone. Like Michael Moorcock (admirers of one another's work, I brought them together at lunch, one of the few positive things a literary agent can do when clients who haven't met are keen to do so), Ackroyd is very much a London novelist, and a novelist of London. *Hawksmoor* exudes, almost viscerally, the sinister forgotten or unwritten history of the capital, tells the unknowable. (I have encountered two people, both well known to me and both as sane as anyone else – one a publisher, Euan Cameron; the other a writer, Alanna Knight – who, within a few months of reading *Hawksmoor* and on separate occasions, visited the Nicholas Hawksmoor church in Bloomsbury, St George's, and heard footsteps. Looking round, they understood that there was no one else anywhere in the building. Neither of them knew of the other's visit. Neither has met

Ackroyd.) *Hawksmoor* is a book of malevolent power. As it is
dedicated to me, I hope I won't come to a treacly end.

A few weeks after he finished writing his enormous biography
of Dickens, which had taken him years, Peter felt that the book
wasn't quite complete. He began writing, and wrote at white-
hot pace, a series of fictitious episodes to be inserted between
biographical chapters throughout the book. They were, essentially,
dialogues between Dickens, his characters (Little Dorrit meets
Charles Dickens), his biographer (Peter Ackroyd) and, in one
case, an encounter between the biographer and some of his previous subjects, including T. S. Eliot and Oscar Wilde, and a reference to the subject of Ackroyd's *next* biography, William Blake.
To me, the intuitive grasp of these episodes reveals much about
Ackroyd's genius. These interludes (they amount to thirty pages
in a tome of almost 1,200 pages) transformed a scrupulous, thor-
ough *tour de force* of a biography into something more than that.
Here was a biographer showing himself at work, his thought
processes revealed, his fears and reservations about his achievement, his hopes; the literary equivalent, if you like, of a Richard
Rogers building with the plumbing on the outside, a virtue made
of necessity. As a device, as a concept, it seemed to me to take
the art of biography, biography as an art form – as opposed to,
merely, chapters about chaps – one stage further even than Michael
Holroyd advanced with his biography of Lytton Strachey, a book
which read as palatably as a sturdily constructed novel.

Peter Ackroyd was uncertain whether the new pages worked.
Sinclair-Stevenson, the book's publisher, hated them. I was asked
to adjudicate. As a result of my enthusiasm, they were included.
They were about the only stick, or bunch of fasces, which the
critics, desperate as always to say something about a biography as
opposed to providing their own *soupçon* of comment on the life
of the biographee, could summon up to beat the book about its
head. I think time will show that Peter's final flourishes, a gloss
upon his own text, are what make the book, putting the narrative
into proportion, into context. In his novels, Ackroyd is very much
a writer of our time. *The Great Fire of London* (1982), his first
novel, builds on Dickens' *Little Dorrit* and portrays a film director
anxious to pin the book down on celluloid – something the film

director Christine Edzard was to do, in two parts, in 1987. His third novel, *Hawksmoor* (1985), plays games with history, and with identity: the architect Nicholas Hawksmoor, student of and rival to Christopher Wren, later to collaborate on Castle Howard with Vanbrugh, is turned into a policeman; and the architect of Hawksmoor's buildings is called Dyer. Certainly you are kept on your toes; little is as it seems. *Chatterton* (1987) is about forgery and originality. *First Light* (1989) is an essay in cod-pastoral, Thomas Hardy revisited with touches of John Fowles: Ackroyd spent much time in a cottage in Lyme Regis in Dorset, where Fowles lives, when writing the book, but the two novelists have not met, nor knowingly espied each other even at Sainsbury's, if Lyme Regis possesses a branch. *English Music* (1992) is a fictional lecture on the Englishness of English art, the conjuring up of the theatrical and pastoral. Above all, Ackroyd's second novel, *The Last Testament of Oscar Wilde* (1983), has to be poor Oscar's last book, written in France after his release from Reading Gaol. It is more than pastiche: it is inspiration and impersonation.

When it was suggested to Peter that he should provide the missing book in Wilde's life, he poo-pooed the idea, declaring without too much conviction that he hadn't read Wilde. (I'm just prepared to believe that he had not seen a Wilde play staged, not even *The Importance of Being Earnest*, outside Shakespeare the most perfect comedy in the language. Oddly, for one who so keenly understands its relevance to the English novel, Ackroyd detests the 'live' theatre, finding it dead or at least dormant. I have twice taken him to productions and on both occasions he has fallen asleep. Once he accompanied me to a modish playwright's latest outpourings at the Royal Court, home of fashionable master-pieces. I was reviewing the evening and thus we had excellent seats, far forward in that lovely little theatre. Not only did Peter keep falling asleep but he was prone to snore. Every ten minutes or so he would shuffle about a bit in his seat and, like the dormouse in *Alice in Wonderland*, wake up. 'What's happening?' he'd ask, in a voice louder than a whisper. I would endeavour to tell him. 'But that's what was going on when I went to sleep,' he'd remon-strate, and quickly nod off again. This happened throughout the well-nigh interminable first half. I was somewhat relieved when, during the interval, he asked if I'd mind awfully if he went home.)

Wilde and the 1890s, especially Aubrey Beardsley (whose schoolboy drawings of Beaumont and Fletcher, knights of the burning pestle, I proudly own, one on each side of a sheet of exercise book), are one of my book collecting obsessions, and I like to think I know a fair amount about the period and its books. Thus when, on a sunny Saturday morning in 1982, I began reading Peter's typescript of *The Last Testament* (improperly called by me, with sparkling wit, *The Last Testicle) of Oscar Wilde* on the balcony of our house in Kentish Town – the Post Office Tower much in evidence then but not, of course, hideous Canary Wharf, which is now visible) – I frowned with irritation when I came to the first of the book's three fairy stories. I read with both the smug pleasure of recognition and the excitement of discovery. (*Surely* I hadn't read this particular Wilde fairy tale before and forgotten it?) I hurried down to my bookshelves, and read through the contents pages of Wilde's two collections of fairy tales. The story wasn't there. Neither, it transpired, were Peter's other two. He had created three new Wilde stories. They went way beyond pastiche. There was nothing synthetic or merely imitative in the writing, or in the sensations evoked. Ackroyd is in danger of proving that there is no such literary skill as originality.

In these last few pages I have mentioned three of the novelists I proudly represent. Others I have mentioned more briefly in this book. Others I have not even referred to. There is nothing invidious in this, nor is it my intention to provide a catalogue in praise of the writers for whom I act. Suffice it to say here that I have a particular penchant for novelists who approach the present by, at least sometimes, writing about the past, and this has led to some remarkable books by Peter Ackroyd, Robert Nye, Allan Massie, Geraldine McCaughrean with the sadly underrated *Vainglory*, Vikram Seth (his 1,600 page *A Suitable Boy*, set in India a couple of years after Independence, is like to prove a genuinely great novel, if traditional in form), Michael Moorcock, Tony Weeks-Pearson with the bewilderingly underestimated *Dodo*,

George MacBeth, Charles Palliser with *The Quincunx*, and Moy McCrory.

For most of my twenty-odd years to date as an agent, my first port of call to a publisher was to Christopher Sinclair-Stevenson, who ran Hamish Hamilton, and was generally regarded (except by some who couldn't stand him because he is an Old Etonian; and others who couldn't see him because he is also exceedingly tall) as our most consistent literary publisher. In 1989 he departed from the Penguin Group, which had acquired Hamish Hamilton some years before, and rather than retire and write (he was born in 1939 and has published five works of non-fiction, the first, I am happy to say, being a history of the Gordon Highlanders), he recklessly started an eponymous imprint without sufficient working capital in a time of recession. Either that or, as some would assert, he recklessly overpaid 'his' authors. His kind of publishing cannot easily survive today. He backed his taste rather than consulting slide rule or pocket calculator, or rushing to Swindon to ask if W. H. Smith approved of jacket or blurb. Generally speaking, his upper-class, middle-brow taste was more applicable to non-fiction than fiction, but he relished publishing the novels of Peter Ackroyd, Robert Nye and Barry Unsworth as well as those of Brigid Brophy, all of whom I sold him.

His Achilles heel was a lack of a visual sense, and his dust jackets were generally regarded, and I'm afraid rightly, as among quite the dullest in the business, and in the eighties this began to matter. Christopher, unlike less energetic or conscientious publishers or those with less of his flair (that's a word you do not hear much these days), would edit as he read, carrying the orchestration and musical detail of a text in his head as he progressed. He was helped by having a wife, Deb, who supported him in everything, and my image is of them at home of an evening, Christopher relentlessly reading manuscripts, Deb ministering to his needs.

He was and is the most congenial of hosts, and thought it important to honour publication of virtually every book with an appropriate dinner-party. When one of his authors, Ackroyd, A. N. Wilson, William Boyd, won a prize – and his authors tended to win prizes, although never the Booker (Unsworth won after

Christopher had left Hamish Hamilton) – he would insist upon another celebratory dinner. Thus he and his wife and Peter Ackroyd and I have had many merry meals. He would always pay an author as large an advance as he felt he could (and sometimes more than he could afford: when he started on his own, I rapaciously asked him for £1 million for Peter Ackroyd's biographies of Dickens and William Blake; he paid somewhat less. This was not, I trust, why Sinclair-Stevenson became a subsidiary of the dully named Reed International about eighteen months after he had set up shop).

# XXII

I ceased to be a publisher in 1972 for various reasons, one of which was that I was writing novels at the time and it is difficult, if not impossible, to combine a full-time publishing job with writing books; although it is noteworthy, or suspicious, how many publishers do find the energy to put together books of their own. Most are workaday. Of the memoirs, Fredric Warburg's *An Occupation for Gentlemen* (the title is ironic; or is it?), although published in 1959, remains the most elegant and entertaining. It is also the most instructive. Sir Stanley Unwin's two books are probably the dullest. I reviewed Sir Robert Lusty's memoirs, *Bound to be Read* (1975), for the *Spectator*, concluding that the anodyne book was 'bound to be remaindered'. The old boy was not amused. I met him occasionally at the Garrick after his retirement and never knew what to say to him, partly because of his deafness and the necessity to shout. He was an indefatigable writer of letters to newspapers, principally *The Times*. Once, when standing next to him at the bar of the Garrick, I vaguely recollected that in the previous twelve months he'd written fewer letters to *The Times*, and I made a jocular remark to that effect. 'On the contrary,' said Lusty, always courteous and stylish of phrase, 'I've written if anything more than usual. The editor has chosen to publish fewer.'

Be that as it may, it is one thing to write reminiscences, another to strive to write lit-ra-ture, and in the years I was writing my novels I definitely thought I was doing that, reaching to Parnassus and an understanding of the human condition. It is singularly sobering that if you believe yourself, as a young man or woman, to be writing 'major imaginative works' and you tell people you are writing literature (that is, 'literary fiction') – which is a qualitative term, not a quantitative one; as in salmon, without mention of whether the salmon is the best you've tasted, or that it stinks – they, too, believe that you are writing literature and tend, except for Martin Amis and his sceptical kind, to give you the benefit of the doubt. The reason why writers are so insecure about all this is that, although no one likes to face up to the fact, they haven't the slightest idea whether what they are doing is masterly or not worth the paper on which it is written and a complete waste of their time, their lives, not to mention the lives and time of potential readers.

I remember in one of those incomparable *Paris Review* interviews with authors, his interlocutor asked Evelyn Waugh what he thought of Edmund Wilson. 'Isn't he an American person?' asked Waugh. The interviewer agreed that he was. Waugh responded: 'I don't think they have anything to teach us.' In a similar vein, Brigid Brophy once wrote: 'The problem for Norman Mailer is that he wasn't born Norman Malest.' Typical Brigid Brophy, and it says almost everything about Mailer's limited macho prose.

I once failed to meet Gore Vidal, in some Fleet Street pub, possibly Dr Johnson's snug, the Cheshire Cheese, but I think it was the more snobbish El Vino's. It was in 1981, when I was commissioning contributions for *Shakespeare Stories*, and I thought that if he could be persuaded to contribute Vidal would turn in a fine one, preferably on one of the Roman plays. He was in London publicising his latest book. I telephoned Nigel Hollis, Heinemann's genial publicity man, and asked if there was any way I could pop the question to Caesar. He suggested I come to El Vino's the next day as Gore was holding court there and Hollis was sure he'd agree. He told me he'd prepare the ground and I was suitably grateful. Gore, as I didn't get to call him, was in such sparkling form and surrounded by so many twittering acolytes that there was no opportunity to pop the question. The book was published without a contribution from him.

When I was at Gollancz I signed up Joyce Carol Oates' *Expensive People*, which I still believe to be her best novel. The first sentence – 'I was a child murderer' – must be one of the most lapel-grabbing ever, whether or not the pun is intentional. Oates and her husband came to London when the novel was published.

She was a tiny, skinny, frightened-looking young woman, with a minute, shrill voice, completely unlike the robust author one envisages writing her bloodcurdling Jacobean novels, not to mention her treatise on boxing. She just about passed out with embarrassment when she asked me where she and her husband Raymond Smith might find a taxi. 'I'll telephone for one,' I said. She stood shivering in the warm room where the party in her honour was being held, shaking and shrinking with alarm as I looked up the telephone directory. 'Oh, this is terrible, we are putting you to such trouble.' As I remember, Smith said not a word. He later edited an eclectic and scholarly book of essays on *Alice in Wonderland*. Hard to fathom sometimes, Americans.

I was at a dinner which Jonathan Cape gave for Harold Brodkey and his wife when they were in London to celebrate publication of *the* Great American Novel, *The Runaway Soul*. Mr and Mrs Brodkey are organic-food nuts, and she told me that when they are invited out to dinner in New York they eat at home at 6 p.m. because they know, wherever they are going, that they will not be able, for reasons of their health, to consume the food provided by their hosts. I waited for her to say what exactly they did (devastated bread rolls, perhaps?) when their fellow all-American diners were tucking into luscious steaks or Caesar salads, but she didn't say and the Brodkeys were so cerebrally intimidating that I could not bring myself to ask. Maybe Harold spent some more time thinking about his novel. He obviously needed as much time as possible as he'd been working on the book for thirty-odd years. I was particularly amused to meet him because, some years before, I'd represented a book by Charles Simmons, a sometime contributing editor to the *New York Times Book Review* and a wry, quiet American. His *The Belles Lettres Papers* was a sardonically witty account in fictional terms of life at a book review journal not a million miles, I suspect, from the *New York Times Book Review*. Chapter Two is entitled 'Who the Fuck is Harold Brodkey?' I didn't know at the time I read and sold Simmons' satire, but was delighted to find out in an austere Japanese sushi bar in Swiss Cottage where David Godwin of Cape gave the dinner. Professor Brodkey's mother is said to have telephoned her son in 1987 to congratulate him on winning the Nobel Prize for Literature. She seemed to think this perfectly natural, even though he hadn't yet published a novel, let alone his *magnum opus*. In fact the Nobel Prize had been awarded to the Russian-born poet Joseph Brodsky.

For some years I represented the New York theatre and film critic John Simon, meter-out of stern opinions. Heavily waspish though he is, he is no WASP, being of Polish parentage. When he was in London in the early 1970s I invited him to have lunch with me at Bianchi's. When I arrived, Elena showed me to a table for three. I told her I'd booked for two. 'I realised that, Giles, but your guest rang up and asked that the table be for three.' Simon was a great romantic, and a lover of female pulchritude. The previous night he'd gone to see a play, and was so smitten by the young leading lady that, without reference to me, he'd invited her to lunch. Simon arrived, followed soon after by the actress, and for most of the lunch he directed his attention exclusively at her. She frequently tried, sensitively and courteously, to include me in the conversation. Eventually Simon ceased to gush about her performance and moved to criticising that of the actor who played opposite her. It seemed to me that from the moment he started she withdrew into her shell. Certainly she went silent, and then reddened. Simon ploughed on and on, saying he couldn't comprehend how she could give such a wonderful performance when acting opposite such a wimp. Eventually she could take it no more, and blurted out that the actor was her boyfriend. The remainder of the lunch was rather difficult. Simon did not offer to pick up the tab.

My first encounter with American writers in the flesh was at the Edinburgh International Festival of 1962. John Calder, the morose Scots publisher of Samuel Beckett, Alain Robbe-Grillet, Marguerite Duras, Nathalie Sarraute and many other of the most worthwhile writers of the last decades, mounted at the McEwen Hall an International Writers' Conference. This was in the days when such events weren't ten a penny. He persuaded a remarkable array of writers to participate, including Norman Mailer, Mary McCarthy, Khushwant Singh, James Baldwin, Truman Capote, Alexander Trocchi, Lawrence Durrell and Henry Miller. I was still at an age when I found it difficult to comprehend that books didn't, perhaps by osmosis, come into existence of their own volition, unrelated to messy, malingering human beings. I was allowed to help on the bookstall because my mother (I still lived with my parents then) thought Henry Miller had written *The Crucible* (although she didn't approve of his being married to that ghastly Marilyn Monroe), and Lawrence Durrell *My Family and Other Animals*.

The bookstall only functioned when the great men and women of letters weren't speaking or debating, and most of the time they were. Thus I spent days being mesmerised by famous writers in the flesh. Somehow I missed the notorious incident of a naked woman being pushed across the McEwen Hall stage in a wheelbarrow. This was a particular disappointment as I had never seen a naked woman and didn't altogether understand what happened to breasts when they were able to flop about. A high point though was when Durrell signed his *Collected Poems* for me ('Lawrence Durrell, 1962'). At least that's what I used to tell people in the hope of impressing them. In fact he signed scores of copies. It was perhaps the only way they could be sold. People somehow feel that books are more worth acquiring if authors have scrawled their signatures upon them. In the case of the majority of authors, not least politicians such as Edward Heath, who is reputed to have signed more copies of his books than were printed, a signature probably neither adds to nor detracts from the book's value. I once heard of a man, obviously unversed in these matters, who went into a bookshop to buy Jeffrey Archer's latest. He picked up what he assumed was a pristine copy and immediately noticed that it was signed by the author. The customer, who bought Archer's books only in hardback, assumed it was the author's copy which somehow had found its way into the bookshop. He took it to an assistant with this explanation and insisted on purchasing an unsigned copy. That may be regarded as literary integrity, a sign of a serious reader, not to be seduced by the bauble of an autograph.

Durrell's verse play *Sappho* was being premiered at the Edinburgh Festival that year, 1962. I had written to him in France months before, asking if he would consider contributing a piece about his play for the literary magazine I was co-editing with Michael Scott-Moncrieff, *New Saltire*, published by the Saltire

Society and successor to the influential *Saltire Review*. The Saltire Society is an association of like-minded people, which protects and sponsors worthwhile things in Scotland's cultural life, and is housed in handsome premises at Gladstone's Land on the Royal Mile. I offered Durrell our top whack of £10 for 1,000 words, almost the entire editorial budget for the issue. To my excitement, Durrell sent a typed postcard back saying he'd do it, and the article arrived – not 999 words, not 1,001, but 1,000 – by the date I'd given him. I thought we would have an international scoop on our hands but no one seemed very interested. To me, though, Lawrence Durrell became a hero, albeit briefly, as soon afterwards I tried to read the clotted prose of *The Alexandria Quartet*. But I still think his best poems lovely, the language much sparer and more precise than in his fiction. He might have signed rather than typed his name on the card, though.

For me the most memorable moment of the conference happened when, during a hard stint of listening or selling books, I went to do what a man has to do. I unbuttoned (zips had still to reach Edinburgh, I think). Two men wandered in, chatting to each other. One stood to my left, the other to my right. One was an American. He wore an old check cap and I think had a scarf and glasses. The other, modest in stature, had on a stiffish coat that looked like a British warm, perhaps left over from the war. To my intense disappointment, they were discussing the merits or otherwise of golf courses surrounding Edinburgh rather than the arcane secrets of literature. One was Henry Miller, the other Lawrence Durrell. I wanted to thank Durrell for his article, but that talk of golf I regard to this day as one of the great betrayals of my young life: how *dared* they talk about anything but books?

I was in New York, on a publishing trip, in February 1983 when Tennessee Williams died. Give or take Arthur Miller, to me he is the finest American playwright. (Eugene O'Neill has something too, but mostly verbal diarrhoea.) I read in the *New York Times* that Tennessee Williams was lying in state in a funeral parlour (it had an exotically American name like the Mildred E. Showerwater Funeral Parlour, but I cannot recall it) a few blocks away in Manhattan from where I was staying with my friends and colleagues, Lois and Tom Wallace. I had never seen a dead body lying in its open coffin for the world to inspect; not even Lenin's or Stalin's as, in common with the three sisters, I'd failed to make it to Moscow (and Madame Tussaud's surely doesn't count). I was far from certain that I could cope emotionally with the experience of seeing the playwright's corpse. *The Glass Menagerie, A Streetcar Named Desire, The Rose Tattoo, Cat on a Hot Tin Roof* and *Camino Real* are considerable works of art. Williams had died from swallowing the stopper of a bottle, or it had lodged in his throat and he had choked to death. The image kept floating into my mind of him lying there on his bier, and the bottle stopper or cork suddenly shooting out of his mouth, striking me in the eye, and my failing to catch it. The image kept recurring, and it didn't seem at all surreal. The *New York Times* gave the hours during which the body could be viewed, and I remember noting that I'd have to go to see old Tennessee before my first appointment of the day as I wouldn't be on that side of town again until after the funeral parlour closed for the night.

I wandered up to the door, which was as grand as those columns and lintel, all fake classical, in the old Pearl & Dean cinema advertisements. A black man in a blue uniform, peaked hat and all, stood outside. 'Can Ah help you, man?' he asked politely. 'I've come to see Mr Williams,' I said, ludicrously, but, I suppose, accurately. 'Mr Williams he no receiving visitors yet, man,' the guard replied quietly. I affected understanding and walked away, though it was later than the time when, according to the paper, mourners would be admitted. It seemed undignified to point this out. It was as if the playwright had had a late night and was sleeping in. I never got to see him, and it is probably as well.

# XXIII

Early in 1982, I received a telephone call from J. W. Lambert, who as well as being arts editor of the *Sunday Times* was much involved with the British Theatre Association, previously known as the British Drama League. As with the National Book League becoming Book Trust, the word 'League' was thought a killer for the times, smacking of patronage, charitable hand-outs and community help, all those things of which Mrs Thatcher didn't approve. Both organisations lost much allegiance as a result of the trendy change of name.

Jack Lambert told me that Ion Trewin was resigning as editor of the Association's quarterly magazine, *Drama*, and would I agree to succeed him? I asked for time to think about this, but he said there was none. Actually, he gave me twenty minutes, after which – on the assumption I said yes – he would ask me to come round and he'd introduce me to the advisory board of the magazine, which would be having one of its four annual lunchtime meetings accompanied by, as I subsequently discovered, the vilest of plonk encountered in captivity outside the offices of the even seedier and equally undernourished Poetry Society. The BTA housed the best theatre library in the world, even better than that of the Garrick Club, and the quarterly journal was the most serious, which is more or less to say dullest, theatre magazine in the country. It was more a record of theatrical progress than a lively companion to the glitter of showbiz, and Ion Trewin had, within its limitations, dragged it into the twentieth century. I agreed to edit it and did so for two years before handing the torch on to a young solicitor specialising in maritime affairs, Christopher Edwards, whom I'd noted as Benedict Nightingale's deputy at the

*New Statesman*. Edwards, ironically, was also to take my job at the *Spectator*.

The administrator of the BTA was a formidable and, in my view, completely eccentric youngish (which is to say, younger than me) woman named Jane Hackworth-Young. Except for the publisher Christopher Sinclair-Stevenson, I have difficulty getting on with people lumbered with double-barrelled names, and Ms Hackworth-Young was no exception. The BTA was (unfortunately it went out of business in the late eighties, owing to lack of funding) particularly concerned with the amateur theatre, and amateur theatre has always been one of my main aversions. Let people have fun doing amateur dramatics, by all means, but please don't expect the rest of us to have to watch the embarrassing results. Jane Young, as, aspiring to democracy, she called herself in the office, kept trying to persuade me to carry articles in the magazine dealing with amateur drama, and this I tirelessly resisted. She could never understand why. She did, to be fair, have more than a case as continued publication of *Drama* was reliant on the fact that members of the Association, and I think there were about 3,000, received the magazine each quarter as part of their subscription.

That apart, I was pretty well left to my own devices. The so-called editorial board was most supportive. Jack Lambert did not want to go on as chairman and I persuaded John Mortimer, over champagne at the Garrick, to succeed him. I have a soft spot for John, my favourite champagne socialist, but he was the worst chairman I've experienced. He would invariably try to skip items on the agenda and I cannot recall him coming up with one idea for the magazine. Nor could he ever remember Jane Hackworth-Young's name. The editorial board included the actor Peter Barkworth (who seemed to be in a permanent state of excitement about the magazine: every issue he thought superior to the previous one; I couldn't have been more grateful), Ronald Harwood, Peter Jenkins (the political commentator and one of my predecessors at the *Spectator*, who nearly always attended, sat there most of the time scowling and was particularly supportive; when he did speak his contribution was shrewd and helpful but, dear man, he thought that editors should be allowed to edit), Clifford Williams, the RSC director, and president of the BTA, and a batch of theatre critics including John Peter, Eric Shorter, John Russell Taylor and Naseem Khan who, being female and Pakistani, wanted more in the magazine on ethnic drama and fringe theatre.

The meetings were rum occasions. Hours were devoted to discussing the rebinding or repairing of the library books, many of which, not least the playscripts, were falling apart. The BTA earned much of its income from lending out 'sets' of plays to amateur groups. The librarian, a pale silent woman named Enid Foster, who looked as if she had a sad past and had swallowed too many acid drops, spent much of her time pasting reviews into cutting books. She had a remarkable memory and could dig out any piece of theatrical data at short notice. One day Jane Young announced excitedly that the Home Office had agreed that prisoners at Wormwood Scrubs should rebind the BTA's library books. I promise you this is true, and I promise you it happened.

When I became editor the doyen of theatre critics, Harold Hobson, wrote reams in each issue, discussing openings in London during the previous quarter. His opinions, it seemed to me, were as nutty as they had ever been throughout his tenure at the *Sunday Times*. I daringly suggested to him that he might instead write memoirs, almost obituaries, of actors, and he graciously agreed to do this and did it rather well. He was, after all, the equivalent of 'Jennifer's Diary' in the world of theatre. I then wrote the London reviews myself. I resigned from the editorial board of *Drama* soon after ceasing to be editor as, like Peter Jenkins, I took the view that editors should be allowed to edit and should not be interfered with, especially by their predecessors. Dismiss them if they're no good, or if their proprietor decides they're losing too much money, but don't tell them what to do when they're doing it. I resigned when I was appointed *Spectator* theatre critic.

Many of the articles we published were first rate. Susannah York was revealing about Hedda Gabler. John Gielgud, out of the blue, submitted an article, written in his small, fastidious hand, on what actors feel as they wait in the wings to go on. I have the manuscript somewhere. We published extracts from James Roose-Evans' journal which he kept when directing Helene Hanff's *84 Charing Cross Road* in New York. We acquired second serial rights in Laurence Olivier's unrevealing and stodgy *Confessions of an Actor*, using up almost an entire issue's budget in the process.

My leaving the editorial chair (there actually wasn't one; nor was the editor particularly welcome at the BTA's Fitzroy Square offices as there was so little room) was hastened by an extraordinary and certainly unlooked for row which I had with an editorial board member, the volatile Jewish playwright, ex-actor (he was a member of Donald Wolfit's company and wrote his biography), novelist and cricketer Ronald Harwood. I have nothing against Ronnie – on the contrary – but he does come on a bit and he came on at me. To his huge credit he is one of the funniest mimics and funniest men in London. (I've met them all.) He asked to write an article about something or other (not, I think, about his beautiful play *The Dresser*, but one of the subsequent ones which all seemed to star Albert Finney) and I readily agreed: our rates of pay were so miserly that any copy volunteered by a professional was gratefully received, especially by someone as ebullient as Harwood. When his piece came in, I made a few minor changes, tightening it up here and there, perhaps (I really can't remember) cutting the odd sentence or paragraph because the article was slightly too long. I did nothing more or less than a responsible, conscientious editor should do, and I believed that Ronnie's article was sharper as a result. He, on the other hand, exploded. He telephoned me at my office, saying that he'd never been treated so unprofessionally in his life, that no one had ever – not even hardly ever – changed a comma of his work before consulting him; and he added, for good measure, that had I consulted him he wouldn't have agreed to any of the cuts and alterations I'd unilaterally made. I was quite shaken by what I took to be his vituperation, and infinitely depressed, whereas I should, no doubt, have shrugged it off.

I took considerable if childish pleasure, when the *London Daily News* was running, to find myself telephoning a review to the paper from the telephone available for members inside the front entrance to the Garrick Club, opposite the porter's cubby hole, one night when Ronnie Harwood bustled in. I leaned out of the box and, raising my voice, entirely for the benefit of Harwood, said, 'And *all* the acting was appalling.' Needless to say, this didn't appear in the morning's paper, as my hand covered the receiver and the copytaker was unaware of what I was saying, but Ronnie went spluttering up the stairs into the Club fulminating noisily about 'bloody theatre critics'. Since I've ceased to be paid to sit in the dark in the theatre, Ronnie and I have always got on swimmingly whenever we've met.

In 1990 I married for the second time (my first wife, who was in the process of divorcing me, having died suddenly from a rare and still incurable illness in hospital on the last, ferociously cold night of 1989), and my new bride and I decided to go to Madeira for our honeymoon. Why Madeira I don't particularly know, except that we both wanted somewhere far from home where neither of us had been before and where we could be in peace. This diminished the planet somewhat, with my being forty-nine (the marriage was speeded up because she declined to be espoused to an old codger already into his second half-century) and she seventeen years younger and each of us having travelled a fair bit.

Most people who have not visited Madeira cannot readily identify it on the map, without initially making a few stabs with a finger and still likely to be hundreds of miles out. It's far closer to the equator, to Africa, than most people realise. Anyway, having established its whereabouts, we arrived at the airport of the capital, Funchal, to have the experience which I had once had before, in Delhi, bad enough when I was on my own, but which seemed an ill omen for our marriage: together with two or three other couples, long after the flight had touched down (and Funchal is not Heathrow), we were still standing by the baggage carousel and there was no further luggage to be unloaded from our flight. It arrived a day and a half later, having apparently spent some time holidaying in Lisbon. (When I was in Delhi my luggage evidently enjoyed itself in Sydney. The Planet of Lost Socks is nothing to what suitcases on air travel get up to.) When we arrived at our hotel, very late and very weary, we were directed along a corridor which was not there to a room which proved not to exist. It transpired that the room did exist but, because the hotel had the builders in, it was necessary to reach it by another route, another floor. In fact the whole saga of our stay at the hotel into which we had booked, culminating in our luggage being delivered to a room which didn't exist, in the middle of the night, easily persuaded us to move to another hotel, half the price and twenty times more agreeable, 'Quinta da Penha de França', a recommendation in case you should ever find yourself footloose in Madeira. But I promised in my first pages that I wouldn't write about myself, and my wife has said she'll leave me if I as much as mention her.

This is not a downward plunge into bland autobiography, or third-rate travel writing, or a shaggy dog story, but an attempt to provide background to the main matter of this chapter, the wit and wiles of Ronnie Harwood. When eventually, if luggageless, we reached our bedroom the night we arrived in Funchal, lying on the prim dressing-table – literally lying, for no one in that mindless establishment had thought to put it in water – was a bunch of roses, somewhat the worse for having been left there in the sun and heat for a day or two, with a congratulatory note from various friends and acquaintances and fellow writers including Harold Harris (the editor who discovered Frederick Forsyth), Morris Fahi, Josephine Pullein-Thompson, Peter Day, Francis King and Ronnie Harwood. When we ventured forth the next morning, almost the first person we encountered was Harwood.

We spent a fair part of our time in Madeira ducking writers we knew. Once Harold Harris, who had been my boss at Hutchinson, looked right through us when we were eating lunch at an outdoor café. Or did he do a double take, remember that we were on our honeymoon and feel that we should be left alone? I like to think so, for Harold is a good man, and a thoughtful one, which isn't by any means the same thing. I did get a bit fed-up with writers sidling up to me in the sub-tropical streets of Funchal to express surprise at finding me there, saying they'd no idea I was a delegate. It turned out that PEN was holding its umpteenth conference (PEN always seems to be holding a conference: freebies for many of the delegates?) in Madeira, and the number of delegates must have just about doubled the indigenous population of the island that May. I had run into Harold Harris a few days earlier in Sackville Street, Piccadilly, on my way to collect my wedding-ring and had told him, in my usual garrulous way, where we were honeymooning and even the name of our unfortunate hotel. He had done the rest.

When the time came to leave, my wife and I arrived at the airport in ample time for our flight back to London; I am neurotic about missing planes and trains, even buses, and thus always arrive early. Bewilderingly, we were told that we couldn't be seated together as we were the last two to check in for the flight, which I thought improbable. Certainly there was no one in the airport we recognised, and the airport was tiny. By the time the announcement came to board, the departure lounge was like a writers' convention. My wife and I were among the first to board the plane, she placed to the left of the central aisle, me to the right. We had been assured that once the plane was in the air we'd be able to sit together.

Suddenly I was aware of Ronnie Harwood and his wife, Natasha, standing in the aisle. He looked dramatically at Maggie, then turned his head to look at me. He enunciated slowly and clearly for all in the plane to hear: 'I see your wife has left you already, Giles.' The world is a bigger place because of Ronnie. And, of course, when I took Maggie to celebrate our second wedding anniversary at the Garrick, the only member who spoke to us was Ronnie, also there for dinner that evening. 'I'm glad you've got back together again,' he said, providing his blessing.

# XXIV

One year when I was editing *Drama*, Judi Dench presented the British Theatre Association's awards for best plays, performances, third spearholder on the left, and so on. The awards had become contentious because that year (1984) they were selected by a small group of us, on an *ad hoc* basis, at a dinner in a private room at the Garrick (or perhaps garrulous) Club, presided over by John Mortimer. John Peter was there, and Eric Shorter. I seem to recall that Ronnie Harwood was against all of our choices, wanting Albert Finney or Tom Courtenay to win everything, or at least something. One of the difficulties was that most of us had not seen the actors and productions we were voting on. It was a thoroughly British, utterly unscientific occasion, but on the whole, as we all knew what we were talking about, I believe that we got it more or less right.

I realised how transitory theatrical fame is when the small, modest man in the queue immediately ahead of me on the way into the awards ceremony at the headquarters (sic) of the British Theatre Association in Fitzroy Square a few weeks later had to repeat his name twice to the young woman noting down names at the door. 'Paul Rogers,' he enunciated clearly, and it seemed to mean nothing to her.

Judi Dench gave out the prizes, which were but 'certificates', for framing or filing or using as scrap paper, subject to inclination, and everybody enjoyed themselves as, really, all present were either prizewinners or those who had chosen the prizewinners. Afterwards it was pouring with rain. I volunteered, leaving the building at the same time as Judi Dench, to hold her umbrella above her head as she progressed from Fitzroy Square to I think it was Heal's in Tottenham Court Road. It's difficult trying to conduct a serious conversation, or even bestow a sycophantic eulogy, with a complete stranger in the pouring rain when you are struggling to hold a wind-swept umbrella over her head and she is much smaller in stature than yourself. Without in any way being other than perfectly polite, Miss Dench (as she then was) didn't give the impression that her life had been transformed when I ventured to say who would have guessed that her horrible Lady Macbeth could be so obsessively evil or her Lady Bracknell so down to earth, and to congratulate her on the brilliant way she disposed of that mighty phrase 'A handbag?' by almost omitting the words altogether. And so I fumbled on. Miss Dench, possibly alarmed by my ramblings, but more likely having reached her destination, thanked me for my pains – pains, madam? Nay, I take none – and scuttled away like a fieldmouse. Later I was to purchase at his Barbican exhibition Antony Sher's pastel of Judi Dench as Mother Courage, almost giving the lie to Brecht.

John Mortimer is one of the relatively few people I know who, when you leave their company, make you feel the world is a more agreeable, tolerant place than you had thought before. He is a sort of male equivalent of Fay Weldon, endlessly benign, hugely tolerant and consumed with interest in the ways of the world. I asked him once what he had thought of Simon Callow's portrayal of him as leading counsel for the defence in a televised dramatis-ation of the *Oz* trial. Callow's performance, possibly for the only time in his fascinating career, had been rather underpowered. 'I hope I had more energy than that,' said Mortimer, recalling a reasonably youthful and undoubtedly energetic court appearance.

On another occasion I remarked upon how pretentious I'd thought a comment by the Canadian pundit Michael Ignatieff in the *Observer* to the effect that you cannot go out to dinner anywhere these days without encountering Salman Rushdie as a fellow guest. 'How true that is,' said Mortimer, not comprehend-ing my objection that this was hardly likely to be everyone's experience. John was forever finding himself at dinner with Rush-die, he said. A few days later I repeated the comment to Fay Weldon and she, too, agreed: yes, indeed, one is always encounter-ing Salman at dinner. Maybe an actor's agency is hiring out Salman Rushdie look-alikes and speak-alikes to attend fashionable dinner-parties in North London and further afield. 'But, Fay,' I said, 'you had dinner with us a few weeks ago and Salman was not there.' 'That is true,' she said, in her still, small voice. A few weeks later she invited my wife and me to dinner. It was an excellent evening, not least because a fellow guest turned out to be Salman Rushdie (accompanied by his security men, who eat in the kitchen).

During my stint at *Drama* Christie's had a big sale of dramatic effects – costumes and memorabilia, and all that conjures up – and the antiquarian booksellers Maggs Brothers of Berkeley Square (no nightingales they) issued a magnificent catalogue of books and pamphlets on the English theatre from the Restoration to 1800. I thought it might be fun to have these two catalogues reviewed together, and who more appropriate to do so, if he would, than Donald Sinden, who is something of a theatrical historian and was much involved with the setting up of the unfortunate, if not ill-fated, theatre museum. Sinden agreed to do the piece, but since he is a famous actor and not perhaps *that* used to writing (although his swashbuckling *A Touch of the Memoirs* had been published by this time), there seemed to be innumerable problems. I began to wish I hadn't commissioned the piece which, in any case, was only to be 1,000 words or so. How could he get the copy, which was handwritten, to me? I suggested the post, but apparently this was too complicated. Finally he telephoned me at home on a hot summer Sunday morning and asked if I'd mind terribly if he brought it round in about two hours' time. He was playing Henry VIII at Hampton Court (I thought he'd done that years before, but maybe this latest appearance as the much-married Tudor monarch was for a commercial – for actors, like the rest of us, have to earn a living – and he'd simply had to dress up as the bloated king and juicily recite a line or two in return for an immodest cheque) and my house was, or could be, on his way home to Hampstead Garden Suburb. (He has a second home, according to *Who's Who*, at Rats Castle, Isle of Oxney, Kent.)

I had this vision of him, arriving in our Kentish Town cul de sac still dolled up as the fat king and causing a sensation. He came, of course, in mufti, but at the wheel of a limousine which seemed to stretch from the top of our modest street to the bottom.

Watching him parking was like watching the captain or pilot of the *QE2* trying to berth the vessel. I invited him to stay for lunch – we had just begun eating, on the top-floor balcony – but he declined, saying that he would, though, be partial to a glass of apple juice.

I said I had something I insisted upon showing him and led him into the sitting-room, where I sat him down on the sofa and showed him an ancient tome with somewhat ragged binding. I have never seen anyone look at a book – and I've seen countless individuals, many of them authors, look at countless books – with an expression so akin to ecstasy as Sinden's when carefully, lovingly fingering the large, rather battered folio, and then the five subsequent volumes. For I was showing him a set of what is colloquially known as *Hanmer's Shakespeare*, the editor being Thomas Hanmer. The first edition was published by the Clarendon Press, Oxford, in 1744. My set is the second edition of 1771, and it is most eloquently printed and illustrated with engravings. On the front and back of the pigskin binding is the stamp in gold of the Society of Writers to the Signet, and inside the front board is the shelf number where, for many years, the volumes lodged. The books were in the Edinburgh lawyers' library, the Signet Library, and in the early eighties they sold at auction many of their non-legal tomes to raise money to continue to buy essential legal books. Why, though, Sinden was excited by the books, and I before him, was that the first volume carries the richly etched bookplate of one David Garrick, actor.

I wrote to G. H. Ballantyne, the librarian at the Signet Library, in the hope that he'd be able to provide me with some provenance. He replied: 'Unfortunately there are no details of the library's accessions prior to about 1850, so that I am unable to say how the library acquired [the six volumes of *Hanmer's Shakespeare*]. On checking the various printed catalogues published in the first half of the nineteenth century, I find that there is a brief entry for this title in the 1826 catalogue. As the previous catalogue was issued in 1820, this presumably means that the volumes were acquired during the early 1820s.

'At that time Macvey Napier was the Librarian and, as ample funds were available, he was given virtually *carte blanche* to purchase what he liked. Presumably he saw the item for sale by one of the London booksellers or, indeed, he may have attended the particular sale where it was being disposed of.'

That, as Michael Holroyd might say, is scholarship, and I am much taken with it.

Had the sale taken place in London rather than Edinburgh I am sure I would not have been the successful bidder. I acquired these priceless books for a very modest sum (this cannot be said of most of my favourite books), which was way below the estimate the auctioneers had set. To watch Sinden looking at the stunningly proportioned and printed settings of *King Lear*, *Henry VIII*, *Othello*, all three title parts of which he'd lavishly essayed for the RSC, was to see and feel theatrical history bridged. It was, for me, most moving and thrilling to behold. I like to think, and do believe, there was even a tear or two as, sipping apple juice, Sinden touched the heavy pages of thick black print with his fingertips. 'To think,' he trilled and throbbed in heaviest black velvet, 'that Garrick learnt his lines from these books. Amazing. Absolutely amazing.'

I am leaving the books in my will to the Garrick Club, on the understanding that women are also eligible for membership by the time my will is read. I suspect I may have to survive to be very ancient indeed if the volumes are to be lodged in the Garrick library.

More than any other leading actor, Sinden has mixed classical roles with lighter parts, frequently in farce. For a period he alternated the RSC with Ray Cooney's Theatre of Comedy. He is thus the Pavarotti of the English non-operatic stage, and maybe when the World Cup is next played in the UK Sinden will inaugurate the proceedings with a mellifluous rendering of 'O for a muse of fire . . .' It may be because he has acted in farce with such thunderous relish and lost his trousers when playing a Cabinet Minister for Ray Cooney that he hasn't been knighted, though many people think he has and he is familiarly known as Sir Donald. (Except by Rowan Atkinson, who in a sketch some years ago portrayed a youthful actor cringingly accepting a theatrical award, of the kind that are twenty a new penny, in front of the theatrical establishment: 'Dame Peggy, Dame Judi, Sir Laurence, Sir John, Sir Ralph, *Donald . . .*')

Actors tend to acquire knighthoods by having their heads chopped off in the classics, particularly Shakespeare, or for stabbing their wives or serving up at table to a mother her sons baked in a pie. I have a mighty respect for Sinden's acting, and for the way in which the one-time Rank matinée idol mastered the great plays. His Duke of York opposite Peggy Ashcroft's Margaret of Anjou in Peter Hall's productions of the *Henry VI* plays was an extraordinary *tour de force* (so acclaimed in Stratford and London that it was not forced to tour). His grizzled, Bismarckian Lear was a thoughtful, political reading, and his Malvolio as affecting as any I've seen. Who else in our time could play Henry VIII as he did (with Peggy Ashcroft as the most serene, poignant Katherine of Aragon)? But out of context, offstage, his fruity voice is just too much, too big and too ridiculous. When he recited some of the Duke of York's lines at Peggy Ashcroft's memorial service it was hard not to laugh at his bombast booming round Westminster Abbey.

Yet actors who have known him for ever, those who were at school with him, confide that he did not speak remotely thus when younger, that the Sinden voice offstage, recognisable a thousand miles away, is a comparatively recent creation, given that he's been an actor for more than half a century. The only one to rival it is Derek Nimmo's, which likewise is apparently a construct of his adulthood. It is an odd thing about actors' voices. You can have a conversation with Gielgud, the greatest voice of them all, and be taken aback that the voice of the man is the voice of the actor, but after a few minutes you accept that the actor is the man, that the voice belongs to the man as well as to his creations. When you're listening to Sinden or Nimmo, it's as if you're perpetually listening to someone playing a part. Every time I hear Nimmo at lunch at the Garrick Club saying, 'Could you pass the mustard?' I want to cackle with laughter. It sounds so silly, mustard being asked for in that voice, though as he usually says it to the actors he's lunching with I imagine they just don't find it that funny.

Only with his Othello, I think, did Sinden adopt a lower register than he regularly employs, or nowadays possesses. Of the younger generation of classical actors, Antony Sher each time finds a totally different voice (the character is the voice as much as the physical embodiment), whereas Kenneth Branagh, to my mind monotonously so, always wields the same vocal instrument; yet both, in their utterly different ways, assume their parts with conviction even if Sher paints in oils, Branagh with watercolours or pastels. I could never fully accept Sybil Thorndike, because she invariably reminded me of two of my elderly great-aunts. Hers seemed the voice of a period and of a class rather than of an individual woman, an actress assuming various parts. Did she really enunciate in *St Joan*, which Shaw wrote for her, as she spoke her roles in later years? If so, no wonder the goddams were so alarmed by this precursor of Mrs Thatcher come to judgement. On the other hand, Peggy Ashcroft never disguised or altered her voice, yet the sounds that came out were unique to each character essayed because the role seemed created from within. This is a rarity: most actors create from without, hoping an internalised characterisation and rationale will be resolved when the external picture is more or less built up.

After Peggy Ashcroft's memorial service, Patricia Parkin and I took a bus up Whitehall. I was suddenly aware of a voice behind me proffering the fare, or rather asking how much it was. It was unmistakably that of Ian Richardson, one of the three or four finest actors to have played major Shakespearian roles for the RSC (which, contrary to general misconception, only came into being in 1961). 'I do wish we could see you again at the RSC, Mr Richardson,' I couldn't resist blurting out. An eyelid rose to see if he recognised me. He has, in recent years, been highly successful in America, playing Higgins in *My Fair Lady*, and on television. 'They haven't asked me,' he said, a little morosely, I thought, even wistfully. They should have done. Actors *are* their voices, although again Ian Richardson with his spun silver and burnished instrument – whether playing Coriolanus, Macduff, Fenton, Richard II, Iachimo, Vendice (in *The Revenger's Tragedy*) never gave the same performance twice.

In 1959 Dorothy Tutin's Juliet was all lyrical, breathless, eagerness, a bell-like nightingale eager to sing, a girl so in love with herself, with her young life and certainly with Romeo that the verse, the lines sparklingly gushed out over themselves (not that every word wasn't crystal clear: it was). When last I heard Tutin, at Dame Peg's memorial service, in her duet with Judi Dench the two voices were virtually indistinguishable (which may or may not have had something to do with the Abbey's acoustics). Dame Judi is another matter, and hers is another extraordinary voice, like Constable's painting *The Hay Wain* come to life. She is also Turner's *Fighting Téméraire*. Her voice is quintessentially English, more the countryside than the court, but when the country comes to court (her Duchess of Malfi, for instance) she is lethal. Her Cleopatra, opposite Anthony Hopkins, was a revelation: she could find the regality at which Glenda Jackson and Melen Mirren could only hint. And yet the voice in itself is not at all *beautiful*: it is how you might imagine farmyard animals talking to one another. Her Lady Macbeth, a really horrible one opposite the slicked-down hellish thane of Ian McKellen – almost Macbeth as fetishistic love object to his adoring queen – seemed as evil as it did because Dench, a person of unusual humanity, had to try to understand real evil in another woman: that she was able to do so became the cruel, terrible tragedy of her Lady Macbeth. I could never get excited by Glenda Jackson with her voice like a dredger sucking up waste from the bottom of the Manchester Ship Canal. She played too hard at not being glamorous, though she could, when she made the effort – the Princess in *Love's Labour's Lost*, for instance – appear to be among the world's beauties and thus the beauty of her performance was enhanced. She will, surely, be at home in the House of Commons, where her voice should command.

Similarly, my withers were never wrung by the self-indulgent and watery-voiced Vanessa Redgrave, all swooning about and grinning inanely whomever she's playing, whose joyful gush seemed synthetic and who always upstaged everyone else by her self-righteous sculptural intensity. I did not, sadly, see her famed Rosalind in 1961, although no doubt Paul Bailey, who played Charles the Wrestler's Second, might have a view. But, of all these actors and actresses, it is the voices that remain lodged in our minds when we contemplate their performances. If Donald Sinden and Derek Nimmo did not speak as they do now, how would they speak? Would they have done better or worse with their 'original' voices, those that God or their parents presumably gave them? And how 'original' are those voices, given that we are all, in that as well as in so many other respects, the children, the victims of our backgrounds, environments, social circumstances? Do you speak any better, more convincingly, after elocution lessons, any more than you write better with a word processor than with a quill pen (what might the Swan of Avon have turned out)? It's endlessly fascinating but ultimately fruitless to try to pin down these mysteries of the theatre. The actor's art is as ethereal as the singer's, but it is the combination of the actor's human frailty and vulnerability, and the authority with which the text endows the character, which makes the theatre so dangerous, so life-enhancing and revealing.

# XXV

The more times I've seen a Shakespeare play the more, almost without exception, I've enjoyed it, because I've derived more from it the better I've known it. The better you know your Shakespeare, the richer the plays seem (including *Titus Andronicus* and *Pericles*). A year or two before he died, the theatre critic J. C. Trewin published a curious but oddly fascinating little book called *Five and Eighty Hamlets* (1987) in which he described and compared all the Hamlets he'd seen, the first in 1922. His recall was remarkable and, plainly, the more he experienced the most famous and intractable play in the world the more he gleaned from it. On the whole he preferred his early Hamlets to his later ones, but that's the way of the world, or at least of the theatregoer.

If you go to see your first *Hamlet* tomorrow and are mesmerised and think it out of this world, little is more crushing and hurtful than to read some critic, too long in the tooth or more likely lacking any, comparing 'your' *Hamlet* unfavourably with some of the previous twenty-odd *Hamlet*s he's seen. (You'll have noted that there are hardly any women theatre critics to speak of.) It is a fact that most of us who become addicted to the theatre believe passionately – and if we do not believe with passion what are we about? – that the first productions of Shakespeare we have seen were incomparably the best. I *know* (I was there) that the Stratford productions of the late fifties – Glen Byam Shaw's regime as well as Peter Hall's – and early sixties were 'better', probably, than Shakespeare has been before or since, and thus I could cheerfully have murdered Harold Hobson when sometimes he ventured to say otherwise in the *Sunday Times*. Every Sunday, reading them in Edinburgh, Hobson's words would incite me to violence, usually taken out on my Pollock's toy theatre. I would shake with rage and frustration at the *wrongness* of most of his opinions. Not so much, though it was bad enough, because he didn't think Ian Holm's Henry V the best ever – theatre is about absolutes – but because he preferred a performance I could not have seen because I was not alive at the time. This historical, elegiac perspective, I felt, was a blow beneath the belt.

Metaphorically, I always sit on the edge of my seat at the theatre, expecting to be astonished; expecting not that something will go 'wrong' but rather that something will happen which I hadn't anticipated. Of course with inventive, imaginative productions of well-known plays this is frequently the case, and text and performances are enriched and enhanced. The experience of regular, religious theatre-going is like the experience of waiting for the bus to take you to work in the morning.

There can be no 'objectivity' in theatre criticism. The young man aged twenty who reviews one actor in *Hamlet* is not the same man who, aged sixty, reviews another actor as Hamlet. I remember wearily watching an RSC *Hamlet* at the Barbican when I had to review it for, I think, Robert Maxwell's ill-fated *London Daily News*. I was envious of the *Evening Standard*'s critic, Milton Shulman, who, with his wife, rose from his aisle seat immediately after the gravediggers' scene (Act V, scene i) and departed. The next day's *Standard* described the production as 'uneventful and hackneyed', or words to that effect. When I encountered him, as daily critics do, that evening during the interval of the play we were watching, I said to the *Standard*'s man: 'Milton, didn't you think the duel scene last night was the most eventful and unhackneyed you'd seen in years?' Milton was concentrating on the present evening's play, or on obtaining his gin and tonic. 'What did we see last night?' '*Hamlet*.' '*Hamlet*. Oh yeah.' (You have to hear that with a Canadian accent. You may well know Shulman's gravelly voice from the radio.) 'I haven't seen the duel scene [pronounced "dool"] in thirty years. I always leave after the gravediggers. Hey, who won?'

Shulman, as must be clear from this anecdote, didn't much enjoy *Hamlet*. In truth, he didn't seem much to enjoy being a theatre critic, and must have been relieved when he finally retired from this job in 1991 at some great age. (It is hard to tell how old as, almost unique among men in *Who's Who*, he fails to reveal a birth date. This cannot have been because he was a foundling or orphan, because his parents' names are listed.) He is a first-rate journalist who should never have had to undertake, and for nearly four decades, a job which appeared to give him so little pleasure. Each time he reviewed a revival of any play, even *Hedda Gabler* or *Uncle Vanya*, let alone a Shakespeare, he would recycle the plot, and many of his notices would consist largely of such interminable summaries. As a result they were uninspired and uninspiring. Once we found ourselves shuffling together into the crowded foyer of the Cottesloe Theatre, part of the National's complex. 'Have you seen this before?' Shulman quizzed. '*Antigone*? Oh, yes,' I said; but however many times I'd seen it, inevitably he'd have seen it more. I knew what Shulman enjoyed of an evening. 'There's no interval,' I said. I could see him wondering if we were about to experience one of those vindictive marathons where the director thinks the message of the piece will only come across if the audience concentrates for three or four hours without a break. That way seriousness in art lies, and the Arts Council subsidy should be increased next year to compensate for the lack of takings at the bar during the non-existent interval. But Shulman took the point. 'It's short?' he asked hopefully. 'Yes,' I replied. 'An hour and a quarter.' I'd read my press release. 'That's great,' said Shulman. 'I'll get home to dinner early.' This *Antigone* received a favourable review from Shulman, which, until his last year or two as theatre critic when he must have known the end was in sight, was something of a rarity.

The oddest thing about the *Evening Standard*'s critic, if you studied him in action, on the job, was that he rarely seemed to stop scribbling notes in cuneiform-like script in the dark, and *without appearing to look up at the stage*. He must, judging by the resultant notices, have been writing the plots down, as if afraid that he'd forget them before he arrived home and wrote his notices early the following morning. He had to file by 8.30 a.m., I think it was, the morning after the night before. For the *London Daily News*, ludicrously described by Captain Maxwell as 'Britain's first twenty-four-hour paper', I had to file by 10.30 p.m. on the evening of the performance. This meant that, whatever the bruising to my artistic sensibilities, I, too, missed the 'dool' if I was reviewing *Hamlet*. I once sat behind Shulman at London's most uncomfortable theatre, the Bush – not only are there no backs to the seats, there aren't any seats: you sit on tiers of steps, your feet digging into the back of the human form in front of you, and I'd swear in the witness box that he wrote his notes, less a plot summary than a novella, even an epic, on an unravelling toilet roll. He limned his chiselled words large, as if to decipher them in a dimly lit room.

He once said to me: 'I don't know what's wrong with you. You enjoy going to the theatre.' For twenty-five years or more, 'going to the theatre' gave me as much pleasure as any other form of human activity, and usually more. Thanks to my friend and client Peter Ackroyd being literary editor of the *Spectator*, the editor, Alexander Chancellor, asked me in the autumn of 1982 if I'd like to take over from Mark Amory, who was giving up the theatre column to edit Evelyn Waugh's correspondence, for six months. 'No,' I said. 'That would terrify me. But could I do it for a week or two to see if I can manage?' 'No,' he said. 'Six months or nothing. Of course you can manage.'

I took the plunge. My first column was to appear in the first issue of 1983, and the copy date – as tends to happen these days with the nation knocking off for nearly two weeks over Christmas and the New Year – was before the holiday began. For my first trick, and with nothing much new opening in theatreland, I chose to pronounce upon Trevor Nunn's and John Caird's production of *Peter Pan* which, like all RSC productions of this period, should have run for three hours five minutes, but invariably overran in first performances by twenty minutes or more. To meet my earlier than usual deadline, I had to review a preview, which is generally frowned upon: good enough for the paying public, albeit at minimally diminished prices, but not good enough for the freeloading critics. I wasn't aware of the restrictive practices which prevailed between theatre and press, and I even paid for ('Darling, you *didn't*! I hope at least you used plastic?') my tickets at the box-office, never being one to put money into the cynical pockets of booking agencies.

So long was that Saturday matinée of *Peter Pan* that children were either screaming or falling asleep long before the end, and there was throughout the Barbican's auditorium that inevitable hum, cacophony and murmur of voices rising to a crescendo which is *de rigueur* when numerous children are brought together to participate in an event which they cannot possibly fully comprehend. It was, though, a terrific production, with Miles Anderson the first male Peter in many a year, if not ever as the management wrongly insisted. In spite of my review being a rave (or so I thought, and certainly intended), the RSC complained that I'd reviewed a preview, even though I owned up to as much in my notice. What they didn't like, presumably, was that I mentioned that the crocodile, harbouring two actors like a pantomime horse, had split open in the middle as it attempted to lumber across the vast acreage of the Barbican revolve in pursuit of Jas. Hook. It was a memorable moment. Some children were distraught, alarmed and appalled – theatrical illusion had been disrupted, the 'real world' introduced – others, mostly the older ones including my three, were highly amused. It made the show.

Not to mince words, I enjoyed being theatre critic of the *Spectator* more than I have enjoyed any other single job I've done. Certainly I didn't regard it as 'a job'. It became not just a way of life but, dangerously, my life. Frank Delaney, then president of the West Ruislip literary society (in succession to Sir John Betjeman), wordsmith, broadcaster and Irish flatterer, once asked me: 'Where was your theatre column, Giles, before you took it to the *Spectator*?' I had to confess that it hadn't been born. 'My God,' he said, 'to think that you've started at the top, in the best theatre critic's job there is. You can't go any higher.' I had to agree. In the eighteen months I went to the theatre for the *Spectator* I did not miss one week, contriving to file two weeks' copy each time I departed on holiday. It could be done, just. I spent most of each Friday writing, polishing and honing my 900 words, once confusing Bill Owen with Bill Fraser, and once writing Edgar when I meant Edmund in a routine production of *King Lear*. The respective actors' agents bustled in self-importantly, demanding that the errors be put right. Otherwise, week followed week, I wrote as well as I could and no one said anything.

Starting as I did at the age of forty-three (Harold Hobson and

Kenneth Tynan had been younger, and for all I know Milton Shulman too, not to mention George Bernard Shaw and Oscar Wilde), I was obviously an amateur, a late beginner, particularly in the eyes of the other critics. Above all, I was probably regarded with suspicion by the other critics as I was working full-time as a literary agent during the day. To the adage 'Those that can, do; those that can't, teach' should be added, either between the two philosophies or after them, subject to your own predilections: 'And those that can't do either, become critics.'

Theatre criticism is, in a way, a hauntingly sterile activity. You can genuinely profess to have the interests of the art form as your only concern, yet why – if you cannot 'do' it yourself, or even if you can – should the creators, let alone those who pay earned income to consume the art, care one iota about your judgements, your strictures, your qualifications and comparisons? If you have high standards for your chosen art, you will all too quickly find that almost everything you witness inevitably falls short of the best. If you lower your standards and seek out matters to praise in unexpected places ('Vanessa Redgrave gave a miraculous performance in the two-line part of the maid'), you are being both absurd and untrue to your own integrity. The truth, unpalatable though it is to those involved professionally in the theatre, is that all theatre critics – and in London there are probably only between twenty and thirty of them – invariably overpraise. Because they sit together in the dark night after night they have to find matters to praise; otherwise they'd either go crazy (which some of them do anyway: it's a very *unnatural* trade) or become sour and cynical (ditto).

There are so many words in most reviews, so many components in a production – play, direction, design, choreography perhaps, music, oh and the acting – that a management can almost always extract a quote or two from anyone's notice which it can employ to help persuade the unwary theatre-going public to part with its cash. How often have I walked out of a theatre, obviously not on a press night, to hear disappointed playgoers mutter, usually in low voices so as not to be overheard, as if their thoughts were blasphemous: 'I don't understand it; Michael Billington raved about it. He's usually so reliable.' The truth is that Michael Billington of the *Guardian*, an exceptionally nice man, seems temperamentally incapable of not finding a great deal to praise in almost anything he sees. Of all the critics, Billington gives the impression of having been at a party every evening.

The second play I reviewed for the *Spectator* was at the tiny New End Theatre in Hampstead, which used to be a mortuary and, judging by the quality of almost every production I've seen there, is bound to become something of the sort again before too much time has elapsed. I spotted Irving Wardle, then and for many years before, the critic of *The Times*, and the critic most admired by other theatre critics – though not necessarily by arts editors. John Higgins, Wardle's one-time boss at *The Times*, once drily complained to me that Wardle's notices were never quoted 'in lights' outside theatres, as in 'A hit, a hit, a palpable hit – *The Times*'. The truth is that Wardle wrote too sensibly, too undemonstrably, to be so vulgarly taken out of context. I once congratulated Eric Shorter, the scholarly erstwhile peripatetic critic of the *Daily Telegraph*, on having some words quoted noisily outside a West End theatre, and he curtly informed me that it was the most insulting thing that could happen to a critic, 'that you can write so badly that some management can wrench your words out of context and use them to drum up business. That is not what dramatic criticism should be about.' Indeed not.

I knew Irving Wardle slightly (unlike most theatre critics, he is a commendably shy and retiring man) from the days when, as editorial director of Gollancz, I persuaded him to write a biography of George Devine. He did so with wisdom and dedication, but for reasons too tedious to go into, it was published not by Gollancz (whence I'd departed before the manuscript was delivered, years later) but by Jonathan Cape.

Wardle looked as if he was doing his homework, as I was later to think of it. I didn't know then that he alone of all the critics (though, increasingly, the elderly J. C. Trewin would remain in his seat) would study the text of a play during an interval, or even, if the play was likely to be a long one, begin to sketch out his review, as those days most self-respecting daily newspapers still printed reviews of first nights on the following morning.

The interval came, not before time, and I moved across the

pocket-handkerchief-sized auditorium to greet Wardle. He looked slightly startled, like a night animal accosted by someone from the daytime world and uncertain how to behave. I suggested a drink, and so taken aback did he seem to be that he accepted. We meandered towards the otherwise untenanted bar. I think he had a half-pint of beer and I had a glass of white wine. All these years later he has not bought me the other half, because we haven't 'socialised' again.

I met J. W. Lambert, who had ever been something of a benefactor to me, a few days later. I told Lambert of my encounter with Wardle, and how in the course of our interval drink I, as a raw recruit to the night-time world of theatre critics, had remarked that being away from home most evenings presumably didn't improve one's private life (except in the case of Mr Trewin, who was accompanied every night by Mrs Trewin; and now that he's dead she goes on reviewing plays). Wardle had responded with surprise, thinking for a while and then saying that being out most evenings didn't seem to make any difference to his marriage. 'How typical of Irving,' said Jack, far from unkindly. 'He's been married and divorced twice and is now on his third wife and presumably hasn't noticed.'

My first wife – five years of reviewing provided the *coup de grâce* (rather than simply, and more appropriately, the *coup de théâtre*) to the marriage – complained, not necessarily without some gratitude to the critic cited, that I spent more nights in the dark with Milton Shulman than I did with her. Admittedly she had a soft spot for Shulman, but then so do most women.

The most tetchy and obsessive critic was Michael Coveney, who in the 1980s wrote for the *Financial Times*, which no one, or hardly anyone, who went to the theatre read, or if they did would not read for its arts reviews, except on Saturdays. Like me, because he reviewed overnight, he was prone to hysteria when, as almost invariably happened with RSC press nights at the Barbican, those long evenings began five minutes or more late: at that rate, in *Hamlet*, we'd even miss the gravediggers' scene. I always thought that Coveney, who privately is a kind man, was as abrasive as he was because he didn't do anything else. He was a full-time, born-and-bred, man-and-boy theatre critic. I think all the other reviewers had various irons in the fire and thus weren't as intense and narrowly based. David Nathan, for instance, the *Jewish Chronicle*'s critic was also its literary editor; Sheridan Morley of *Punch*, no one could stop from writing books, sometimes before breakfast; Michael Ratcliffe of the *Observer*, kept flying to Germany to research a still unpublished biography of Goethe; Jack Tinker of the *Daily Mail*, like a Babycham cork, kept popping up on television quiz shows; and so on. Coveney's wife, the regal Sue Hyman, was even a theatre PR. Most theatre critics grow up with other ambitions than to be a theatre critic, perhaps to be an engine driver or a great actor, or a second Edward Bond. Coveney was born, he insists, wanting to be a theatre critic.

He's a decent, moody man whose slightly histrionic command of the English language is commendable. Yet his theatrical taste and judgement (he's a working-class lad made good who not only 'appreciates' soccer but used to spend a fair amount of time kicking a football about on Hampstead Heath with his young son) seem to me almost invariably wrong. He is a prime example, I'd submit, of a critic so in thrall to his subject matter that he becomes too close to it. I expect he's mellowed since I last met him, if only because he's published two books, *The Citz* (a history of one theatre company that for him can do no wrong) and a biography of Dame Maggie Smith.

I'm positive that young Coveney (I was born eight years before him) was pretty contemptuous of my critical evaluations, for once, as we brushed against each other as we stumbled towards our seats, he said: 'I must have got it wrong last night because I see in your paper today that you agree with me.' Unlike most critics, Coveney read all his *confrères*, and if they needed a wigging he'd give them one. The great thing about him, though, is that he cares. Reading him, you feel that the live theatre is the most important activity in the firmament.

He succeeded Michael Ratcliffe at the *Observer* in 1990, and seems less happy with a relatively short weekly column than he did in lengthy daily notices in the pink 'un, where his enthusiasm could instantly and eloquently communicate itself. He was – no doubt still is – a master of the overnight 1,000-word review, which at Stratford he'd write in forty minutes or so and telephone to the copy-takers, before turning up for supper at the Dirty Duck with fellow critics, most of whom did not have to file overnight, or even with some of the actors. He would usually escort Pam, the capacious and partisan landlady of the Dirty Duck, to Stratford first nights as it annoyed him that the management of the theatre declined to give her complimentary tickets. Perhaps the actors expected complimentary drinks in her public house. I once offended Pam by referring to her in print as the Mistress Quickly of Stratford, but she was, she is, the Elena of the Avon.

John Peter of the *Sunday Times*, who succeeded Harold Hobson (the first, and may he be the last, theatre critic to be knighted for being a theatre critic) after the unsatisfactory interregnum of the poet James Fenton, is, in spite of his name, not English but Hungarian, which possibly explains why his language sometimes seems an approximation of what you suspect he intended to say. Like George Steiner, Professor of English and Comparative Literature at Geneva University, he employs English as a blunt rhetorical instrument, a cultural shillelagh, a weapon of prodigious passion, but with an abbreviated vocabulary. He wrote a much-admired book about modern *Kultur* called *Godot's Carrot*, which no one acknowledges having read but everyone intends to read.

Michael Ratcliffe wrote as an artistic intellectual, an exquisite don *manqué* balancing and counter-balancing. His passion for theatre, his cultural credentials, are second to none, but his erudite essays in the *Observer* were too refined, too polished, too tentative. He preferred, to the chagrin of the theatrical profession, to analyse the play rather than the performances, and had a particular penchant for matters German.

When I was reviewing, the fledgling *Independent* used a roster of critics of whom the best was a nervous young man named Andrew Rissik, who exhausted himself on the job and for a period had to be hospitalised. He will, perhaps, go down in history as the biographer of Sean Connery (when shall we see *his* Macbeth?) who wanted to confide to his readers his belief that Connery's chest was completely hairless, and the jungle on that area of his anatomy which the actor revealed in the James Bond films was but a chest mat. This, of course, is fantasy on poor Rissik's or his informant's part. I think the revelation (which wasn't) was cut even before the book reached proof stage, as the publisher's lawyers correctly pointed out that countless (well, not quite countless) individuals could presumably be found to testify to the thickness of the actor's chest hair.

It is depressing that there are so very few women critics, not least because the most astute critics of theatre tend to be female, and more women buy theatre tickets than men do. I see the *Daily Express* now has one. *Punch* in its dying days employed the vulpine and acerbic Rhoda Koenig, who is a New Yorker, which can only explain her embarrassing addiction to musicals (provided they are not by Sir Andrew Lloyd Webber and Tim Rice Paper). Ms Koenig began at *Punch*, where she succeeded the avuncular Sheridan Morley, by meting out severe judgements on almost everything. Within a year, like almost all the rest of us, she'd become a camp follower, succumbing to the thespian sirens, the Scylla and Charybdis of showbiz, although she still resisted the ubiquitous megaphone pronouncements of the short-back-and-sides compère Ned Sherrin.

Many great writers have been theatre critics, their insights usually more valuable than the journalistic variety, but more often than not they've kept, if not made, their reputations writing, let us just say, more originally than commenting on the work of others. Critics throughout history have usually got it wrong, although you have to hand it to Harold Hobson that he saw the point of *Waiting for Godot*, a rare masterpiece and key work of the nuclear world, perhaps because his command of spoken French was, it is said by those who tried to converse with him in it, minimal, and of the early plays of Harold Pinter, that strange litmus paper of inarticulate menace.

The first letter I received from the *Spectator* was Alexander Chancellor's inviting me to become drama critic. When the second arrived, on a Saturday morning less than two years later, Charles Moore having replaced Chancellor as editor, I said to my wife: 'This'll be the new editor sacking me.' I was right. Moore insisted that it was nothing personal – how could it be? we hadn't met – but, he wrote, he wanted to make his mark on the paper as soon as possible, and as I was almost the only regular columnist he didn't know (or who, it sardonically occurred to me, hadn't smarmily written to congratulate him upon his appointment) he hoped I wouldn't mind too much if he dispensed with my services. I replied courteously, told him I minded desperately, and that he had sacked me from the job I'd most enjoyed in my life. I didn't tell him that my response, in the privacy of our bathroom, had been to weep, something I hadn't done in years. It was so *unfair*. I'd have understood if only Moore had said that my column was no good. Maybe he did think that, but his letter suggested otherwise. When you are sacked, of course, you feel inadequate, a failure, and compliments from the person who has dismissed you are particularly resented. At least I wasn't on the dole as I had continued to practise as a literary agent, not that anyone could live off the *Spectator*'s stipend.

Some months later, at the end of 1984, Alan Coren, editor of *Punch* (whose first book, *All Except the Bastard*, I had published at Gollancz), telephoned to ask if I'd like to fill in for ten weeks as Sheridan Morley was going to Hollywood to research a biography of James Mason. I accepted with alacrity and, during those ten weeks and at other times during the next three years when Sherry was away, I enjoyed writing his column, accompanied to the theatre once a week by Bill Hewison, who did the cartoon and who, like Morley, enjoyed an ice-cream in the interval. Sometimes he urged a choc-ice upon me, but I resisted, preferring a minuscule glass (and it was minuscule, especially if we were at the National or RSC) of overpriced warm white plonk.

A week or two after Coren had hired me, Morley, whom I hadn't met before, took me out to lunch and made it clear that it was he who had wanted me. Oh well. I started, affectionately (because it's not possible to dislike the effusive, garrulous Morley) to think of him as Sheridan Mostly – partly because he is quite substantial but more particularly because he seemed to contribute, and more or less simultaneously, to almost every publication in the land, as well as overseas. He was and is a walking goldmine of theatrical facts and statistics, a kind of Bill Frindle of the theatre. (And if you are not familiar with Mr Frindle's curious name you cannot be seriously interested in cricket.) I asked Morley on one occasion if his biography of Gielgud, whose official biographer rather improbably he is, would contain any surprises: 'Only that John is a closet heterosexual.'

My tenure at *Punch* was terminated when in 1987 I was appointed theatre critic of the *London Daily News*. So time-consuming and demanding was my work on the paper that I anaesthetised myself to the extent to which my private life was spiralling out of control. My son Callum was, to my regret, quite uninterested in the tradition of English Literature and Drama at King's College, Cambridge, but volunteered after about a year that there was a very elderly Fellow called Dadie Rylands who seemed to have had a bit to do with drama. I explained to him that, in effect, he was the forefather of the RSC, having influenced generations of undergraduates at Cambridge – he had even directed Gielgud as Hamlet in 1945. My younger son, Gareth, had his problems, and was away from home, at a therapeutic school in Hampshire, and my daughter Harriet was largely under the control of her mother, in so far as she was under control at all. We were, Margaret and I, more or less living separate lives and, in our different ways, miserable about that. Certainly I was consumed with a very Presbyterian guilt.

The *London Daily News*, from beginning to end – and the end came unexpectedly – was a nightmare. I had been told by Sue Summers, the arts editor, whom I never took to – or she, I think, to me – that I had been her first choice as theatre critic. As I was to find out, I was about her sixth choice; I didn't mind that – I considered myself lucky to be offered the job.

I was first taken out to lunch by Sue Summers, presumably to be vetted, although by then the incipient daily required a theatre critic rather urgently. I was particularly gratified to learn that the volatile veteran film critic Alexander Walker had been persuaded away from the *Evening Standard* in return for, reputedly, a king's ransom of a salary. Walker was the most colourful film critic around: as writers, most film critics seem to espouse black and white rather than Technicolor. He was, like his colleague Milton Shulman, something of a plot man, but maybe *Standard* readers like absorbing the minutiae of plots on their commuter buses and Underground trains. He is small but fiery. Once, sitting in the stalls of a cinema one weekday morning (as is the *modus operandi* of film critics), he noticed that a critic a few rows in front of him had lit up a cigarette. Ferociously anti-smoking, Walker reached under his seat for his umbrella, leant forward and swiped the offending tobacco inhaler on the shoulder, insisting he extinguish the vile weed immediately. Alex Walker was indisputably one of the *Standard*'s prime assets, and his move to the *London Daily News* would woo readers to what was intended to be a more up-market and arts-orientated rival London evening newspaper.

After presumably passing muster with Sue Summers – who hadn't seemed much interested in discussing either the theatre or how I might do my job – I was dispatched to see the paper's editor, Magnus Linklater. He was the elder son of the peppery Scots novelist (*Magnus Merriman; Juan in America*) and play-wright Eric Linklater, whom I'd been thrilled to see in 1958 wearing moustache and black tie at the first night of one of his own plays, *Breakspear in Gascony*, at Edinburgh's repertory thea-tre, the Gateway, which, quirkily, was owned by the Church of Scotland. People didn't wear black tie to the Gateway, half way down Leith Walk, even during the Edinburgh Festival.

As to black tie, I have always disliked wearing a dinner jacket because, by definition, it does not allow any sartorial quirks and character revelations on the part of the wearer, which, surely, is the main point of both dressing and dressing-up, other than, figleaf-like, to conceal private parts and to keep yourself warm. It is curious that virtually all women with whom I've discussed the matter insist that they prefer men in black tie as it makes them look more handsome, distinguished, desirable. This is hardly, I'd have thought, a compliment to God (unless Adam initiated black tie in the Garden of Eden), or to the designers of our everyday clothes, or to our collective dress sense. Maybe there is something in the psychological make-up of women which causes them to prefer that all men look essentially the same; and like penguins.

Magnus Linklater, in his office in the annex of the *Mirror* building at Holborn Circus which temporarily (and, in practice, permanently) served as the *London Daily News* offices, did not wear black tie. I can't remember what he wore, something nonde-script, and he always had strong seven o'clock shadow – but journalists seen on the job or *en masse* do tend to resemble hedgerows somewhat out of control. It is as if printer's ink has infiltrated their skin. He was calm and charming, which was not how I expected editors to be – or was I subconsciously confusing him with his proprietor, Captain Maxwell?

Sue Summers sat silent beside me. Linklater asked if I'd need to go to the theatre two or three times a week. I pointed out that, if we were to cover the better fringe productions as well as the national companies and the West End (which, for reasons of the economy and lack of foreign visitors, was fairly moribund at the time, although *The Mousetrap* seemed as ever to be surviving), there were, on average, seven to ten London openings per week. He clearly did not believe me. This was partly, it occurred to me later, because he was about to make me a financial proposition and, generous though it was – foolhardy, I'd say, but Fleet Street salaries still were, then, and the demise of Maxwell was some years away – he had calculated it on the assumption that I'd be covering two to three plays a week. In fact there was hardly an edition of the six-day newspaper in which I didn't have a review, and occasionally two. This was the last time I saw the editor until, nearly a year later, the wake to commemorate the death of the paper.

There were intended to be six or seven editions throughout the day, an ambition which disintegrated within weeks if not days of first publication as so few people were purchasing the sheet. If you tried to purchase it from a news-vendor he'd invariably proffer the *Standard*, even if you asked in a loud, clear voice for the *London Daily News*. (Whether the news-vendors had been flattered by the *Standard*'s proprietor, Lord Rothermere, or were, like taxi drivers, just irredeemably conservative, I do not know.) The paper was infinitely more anorexic than its rival because it secured precious little advertising, and Maxwell never got to grips with the potential of classified advertisements. There was some news, tabloid-style, and many feature articles. Sue Summers had elected to call the arts section Metro (but industrial espionage at the *Standard* discovered as much and that paper renamed its arts pages Metro before the LDN could use the name). It was generally highly praised, but I found it pretty nondescript. There tended to be a page of reviews, all huddled together in thin, short columns, one after the other, as if they were a necessary chore, with no editor or layout person deciding whether one event covered on a particular day was more important than the others.

Alexander Walker was persuaded to stay at the *Standard*. Milton Shulman, thereafter thought of as the *Standard*'s secret weapon, had been deputed by the editor to take Walker out to lunch at the Savoy or Ritz and twist his arm to make him remain. Uncle Milt's flattery or powers of persuasion clearly triumphed, because Walker of the Technicolor prose remained with the *Standard*.

Michael Pye was infiltrated as the LDN's film critic, and he was rather bright. As soon as the paper folded, he went to live in New York, which was one way of coping with the débâcle. Celia Brayfield, the popular novelist, was the television critic. Sue Summers treated her as if she were a *prima donna*, if not quite *prima donna assoluta*. Because Ms Brayfield was a single parent, she was allowed to watch her television programmes at home in the evening, or whenever they were transmitted, and didn't have to attend previews as other television critics did. Because more readers watched television than went, say, to the ballet, Ms Brayfield's reviews would be phoned in (to the most creative, not to say interpretive, copy-takers in the history of journalism) late in the evening and the rest of us telephoning in copy from all over London would have our pellucid prose cut and trimmed to fit around her.

The ballet critic was a raunchy-sounding Canadian named Jan Murray, not to be confused with Jan Parry of the *Observer*, who addressed me, and everyone else, as Sweetie and took to telephoning at all hours of the day and night to complain about Sue Summers. When the paper closed Ms Murray became a travel tour operator. She cared passionately about everything, and seemed hugely professional.

Press nights usually began at 7 p.m., to allow critics to publish their notices the following morning but, by the time the LDN was running, most other newspapers had already given up the unequal struggle. It is, of course, ironic that the industry's 'new technology' means that papers go to press earlier than was the case in the days of hot metal and filthy ink. *The Guardian* and *The Times* no longer reviewed overnight, meaning that Michael

Billington had longer to insert effusive adjectives and hyperbole into his glowing copy, and Irving Wardle could do more home-work in the morning. Only the *Daily Telegraph* and the *Daily Mail* reviewed overnight, and then even the *Torygraph* stopped. Its critic was the notorious Charles Osborne, an Australian opera freak with many books to his credit, who had, as I have mentioned, spent years running, some would say running down, the so-called Literature Department of the Arts Council.

Max Hastings, the *Torygraph*'s haughty and swingeing editor, had been looking for a theatre critic to succeed the enervating and long-running John Barber. Instead of replacing him with his admirable deputy, Eric Shorter, who had already spent decades of his life travelling the world with a shoulder bag in search of stimulating and original theatre for *Telegraph* readers and whose style was quite lively, Hastings ordered his arts editor to find a new theatre critic who was likely to be more critical. Colonel Hastings, as he was known because of his military demeanour and because he was the first British journalist and war correspondent over the top and into the Falklands during Thatcher's War, was not much interested in the arts. As a hunting and shooting man (I know nothing of his attitude to fishing, but I can't imagine he abstains), he didn't appear to have much time for quieter, more sensitive pursuits. The arts editor hired the sharp-tongued Charles Osborne, presumably assuming that the previous night's thespian charades would be blitzed in contemptuous prose the next morn-ing. At heart Osborne is an old sentimentalist and, poacher turned gamekeeper (thank you, Max), he penned some of the softest, least grumpy reviews of them all. His friends, and even some enemies, were safe with Charles.

I've devoted so much space here to theatre critics because, though they may not, in London, be as powerful as the 'butchers of Broadway' – a couple of whom, or even one, can kill a show overnight – there are so few that their opinions may matter, and thus matter more than they should. My 400 words for the *London Daily News* were rough-and-ready work, and not once was I remotely satisfied with what appeared in print. With most pro-ductions, I'd be obliged to write half the review or more during the interval. Frequently, with classical productions and especially if mounted by the RSC, I'd have to creep out of my aisle seat in the dark and blink my way, mole-like, to an exit and compose my final sentences and telephone the review through while the performance continued. It was surprisingly difficult to find a telephone on occasions, though the RSC press office, knowing that their press nights overran, would wire up Jack Tinker of the *Mail* (the liveliest and arguably the most accurate assessor of plays reviewing during my years) and me.

With hindsight, I think the experience of writing (not that it really was writing) for Captain Maxwell's increasingly tacky rag poisoned my pleasure in penning theatre criticism, and even in going to the theatre. Ironically, the last notice I had published (I did one the following night, but by then the paper had been declared a corpse) was of Stephen Sondheim's glorious, nostalgic, romantic *Follies* where, for I think only the second time, I was promoted to the front news pages and had to write 750 words as the première of *Follies* at the Shaftesbury Theatre was news. If memory serves, the show began half an hour late – no doubt Joan Collins or someone had difficulty finding her seat – and I was frantic. I had to leave the auditorium long before the end and was escorted up to the deputy manager's tiny office, where I began telephoning in what I'd written during the long interval ('Darling, how *wonderful* to see you') as I was simultaneously trying to compose my concluding paragraphs. I began scribbling with my left hand as I held the telephone receiver with my right.

As I dictated and wrote, somehow (where did the third hand come from?) I was slurping white wine. The deputy manager, penguin-suited, had heard that my notice, the very first to be filed, was a rave. I reached the end, sweating profusely (it was a sweltering evening in July). The copy-taker confided that I was two sentences short, then three words. 'Another drink?' I heard the deputy manager say. 'A stupendous production,' I heard myself breathe sardonically down the telephone. Those words – 'A stupendous production, *London Daily News*' – were to haunt me outside the Shaftesbury for the year's run of *Follies*. No doubt it was the nearest I'd ever come to seeing my name in lights. But how bizarre that the management should have regarded it as profitable advertising to use a quote from a moribund newspaper to boost a vibrantly living show. Yet who, of those tempted to experience *Follies*, would have cared whether the LDN was dead or alive, or would even have heard of it?

I returned to *Follies*, on the last night, having paid for a ticket. I spent much of the evening in tears. The show was as wonderful as on the first night.

# XXVI

On my first night in London in 1962, the novelist, raconteur and jazz fancier Roland Gant (who died in March 1993), was editorial director at Secker & Warburg. Having met me once previously in Edinburgh, he took a paternal interest in me, and invited me to dinner at the Garrick Club. From that evening I aspired to become a member. The room in which we dined, with the long table down the middle around which sat members without guests, and the smaller tables on either side where members could entertain guests, all dominated by the grandest collection of theatre paintings anywhere, the chandeliers and the twinkling candles on every table, made London seem a more intriguing place than I'd anticipated. At the table to our left, I immediately identified Hugh Gaitskell, Leader of the Labour Party; at the table to our right was Donald Wolfit, whose towering King Lear had awed me at the King's Theatre in Edinburgh some years before. And Roland seemed to be on first name terms with everybody. The evening was not in any way diminished, rather the contrary, by my being sick on the walk home to my bedsitter in Bloomsbury. Too much Garrick claret, and I shouldn't have had that cigar which the hospitable Roland pressed upon me.

In succeeding years, I always experienced a frisson of delight on the infrequent occasions when an author or publisher invited me to lunch at the Garrick. The atmosphere was different from any I had experienced elsewhere, and I thrilled to the theatrical and literary associations.

When at Gollancz, I published rather an important book (and being important it didn't sell), *The Punitive Obsession*, an argument against prison and a rational, eloquent plea for prison reform, by Giles Playfair, whose father was Nigel Playfair, the man who revolutionised theatre production at the Lyric, Hammersmith, in the thirties. He took me to lunch at the Garrick on his publication day, although it would have been more to the point if I'd taken him. Perhaps he realised even then that the modest advance against royalties would never be earned. 'Have you ever thought of becoming a member here?' he asked. I confessed that it had been a pipe dream of mine since that evening with Roland Gant. 'I'll put you up,' said Playfair. We talked a bit about who might second me, and I mentioned a number of publishers and writer members. 'I'll put your name in the book,' said Playfair, 'and we can decide upon a seconder later.'

The waiting list at the time meant that it was five or six years before a name came up, subject to how quickly members popped off, the Club's rules limiting the membership to 900. (It's now slightly more.) The waiting time was to grow to eleven or twelve years by the late eighties. In future, perhaps members will be proposed at birth. Some months later Playfair and his wife invited my wife and me to dinner. To my alarm we found on arrival that the other guests were Peregrine Worsthorne and his wife. Being an ardent Leftie in those days, or so I liked to think, I doubted whether I could cope with one of the high priests of Conservatism. I cannot recall much about the evening, but I'm sure it was amusing and cultivated. Worsthorne was courtesy itself, and his wife most jolly.

A few days later Playfair wrote to me at my office, something about the sales of *The Punitive Obsession*, I expect, adding at the end of his note, 'By the way, Perry's agreed to second you for the Garrick.' I thought this remarkably decent of him. As he had only met me on the one occasion, he clearly was doing Playfair a favour.

Years passed, and I almost forgot the Garrick. (Oh no, I didn't.) In 1972 I left Gollancz and ceased to be a publisher when I joined Anthony Sheil and became a literary agent. One day Playfair, for whom I was acting as agent, telephoned me at home to say that my name was on the list of potential candidates to be considered for membership at the following month's committee meeting. He needed me to provide him with some biographical particulars, which of course I supplied by return. A few weeks later he telephoned again, to say he was sorry but the committee had received two letters objecting to my candidature. I was stunned. If, at the time, I had one remaining ambition, trivial though it may seem, it was to become a member of the Garrick. 'Well, that's that,' I said, trying to shrug it off, and pulling myself together sufficiently to tell Playfair how sorry I was that, albeit inadvertently, I had caused him embarrassment. He said that he was not embarrassed at all, and that one of two things could happen: either he, as my proposer, could withdraw my name from the list, or he could allow it to remain there with the almost certain result that I would be blackballed. 'Which would be the better course?' I stammered. 'I really don't know,' he said. 'The last person I proposed was Bernard Levin and he was blackballed.' Levin was infamously blackballed from the Club, no doubt by some judicial members; he had written a coruscating article about the 'hanging' Lord Goddard soon after the Lord Chief Justice's death, which also accused the legal profession of hypocrisy in declaring in obituaries what a wise and learned judge Goddard had been. I was content to pass the way Levin had gone, and suggested to Playfair that I be blackballed, or rather allow my candidature to go forward.

Three or four nights later, he telephoned again. 'It's absolutely astonishing,' he said. 'You've been elected. The two members who had written letters to the committee objecting to you decided not to go through with the blackball.' It was all most mysterious. Years later I discovered who the objectors had been. They were both, as I might have surmised, publishers. One was Hamish (Jamie) Hamilton, who felt unequivocally that agents, who presumably were trade and therefore to be seated below the salt, should not be eligible for membership of his club, which housed quite a few publishers. This was surprising if only because Hamilton, whom I hardly knew (although he once offered me a job which I decided not to take; maybe he held that against me), invited me to the Christmas party for agents and authors which he gave at his house in St John's Wood each year, and more than once I went. Trade's all right in your home, once a year, I suppose, even if you have to grit your teeth, but not in your Club.

The other objector was my erstwhile boss at Hutchinson, Sir Robert Lusty, whose objection, I gathered, was much the same as

Hamilton's, that if agents were allowed into the Garrick they'd insist on talking business at lunch. To which I had to respond: British publishing might be in a healthier state than it was if *publishers* could bring themselves to discuss business at lunch – but not, of course, at the Garrick, whose rules forbid business to be conducted on the premises and which has charitable status. Bob Lusty, a publisher of whom I could never see the point (he'd have been in good company were he practising his skills today), described me, a committee member later informed me, as 'the thin edge of the wedge. If we allowed Gordon in, we'd be opening a floodgate to agents.' I had not, as far as I knew, previously been described by anyone as the thin edge of any wedge. I think I was flattered. I believe I was admitted formally to membership of the Garrick not as a literary agent but as a writer and editor, and so, I gather, were the agents elected after me, Michael Sissons, Hilary Rubinstein and Rivers Scott. Mike Shaw of Curtis Brown became a member in 1990, by which time it must have been respectable, or respectable enough, to be an agent.

The publisher Liz Calder has always scolded me for joining the Garrick because there are no women members. Yet she was, I think, sufficiently frustrated at not being eligible for membership that, with a few others, she was instrumental in setting up the Groucho, a club of a somewhat different sort. On the other hand, Carmen Callil, another founder member of the Groucho and creator of Virago, loved going to lunch at the Garrick, and to dinner. Women may lunch there but not in the members' main dining-room. In the evening they may dine or have supper after the theatre (or whatever) in any of the main dining-rooms.

I'm sure it is only a matter of time until women become members. Strictly speaking, they are eligible for membership now, but in practice they would not be elected. Occasionally gossip columnists, raking through old files, come on a press-cutting which asserts that one or two other members and I were 'leading' a campaign to have women admitted. I have never done any such thing, nor am I aware of such a campaign. Once a story has appeared in the press, even if it is wholly inaccurate, it's impossible to persuade journalists who want to embellish it later that there was not an iota of truth in it originally, and nor is there now. The

Garrick's AGM in 1992 voted on the matter of whether to admit women and by a substantial majority decided against.

Garrick stories are legion, if only because so many members are beguiling storytellers. My favourite concerns Donald Sinden, who was showing a party of American art historians round the Club one evening, pointing out in particular the paintings. Sinden paused dramatically outside the dining-room, and raised an eyebrow to whet the Americans' appetite. 'The Zoffanys are in here,' he said proudly. 'Oh well, in that case we'd better not go in,' said the leader of the art historians' delegation. 'We don't want to disturb them at dinner.'

I was once waiting at the Garrick in the small open room off the hallway, for my lunch guest, and idly reading the *Evening Standard*. Three or four other members were chatting to each other in the room. Lord Longford wandered in, and nodded genially to everyone. After a minute or two, seeing I was trying to concentrate on the newspaper, he addressed the group of members. 'I expect you'd disapprove of my guest today,' he said. The men stopped chatting, and turned politely towards Longford. 'Oh, I'm sure we wouldn't,' said one of them, laughing. This was not the kind of remark regularly made at the Garrick. 'I think you would,' the Labour peer persisted. 'He's black, you see.' The men made some fumbling remarks – what else could they do? – to the effect that even if Longford's guest were green they would not object nor would it be any of their business, but it was an extraordinary performance by the ex-leader of the Government in the Lords. Perhaps he was just lonely, and wanted some conversation.

On another occasion, when our agency's offices were just off Bedford Square, I went to have lunch at Pizza Express in Coptic Street, after decades still the best pizza restaurant in London. It was latish, probably past two o'clock, and the place was emptying. Lord Longford at the time was chairman of publishers Sidgwick & Jackson, whose offices were just round the corner next to St George's Church, in a seedy-looking, crumbling building which made Gollancz's former banana warehouse in Henrietta Street seem palatial. He shambled into the restaurant and sat down at a table on his own. After a minute or two he got up and wandered across to a table at which a young woman was eating alone and reading a magazine. 'Good afternoon,' he said. 'Do you eat here often?' Looking alarmed, and without responding, she picked up her plate of pizza and hurried to another table.

Another Garrick member is the actor Derek Bond, a most affable fellow born in 1920. He is tall and a bit red-faced, as if somewhat broiled. He looks preserved, if not in aspic, in after-shave, and is invariably turned out like an older male model, most natty. He apparently missed the Garrick votes-for-women AGM because he was at home babysitting. I respected that. When I was young he was forever visiting Edinburgh in Agatha Christie plays, usually playing the lead. He walks stiffly, like a marionette, as a number of tall older men do. I do not mean he is arthritic, or anything of the sort; his walk is closer to that of a Guards officer. I remember being moved to tears when we were taken from school to see the film *Scott of the Antarctic* (1948), a movie I always confuse in my mind with *The Conquest of Everest*, which we saw at the Roxy cinema in Inverleith in a double bill with the film of the coronation of Queen Elizabeth II. The heartbreaking moment in the Antarctic film was Derek Bond as Captain Oates saying, 'I am just going outside and may be some time,' then crunching his way through the tent flap and into foul weather and history. Whenever I find myself in conversation with Derek Bond, he will always manage early in the chat to insert a sentence which begins: 'When I played Captain Oates . . .'

It was, of course, that famous Fellow (of the Royal Society of Literature), James Morris, who as a young journalist reported the conquest of Everest on the front page of *The Times* a few days before the Queen's coronation. Some time in the early eighties, the American publishers Doubleday, who had an office in Wigmore Street, threw a party for one of their editors, visiting from the Big Apple. I was there only briefly, since I had to rush off to a first night. The Doubleday offices were on the second floor of the building. I must have been feeling tired, because I waited for the lift to descend rather than walk the two brief flights. As I waited for the lift, three people joined me. One was the agent George Greenfield, and we greeted one another. I had hardly seen him since the George Brown days. 'Shall we walk?' he said to the elderly couple with him. 'By the way, Giles; do you know Sir Edmund and Lady Hillary?' Very Greenfield, that.

Why, as a man grows older, does he tend to move politically from the Left to the Right? I say 'tend' because some young men seem to have been born Tory, and proceed through their lives without a hint of social rebellion or doubt. Women appear much less immune to this rightward march, mainly, I think, because they are less hysterical about politics, being more sensible and pragmatic by nature. The progression from Left to Right except among fire-brands and freethinkers would seem to suggest that Right is right and Left is wrong, as in his or her maturity a person's thinking and opinions are likely to be based on the learning, even the wisdom, of a lifetime or a substantial part of it.

This, surely, is the opposite of the truth. In his or her giddy youth, a person is open to experience, and more or less lacking in prejudice. He takes things, people, events as they come, without much preconception, without built-in judgement and censorship. If he has – and heaven help him if he hasn't – a keen sense of humour, of the ridiculous, he should survive with brio and scepti-cism intact. Most things in life are ridiculous, starting with concep-tion and birth. It's all very odd. If babies come that way, and we know they do, shooting out of their mothers' bodies like slippery salmon, why then it's hard to take anything subsequent to birth too seriously. Yet we are required to make the effort, for much of our lives, to keep a straight face, as otherwise how would we find life's adventure or drudgery (depending on our persona and Jonsonian humours) bearable? Without a strong sense of humour with which to confront the daily grind, the moral ambivalence of 'reality', we should surely go mad.

Has – and I pick their names pretty much, but not entirely, at random – Enoch Powell or Max Hastings, the editor of the *Daily Telegraph*, a sense of humour? I would suspect not, and if I am correct it explains much about their public stances on divers topics. Yet, no doubt, they and their friends and families would assert that both gentlemen possess highly developed senses of humour, albeit perhaps sly and subversive. If I say that I did not find Benny Hill funny but think that Frankie Howerd was a hoot, which is the case, would I be regarded by Benny Hill aficionados as humourless? For nothing is more subjective than humour. You can pass examinations in Latin and Mathematics and Electronics and even English ('Which is the funnier novelist, P. G. Wodehouse or Evelyn Waugh? Discuss') but who would dare mark a Humour examination paper? You may believe that you have an awesome, all-embracing sense of humour and still find, as I have always done, that Charlie Chaplin is seriously unamusing. Humour dates. (Do not tell me you find Aristophanes a laugh a line.) Although it is difficult these days to find many who revere or idolise Chaplin (I'm a Buster Keaton man myself), during his lifetime he obviously came across as a kind of genius.

One of the superficially oddest progressions from Left to Right has been that of Sir Kingsley Amis, the quaintly named novelist, poet, critic and memorialist. Why do some people seem to need to change their political or social stance, and need to be seen to do it? Most do it quietly if not necessarily subtly, or subversively. My eighteen-year-old daughter, for instance, told a canvasser that the way she was going to vote in the 1992 general election was none of his business, nor of anyone else's. Perhaps this explains why Labour lost that election. Old Kingers, the toast of the old soaks at the bar of the Garrick Club, scourge of Lefties and pooftahs, is amused to do it publicly. His public persona, culti-vated entirely by himself, is so disagreeable that he becomes almost likeable. He is a kind of walking – waddling and shuffling, rather – fossil encrusted with experience and prejudice, a besmirched schoolboy swot perceptively refusing to accept that he really should grow up (he was born in 1922), or that the world's sup-posed to be a serious place. That's why we have bankers and businessmen and scientists. For if we do not take the world seriously, our working and living lives, our little triumphs and tragedies, our breeding of the next generation (the novelist Kings-ley begat the novelist Martin: wait for the grandson's first novel; this is not, surely, what Dr Leavis meant by the Great Tradition), how can we manage other than through laughter? Yet you cannot laugh all the time, or humourless men in white coats will man-handle you off to the funny farm, where, of course, nobody laughs.

The same question may be asked of Kingsley Amis as is sometimes asked of the Queen: what is this person for? His 1990 novel,
*The Folks that Live on the Hill*, is partly set in a gentlemen's club,
the Irving, 'just around the corner from the Garrick'. Patricia
Miller, the American literary editor of the London *Evening Standard* at that time, had the bright journalistic idea (and that is what
editors on newspapers are meant to have) of asking an Irving –
that is, Garrick – Club member to review the book. I imagine she
must have been turned down by some eminent author members,
because I was invited to have a go and, being a man who's more
inclined to say yes than no to almost anything, I foolishly agreed.
Unfortunately, my review began: 'I have failed to finish more
novels by Kingsley Amis than by any other living novelist.' You
will understand that, *Lucky Jim* apart, I am not a relisher of the
Amis *œuvre*, but I'm sure he can live with that.

My review of *The Folks that Live on the Hill* was scheduled to
appear on the day the novel was published, 29 March 1990. I was
somewhat thrown to see from my diary that I was to have lunch
that day at the Garrick with a very old friend (I mean that he had
been a friend for three decades, not that he was decrepit), Euan
Cameron, who had recently become a member. The Club takes
delivery of two or three copies of the day's *Standard*, so that it's
available on the premises for members to peruse at lunchtime. I
did not want to run into Amis within minutes of his reading my
review, the novel's first in a newspaper. Although Amis once
famously said that a bad review may spoil your breakfast, but you
shouldn't allow it to spoil your lunch, this was presumably on the
assumption that the review had appeared in a morning newspaper.
I didn't flatter myself that Amis would have bothered to read the
review himself, but I was certain that some member would have
drawn his attention to it. 'A stinker for your new one in the
*Standard*, Kingsley. The chap's obviously a shit. Member of the
Club too.' Then I reassured myself that the one day of the year
when Amis wouldn't be at the Club at lunchtime was his publication day, that Messrs Hutchinson would be wining and dining
or, perhaps more precisely given his penchant for malt whisky,
spiritualising him.

When I arrived at the bar, Euan Cameron was already there. I told him, with my usual relish for self-dramatisation and insistence, by nuance and innuendo, that the world revolves around me, of my baseless anxiety about encountering Amis. 'Don't look now,' said Euan, 'but Amis is here, and standing immediately behind you. I think he could be looking at you.' '*Could* be looking at you' is very Euan; he's not a man given to overstatement. We went down to lunch, and sat next to each other at two of the few remaining places at the long table. I remained nervous of a confrontation with Amis, rather childishly. 'Don't look now,' said Euan once again, 'but Kingsley and three of his cronies are standing in the doorway, looking for places to sit, and there are only three empty places around the table, and they are immediately opposite us.' If Amis sat down opposite us, I knew I'd pass out. I didn't in any circumstances want him to spoil my lunch, although, insensitively, I hadn't given a thought to his. Amis and his companions departed from the dining-room, not having ventured further in. Perhaps they hadn't liked the company they would have had to keep.

Ten minutes or so later Euan, all eyes that day, told me that Amis and his chums had reappeared, and they'd gone to sit at one of the two smaller tables for members, placed at each end of the long table. This was the table where Sir Robin Day regularly used to hold noisy and bombastic court, unless Lord Rees-Mogg was there, when lunch seemed to be eaten more politely. Milton Shulman, a newish member, seemed naturally to gravitate to that table of higher journalism. I relaxed, and Euan and I ordered coffee. After a while, Euan said: 'Kingsley Amis is trying to attract your attention.' I thought this most improbable, and deliberately kept averting my eyes from the old devil. Euan repeated his remark, as if he were in league with Lucky Jim to persuade me to meet his gaze, and charily I peered across the dining-room. Amis was sitting there, his back to the wall, grinning manically at me and stabbing two fingers in the air, over and over again, jerking his arm up, an unmistakable V sign, and not of the Churchill variety.

Garrick Club stories, which must not be told outside the confines of the august Club, are legion. Here are a few. One of the more eccentric, more complicated men I know (I act as his literary agent and am fond of him) is George Bull. For years he was editor-in-chief (a more fitting title for George than mere editor, which he was before; not that the later job seemed any different from the earlier) of *The Director*, the self-serving and anodyne glossy monthly of the Institute of Directors. Bull (known inevitably as Papal Bull) is one of the country's leading Roman Catholic laymen (whatever *that* means) and was always slipping away to interview Graham Greene and Shusaku Endo, both novelists of the Roman Catholic liberal establishment. Greene, a one-time journalist with moralistic overtones and a sense of guilt, made to pose as an artist by his middle-brow readers, is ludicrously overrated, because his novels are not as straightforward and as accessible as Agatha Christie's. Endo I haven't read, either in Japanese or in translation into English.

George Bull, arguably the fourth most messy typist in the history of the world, translates Italian classics for Penguin, notably Machiavelli. Once, standing at the bar of the Garrick at lunchtime, he said to me, 'Do you see that man?' directing his gaze at a capacious pin-striped back. I nodded. 'And that man,' indicating another. 'And that man,' pointing to a third. He paused, then, *sotto voce*, as if God had joined us, confided: 'They don't know it but I've written their obituaries for *The Times*.' George provides obituaries of businessmen and industrialists for the one-time 'Thunderer', and clearly derives a kick from the sense of power this brings him, of enhancing or diminishing the reputations of men still alive while those same men shall not know what the newspaper of record will say about them until they aren't around to read it.

The best George Bull story tells of how, early one evening, he went to the Club for a drink or two and found himself conversing with a tall, handsome man. George identified the man's accent. (On one level George always seems somewhat abstracted, as if he is communicating with extra-terrestrial beings.) 'I think you're an American friend,' said Bull. The man admitted that he was, and George asked him where he came from. 'California,' was the answer. 'Do you ever go to New York?' George asked. The man admitted he did. 'I stay at the Travellers' Club,' said George. 'Where do you stay?' 'The Pierre,' the American replied, naming one of New York's most exclusive hotels. 'Are you in our country on holiday?' George gently enquired. 'No,' the man smiled, 'I'm working over here.' 'Ah,' said George, 'how interesting. What sort of work do you do?' 'I work mostly in the evenings,' said the American. 'That's *very* interesting,' said George, his mind presumably elsewhere, in Renaissance Florence or Venice perhaps. 'In fact,' said the man, looking at his watch, 'I've got to work this evening and really ought to be getting along.' 'Do tell me your name, and what line of work you do, so that I'll know who you are the next time we meet.' Being a good Catholic and a gregarious clubman, George assumed that people kept meeting one another, presumably at the great convocation in the sky if not in the bar of the Garrick Club or elsewhere on the planet. 'I'm an actor,' said the man. 'My name is Charlton Heston.' (Or did he say 'Chuck'? Or could George have got the wrong actor?)

On another occasion George Bull and his wife attended the party my wife and I gave in May 1990 at our home in London (no, we don't have more than one home) to celebrate our wedding in Glasgow the month before. Martin Seymour-Smith, the deranged-looking bearded sage of Bexhill-on-Sea and, I insist, the most learned literary critic in the UK, was also there. I introduced them, in some desperation it has to be admitted, because Martin kept falling into the flowerbeds. We have a small garden and it's mostly paved. 'Martin Seymour-Smith,' said George, 'I haven't seen you since Oxford. You were at Brasenose. 'No,' said Martin, 'you were. I was at Keble.'

I wouldn't be surprised to discover that George worked for MI5. There is even more going on in that mind than meets the eye.

For years he thought that David Hughes, at Oxford with him but *not* a member of the Garrick, and I had no grasp of the practical life of business and money, which in David's case cannot be true as he married a well-off wife. David, with whom I have since 1986 co-edited Heinemann's annual *Best Short Stories* anthology, has written a number of distinguished novels, not least *The Pork Butcher* (1984), which won him the genuinely prestigious W. H. Smith Literary Award. The novel, about the German destruction of the French village of Oradour-sur-Glane (renamed Lascaud-sur-Marne in the novel) in retaliation for the killing of a

German soldier, is a minor masterpiece of prose fiction. The villagers are herded together in the village church and locked in. The church is then torched, the villagers burned to death. The film rights were acquired and, after the usual chaos, artistic and financial, of the neurotic, narcissistic film world, a movie was made. Mercifully, but confusingly, the title was changed, the film being called *Souvenir*. It was made, as most films are, on what the film world regards as a low budget, so much so that the same four or five extras seemed to essay, without even changing their stuck-on moustaches, the entire German garrison of Oradour. David invited me to accompany him to a preview on a summer Sunday at the Curzon Cinema on Shaftesbury Avenue. Christopher Plummer played the eponymous (if we stick to the title of the novel) ex-Nazi pork butcher from Lübeck who, with his grown-up daughter, returns to the French village forty years on, expecting somehow to be greeted with open arms and tears of welcome.

At the Sunday preview, intended mainly for friends and relatives of the actors and technicians, I was aware that David, sitting next to me, had begun snivelling and even snorting, and was wiping his eyes. I nearly joined in, being one who weeps easily, especially when others weep (Ralph Richardson, crying on stage in Robert Bolt's *Flowering Cherry* in 1958 when the character he was playing proved not to have the strength to bend a poker, immediately reduced me to tears, yet only now, as I write, have I understood that his tears were artistry, mine genuine), so affected was I that David was moved by witnessing his novel translated to the screen.

As we walked out of the cinema, blinking in the summer light, David made it clear that he wanted to get away as soon as possible without having to encounter and congratulate the gushing and self-congratulating film makers. 'Darling, you were *wonderful*.' 'Don't *mention* it, darling.' I continued to be moved by how moved David was, particularly as I had thought the film banal, crass, unsubtle and unsophisticated, whereas the novel was the opposite of all of that. 'That was terrible, terrible,' whispered David, who had another life as a film critic. That was all he would say. He was crying because he'd seen his lovingly crafted novel destroyed.

David is a mighty luncher, possibly the last author of the breed.

He contrives to convey the impression, and more or less succeeds, that his literary progress is enhanced by an almost religious lunching activity rather than as a consequence held back, and this is reassuring to others like myself who enjoy a stylish lunch – the venue, the menu, the wine list (no Perrier or other water, not if you can help it), your fellow luncher, your fellow guests – while feeling guilty about all the work to be done back at the office. (Somehow you rationalise this by starting early in the morning and by staying late in the evening, quite possibly not in a state to achieve much of a constructive nature.) My wife tells me that this is Presbyterian guilt.

David and I have three lunches every year, in November, December and January, the months during which we wrestle with *Best Short Stories*. The November lunch takes place at the Garrick Club, and I pay, as David is not a member. Nevertheless, he eats there so frequently and has so many member friends that some of the staff greet him as the member and me as the guest, even presenting him with the priced menu and me with the priceless one intended for guests. Maybe one year David will order sausages and mash. The second lunch takes place at Café Fish in Cranbourn Street off Leicester Square, where the chef presents his compliments to you with a little fish (what else?) pâté before you order, thus giving the impression – which is pleasing to a Scotsman, even though a Welshman pays for this lunch – that you get summat for nowt. At the end of lunch, each December in Café Fish, we decide that, on the advance Heinemann pays us, we cannot afford to eat at Café Fish again, yet every year we return. The final lunch, in January, happens at Bertorelli's in Floral Street, not of course to be confused with Bertorelli's in Charlotte Street, which is no longer Bertorelli's.

At the first lunch we discuss editorial approach – more Irish or Blacks this year, and what about the Caribbean? Are we monitoring their magazines sufficiently? Are we monitoring their magazines at all? More seriously, are we *reading* their magazines? How can we keep William Trevor out with a mediocre, by his standards, story when his worst is inevitably better than more or less anybody else's best? What about that man who year in, year out *submits* about twenty stories, all published in magazines none of which anybody has heard of or reads? Why are women better short story writers (novelists too, for that matter) than men, whatever their colour or sex? Ah, the cut and thrust of editorial decision-making, of prejudice, passion, discrimination and taste!

At the second lunch we exchange stories, each of us by then having read dozens, scores. We hand over, too, lists of our likes and dislikes, highly libellous notes, putting down the famous and raising up the young and unknown. At the third lunch, each of us having read everything, we do not arise and go until we've made our final choice for the year's volume or Messrs Bertorelli's delightful middle-aged waitresses show us the door.

The best lunch I've had with David, though, took place on Monday 16 September 1985 in Boulogne. He wrote a novel, at my suggestion, called *But for Bunter* in which the narrator, Frank Richards' Fat Owl of the Remove at Greyfriars School, in his declining years presents his version of twentieth-century history. It wasn't, for instance, Winston Churchill (another portly owl of the Remove) who won the war but Billy Bunter himself; and so on. Bunter, older readers may recollect, was a prodigious eater, waiting for the next tuck box to arrive from home. David Hughes, however, is infinitely more gourmet than gourmand, as well as being charm and gentlemanly conduct personified. He persuaded Susan Boyd, wife of the lightly satirical novelist William Boyd and at the time Heinemann's publicity director, to blow the entire publicity budget for the book (in truth, there probably wasn't one) on transporting the five dedicatees of the novel (the Famous Five, another Bunteresque joke) to France for lunch. The dedicatees are Jeremy Bullmore, David's wine merchant and a fundamental figure in the novelist's life; Godfrey Smith, novelist and sophisticated columnist on the *Sunday Times*; Miles Huddleston, David's erstwhile publisher at Constable; actor Michael Gough; and myself, David's literary agent. Messrs Bullmore and Smith were otherwise engaged and couldn't be present. The remaining three of us, together with David's endlessly patient and long-suffering wife, Elizabeth (each year she reads the proofs of *Best Short Stories*), publisher David Godwin, Susan Boyd and, of course, David himself, boarded an almost empty early morning ferry at Dover and presented ourselves, shortly before 1 p.m., at La Matelote restaurant on the keyside at Boulogne.

We had what Bunter would have described as a memorable meal at the one-star Michelin establishment, and only just completed the eating and drinking in time to catch the ferry back to Dover four hours later. The sole item of publicity resulting from our gourmandising was a paragraph or three in the Londoner's Diary of the *Evening Standard* which commemorated the meal (what publishers are reduced to in the attempt to sell books which, frequently, people don't want) and those present. Poor Micky Gough had palpitations at the inclusion of his name in the middle of making a film for Sam Spiegel or Otto Preminger, or some other Hollywood mogul. Although he had leave of absence from the set for the day, his contract with the film company did not allow him to leave the country before his performance was finally in the can – he might have been captured by brigands, or even French farmers – and shooting of the entire film might have had to start again from the beginning. Why he was regarded as at more risk abroad than at home is not clear: in Britain he might, say, have broken a leg or, heaven forbid, been blown up by the IRA. Anyway, Michael Gough survived to complete the film, and if anyone connected with the movie read the piece in the *Standard* nothing was said about it.

# XXVII

Some time in 1982 at the bar of the Garrick Club (where else, except perhaps Lord's or even the Army and Navy Club; not that I am a member of either institution), the publisher Leo Cooper asked me if, as literary agent, I'd be interested in representing the Tory MP Patrick Cormack, whose *Westminster: Palace and Parliament* Cooper had published at Warne. Not having heard of Cormack (whose constituency was Staffordshire South-West before it became Staffordshire South) or of his book, I said that I doubted it. 'You should,' said Cooper, a genial man of a magnanimous disposition, 'if only because he has . . .' Cooper surveyed the bar, whether to ensure that his remark was overheard or not heard I can only speculate, '. . . the Speaker's memoirs in his giving.'

Soon afterwards I met Cormack and rapidly agreed to become his agent, and shortly after that I became George Thomas's agent. 'You're a good boy, Giles,' the Welsh Speaker would pronounce, patting me on the knee. I do not know how the relationship between the two parliamentarians, from opposite sides of the House, came about – perhaps through parliamentary prayer meetings as both are staunch (and that has to be the word) Christians – but George Thomas is godfather to Mary and Patrick Cormack's two sons. The godfather, in the presence of the boys, was always referred to as 'Uncle George'.

Viscount Tonypandy, as he was to become in 1983 upon retirement from the Speakership of the House of Commons, was a man, and a Welshman, who liked to be liked, and thus seemed not inclined to say no. As he explained to me, circuitously, he had promised at least three publishers his memoirs, and there was a degree of resentment among them (what parasites agents are) –

though none knew of the others – when I appeared on the scene. George Thomas, still in the chair of the Commons, made it plain that I should tread warily, and understand that there was no question of his signing a contract until he'd ceased to be Mr Speaker. Nevertheless, he made it clear, cutting through the nitty-gritty (and it's surprising that the nitty-gritty is nearly always cut through in such instances) that he would sign up with the publisher who made him the best offer, since, naturally, the book would mean most to that publisher. Why had I never thought of that?

I spoke to all the publishers who had expressed interest direct to George, and to two or three others. I tried for some weeks to track down George Weidenfeld, who liked to publish political memoirs. Eventually we agreed to meet in a greasy spoon café in Floral Street, when George was either on his way to or emerging from a board meeting at the Royal Opera House. By way of encouragement, I even paid for his lordship's tea, not something agents do regularly when with publishers. Weidenfeld perused the outline and shook his head. 'Giles, my friend,' he said, exuding great frankness, 'do not have anything to do with this book. George Thomas is a very boring man. I know him a little from the Lords.' And he shook me by the hand and was on his way to his next mighty meeting. That was one book that got away from Weidenfeld & Nicolson.

One afternoon I found myself waiting to cross Tottenham Court Road when I espied Anthony Cheetham, then head of Century, Hutchinson and Arrow, standing close by. I asked him if he'd be interested in Thomas's memoirs. He was, and we more or less made a deal on the kerb. The fortuitous or at least unforeseen is often the best way forward in the book trade. By chance, much later Anthony Cheetham ended up buying George Weidenfeld's firm.

When *George Thomas, Mr Speaker* was published in 1985, it was – and no one was more surprised than I, who had lived too long with the idea and a lack of the text – a significant bestseller, largely thanks to Thomas's radio following, but in no small part because Michael Foot and Lord (as he had become) Callaghan wrote to the editor of *The Times*, remonstrating about disclosures made in the book's pages.

Before he became an MP, Thomas was a schoolmaster in Cardiff. He taught another client of mine, the poet Dannie Abse, who should, upon the death of John Betjeman, have been appointed the first Welsh Jewish Poet Laureate. Dannie's brother Leo was a fellow Cardiff MP with George Thomas (as was Jim Callaghan), although Thomas had entered Parliament eight years earlier. Way back in 1950, when Dannie wanted to marry his non-Jewish sweetheart, Joan, he pondered as to who might be the person to persuade his parents, they being set on his marrying a nice Jewish girl, not to say a nice Welsh Jewish girl. Dannie thought his primary school teacher Mr Thomas might, given his gift of the gab in the Principality where everyone harboured the gift of the gab, be the person to persuade his mum and dad. George Thomas pleaded young Dannie's case to Rudolph and Kate Abse, and Dannie is not only still married to Joan but they have a splendid son and two magnificent daughters and are wonderful grandparents, and it's as happy a marriage as the world could imagine.

Once I took George Thomas to the Garrick for lunch. It was the only time I witnessed the squint-eyed wine waiter, Sidney Powell, become overexcited. He bustled to my table as we were sitting down, and congratulated George on his recently bestowed viscountcy. 'Congratulations, my Lord,' said Sidney with the degree of sycophancy that his lordship enjoyed. The peer and the waiter then chatted strenuously about the town of Tonypandy, and discussed knowingly the progress through life of various Joneses and Davieses. Sidney hadn't previously boasted of his Tonypandy background.

I do not know if it was as a result of this lunch or not, but Thomas decided he'd like to join the Garrick. Some distinguished member offered to put him up, and another to second him. I think he genuinely assumed that he was thus already a member, and might as well book a table for lunch the next day. When he learned that the waiting list was, at that time, about eleven years, he reared like a whinnying horse and immediately joined the Athenaeum. (He must subsequently have resigned from it as *Who's Who* lists his clubs as the Travellers', the Reform, the English-Speaking

Union, the United Oxford and Cambridge University, and the County, Cardiff).

On another occasion he took me to lunch at the Athenaeum. In the course of the meal, amidst the general silence of distinguished men chomping away and discussing matters of pith and marrow, he demanded in stentorian tones to see the head waiter. 'This lamb chop is pink,' he pronounced dramatically. The waiter looked puzzled. 'No one can eat it that way. It's raw.' The head waiter, Uriah Heep of the moment, cringed and fawned. 'Fancy serving a lamb chop like that,' said Tonypandy, when the offending object had been dispatched back to the kitchen. When it reappeared, it resembled a cinder. George smiled all over his face. 'That's better,' he said; and to the waiter, 'You didn't mind, did you? That's a good boy.' He consumed the charred object with relish.

When he was Mr Speaker, he liked to have people to dinner in his wood-panelled Victorian flat in the Palace of Westminster. It was a gloomy place, like a set for *Ruddigore*, with a splendid view across the Thames. George's beloved mother had died shortly before he was elected Speaker, and that was a great sorrow to him. As a bachelor, living on his own in that gaunt flat, and being as garrulous as he was, he would have been lonely had he not constantly been entertaining guests. The evening meal was taken early so that Mr Speaker could be back in his chair in the Commons for the division when the House was sitting at 10 p.m.

My wife and I were invited to a meal at Speaker's House, as the flat was grandly called, in April 1982. The evening coincided with the war in the Falklands – it was, I think, the night before the *Belgrano* was hit – and dinner was consumed even more quickly than usual so that Mr Speaker could watch the television news before descending to the Chamber. The only other guests were a Tory MP and his wife.

We settled down around the television set in the living-room, and listened to the Ministry of Defence spokesman, Ian Macdonald of the robotic voice, sonorously reporting on the day's unfortunate events. The wife of a naval rating who had been injured in the conflict was then shown, tearfully insisting that her husband had joined the navy not to be slaughtered but to see the world. My

wife expressed sadness on her behalf. The Tory MP expostulated
that it was outrageous, and singularly unpatriotic, of the TV net-
work, at this time of war, to allow a woman like that to make
those sort of remarks. The widow of a naval officer was shown
next, very stiff upper lip, saying in effect that she was heartbroken
that her husband had been killed, but that sort of thing was likely
to happen when a country went to war and she was proud that
he'd done his duty. The Tory MP purred with pride, and my wife
sniffed her contempt and said how much she disagreed. Mr
Speaker patted her on her knee and said, 'My dear, you don't
argue with an MP when you're in my house.' I could never
bring myself to forgive George Thomas for this quite unnecessary
rudeness, and I was not invited to dinner again, although I'd been
a frequent guest before. George never subsequently asked after
my wife.

He is, it seems to me, a decent if vain man from the 'humblest'
of backgrounds, beguiled throughout his career by the blandish-
ments of the Establishment. Even in his declining years, after two
major operations for cancer, he remained as sharp as a needle.
When his second book, *My Wales*, with photographs by Lord
Snowdon (how George appreciated that), was published, Century
Hutchinson gave a reception at Cardiff Castle, followed by a
dinner for Welsh booksellers. At midnight George whispered to
me that he'd have to leave as he was obliged to be up early the
next morning for a television interview. 'What is the name of our
host?' he asked to be reminded, gesturing towards the publishers'
young sales director down the table. 'Dallas Manderson,' I replied.
'Lucky his parents didn't christen him EastEnders,' responded
George, quick as a flash.

It is quite clear from his memoirs what he felt about the conflict
in the Falklands:

Britain would have lost all influence in international affairs if
Mrs Thatcher had submitted to the pressures and gone back to
the United Nations. It would have meant that never again would
Britain take any decisive action to defend her people . . . by her
action she saved the good name of Britain.

The whole exercise showed that British youth, who never

thought they would have to do that sort of thing again, could respond magnificently to the challenge. The Falklands affair reinforced my belief that the British character has not really changed, despite all the troubles that we face with violence and sometimes appallingly selfish behaviour. We are still a tough little race, and now the world knows it.

*George Thomas, Mr Speaker* sold extremely well, Tonypandy being a much-loved character. His successor in the chair, Bernard Weatherill, had said from the beginning of his Speakership that he wouldn't write his memoirs. Nevertheless, when he resigned in early 1992, I couldn't resist trying to corral him. He replied.

You may know that, shortly after I became Speaker, I told the House that, unlike my predecessor, I did not propose to write my memoirs. The result of that is virtually everything that happened in the Chamber *and* outside the Chamber was disclosed to me in confidence. I hope, therefore, you will understand why I propose to honour the pledge which I gave in 1983.

Within weeks of Betty Boothroyd having been elected Speaker, the first female Speaker in the history of our Parliament, at least one publisher had written to her enquiring whether he or she could sign up her memoirs. Such is the hunger of publishers for books thought to be saleable.

Roy Hattersley became Deputy Leader of the Labour Party in 1983 and he was, though more sophisticated – a generation on, and university-educated – somewhat in the George Brown mould. I once encountered him at a *Punch* lunch when the dentists' waiting rooms' humorous weekly magazine still lodged in Bouverie Street. Hattersley sat on the editor Alan Coren's left, and I opposite Hattersley on Coren's right. When the meal was nearly completed, the waiters enquired of the twenty-odd lunchers who would like dessert. 'Nice profiteroles. Or fruit. Or cheese?' The only taker, at least of the sweet, was the Deputy Leader of Her Majesty's Opposition. The rest of us chatted noisily, as was the fashion at *Punch* lunches, finished our wine and vaguely waited for the brandy and cigars to be brought, the port to be passed.

Suddenly there was a fascinated silence. Everyone had noticed that Hattersley was tucking into his pudding. Hattersley looked up and down the table. 'If I read in *Private Eye* that Hattersley devoured profiteroles at the last *Punch* lunch . . .' there was a dramatic pause '. . . then I will know that there's an SDP supporter here.'

His remark seemed more threat than good humour, but I suppose it was to his credit for, at the time, the *Eye* reported in almost every issue sightings of Fattersley, as he was known in its pages, at expensive restaurants. It's puzzling that Hattersley, who resigned as Deputy Leader of the Labour Party after Labour's inevitable defeat at the 1992 general election, is regarded as an unattractive man, since he's agreeable, able and intelligent. He's also a useful writer. And why shouldn't the Deputy Leader of the Labour Party, particularly subsequent to the jettisoning of socialism, enjoy his puddings?

Hattersley and Neil Kinnock made an odd pair, destined not to head a much-needed alternative government. Kinnock always seemed like some down-market brand of mottled sausage, long past its sell-by date. I found it impossible to be reconciled to his relentless jolliness and frightful pinched anoraks, a garment which more than any other makes men and women, particularly men, look mediocre and uninteresting. It is the garment, whether an expensive 'designer' version or a cheap 'off the peg' one, which condemns the affluent working class climbing up the snobby social pole or clambering on to a classless bandwaggon to remain irretrievably proletarian. You cannot enjoy Mozart and choose to wear an anorak. This may sound trivial and snide, but clothes are 'important' in so far as they indicate an attitude of mind, an aesthetic style and sensibility.

Something else which must have punctured Kinnock's endeavours to become Prime Minister was the way in which he jerkily stabbed his face forward at the dispatch box in the chamber of the House of Commons when making a speech, as if he were being manipulated from behind like a puppet. But I am convinced that what did for him was something which, in our post-feminist years, should have been his greatest asset. It was the 'Glenys and I' stance, not to be confused with the Queen's 'My Husband and

I'. Mrs Kinnock looks a decent soul and seems intelligent enough, but none of us had occasion to vote for *her* any more than we did for Mrs Thatcher's consort, who, sensibly and invariably, was kept in the background. Whether this was Denis Thatcher's doing or his wife's matters not one whit. Ironically, we all came to appreciate Denis because he remained in the background, vaguely assumed to be providing personal (but not political) support to his wife. Mrs Kinnock always seemed to be pushed forward by her husband.

# XXVIII

In 1958, when I spent two terms studying book design and typography at Edinburgh College of Art, the Edinburgh University literary magazine, *Gambit*, accepted five poems of mine, and they were printed as a double page spread. Almost a decade later, when I was editorial director at Gollancz, a caller was put through whose name was vaguely familiar. It was Michael Shea, who'd been editor of *Gambit* and had been the first to spot me as a potential Poet Laureate. He, in his turn, was now looking for a publisher as he'd written a thriller. I could hardly refuse to read it but, as always in these instances, feared the worst. In fact it wasn't discreditable as a first effort and *Sonntag* by Michael Sinclair did rather well – rather better, I seem to remember, than his subsequent novels. (Because Shea was a diplomat, the book had to be published pseudonymously.) Later, he moved on to become press secretary to the Queen, and was allowed to publish novels under his own name, all of which might seem a bit ridiculous and very British.

In 1972, when I left Gollancz to become a literary agent, Michael Shea signed on as a client. Near the end of 1979 he telephoned me at the office. 'A friend of mine has just written a children's book. Would you take a look at it?' Friends of authors were forever writing children's stories, usually illustrated by other friends who were said to be very talented, but I'd yet to encounter one that was any good. 'Sorry, Mike,' I said, in as sepulchral voice as I could summon up, 'we don't handle children's books.' 'That's a pity,' said Shea, in his self-confident, slightly saucy way, 'because my friend is the Prince of Wales.' 'Wait a minute, Mike,' I squeaked. 'We do now handle children's books.' This was to be the beginning of an association which I have hugely enjoyed, acting as literary agent for HRH the Prince of Wales, HRH the Duke of Edinburgh and, on one book, HRH the Duke of York when he was Prince Andrew. Over the years, I sold all three authors' works to Christopher Sinclair-Stevenson, then running Hamish Hamilton, and joked with him that, he being a publisher and thus a gentleman (he is, as you may have surmised from his name, a gentleman in any case), he'd receive the knighthood and I, being trade, would be lucky to end up with an MBE. Indeed, *Private Eye*, in 'Heir of Sorrows', knighted him as Sir Christopher Hamish, Publisher Royale.

One of the pleasures of doing the occasional piece of work for members of the Royal Family, if you are permanently amused by the human scene, is to watch how usually sane and rational people are transformed into salivating, sycophantic morons when there is the possibility that royalty, even minor royalty, may smile upon them, or rather us, insofar as I was – am – part of the coterie. Thus it is hard to see how members of the Royal Family, not least the Queen, can assume other than that every human being is not only intellectually inferior to them but a gibbering idiot as well.

It is, in my experience, extremely difficult for 'ordinary people', such as myself, to communicate on any but the most Ruritanian level with members of the Royal Family. I have no strong feelings one way or the other about our monarchy as an institution. After all, the present lot are there because their ancestors got rid of a previous lot, and so it has gone on back to the Norman Conquest and before. The Divine Right of Kings had more to do with the divine right of the sword. In that they are professionals born and more specifically bred to do particular jobs of work, which may or may not need doing, I applaud their commitment. I feel safer with the Queen in Buckingham Palace and her relatives scattered about in other palaces than I would with, say, Mr Kinnock, Sir David Steel, or the Countess of Finchley as President. Maybe all other qualities than service and enjoying themselves have been bred and brainwashed out of the Royals, but I doubt it: they are of resilient stock, survivors. Whether they would wish to live ordinary lives is not a question that leads to realistic or instructive answers. What they discreetly crave and desperately need, it seems to me, is to be surrounded by people who aren't, in any pejorative sense, courtiers. I particularly admire the beleaguered Prince of Wales for his attempts to live in what he regards as the real world, to relate to it and understand it; and who would blame him, even if they disagree with some of his diktats, for trying, as he sees it, to improve both the lots of his fellow countrymen and his own lot? And this in spite of the fact that he's likely to be completely bald before he's called to be king.

Most people in this country – *most* people – are intrinsically conservative, and thus it is hardly astonishing that the heir to the throne should wish to preserve the *status quo*, preserve or resurrect what he sees as the best from the past, whether it is classical architecture, the English language or organic farming. The irony is that if our mass market factory farming methods were less offensive, less brutal to animals and to the nature of the land, or contemporary English more expressive and eloquent, or contemporary architecture more aesthetically pleasing and sturdily built, the Prince wouldn't need to evoke nostalgia and our so-called romantic past; to those wrestling with the daily grind at the time the past palpably wasn't romantic. He is, I believe, while not a way-out aesthete like Richard II or a holy fool like Henry VI, a kind of idealist who, cocooned and insulated in his strange role, has little to bite upon, to engage with, but arcane flattery (not intended that way) and mediocrity (not aspired to). By Machiavellian definition, anyone attending upon and surrounding a prince is a courtier, and can courtiers ever avoid being essentially flatterers? (Why does a parallel with Robert Maxwell spring to mind? There is a difference, of course, apart from the obvious one of birth. Maxwell knew that his bullying tactics persuaded his acolytes, journalists as much as management, to lie to him, and he didn't care. The Prince of Wales must assume – how can he think otherwise and remain sane? – that those who sup at his table are telling the truth as they perceive it; which, according to their fashion, no doubt, most of them are.)

Before Transworld published the Prince of Wales's *A Vision of Britain* (1989), it arranged for twenty or thirty leading booksellers (yes, there are as many as that) to meet His Royal Highness at Kensington Palace. Everyone was told to behave naturally, as if booksellers were in the habit of behaving unnaturally when together. At the appointed hour the Prince of Wales appeared – he was suddenly a presence in the room, chatting to a couple of booksellers – as if he'd materialised from under the carpet. He talked to every bookseller, individually, asking each one about his or her shop, its city, the state of the trade, and so on. It would be impossible to fault his application or the intelligent interest he displayed. If, occasionally, he ventured to ask a particular book-seller how he thought *A Vision of Britain* would sell in his shop, find me an author who would not have behaved similarly. The time allotted for the royal walkabout and chat was, let's say, forty-five minutes. After an hour, with the Prince engrossed in conversation with two booksellers from W. H. Smith, a small dog was released into the room. I watched it sniffing its way to the royal feet. The Prince looked down and soon thereafter bid his farewells and departed. Later I enquired as to the provenance of the dog. It belonged to the Princess of Wales. She'd been hovering in an adjoining room, fuming as her husband overran his time with the booksellers. She was waiting for him to whisk her off on holiday.

For some years, Mark Le Fanu, the discreet and capable sec-retary of the Society of Authors, had been trying to persuade Prince Charles to attend the Society's annual prize-giving jam-boree in June and to do the honours. Eventually it was agreed that, in the year of publication of *A Vision of Britain*, His Royal Highness would, in the Banqueting Hall, Whitehall, present the year's prizes to poets and novelists and biographers. Le Fanu, a tactful man and thus well equipped for his job, telephoned me in advance and asked if I wanted to be on the receiving line. I suggested to Mark that on this occasion I shouldn't be presented to my client, so that he could meet as many other members of the Society of Authors as possible, particularly the likes of Sir Victor Pritchett. On the appointed evening, the Prince arrived and chatted to authors before making an amusing and even subversive speech (free from expected platitudes) which began something to this effect: 'My family has always had difficulties with publishers.' He started by recounting the problems Queen Victoria experienced when Messrs Smith, Elder published her *Leaves from the Journal of Our Life in the Highlands* and then *More Leaves* . . . It was

witty, refreshing stuff, perfectly calculated to its audience, culminating with a remark about his difficulty in keeping up with the
name of his own publisher, which had been called Transworld, or
was it Bantam, or Bertelsmann, or Corgi, when *A Vision of Britain*
was signed up, and now seemed to be called Doubleday. There
was more to this than knockabout. It was a coded comment on
the take-over of publishing houses, and of the understandable
confusion of authors as to who owned whom.

(At the time Transworld offered for the book, Sir John Riddell,
then the Prince's private secretary, asked if Transworld was a
British company. I explained that it was American, hence, it being
a UK publisher as well, the corporate name. 'Oh dear,' he said,
in his debonair way, 'can't you find a British company? The press
won't like the Prince being published by an American firm.' I
reminded Riddell that no British house had come up with anything
approaching the advance against royalties which Transworld had
proposed. Then I remembered that Doubleday, and thus its parent
company Bantam, and thus Transworld, had shortly before been
acquired by Bertelsmann, the German conglomerate. Sir John was
much relieved: keeping it in the family, in a manner of speaking.)

A few minutes after Prince Charles had presented the prizes, a
young woman bustled up to me and asked if I was Giles Gordon.
His Royal Highness, evidently, had asked Mark Le Fanu why I
wasn't present; meaning, presumably, why hadn't I been presented
to him? Eventually, before he went off to a film première for
which he must have been late, and probably keeping the Princess
waiting and fuming again (he seemed in no hurry to leave), I
joined the receiving line, close to the exit, and was in fact the last
person to meet him that evening. 'Ah, Giles,' he said. 'Nice to see
you. Aren't we due a royalty statement from Doubledays?' You
do not, in my limited experience, so much think on your feet as
react when asked a wholly unexpected question by royalty. 'It's
due next week, sir,' I mouthed, ad-libbing, having at the time no
idea. He had gone before I realised how very funny his question
was. Did he imagine that royalty statements were something which
publishers provided exclusively for him and the fellow writers in
his family? Or was he about to make another speech? Or was he
genuinely concerned to discover how many copies his book had

sold? Or, even more surreal (though why should it be?), was he anticipating that the considerable advance had been earned already and that there might be a further cheque for his charities trust?

In 1985, when awarded the OBE, certainly not in her case for Other Buggers' Efforts, Catherine Cookson was too ill to travel from the north of England to Buckingham Palace to receive it, but she was well enough, some months later, to go to Newcastle University where, I think, the Prince of Wales was to receive an honorary doctorate and was also to declare open a new wing – something of the sort – at Newcastle General Hospital, which had been endowed with some highly sophisticated and advanced laser equipment by Mrs Cookson (to become Dame Catherine in 1993).

Prince Charles presented her with her OBE, and there was a silence. The seconds ticked away. Catherine, if not the Prince, can always be relied upon to fill silences. 'We have something in common, Your Royal Highness,' her voice rang out, no doubt to the alarm of courtiers. The Prince looked quizzical. 'We share the same literary agent.' The Prince seemed perplexed, then smiled. 'Oh, do we?' he said, then summoned a name from the resources of his memory. 'Curtis Brown.' 'No!' shrieked Catherine. 'Anthony Sheil Associates.'

I have no idea how the conversation continued, if it did, or why the Prince of Wales thought he was represented by a firm other than ours, unless he was thinking of Princess Michael of Kent, who is, I believe, 'handled' by Michael Shaw of Curtis Brown. Perhaps he ducked presenting Britain's most successful author in the public libraries with her DBE in 1993 as she received it from the Lord Lieutenant of Tyne and Wear – not, to my knowledge, a client of either Sheil Land Associates (as we now are) or Curtis Brown.

In connection with publication of the Prince of Wales' third book, *Watercolours* (1991), Little, Brown, the American publishers, gave a reception for booksellers in a stunning Georgian house in Salisbury cathedral close in the summer of 1991, an hour or so before 'Symphony for the Spire', a grand fund-raising concert and event which took place in the open air in front of the cathedral. Among those taking part in the concert were Phil Collins, Grace Bumbry and Ofra Hanroy. There were interminable extracts from *Henry V* with Kenneth Branagh declaiming hoarsely against the film score being played frenetically on stage behind him by a scratch orchestra, and Charlton Heston playing other parts, notably the French herald, Mountjoy, and wearing an expensive-looking tracksuit that in Hollywood possibly qualifies as royal garb.

Before the Prince arrived we all rather self-consciously viewed a modest exhibition of a few of the 'originals' of the Prince's watercolours reproduced in the book. At the reception he congratulated me on the contract I'd negotiated for the book. I reciprocated by congratulating him on the quality of his paintings. 'I'm not so sure about that,' he replied, laughing self-disparagingly. This is the nature of the dilemma of any dialogue between Prince and commoner: royalty compliments you, and your instinct is not only to absorb and believe the compliment but to lob it back, with interest. Royalty nonchalantly shrugs off the compliment but, if it is given to brooding or worrying or its ego is insecure, it must to a degree accept and believe the compliment and, unless it is encouraged or encourages itself to read the 'wrong' newspapers, it must vaguely believe that the world, Mr and Mrs Everyperson, are happily approving of it and its lifestyle – which may well be true.

On this occasion the Princess of Wales accompanied her husband. Tall and elegant she was, all legs and arms and elbows and seemingly little in between. She wore more make-up than I'd have expected but, living a soap opera life for television and countless other cameras, this, I suppose, is inevitable, although the make-up department didn't appear to have attempted to disguise her husband's increasingly bald patch. I was at the back of the group being introduced to her. She seemed all the while to be looking through me, peering behind me, through the open door and beyond into the handsome garden where other of the evening's guests cavorted with champagne and canapés before the concert. 'Is there any one else?' she asked, giggling, and remarked that she hadn't realised that it took so many people to publish a book even, you felt her thinking, such a handsome volume reproducing almost in facsimile so many of her husband's precious watercolours. 'It takes many more than this, ma'am,' I replied, and she giggled again, her face suddenly seeming to move down below her neck before she insinuated herself in the direction of a lady-in-waiting standing guard in front of a closed door. Words were exchanged *sotto voce* between Princess and lady-in-waiting, then the latter banged on the door. 'Wait a minute,' called a distraught voice from within, and another woman standing near the door remarked a little crossly that there was a queue. This was not Camilla Parker-Bowles, although she put in an appearance. When this person saw who was standing behind the lady-in-waiting she yielded her place to the Princess, who shortly thereafter, when the throne was vacated, disappeared into the smallest room.

In the summer of 1992 I spent a day, with his latest publishers Ian and Marjory Chapman, in the company of the Prince of Wales at his home in Gloucestershire. He was being filmed for a programme on organic farming at Highgrove to be transmitted by Anglia's *Survival* unit, and the book *Highgrove: Portrait of an Estate* was to be published around the same time in early 1993. Although he treated us guests, hangers-on if you insist, in an utterly courteous way – and the Chapmans to their pleasure zoomed about the estate with the Prince in his Land-Rover – what was fascinating to observe was his passion for his estate, his real concern for the land and those who worked upon it. Here he was in his element. This was a man who had broken through protocol, and was content and fulfilled in a life as near to private as he could ever achieve.

At this very time, the tabloid press was baying for a royal divorce. For the day at least, he had put such matters from his mind. His children were there too, playing about with horses; and Prince Harry even let my baby daughter Lucy sit on his horse, although he quickly declared she was too small for it. Not, I hope, a future Richard III.

The first time I met the Duke of Edinburgh I was introduced to him in his study at Buckingham Palace by Michael Shea, still at the time the Queen's press secretary. 'A member of the Garrick, I see,' said a gravely smiling Prince Philip as Shea disappeared, almost genuflecting. Afterwards Shea asked me what the Duke had said. Later Michael was to become a member of the Club, of which Prince Philip is Patron, and would, presumably, have no difficulty in recognising the salmon-and-cucumber-coloured striped tie.

The meeting was short, practical and sensible. The Duke addressed me as if I knew my business, which was his. I negotiated the contracts for three or four of his books. The last, perhaps unfortunately entitled *Down to Earth* (1988), was a deeply felt and intelligently edited volume comprising, in the main, extracts from speeches and lectures which down the years the Duke had given on the environment and conservation. This book of gravity, passion and informed common sense achieved the distinction of not receiving one review in the British national press. Sometimes the Royals can't win.

I was more than a little surprised when, some months after my first meeting with him and after publication of his book *Competition Carriage Driving* (1982), he invited my wife and me to be his guests at the annual meet of the Carriage Club of Great Britain and to the Club's dinner afterwards at Hampton Court. The Duke either was or had just ceased to be president of the club. It was an alarming day: I had to dress up in morning suit and grey topper, foolishly purchased second-hand from a shop in Charing Cross Road rather than hired from the Brothers Moss. The Duke's other guests were the director of an educational video being made to accompany the book, which explained the skills of competition carriage driving, and his wife. We charged manically around Hampton Court Park on the open top of a plunging, hurtling coach with the Duke driving the archaic vehicle and urging on the horses. The coach lurched and creaked as the rain constantly slashed and slewed down round us. We seemed to indulge in this utterly futile and unpleasant activity for hours, and certainly until long after we were all thoroughly drenched, my newly acquired second-hand finery and my wife's best dress and coat all pickled in wetness. Eventually the Duke and all the other carriage drivers had had sufficient fun, and we were ushered from the coach under the largest black umbrellas I've seen, into a room of the palace where, after we'd brushed ourselves down and tried to dry out, Prince Philip re-entered, his suit dried out, and entertained us to drinks before dinner, with the odd whiskery, mahogany-visaged military man and his ancient wife hovering. There was a large log fire burning in the grate and it wasn't too long before we recovered some body warmth.

At dinner the five of us – the Duke and his four guests – sat at a small table, while Prince Philip fired questions. I can remember hardly anything of the conversation beyond 'Have you been to New Zealand?' and 'What are your views on the decimal coinage?' The Queen had been taking the salute, her official birthday, at Trooping the Colour that day, and was dining elsewhere. The Duke couldn't have been a more courteous host, even though the conversation was, as I recall, somewhat narrow in its range – lots about competition carriage riding. There again, the Royals mustn't, presumably, be seen to initiate a conversation that can turn controversial, which for a start must preclude any mention of politics. On the way home in her old third-hand boneshaker (the only non-grand car parked at Hampton Court) my wife expressed a certain bemusement that she'd been groped by a royal groom, both as he helped her up on top of the carriage and, hours later, as he assisted her down. Perhaps the 1992 fire at Windsor Castle was a kind of retribution.

For some years my architect father was honorary secretary of the Royal Scottish Academy in Edinburgh, and one of his duties and pleasures was to accompany the Duke around the annual summer exhibition of the Academy (which, it might be said, is more than a cut or two above the Royal Academy's annual summer show at Burlington House). Each year the Duke tended to buy a number of paintings off the walls for his personal collection, and my father was ever taken by his eye, the instinct and sensibility as to the pictures worth acquiring. He was even more impressed, year after year, when the Duke would remark, as he toured the exhibition and looked at individual pictures, that he'd bought a painting by that artist – indicating a particular canvas – last year. My father made a point of checking up afterwards, and the Duke had invariably identified the painter correctly.

Years ago my father learned that Prince Philip was thought to be an accomplished painter mainly in oils (unlike his eldest son, who prefers to work in watercolour) but he wouldn't admit to wielding a palette and brushes. Tim Heald, in his 1991 biography of the Queen's consort, revealed that Prince Philip enjoyed painting, and I took the opportunity of writing to him to suggest a book. I received a reply from his private secretary declining the proposition. I suspect he didn't want to be seen as following in the Prince of Wales's footsteps, even though he had been a painter years before his son.

Of the three members of the Royal Family for whom I have acted as agent (a further two I declined to act for: whereas most of my more republican-inclined authors could stomach my representing three, they might have found five to be over-egging (even over-Fabergé-ing) the pudding and departed to a less sycophantic agent), the one whom I grew to know best was Prince Andrew. My assistance – again via Michael Shea – was enlisted to find a publisher reckless enough to commission from him a book of photographs. Again, Christopher Sinclair-Stevenson did the honourable thing. Books by Royals (as opposed to books about the Royal Family) are not remaindered – that is, sold off cheaply when the market declines to purchase them at the publisher's marked price – but let us agree that Messrs Hamish Hamilton printed rather more copies of Prince Andrew's book, plainly entitled *Photographs*, than were eventually called for by the book-buyers of the world. Prince Andrew never pretended that he was a master photographer to rival the Lords Snowdon and Lichfield, let alone his revered Norman Parkinson. Rather, the book was a selection of photographs taken during his first year with a camera, the pictures being reproduced in chronological order of shooting, the first section pretty indifferent (but never wholly without interest, if only because, say, shots were taken from the windows of Buckingham Palace), the later ones more professional.

Something you learn if you are unfortunate enough to have to spend time with photographers is that what might seem the simple act of aiming a lens at landscape (or whatever) and then squeezing the trigger is turned, pretentiously or not, into one of life's more significant, time-consuming and tedious activities. The composition has to be immaculate, the light as good as it may be, the speed of the shutter, especially if the picture is being shot indoors, exact. Prince Andrew invited me, one Saturday in 1984, to come with him, together with his photographic guru and printer, the Filipino Gene Nocon, and his buxom English wife, Liz, to Windsor. I met the Prince at Buckingham Palace where, prior to his marriage, he lived and where he'd converted – or, more likely, had converted – a light room into a dark-room. The Prince at the wheel, we roared out of the Palace gates in his Range Rover, the odd military or police hand twitching into a salute as the Prince made for the open gates. I sat in the front seat next to him, his detective behind us. I'd failed to bring my detective with me. The drive was a bit like being with Toad of Toad Hall on the high road, all immensely jolly with a great deal of laughter, the Prince all the while trying to give his poor police escort the slip. Occasionally, when forced reluctantly to slow down at a traffic light, the Prince would be recognised by other motorists, and he'd respond as presumably Nigel Mansell or any other sporting hero of the moment does, although drawing the line at autographs or squirting champagne over everybody.

At Windsor we were met by Dean Mann, empurpled and unctuous, who welcomed the Prince to St George's Chapel where the cub photographer was setting up his tripod in the nave to take a shot (commissioned for next year's Ilford calendar) of the magnificent West Front window. An additional picture was taken of the Dean sitting in his own transept, with an expression on his face as if he wished he were anywhere but in his own pew. He was, I think, as bored as I was by the time it took to squeeze the shutter for the last time. We seemed to be there for hours (we *were* there for hours), as every piece of equipment was adjusted, and readjusted, again and again.

Eventually we adjourned to the private apartments of the Castle where Prince Andrew ('Let me be mother') served a picnic lunch. Again this was reminiscent in a slightly surreal way of *The Wind in the Willows*, a touch of the Toads, a vast hamper disgorging goodies, including linen napkins, crisply starched and perfectly ironed, and some of the Palace silver cutlery. After eating, we lounged about in a drawing or drawling room, idly watching the rugby international on television. Gene Nocon – who bore the lean and hungry look of a famine victim in an Oxfam advertisement, then as always, and always disconcertingly – inserted the word 'sir' into every sentence directed at the Prince. I tried to remember, every tenth sentence or so, to slip in the word 'sir': he noticed, you could tell, if you omitted the expected and required formality for too long. However 'friendly' you may have felt you were with him – or with any of the Royals – you were never permitted to become so friendly that your relationship, even for a few minutes, was reduced to that of equals. This must, ultimately, result in the discreet demise of the Royal Family, a consummation to my mind not devoutly to be wished.

From his capacious armchair in the television room, the young Prince lobbed a heavy cushion, balloon-like, across the room to Liz Nocon, who lobbed it back. (Gene probably didn't notice, so busy was he saying 'sir'.) This mildly louche game went on for some time – the boredom of the Plantagenet – the throwing of the cushion becoming more aggressive, more serious on both sides. Eventually Liz, no weakling, hurled it with all her might and Prince Andrew stopped it from striking his cheek only by raising his hands suddenly to catch it. His face froze and his lips pursed, Hanoverian-like, as if he were about to sentence Liz Nocon to the Tower. It was a dangerous moment. Time stopped. On the television Bill McLaren became particularly excited about the rugby. Then Prince Andrew controlled his anger (breeding will, presumably, out, or in), his face slowly relaxed, and he thrust the cushion behind him, the game that almost got out of hand and ended in tears, over. Richard III, I thought, had executed peers of the realm for less. The Prince was, it should be said, immensely fond of Liz, and he had a touching respect for Gene's professionalism. My wife and I once spent an enjoyable evening at the Nocons' house at Beaconsfield with the Prince, and I have never seen him more relaxed, although after his marriage he saw infinitely less of them.

On the way back to London from Windsor the Prince again tried to throw off the police escort – and, from the back of the car, his detective bravely admonished him for this – but presumably they were always in touch, if only by radio. He asked where I wanted to be dropped off and I suggested Buckingham Palace, if he was returning home. He asked where I lived and I told him Chalk Farm, Kentish Town. His policeman expressed some interest as, he said, his first posting had been at Kentish Town police station in Holmes Road. The Prince insisted that he'd drive me to my front door. I demurred. He continued to insist and, obviously, I had to direct him. Eventually his high Range Rover (I remember feeling as if I were jock-strapped in a parachute above the rest of the traffic) pushed up our tiny cul-de-sac.

I took a deep breath, closed my eyes and thought of Scotland, then asked him if he'd like to come in for a drink. I was praying that the answer would be in the negative. The plaster rose had, a few days before, fallen off our sitting-room ceiling, within inches of a visiting baby, and the mess of plaster and the gaping hole in the ceiling remained. We also, *en famille*, invariably had fried chicken and chips on Saturday evenings and I knew that, at this hour, my wife would be presiding in a smoky kitchen. To my alarm, Prince Andrew consulted his wristwatch and said that he'd come in but only for a few minutes and he'd have, please, a soft drink.

I rang the bell, to give warning, to suggest that it wasn't just me returning; I'd normally have used my key. My wife, in her striped butcher's apron, came to the door, looking a bit annoyed at having been summoned from the cooker, and by me. She was immediately followed by the alarming if lugubrious lolloping Sniffy, my second son's white boxer dog. 'This is my wife, Margaret; Prince Andrew,' I said, making the unexpected introductions on the doorstep, and my wife batted not an eyelid. She had coped stoutly with that improbable visitation from Lord George-Brown years before and was, generally speaking, accustomed to unexpected visits from surprising 'authors'. We entered the house and Sniffy, unabashed by the royal visitor, leapt up, apparently to greet the royal balls. He scratched and scraped, stimulated, as he always was, by a visitor. I ushered the Prince into the sitting-room, and somehow throughout the visit no mention was made of the plaster on the floor, the hole in the ceiling. We all chatted away for longer than the Prince had intended, with my wife and he and the detective sipping orange juice, while I, I recall without surprise, imbibed something a little stronger. Children, not all ours, wandered into the room, gaped at and greeted the royal visitor, and drifted out. Eventually it was time for the Prince and his detective (who had kept a low profile) to depart.

## Chapter XXVIII

To my horror, the pavements of St Ann's Gardens seemed crammed with small children, all – in my memory, but no doubt only in my memory – clutching tiny Union Jacks and the occasional Royal Standard and waving them fervently. My ten-year-old daughter, Harriet, had flitted from house to house in the street, announcing to everyone that I'd brought Prince Andrew home. No one believed it until they saw the Prince leave the house, re-enter his car and roar backwards down the street, waving, and flashing his teeth at the assembled residents. He needed his gallery.

A few months later, again on a Saturday, I was summoned to Buckingham Palace to help His Royal Highness with the writing of the book's introduction. When I was ushered into his apartments, bits of typescript were strewn all over the floor. He was down there on the carpet, wielding scissors, cutting up sentences and paragraphs, sellotaping and resellotaping pieces of prose in different sequence. He had been incredulous at my insistence that he must express himself as precisely and as accurately as possible, and that it was at least as difficult to write prose decently as it was, well, to take photographs. We worked at it for hours, until we ran out of royal Sellotape. He was particularly surprised at my humourless bullying about split infinitives, a grammatical nicety he hadn't previously encountered. I would not let him get away with it. His memorial to me, and to his publisher, resides in the acknowledgements: 'There are a few who have been particularly helpful and I mention them here for special thanks: firstly, Giles Gordon, who guided my pen in its wanderings around split infinitives and other traps waiting for me in the English language, and secondly, Christopher Sinclair-Stevenson, the publisher, both of whom think I'm mad delivering a book and then, virtually immediately, sailing off to the South Atlantic and the Falkland Islands for five months, when most first-time authors are either biting their nails or ringing their publishers up every ten minutes.' He survived the Falklands, if not necessarily to publish another book.

Publication of *Photographs* was preceded by an exhibition of the Prince's prints at the Barbican gallery, and after the private view HRH invited ten or so of us, including ex-girlfriends, the Nocons and me, to supper at L'Escargot where, needless to say, the wonderful Elena was much in evidence, billing and cooing.

One girl who was not present was the ridiculously named Koo Stark, who came to England wanting to be an actress or a photographer, preferably both, and was certainly a photographer before he who was not destined to be her Prince began playing about with a camera.

She, too, found a publisher. Her *Contrasts* (1985) was the second title to be published by Bantam Press here, the first being a history of the Oxford and Cambridge boat race, which says something about the indiscriminate eclecticism of publishers. The great Norman Parkinson provided the foreword to Ms Stark's photographs. He began: 'A dark-haired wisp of an American girl was plonked, some years ago, on the English social scene and was soon goaded and pestered by the expert English gossip columnists because of some amatorial association which we need not discuss here,' and went on for paragraphs. How knowing and winsome it all was, but all's well that ends well, for Koo just loves taking pictures, and is most accomplished at it.

I was introduced to her at the launch party for *Contrasts*, held, rather surprisingly, at the Institute of Directors on Pall Mall, a building I'd previously associated only with my client, George Bull, when he edited the IOD's monthly journal, and his eager young Irish assistant editor, John Walsh, who went on to become literary editor of the *Sunday Times*, then editor of the *Independent* magazine. When Koo realised who I was – that is to say, my 'relationship' with Prince Andrew – she said she had to have a private word with me. We left the handsome room in which the party was being held, and she walked me along a corridor to the ladies' lavatories. There, hovering in the doorway, between the basins, we conducted our talk, which was, I can now reveal, not about matters of state. We must have been there for all of sixty seconds.

The next evening Prince Andrew telephoned me, in a state of high old excitement. What japes. 'I hear, Giles, that Koo took you to the ladies. I do think that's the funniest thing.' And there was much royal laughter down the line.

The last time I encountered Prince Andrew was at the ball at Windsor an evening or two before his marriage on 23 July 1986. My wife declined to accompany me, loathing that kind of event and disapproving of what she saw as my enthralment to the Royals. Of all my female friends, I thought that the journalist and travel book writer Louise Nicholson would enjoy the evening most, and what's more she had access to a car, which I, as an embarrassed non-driver, hadn't. We had dinner first at Marlow and then, in our finery (Louise that evening looked like a painting by Gainsborough with a touch of Holbein), we meandered with, it seemed, thousands of other cars towards Windsor's polo park. The occasion was, inevitably, a most lavish one, the nearest to the Field of the Cloth of Gold I'm likely to witness, let alone participate in. David Hicks had provided the *mise-en-scène*, decorated the largest tent imaginable (infra dig. to call it a marquee, or rather series of marquees). From the outside, it glowed like a gigantic island, illuminated from within, casting an orange aura over the countryside. Inside, it was like a floating palace, all hangings and false ceilings, coloured ribbons and cornucopias wherever you looked, pilasters and curtains, a red carpet and tables, less groaning than coolly presenting their sumptuous dishes, waiting to be approached, admired, abused, dismantled, consumed down to a naked silver salver. Hours later, when evening became night, night dreamed towards morning, breakfast appeared and was served out of bubbling silver tureens and ashets, then everyone stole away, back to the mundanity of another ordinary day, disappearing like hundreds of Cinderellas from a palace erected for the night, as if it might be tempting fate to remain a moment longer.

In between the two meals (we should not have dined beforehand), hundreds of people danced the darkness away, and chatted and drank. There were various groups, various factions. The Queen, looking timeless and ageless, danced with someone I didn't recognise, and so did the groom's father, and then I saw them dancing together, the Queen and the Duke. Princess Anne swept past, purposefully, and Prince Michael of Kent, looking more like a Romanov than ever, stood next to a tent pole chatting to a couple of people. There was a noticeable show business contingent including Elton John, rather smartly dressed, a pregnant Pamela Stephenson with a still bearded Billy Connolly, and David Frost, not yet knighted, without whom even this event could not be complete. If they were there, I missed Ned Sherrin and Sheridan

Morley. At one point, early on, Major Ronald Ferguson, the bride's father, shook me steelily by the hand and glared with fierce bonhomie into my eyes, then gripped someone else's hand. As we arrived, swinging through from the tented antechamber to the palace of lavish illusions, Prince Andrew happened to walk in our direction. Louise Nicholson had, on the way, teased me that he wouldn't know who I was, and wondered how *had* I managed to procure two tickets for the event of the season? 'Good evening, Giles,' he said. Louise's mouth fell open, and I imagined that her eyelids fluttered. 'You ought to meet Sarah,' said the Prince. 'You're both in the same business,' he added as, appearing behind him, she threatened to thunder past, plainly on her way to find someone more interesting. She stopped, realising she was being introduced, looking a little irritated, quizzical, but not unhappy. 'The book trade,' he said, in his deliberate way, as if her occupation (as assistant to a book packager) needed to be spelt out to her. She continued on her disdainful progress after the briefest of acknowledgements.

A few days later my wife and I attended their wedding in Westminster Abbey (we could see nothing, really, from where we sat), and that Christmas we received a card, on which Prince Andrew had written 'Dear Mr and Mrs Gordon, Kind regards, Andrew & Sarah'. Opposite was a colour photograph, presumably not taken by himself, of the gleaming couple on their wedding day, he all naval uniform, gold braid, medals and teeth; she all flowers, hair and eyes. This was the last time I heard from him. It was as if the Duchess of York persuaded her Prince, like Prince Hal banishing Falstaff, to drop those commoners whom he may have enjoyed being with before his marriage.

I like to think he occasionally appreciated the company of people who were neither in the services nor courtiers, who would let him see how the other 99.9 per cent thought. I enjoyed my dealings with him and never found him boorish or thick, as he tends to be presented by the media; on the other hand, he is plainly not a genius, but how many of us are? Looking back, I feel like an uncle to him, a slightly older, more staid and undoubtedly nervously pompous relative, trying to keep him calm and collected. I find it difficult to dislike people I come into contact with and grow to know, however much I may have been prejudiced against them. Prince Andrew was a case in point.

(Since all the above was written, the Duke and Duchess of York have separated. As with Labour losing the 1992 general election, I suspect the tabloid press has a lot to answer for. On the other hand, it always seemed to me – even before there was evidence – that some of the younger Royals flirted with it, you might even say courted it. If the tabloids could hardly exist these days without the antics of the pleasure-seeking Royals, the pleasure-seeking Royals hardly have a *raison d'être* without the tabloids. Reluctantly, I have to admit that they probably deserve each other.)

I invited the Duke of York to the publication party for Sue Townsend's *The Queen and I* but he couldn't come. I hope he had time to read the proof copy I sent him, and passed it around the Palace.

# XXIX

When Prince Andrew was putting together his book of photographs he was, for much of the time, seeing service, as the phrase has it, in the Royal Navy. He was stationed at Portsmouth, and was given to telephoning me at home in the evenings. I suspect he was bored. He wasn't a young man who gave the impression of enjoying being closeted with himself on long winter evenings, particularly after a day spent flying helicopters and otherwise energetically exercising his naval skills. He also liked to share his enthusiasms of the moment with anyone prepared to be button-holed. He would, during this period, telephone me two or three times a week, and sometimes he'd ask me to ring him the following evening with information he'd requested, which I did. (The first time he rang me at home my streetwise son Gareth answered the telephone: 'Dad, there's a bloke who says he's Prince Andrew to speak to you.') I was surprised how often the Prince would pick up the receiver himself – oh yes, he has many skills – though never revealing his identity until I had revealed mine.

At the same time as my evening conversations with the Prince were taking place, I was receiving telephone calls from Tasmania which, according to Peter Hennessy, Whitehall historian and enthusiast for the Civil Service, resulted in our home telephone being bugged by MI6. I would not have believed that, but Hennessy, something of an authority on the subject, insisted that certain clicks and noises on the line could indicate nothing else. There was, indeed, the occasional click. I, naïve and romantic in these matters as in most others, assumed merely that this was the general and unparticularised shuffling and heaving of the telephone system.

My caller from Tasmania, who couldn't easily reach me during office hours because of the time difference between the two continents, was Peter Wright – who was to produce a notorious book called *Spycatcher* – or his wife Lois. It amused me greatly, as a sceptical Scot, to imagine a puzzled person from Porlock at MI6 hearing me chat with HRH the Prince Andrew, hang up, then talk to 'the traitor' Peter Wright. At this time, because of the television programme in the course of which Wright first went public with his allegations, he was *persona non grata* in the United Kingdom. What *would* the Prime Minister, Margaret Thatcher, say? And what would she have said to Sir Michael Havers, her Attorney-General, if she'd known that more than once he and I chatted away about the state of the world when sitting next to each other at the Garrick Club's members' table? One thing that may be confidently asserted is that such Alice-in-Wonderland connections could thrive only in Britain.

Some years later, after Mrs Thatcher was deposed as Prime Minister by her own party, those acting on her behalf invited our agency, and specifically me, to provide a paper setting out how we could conduct ourselves were we appointed her literary agents. We were asked to provide a list of clients. We included Prince Andrew but, by a strange oversight, omitted the name of Peter Wright. It hardly mattered because Mrs Thatcher, presumably regarding British agents as too feeble by half (maybe she connected them in her mind with British secret agents, or even with estate agents, given the problems she and her husband experienced in disposing of their unloved house in Dulwich), chose an American to negotiate the sale of her memoirs. The same agent also represented President Reagan, General Schwarzkopf and the authoress of the *Budgie the Helicopter* books.

*Spycatcher: The Candid Autobiography of a Senior Intelligence Officer* (as the US edition was subtitled) is, I suppose, one of the two best-known books I've been associated with. (The other is *The Secret Diary of Adrian Mole*; a different kind of secrecy, and a different kind of mole.) In the days when I still read *The Times* at breakfast (not that I eat breakfast except on holiday), a front-page story on 9 July 1984 by my client Peter Hennessy, the paper's Whitehall correspondent, disclosed that on that evening's Granada Television *World in Action* programme a former MI5 man (indeed, a former assistant director of MI5), Peter Wright, would be interviewed on camera about, among other matters, an almost successful campaign to overthrow and oust Prime Minister Harold Wilson and his government in the mid-seventies. There were, in Hennessy's scoop, or scoopette, hints of much more to be revealed.

I rang Hennessy, one of the most generous of individuals, and asked him whether there was a book to be written about all this, and if so whether he might be inclined to write it. He reminded me, not that I needed reminding, that he was engaged upon his *magnum opus* on Whitehall which, he further reminded me, I'd talked him into writing approximately twenty years before he had intended writing it. In any case, he said, the Peter Wright story was not for him. Why didn't I watch the programme and, if I thought there might be a book in it, let him know. I watched *World in Action* that evening and telephoned Hennessy at home as soon as the credits rolled. I remarked to the chuckling Hennessy that not only was there a book in it, but Wright's story, if he'd tell it and reveal all or much, would surely bring down Mrs Thatcher's appalling government. Hennessy suggested that the person to write the book – that is to collaborate with Wright – was Paul Greengrass, the co-director of the film I'd just watched, and Wright's interlocutor. No, Greengrass hadn't written a book before but that, in the context, hardly mattered. He and his co-director, John Ware, had spent months gaining Wright's confidence before the spycatcher was prepared to allow the film to be made, let alone transmitted. Wright was shrewdly, or perhaps obviously, aware that the wrath of the Thatcher government would descend upon him for asserting and revealing what he did: that there was incompetence in high places and that the Tories hadn't cleansed the Augean stables adequately subsequent to the misrule and abuses of the Labour years, when Harold Wilson and his cronies were allegedly in bed with the Muscovites.

What Peter Wright, presumably, had not bargained for – and a positively Faustian bargain he'd taken out – was that Mrs Thatcher wouldn't begin to thank him for his revelations, for exposing incompetence and corruption (who *was* the Fifth Man?), but instead would hound him, refuse to allow him to set foot in the

UK or leave Tasmania, where he'd lived, very modestly, since retiring from the service in 1976, aged sixty.

But all this lay in the future. I contacted Greengrass and we met. A somewhat dour, melancholy and pragmatic Northerner, who looked and dressed like a successful (or even unsuccessful) soccer player, he was a veteran of Granada's *Newsnight* programme, and took nothing on trust. Like so many television reporters, he seemed to have the luxury of making programmes at his own pace, and thus was able to check and recheck everything, to achieve the balance, the effect he wanted. Certainly he'd studied Peter Wright for years, and all this, it must be understood, in the days before Wright's face became a familiar icon on television news, the gnarled head topped with wide brimmed hat, at least metaphorically speaking festooned with corks, as if he were flying Qantas. Wright could land anywhere on the globe except in the UK, where he would undoubtedly be arrested and, if the Prime Minister had her way, be clapped into irons and arraigned for high treason for violating the Official Secrets Act (which he had signed, wittingly or not, voluntarily or not, as a youngish lad when he joined the service), by revealing events which he'd participated in when employed by Her Majesty's Governments.

Greengrass, whose reactions, perhaps as a result of having collaborated with Wright for so long, always seemed unnecessarily convoluted, as if he were trying to discover misunderstandings where there couldn't logically be any, thought that there *could* be a book in Wright but that the old buffer couldn't possibly write it himself. Would he, Greengrass, consider writing it with Wright? He thought he might, but it would mean giving up his television job, or at least arranging extended leave of absence. And there was his personal life. Greengrass managed to sustain an unusually complicated, or paranoid, private life, seeming rarely to be found at the same telephone number twice; if he was, a different female voice would answer the phone. Yet in spite of all this – and the frustrations involved in the simplest of meetings with him took forever (but this, I've noticed, is a particular fetish or conceit of television journalists) – he was and is a likeable, honest man; on the one hand in need of endless if not necessarily extravagant reassurance, on the other quietly confident in all he did or appeared to do.

It so happened that I had arranged a few days after this conversation to take the effervescent David Godwin, then editorial director of Heinemann, out to lunch, and had booked a table at a small Greek taverna just off Charlotte Street. Godwin's career, it seemed to me, had been meteoric, although his detractors insisted he'd been plugging away, trying to make a splash, for years, since, aged twenty-five, he had persuaded the anarchic head of the academic publishing house of Routledge & Kegan Paul, an eccentric named Norman Franklin, to let him publish a handful of general books. Godwin was uninterested in politics, perhaps because he'd attended as an undergraduate that most politicised of the new universities, Essex.

As a result of his perceived success at Routledge, Brian Perman, the somewhat driven managing director of Heinemann (all interesting publishers are probably slightly unhinged), had invited Godwin there as editorial director. William Heinemann was, historically, a middle-brow fiction house – in days of yore it published Maugham, Heyer, Priestley, Greene, and Catherine Cookson – where all the executives appeared to be male, fat, bald, and wore pin-stripes. Perman, much younger than the pin-stripe brigade and with a background in marketing at Hutchinson, was a restlessly intelligent and ambitious man who favoured the Left in politics. He was not, on the face of it, a bookman, yet he understood the seductiveness of publishing, the power of the book. I never warmed to him the way I did to the wild, passionate Godwin, but I thought he'd see the point of Peter Wright's projected book and thus suggested to Godwin that he bring Perman to lunch, even though I was picking up the tab. For an agent to take two publishers out to lunch at the same time might be regarded as dangerous profligacy.

Godwin was arguably the most 'committed' publisher/editor of the last decade or so, but it is difficult to establish to what he was committed. His forte was for 'creative writing' with all its connotations. He had an instinct for quality, 'flair', that now disregarded publishing commodity which few in the industry possess to the same degree. (At Heinemann he went wrong only when he embarked on a short-lived phase of signing up a number of superficially fashionable young women, mostly journalists, to write fiction and non-fiction.) It is harder to have it and hold on to it in the present climate of the troublesome conglomerates (akin to the Labour Party adhering to socialism in the 1990s) than it was in the days when André Deutsch, Victor Gollancz, Fredric Warburg, Stanley Unwin and Allen Lane hung out their shingles. (The charming Hungarian Deutsch's flair, it might be added, was said to be for meanness, although he was not alone among energetic publishers in trying, like a punch-drunk fighter, to continue talking terms down *after* a contract had been agreed. Like most agents, I only saw the charm in André once he'd lost the authority to sign up books.) Perman dressed conventionally, that is, wore business suits off the peg, or so they looked. Godwin's physical appearance generally evoked an unmade bed, and he seemed particularly ill at ease and ridiculous on the few occasions I encountered him wearing black tie, looking like a waiter who'd failed to go down with the *Lusitania*. His straw-coloured hair had either rarely encountered a brush or was permanently in artful disarray. His somewhat pink face beamed behind what looked like National Health spectacles. He was witty, energetic, self-centred, obsessive, the qualities possessed by all the best publishers.

Against a background of the theme music from *Zorba the Greek* I explained to Perman and Godwin what I wanted to sell them. Godwin began by being terribly excited – he'd read Hennessy's preview in *The Times* a few days before, although he hadn't seen the programme; Perman, who also hadn't seen the programme, had read the reviews and news stories. (Publishers infrequently watch television; inevitably, they spend most of their waking hours reading, at least those whose books have old-fashioned words in them.)

I arranged for Greengrass to meet Perman and Godwin. Greengrass, with difficulty and after at least one more visit to Tasmania, had persuaded Wright to collaborate with him on a book. Eventually a contract was signed. Wright would be the author; Greengrass as co-author would receive a percentage of the advance and subsequent royalties but his name would not appear on the book.

Subsequent to the Granada television programme, questions

were asked in the House of Commons about the traitor Wright, and what the Government proposed to do about his revelations. It was all terribly British, our self-conscious and self-referential obsession with secrecy, espionage, double-dealing, if not – on this occasion – any whiff of homosexuality in the wind: more anal retention than disgorgement. Somehow that seemed to make matters worse: you'd expect this sort of thing from buggers like Burgess and Blunt, but not from chaps like Wright. But soon enough it was revealed, the way the Establishment reveals these matters by using the press, that he hadn't gone to a top-grade public school, and that he'd entered the service as a *technician*; that is to say, he was not a gentleman. These facts, frankly, explained almost everything. He wasn't really one of us, the *élite*, the *crème de la crème* puffs.

Greengrass went out to Tasmania and commenced work on the book. It was a slow, laborious process. The old boy couldn't remember names, dates. Back in London, Greengrass had to burrow deep, checking and double-checking everything, and establish cross-references where humanly possible. But this was where he was meticulous, doggedly brilliant. He was the Geoffrey Boycott of his trade, building his case by accumulating a wealth of watertight detail. It is for this reason that, to me, *Spycatcher: The Making of an Intelligence Officer* (no one ever remembers, or cites, the ironic, terribly British, subtitle) is such an intriguing, damning book. Wright and Greengrass between them may not have achieved the high gloss in their prose, the dextrous sleight of hand and panache of, say, John le Carré 'On Writing Longer and More Way-out Spy Stories', but the book's very bottom, its ballast, the relentless nuttiness of almost everyone involved in Cold War espionage, makes it an irrefutable monument to an era which now seems absurd, to human follies on a relentless scale.

It is nowadays fashionable to refer to *Spycatcher* as boring ('Darling, I couldn't get through it'), but this is a blasé response to that rarity, a book which assisted in cleansing those Augean stables. An additional irony, again most British, is that everyone involved with the book and its publication in the UK was instinctively and intellectually of the Left, not of the Right, though we found Peter Wright, in his belief that the Right was too wishy-washy and in his nostalgia for Empire, a Baden (or even Enoch) Powell-like figure, yearning for the stiff upper lip he never possessed.

Paul Greengrass used up more than the advance paid to him by Heinemann on signature of the contract, because of the time it took him to write (no pun intended) the book. It had to be accurate, and Greengrass was seeing to that. It had become his life. Godwin became bored and concentrated on cultivating his more ethereal creative writers. Perman became obsessed with *Spycatcher*, driven, as though it were his mission to publish it to the exclusion, if necessary, of all other books. There are those, including myself, who felt that his commitment to see the book published unhinged him for a while, and certainly caused him, though no one will admit as much, to lose his grip and then his job at Heinemann. During the period of *Spycatcher*, Paul Hamlyn, who was chairman of the Octopus Group of which Heinemann was a component, sold the Group to Reed International. Perman resigned in 1987. I don't think that even he realised that *Spycatcher* had terminated his Heinemann career – and overall he was an efficient managing director – but I believe it did. For years thereafter he sailed his yacht, threw pots with some dexterity, and spent time with his two young children. Only recently has he become secretary of the Poetry Book Society, a decidedly improbable job for him.

But this is to look ahead. Greengrass delivered the final manuscript of *Spycatcher* in 1986, and Heinemann prepared to publish. We all kept it as confidential as possible. The book wasn't, for instance, announced in seasonal lists or advertised. One day, at the agency, Neville Burrell, the head of our accounts department, mentioned that two HM Customs and Excise inspectors were coming to visit us. Burrell couldn't think of a reason why we merited our first ever call from VAT inspectors, and why they were visiting in tandem. My managing director, Anthony Sheil, and I were suspicious of these two men, who may or may not prove to have been from MI5. We joked about whether they would wear bowler hats and carry rolled umbrellas, as if essaying Alec Guinness in a misty remake of some long-forgotten Ealing tragi-comedy. As a precaution, I removed Peter Wright's and the book's files and took them home, concealing them under my bed. All mention of Wright and *Spycatcher*, and Greengrass, was expunged from our computer and other systems. Wright and Greengrass did not exist in our lives, nor did the book.

Prior to my lunch with Godwin and Perman, I had agreed terms for publication of what was to become *Spycatcher* with Christopher Sinclair-Stevenson. I had drawn up contracts and sent them to him. A few days later he telephoned to say that he was terribly sorry but he wouldn't be able to proceed with signing the contract or commissioning the book.

In all my years of dealing with Christopher, and as agent and publisher we must have had fifty books or more between us, he'd never reneged on a deal. I was astounded, both worried and, to be candid, rather excited. Clearly the book was a hot potato. Some time later Sinclair-Stevenson told me that he'd had a visit from, I'm delighted to record, a gentleman with a bowler hat and a rolled umbrella from whom, for a number of years, Christopher had received an annual Christmas card, signed 'Edward', or whatever the man's Christian name was. No, Christopher couldn't remember *exactly* why he received a greeting from the man each year and, no, he didn't reciprocate the card, because 'Edward' never provided an address or, I surmised, even a surname. Sinclair-Stevenson, a combative and assertive Old Etonian and nobody's fool, seemed quite shaken by the visit and by whatever was said to him. Nor has he since alluded to *Spycatcher*, which, as he appreciates the cut and thrust of publishing as much as I do, shows dangerous and unusual restraint on his part. And I have not chosen (until now) to embarrass him by raising the subject. But it should be on the record.

Back at Doughty Street, Anthony Sheil Associates duly received its visit from two VAT inspectors. Neville Burrell kept his well-honed eyes upon them throughout their investigation as they riffled through invoices and invoice books, statements and ledgers, checked columns of figures and double-checked them. The only suspicious thing about the visit, Burrell reported afterwards, was that he kept finding them gravitating towards the 'W' drawer in the filing cabinet and he would have to keep directing them back to the files they'd purported to be consulting, pointing out that, say, 'A' for Ackroyd was there, 'F' for Fowles there, 'C' for Cookson there. Oh, all right. 'W' for Weldon was indeed in that file. Maybe they'd been searching for 'Wales, Prince of', I suggested, seeking to discover whether we'd raised an invoice for Value Added Tax on his royalties. Sheil and Burrell smiled at me wearily.

Events soon speeded up. Brian Perman at Heinemann's Mayfair offices had a visit from, presumably, the same stuffed shirt, bowler hat and rolled umbrella which had called on Sinclair-Stevenson in Long Acre. That very day Perman came to see me. In some excitement, tense and tight-lipped, he told me that Heinemann could not publish *Spycatcher* in the UK or they would be injuncted and the book suppressed. He had a favour to ask: would I be prepared to extend the territory within which Heinemann had the legal right to publish and distribute the book from, as is conventional with publishing contracts for books by British authors, the UK and Commonwealth to, well, the world? I immediately concurred, on one condition: that Heinemann would permit Viking to publish in the USA, Viking having already acquired the US rights through Wallace & Sheil, our agency in New York. Immediately prior to the visit from the Customs and Excise officers – or were they Special Branch officers posing as VAT inspectors (*that* is sheer Joe Orton)? – I had transferred all the agency's documentation regarding the book to our New York office, including the papers on which I had slept. Wallace & Sheil became, as legally was necessary, the agents and agents of record for *Spycatcher*.

Viking quietly slipped the book out in early 1987 and very handsome the volume looked, bound in black boards with silver lettering on the spine and protected by a black dust wrapper also with silver lettering. They did a small first printing, but were obliged to return to press quickly. Copies of the Viking edition were posted to the UK from the USA, and if you returned from the States with a copy or three in your luggage you were much admired, rather like those who infiltrated Maurice Girodias' green-covered Traveller's Library – whether Durrell or dirt, Beckett or bucket, literature or pornography – from naughty France to staid England in the fifties and even the early sixties.

Paul Greengrass's name did not appear on those early printings any more than Oscar Wilde's had been on the first six impressions of *The Ballad of Reading Gaol*, a book equally if differently notorious in its day. (Odd, come to think of it, that I should possess a copy of the *Ballad* signed by Wilde but lack a *Spycatcher* signed by Wright or Greengrass.) The co-author's name was added to the title page of the sixth printing, authorship being described as 'by Peter Wright with Paul Greengrass'. Wright was reluctant to see his collaborator's name on the book but was eventually persuaded.

Then one day, in spring 1987, Heinemann Australia, master-minded by their managing director, Sandy Grant, casually sneaked the book out. Mrs Thatcher at once requested activity and results from her law officers, the point being that the British Government had no jurisdiction within the US courts but it did, or so it was assumed, in Australia as part of the Commonwealth. Besides which, British books published in Australia could legally and without impunity be brought into the UK. *Spycatcher* was then published in the Republic of Ireland in October 1987.

In July 1987 I had accepted an invitation to a party being hosted by Paul Hamlyn and Terence Conran in the restaurant at Heals shop in Tottenham Court Road to inaugurate their new jointly owned publishing house, Conran Octopus. The party commenced at 6 p.m. and I arrived a minute or two early as I had a play to review an hour later on behalf of the *London Daily News*. Paul Hamlyn, an immensely complex and shy man who was conversant with at least some of the background to *Spycatcher*, hovered vaguely around the young women preparing the room and the spread, playing with the canapés, juggling with wine bottles and glasses. I walked straight up to him, took him aside, presented him with his Heinemann managing director's compliments and told him that, an hour or so earlier, the British Government had taken the decision to injunct *Spycatcher*. Hamlyn, a life-long Labour man, puffed his slender frame up with real indignation and looked outraged. A man not given to over-employing the English language (it was no accident that he made his initial repu-tation publishing books with many pictures and few words), he muttered that as soon as the party was over he'd telephone his old friend Bob Hawke, Australia's Prime Minister, and discuss the matter. The printed word must not be suppressed. Hamlyn's influential dander was up.

I shall not, you will be relieved to learn, rehearse what subsequently occurred in the *Spycatcher* trial in Australia, as events have been remorsely documented by the participants, notably by Wright's and Heinemann Australia's barrister, Malcolm Turnbull, whose career was made as a result of his cross-examination of Mrs Thatcher's Secretary to the Cabinet, Sir Robert Armstrong (later Lord Armstrong of Ilminster) and David Hooper, their solicitor.

It was only in December 1991, with Mrs Thatcher gone for a year and a month, that the European Community courts ruled that the British newspapers which had published extracts from the book when it had been readily available almost everywhere else in the world were not in breach of the law as the British courts had insisted. Even then, although copies of the paperback were still to be found in British bookshops (for months they'd been stacked, in many shops, by the till, like condoms in a pharmacist's shop: 'Oh, and I'll have my *Spycatcher*'), Heinemann coolly declined to publish in the UK. Bookshops had consistently ordered the Heinemann Australia paperback edition, which was printed 'abroad', from exporters and wholesalers in the Netherlands.

In Sweden, to capitalise on the relentless publicity, the publishers put twelve translators to work simultaneously, each one being requested to do thirty-odd pages in a very few days, and the book was on the market rapidly. Most of the foreign editions, in paperback, used the basic cover design of the US and Australian editions, carrying a device of the Union Jack and the Stars and Stripes *in flagrante delicto* with the now defunct hammer and sickle. Only in one of the Chinese translations was the Chinese flag included on the cover, presumably a marketing ploy somewhat analagous to portraying Lolita, in the Chinese translation, as a doe-eyed oriental nymphet in a slinky Suzy Wong sheath dress. There is no mention of China or matters Chinese in *Spycatcher*.

In October 1988 I paid a visit to China, the only literary agent member of a Publishers' Association copyright delegation. Greengrass and my foreign rights colleague Paul Marsh had asked me if

I would try to bring back a copy of the pirated edition of *Spy-catcher*, which they'd heard existed. The bookshops of Shanghai and Beijing (Peking), the two cities the delegation visited, have many bookshops, piled from floor to ceiling with paperbacks (but they don't resemble branches of Waterstone's). Particular shops, or section of shops, specialise in pirated books, translated from other tongues into Chinese languages. Every time I spotted one of these shops and tried to gravitate towards it (I grew to recognise the fascia board, or the Chinese equivalent thereof), a Chinese official accompanying our delegation would gently but firmly direct me away. Our task was to try to persuade the Chinese to sign and adhere to one of the world's two leading copyright conventions, either the Universal, which the Americans espouse, or the Berne, which gives wider protection. Ours was the eighth British delegation in ten years, and there had been almost as many official visits from the Americans. The Chinese were on the verge of becoming signatories to one or other convention, realising that only if they did so was there the possibility of many Chinese books being reciprocally translated into English or American. Agreement would have been reached earlier than 1992, had the horrors of Tiananmen Square not erupted in June 1989.

My ten days in China did not seem likely to disclose a copy of *Spycatcher*, pirated or otherwise. On the way to Shanghai airport to catch our long flight back to London, we stopped off – rather reluctantly, as we were all exhausted after days of bowing and scraping, receiving and presenting visiting cards, drinking gallons of tea and concentrating on hours and hours of Chinese languages translated into English – at the house of a friend of one of the delegation for, yes, tea. Our final tea.

He enquired of the eight of us whether we'd enjoyed ourselves and had found our visit both constructive and instructive. We responded, inevitably and truthfully, to the effect that we had. I jocularly mourned the fact that I'd failed to unearth a copy of the pirated edition of *Spycatcher*, a book that interested me. (There was, I should explain, no unpirated edition of *Spycatcher* in a Chinese language. There was, in practical terms, no unpirated edition of any English-language book in a Chinese language, which was why we, and the Americans, joint custodians of the book in English, were so concerned that the Chinese should become signatories to a copyright convention.) Our host excused himself from the room, then returned with not one but three distinct pirated editions, different translations, of *Spycatcher*. The one that had been published first sold at 33 yen, the next at 30 yen, the latest at 28 yen. *Spycatcher* was a hot property in China, each new publisher undercutting the previous one in an attempt to capitalise on sales. Our friend generously presented me with all three copies, saying that he could pick up further copies more easily than I could. I displayed them triumphantly to Greengrass upon returning to London.

A not unrevealing footnote to the story is that, apart from his initial advance from Brian Perman's Heinemann, Paul Greengrass has been forbidden by the British Government to receive a penny by way of royalties. Peter Wright has received, via Australia and New York, his contractual remuneration. Greengrass would have had to go into tax exile to benefit from his stipend, but for all kinds of reasons – not least that his children are at school in the UK, and why in any case should he flee the country as this is where he was born, grew up and works in television and film? – he deliberately declined to rat. Even so, his bank statements were impounded and scrutinised, and he was, and probably still is, treated not as the scrupulous professional he is, but as a pariah.

When the *Spycatcher* trial was taking place in Melbourne, Heinemann besought Greengrass to fly out there and brief them in the courtroom. He felt it his duty to do so. It is probably the case that without his advice, his detailed knowledge of the facts and of Peter Wright's life (Wright was, understandably, pretty unwell at this time), Heinemann would quite possibly not have been granted permission to publish the book worldwide. Although Greengrass's air fare was paid, he received no further expenses. Perman believes that Heinemann should have made a profit of around £4 million from the book. They paid Greengrass £3,000 on signature of the contract, and my remonstrations on my client's behalf to Perman's successor that Greengrass should receive further payments were met merely with raised eyebrows and scepticism. My point was that had Greengrass attempted to bring his royalty earnings into this country where he needed them (rather than spend them in the USA or Australasia), they would have been impounded. In a manner of speaking, Mrs Thatcher might be thought to have won after all.

There were a number of spin-offs of *Spycatcher*, including a packet of Fundoms: 'Spermcatcher: MI5 Penetrated by Russian Sperms. Contras used by CIA – big cover-up expected. Wilson government laid bare by secret service agents – all exposed!' The author of this work, apparently, was one Peter Tight, and other available titles included *The Sperm Who Came in from the Cold* and *The Sperm Who Loved Me*. Good dirty fun, the packet contained, it was claimed, three real contraceptives, to be used before 1993.

*Spycatcher* was legally published in translation in fifteen countries – Spain, Finland, Sweden, Norway, Denmark, the Netherlands, Germany, France, Turkey, Argentina, Brazil, Greece, Japan, Italy and Israel (in Hebrew) – and pirated in various Far East countries including China, Taiwan and Korea, and in Arabic.

Another political book which hit the headlines and which I handled as agent was *The Minister and the Massacres* (1986) by the self-styled Count Tolstoy (why should he, born and certainly expensively bred an Englishman, acknowledge the Russian Revolution?). Nikolai Tolstoy's infinitely, patiently documented history is an indictment of Harold Macmillan and his ADC, Brigadier Toby Low, later ennobled as Lord Aldington, who Tolstoy alleged were responsible for sending thousands of White Russians to their deaths at Klagenfurt in Austria in May 1945. Aldington insisted that he wasn't in the area on 22 May, when the order to dispatch the Chetniks to Marshal Tito and certain slaughter was given, and the jury at the Royal Courts of Justice found in his favour. At the time of writing, Tolstoy is considering an appeal.

Tolstoy, who sports elegantly cut check suits, is a man of shining conviction. To say he is more British than the British is apt only in that his father was an *émigré*. Yet he doesn't rate an entry in *Who's Who*. He is a Jacobite and an incorrigible romantic; and, like Peter Wright, of the Right rather than the Left. His supporters have ridiculous names and titles and include (I take this selection from his appeal letterhead) Count Leopold Goëss, Countess Casimir Grocholski, Prince Dmitri Galitzine, Princess Tatiana Metternich, Mrs Zoe Polanska-Palmer, the Very Revd Father Michael Protopopov, Prince and Princess Lew Sapieha, Philipp von Schoeller and the Duke of Valderano. Ronald Firbank could not have done better, nor Offenbach's librettists. Other patrons include Peter Ackroyd, Lindsay Anderson, Sir Nicholas Fairbairn, Richard Ingrams, Lady Olga Maitland, Chapman Pincher, Professor Roger Scruton, Gavin Stamp, Colin Thubron, Alan Watkins, Auberon Waugh and, perhaps most appropriately, Michael Wharton ('Peter Simple').

Tolstoy, like Wright, is in many respects a simple soul who believes in right and wrong, in St George and the Dragon. He deals, as he sees it, in facts rather than in interpretations of facts or in opinions. He does not, as an historian, believe in creative thinking. He does not have the mind or imagination of the novelist, yet he has published a mammoth novel, *The Coming of the King* (1988), a hugely ambitious first part of a trilogy about the Arthurian legend (no legend to Tolstoy), heavily weighted in the direction of Celtic studies and scholarship rather than derived from the fiction writer's soaring flights of imagination.

Tolstoy's tragedy was to convince himself that his belief in the rightness of his historical documentation, evidence and argument was bound to triumph in the courtroom when Lord Aldington sued him (Macmillan, who declined to grapple with the matter, had died in 1986) and a man called Nigel Watts – a sprat to ensnare a mackerel – for libel.

Bolstered by what he regarded as a cast iron, irrefutable case, Tolstoy couldn't countenance the possibility that he might lose the action. I, and no doubt countless others, warned him about the risks of defending a libel action, particularly where the plaintiff was a member of the British Establishment, but he laughed such worries off.

The fact that Harold Macmillan had declined to prosecute Tolstoy, or collude in a prosecution, both strengthened and weakened the historian's case. One school of thought suggested that the ancient, dying Macmillan – a bit like King Lear run to seed – couldn't raise the energy to sue the Count, thinking it more dignified to leave well alone and allow history to adjudicate. The other view, to which Tolstoy adhered, was that the first Earl of

Stockton, as Macmillan had become, didn't dare risk an action in case Tolstoy was proved right and Macmillan's reputation was severely dented. The fact is that, forty-five years and more after the end of World War II, it was most improbable that what actually happened on a particular day in the north of Italy in the aftermath of five years of hostilities, with the world shattered and exhausted, would be unravelled with the precision and clarity of, say, a poem by W. H. Auden. Besides which (Tolstoy never made sufficient allowance for this), Aldington was a respected workaday politician who had been favoured by Macmillan and who, after being a junior member of his government in the fifties, rose, at the end of the decade, to be deputy chairman of the Tory Party. He also became chairman of Sun Alliance and the London Insurance Company, and insurance and assurance were the names of the game. He was as British as roast beef. Tolstoy, on the other hand, was the son of White Russians who had settled in England in the twenties. He was but a distant relative of the author of *War and Peace*, yet his continuing use of the rank of Count implied, rather preposterously, that certain historical events hadn't occurred. Tolstoy is such a charming, disingenuous gentleman that it seems reasonable, if he enjoys the epithet, to indulge him in the petty vanity of calling himself or even being addressed as Count rather than Esquire or Mister, let alone Comrade.

To those who know him it seems clear that Tolstoy is genuinely concerned to establish the truth about what happened at Klagenfurt. That the jury, after a wearisome trial, awarded damages against him greater than had ever before been awarded in a libel case (£1½ million) merely endorses for me the self-serving vindictiveness of our libel laws. Tolstoy, striving to go on writing history and novels under the outrageous weight of his bankruptcy, believes that he will soon be vindicated. I hope so too, because of the man's integrity.

# XXX

When I was at Gollancz, I became involved with a number of politicians' books in addition to George Brown's. They were mostly of the dry and worthy sort. Gollancz, in the late sixties and early seventies, paid lip-service in yellow, magenta and black covers to the bequest of the Left Book Club, but book readers and buyers, even those still politically committed, resisted reading, let alone buying, didactic books written in workman-like prose about the way forward. Even Penguin Specials, which had been an influence in the land of the intelligentsia a few years earlier, were no longer selling as they had done. People, on the whole, were getting their fill and fix of politics and current affairs from rapidly fattening newspapers and colour supplements and from television. But Gollancz, understandably, did not want to lose its links with its historic past. After all, politics was the reason why in the thirties Victor Gollancz established his imprint and became a publisher, dispensing his largesse ever leftward, though not to George Orwell when the pseudonymous author turned up in 1944 with the manuscript of *Animal Farm*, which Gollancz thought put the cloven hoof unfairly into Marshal Stalin. Orwell's allegory was rejected by a clutch of publishers, including the eponymous Jonathan Cape and T. S. Eliot at Faber and Faber, before being put under starter's orders by the patrician Fred Warburg.

At Gollancz in my time, we published the then youngish MP for Motherwell, Dr Jeremy Bray (he always liked the Dr), on science and technology, an especially dry tome of which I recall only the stultifying charts and graphs which were legion and no doubt justified the white-hot heat of Harold Wilson's and Dr Bray's technological revolution. We published Eric Moonman, a decent man and honourable Member, whose main distinction, with hindsight, was to have been addressing the House of Commons at the moment the first spacemen landed on the moon. We published, most regal of all, the generous-minded and astringent Judith Hart, on overseas aid and development.

These books, and others nearly as worthy, came to us through the contacts of Ben Whitaker who, until Glenda Jackson won the seat at the 1992 general election, had been Hampstead and High-gate's solitary Labour MP (1966-70). In the wake of his exit from the House, I appointed Whitaker as Gollancz's political books adviser, and it was a useful appointment. He had succeeded Henry Brooke, arguably the most illiberal of Home Secretaries in decades (there's a lot of competition), as Hampstead's MP, and as I lived in the constituency at the time, he had my vote. On the steps of Hampstead's Old Town Hall where he and Brooke emerged after the count, Whitaker made a brief but gracious speech: 'The victory is not mine, but Hampstead's.' Bliss was it in that dawn to be alive. Since his departure from the House, Whitaker has been director of the Minority Rights Group, and is currently director of the Gulbenkian Foundation, UK. Presumably, given the fact that he was educated at Eton and Oxford and practised as a barrister, and that he and his wife Janet (who before their marriage worked for André Deutsch) live in an idiosyncratic mansion over-looking Primrose Hill, Whitaker is well-heeled. Certainly he's that increasing anomaly in the nineties, a moneyed, sophisticated socialist who remains so for reasons of history and conviction rather than self-interest. Yet when you go to parties or dinner *chez* Whitaker you meet not the working class but successful middle-class freethinkers and intellectuals, as if Ibsen and Shaw had newly arrived in NW3. I remember in the early seventies going to dinner there, accompanied by Liz Calder, publicity director at Gollancz. Liz had only recently returned to this country from working for some years in Rio de Janeiro and wasn't, at that time, well up on British politics. When we went in to dinner there were name cards by the place settings. Liz was put next to someone called 'Edward'. On enquiring of her neighbour what his occu-pation was, he revealed modestly that he was a politician. In fact he was the sometime Minister for Education, the Rt Hon. Sir Edward Boyle.

Until the 1992 general election, I always voted Labour. The only exception was voting Green one wild morning in some EEC election or other. In 1992 I voted Green again, as I couldn't stomach the William-and-Mary duo of Mr and Mrs Kinnock. Yet I would rather be carted away to the funny farm than place a cross on a ballot paper against a Conservative candidate. My middle-class generation still believes instinctively – it is our inheritance – that the Liberals, whatever you call them, do not win, or even come second, should you wish to back the underdog. (Tell *that* to Sir Clement Freud.) Besides which, and not forgetting the intellectual buccaneering of Dr David Owen and his pals, they're frankly wishy-washy, betwixt and between. Politics is not about niceness; if anything it's about nastiness. It is not about reasonableness; it is about unreasonableness, extremes. Thus those of us who hate to think of ourselves as moralistically liberal, had to admit that Mrs Thatcher transformed Britain in the short term, restoring to us much of our pride as a nation. But this has already evaporated. And was it worth what the Iron Lady did to the individual soul, the innate decency of the individual, the almost Dickensian sense of fair play and richness of character that pertained in most breasts before her eleven-year wallow in Downing Street, her reign of (however necessary it may have been) ruthless humourlessness or humourless ruthlessness?

During the Thatcher years, and as the nation grew to accept them, I became intrigued by the career of Bernard Ingham, the Prime Minister's press secretary. From television and newspaper pictures he looked like the archetypal fall guy, the stooge, of a comic duo. But there was some confusion there as, whatever else she was, Mrs Thatcher was hardly a comedian. I was intrigued by how this ex-*Guardian* journalist, obsessed not just with Yorkshire but with, specifically, the West Riding thereof, could transform himself into a civil servant and serve as press officer to Tony Benn, then Barbara Castle and then, becoming an influence in the land, the Prime Minister herself – not unlike Paul Johnson, the one-time socialist who red-headedly and vigorously edited the *New Statesman* when it was more read and influential than the *Spectator*, and then overnight, or so it seemed, became the scourge of the Left and one of Mrs Thatcher's greatest advocates, even acolytes. There was a crucial difference though. Johnson, as a professional freelance writer, was perfectly entitled, provided he continued to receive commissions, to change the colour and temper of his politics as frequently, and as arbitrarily, as he desired or felt the need to do so. Ingham, as a civil servant, was not permitted to allow his personal politics to intrude upon the job. Thus whether by background, education or conviction he was of the Right or of the Left, or shifted his view at the drop of a hat, was irrelevant, provided that he conducted his job as press officer impartially. Yet in his years with Mrs Thatcher, he was increasingly regarded, like the St Bernard he came to resemble, as His Mistress's Voice; which, in a professional sense, he was and was paid to be. I chose to believe, without too much evidence one way or the other, that Ingham remained, in the dull and isolated privacy of the clapboard polling booth, a closet socialist.

After the fall of Mrs Thatcher and the subsequent hasty departure of Ingham, soon to be Sir Bernard, from Downing Street, he began to write a weekly column for the *Daily Express*. It was at once plain that the civil servant's objectivity and impartiality had been swamped by the charismatic force of the Prime Minister. I reluctantly had to accept that the ranting in the *Express* and the directorship of McDonald's the hamburger chain were the real man, although I never found him anything other than completely charming, easy to work with and professional in all my dealings with him in connection with his rumbustuous memoirs, *Kill the Messenger*. But the tone of his *Express* column was a combination of Samuel Smiles and Attila the Hun.

Forget that Ingham was originally a journalist. Can there ever have been a more influential espouser of the petty bourgeois, nine to five, I'm-all-right-Jack brigade in Britain than big Bernard? He didn't believe in the healing powers of the social services only because he was convinced that we all, like himself, should and could work, and work hard, and could, with a modicum of application, pull ourselves up by our bootstraps and not only make a decent living, but in addition to that better ourselves. In truth, we surely are the most conservative of nations. We're happy for Shakespeare and Dickens to have produced our great written art for us (and they weren't nine-to-five men), but we wouldn't have wanted to lead such erratic lives ourselves. (At least writers – and writing is the art in which we have excelled – can endeavour to pin down experience precisely, unlike artists and composers, who can only make a stab at a non-verbal equivalent. The English language is, or so we like to romanticise, our greatest asset and visible export. This, ironically, is why we are such lousy linguists, so bad with other people's languages. If ours is the lingua franca, as increasingly it is, why should we trouble, even condescend, to learn other tongues?)

I stalked Ingham for his memoirs years before he was in a position to write them. Even before I met him, I surmised that his account of the Thatcher years, not least because he was a professional communicator, would be as interesting as any Cabinet Minister's, especially if he got them out quickly, which is a primary requisite in the marketing of political memoirs these days. He did, and he became highly successful on, as he put it, the rubber chicken circuit, preaching to the faithful at luncheons and dinners, day after day, night after night.

Conversations with Ingham in the months following the departure of his mistress could assume a surreal quality as he would invariably refer to her as 'the Prime Minister'. You would think: I'd no idea that was John Major's view. Or that John Major had done that. Good gracious me. Then you'd adjust your sights and quickly realise that Bernard was talking about the Queen Across The Water. He indulged in this sort of talk particularly at the end of the day, over a glass of spirits. He was often described, unlovingly, in the press as the Prime Minister's poodle. In truth he looked more like a sheepdog after a night out, or even Nana in *Peter Pan*. It wasn't that he was untidy, just that somehow he had a recalcitrant body and a face that looked permanently windswept. But his craggy features could break into a guileless, unselfconscious smile.

The other press officer I knew well, indeed much better, was Michael Shea, who did the job at Buckingham Palace for almost ten years. Shea is a much smoother man than Ingham, Isaac to his Esau. He gleaned a great deal of satisfaction from his own career. He started in the diplomatic service, and was seconded to the British Information Services in Washington in the mid-sixties to massage the Prince of Wales's 1976 tour of the States. So satisfied was the Prince with the smoothness of the arrangements and assistance provided by Shea that he recommended Shea to the Queen and, in 1978, Shea became her press secretary.

His influence at Buckingham Palace was considerable, although journalists didn't take to him. Journalists are an exceptionally insecure, neurotic, self-righteous lot without, if truth be told, a responsible role in society. Unless a journalist is a star and commands his or her own column – Barbara Amiel, Bernard Levin, Alan Watkins, Bryan Appleyard – it is not really an occupation for a grown-up, the way that being a doctor or a barrister or a shopkeeper (subject to what you're selling) is; and most journalists are all too aware of this. Yesterday's great utterances are indeed destined for tomorrow's fish and chips. Hence the huffing and puffing of hacks, the self-righteous lather they work themselves into if they're denied access or flattery. Shea single-handedly did more, for better or for worse (and that is a very different matter, a much more significant subject), to democratise the image of the Royal Family to the British public than any of his more naturally cautious predecessors.

His was, to say the least, an interesting job but, I'd have thought, a virtually impossible one. Ingham's task was to put forward Mrs Thatcher's policies to the British press, and thus the public; Shea's, in a manner of speaking, was to keep the Queen's policies from press and public precisely because Her Majesty, by the nature of her constitutional role, was kept in office by the taxpayer on the tacit understanding that she had no policies, no political views. Even her opinions, trivial or profound, had to be protected from public scrutiny. Shea's job was on the one hand to ensure that the mystique (if not quite the mystery), the sanctity almost of our constitutional monarchy was not weakened or, worse still, violated; on the other hand to make the Royal Family, and especially the monarch, seem relevant to our lives in the latter part of the twentieth century. Somehow, despite the increasingly frenetic antics of the odd duchess or princess and Hooray Henry member of the extended Royal Family, Shea achieved that objective – just. The Queen is still secure on her pedestal, significantly because we still don't know what she really thinks about anything, with the possible exception of horses and headscarves and corgis. This is as it has to be. Perhaps she holds fervent views on every topic under the sun, but somehow I doubt it. The Queen's job is simply to be Queen.

Once when I was visiting Shea in his press office at the Palace (a somewhat dowdy, underlit room with long-legged, large-footed Sloanes clumping about and forever hovering breathless) Prince Philip wandered in and sat down, looking diminished and tired. Improbably, the television journalist and 'personality' David (now Sir David) Frost then bustled into the room (maybe he's an honorary Royal?) and immediately struck up a conversation with the Duke. Then Prince Andrew, sweaty in white open-neck shirt and shorts and clutching a tennis racket, joined the mêlée. Whether it is BBC1 or 2, ITV or Channel 4, we need our royal soap opera, if only because, like Everest, it is there (at least at the time of writing). It is, indeed, much more precarious than we may think, and the tabloid editors, court reporters and Andrew Mortons play with it at their peril.

The democratisation of the Royals during the Shea era was essential if the tumbrils weren't to roll. I don't know why I am relieved that the Queen remains in place, but I am. You cannot argue intellectually for the Queen any more than you can prove that Christ exists. You accept her or you don't, like, I suppose, God or the Pope. Yet my Presbyterian gorge rises at the exotic conceit, a clash of matters temporal and spiritual, that the monarch down the road at Buckingham Palace can also be head of the Church of England at Westminster Abbey or Canterbury Cathedral.

The press corps, as they like to think of themselves, were unenamoured of Shea chiefly because he wasn't a journalist, he wasn't 'one of us'. He refused to accept, rightly, that their jobs were, in essence, different from other people's jobs. Five years after he left the Palace, he was moved from what had been an anguished silence to pen three articles about the press hounding of the Royals for, ironically, the republican Rupert Murdoch's *Times* in December 1992, which caused the self-righteous rat pack, the Peter Mackays and Andrew Neills and a particularly virulent fellow in the *Sun*, Richard Littlejohn (clearly no Robin Hood he), to accuse Shea of hypocrisy. He may prove to be the Danton of the second British Revolution; certainly he is no Robespierre.

Anthony Rudolf is a loquacious and enthusiastic poet and translator who makes a modest living working for the BBC World Service. He ploughs all his savings into a small publishing house, the Menard Press, which specialises in publishing poetry, chiefly by Jewish writers, translated into English. Some years ago, a bit like Laura Riding's denunciation of her art, Rudolf decided that poetry wouldn't save the world and instead he'd publish material that denounced the nuclear bomb and atomic warfare. One of the worthy pamphlets he published was by Lord Zuckerman. Zuckerman wanted to publish a volume of autobiography next, which wasn't right for the Menard Press, and Tony put him in my direction.

I represented Zuckerman for almost a decade, but I was never able to address him either by letter or in person as 'Solly'. Although he always wrote to me as 'Giles', he continued to sign himself 'S. Zuckerman'. As he was a generation older than me, born in 1904, and hugely distinguished, I could live with this. Zuckerman was prone to telephone a great deal, and was always annoyed – he was known in the office as Lord Grumpy – when I was either on the telephone, in a meeting or out of the office. A man who clearly hadn't wasted much time in his long and successful life, he didn't want to start wasting it in his final years. He lived with his wife, who on the telephone sounded even fiercer than he did, at a house in Norfolk preposterously called The Shooting Box, the thought of which always made me laugh, given that for many years Zuckerman was the secretary, then president, of the Zoological Society of London. Although he was a great buddy of the Duke of Edinburgh, I cannot imagine he approved of shooting, at least not of animals. On the other hand, Auberon Waugh used to get very cross with Zuckerman in his *Private Eye* diary for advocating the gassing of badgers in their sets.

Zuckerman, who died in April 1993, must be one of the great men of our era, not just because he was chief scientific adviser to *every* British Prime Minister from Churchill to Thatcher – surely a unique achievement – but because of the wider use he made of his extraordinary influence and because of his persuasive, unrelenting efforts to halt the nuclear struggle. In his later years he was more highly regarded in the United States than in Britain.

In the way of publishing, the American editor of Zuckerman's second volume of autobiography, *Monkeys, Men and Missiles* (1988), suggested that the eminent baron might follow it up with a book about some of the influential people whom he had known and worked with. Zuckerman came up with the idea of a volume comprising six pen portraits of three Americans, three Brits, the idea being that the book would be of equal interest on both sides of the Atlantic. I knew when the manuscript came in that it would be virtually impossible, in the difficult publishing climate that prevailed in 1990, to find a publisher, and HarperCollins, which had brought out Zuckerman's last books, was not interested. I offered the manuscript to Peter Owen, who has published more minor books by distinguished writers than anyone else. Owen acquired *Six Men Out of the Ordinary* (1992) for a minuscule advance, and promptly wrote to the Duke of Edinburgh asking if he'd write a foreword. Prince Philip, I suspect, assumed Zuckerman had suggested this. On the contrary, Zuckerman was livid as he'd specifically told Owen that his friend the Duke was not to be approached. By return of post, Prince Philip sent a foreword, and Peter Owen persuaded Christina Foyle to give a luncheon when the book was published. It took place, rather oddly, some two months before publication, and was sparsely attended.

I found myself at the top table, sitting next to the very eminent physicist Sir Rudolf Peierls. The luncheon was presided over by Lord Jenkins of Hillhead, who told a story about how once, when he'd been sitting on the verandah of a house he was staying at in India, a monkey hopped down beside him. Roy Jenkins, looking up, enquired of the monkey whether it knew his old friend Solly Zuckerman. The monkey nodded, then departed.

Sir Rudolf Peierls, born in 1907, was pretty old, obviously, and pretty decrepit: Zuckerman told me later that he had recently suffered a stroke. In the course of his speech, Zuckerman revealed that Peierls had advised both Churchill and Attlee what the effect of dropping the atomic bomb on Hiroshima and Nagasaki (and anywhere else) would be, yet the Prime Ministers denied in years to come that any scientist had told them. When Zuckerman was praising Peierls, I noticed, looking sideways, that Sir Rudolf's head was bowed down and his chin rested on his chest. How very modest, I thought.

Not so the *Daily Telegraph*, which reported the next day that Peierls had fallen asleep in the middle of the luncheon. I wasn't having this, and penned a letter to the editor which, to my surprise, was published. Some days later I received a letter from Sir Rudolf:

> I am writing on the assumption that you are the Mr Giles Gordon who was my neighbour at the Foyles Literary Luncheon for Lord Zuckerman the other day. If you are not, please disregard this letter.
>
> If you are, I would like to express my appreciation of your coming gallantly to my defence against the comments by Peterborough in the *Daily Telegraph*. I am most grateful, but I must confess that I did fall asleep, and woke up only to the tail end of Zuckerman's remarks about me. This, no doubt, resulted from a combination of old age with plenty of good drink.

I treasure that letter. If only the young, and even more the middle-aged, possessed the grace of the old.

Once, when I took Zuckerman to lunch at the Garrick, he spotted Lord Cudlipp (probably recognising him by the length of his cigar). Zuckerman told me how, years before, when he had been secretary of London Zoo, he had arrived very late at that year's Royal Academy dinner. So late was he that the speeches had begun. Zuckerman slipped into his seat, next to Hugh Cudlipp, who whispered to him, 'Where have you been?' Cudlipp must have noticed, too, that Zuckerman was wearing black tie and dinner jacket whereas every other male present was wearing white tie and tails. 'I'll tell you later,' Zuckerman whispered back.

He'd been dressing for the dinner in his flat at the Zoo when his preparations were interrupted by a knock on the front door. He had already struggled into his starched shirt, striped trousers and tails. At the door was the keeper of the tortoises, who had some sorrowful news for the secretary. The giant tortoise was dying. He hadn't taken any food for days and the keeper thought that the secretary should know about it. Dressed, or partially dressed, as he was, Zuckerman hurried with the keeper to the giant tortoise's quarters. Zuckerman took one look at the poor creature and pronounced that it was merely constipated. 'Fetch a gallon of castor oil,' he said, and ordered that the heavy animal be chained, winched upwards and left dangling above ground. The castor oil was brought, the creature chained and heaved up. 'Pour the tin of castor oil into the tortoise's mouth,' said Zuckerman. The keeper, presumably standing on a stepladder, poured the entire gallon of castor oil slowly into the animal's mouth, then stood back. Zuckerman and the staff members in attendance looked up anxiously. Eventually there was a bit of a noise from inside the giant tortoise, but nothing else seemed to be about to happen. 'Get another gallon of castor oil and give it to the tortoise,' said Zuckerman. The keeper did as requested, and a second gallon of castor oil was poured into the animal. Suddenly there was the most incredible sound of rumbling and exploding from the innards of the great beast. The tortoise slowly began to spin on its chains, and then the spinning began to speed up. Lord Zuckerman, the head keeper and everyone else in the vicinity was showered, pelted, saturated with excrement and liquid from the poor animal.

'That,' explained Zuckerman to Cudlipp at the end of the Royal Academy dinner, 'is why I am late.' And why he hadn't been wearing his tails.

Some time in 1985, Michael Shea rang me from Buckingham Palace to say that Rex Fleet, the arts-loving and philanthropic chairman and chief executive of the British arm of NCR, the American computer company, wanted to put some cash into fiction, preferably a prize. Had I any ideas? Shea had encountered Fleet and NCR when the company had sold some computers and word processors to Buckingham Palace. Knowing that Shea wrote books had presumably suggested to Fleet the idea of literature.

I put it to Shea that there were, if anything, already too many prizes for fiction, not least the Booker. Did he realise, did Rex Fleet and NCR realise, that almost 90 per cent of all new *titles* published in the UK each year were non-fiction? In 1985, 5,846 new novels were published, out of a total number of 52,994 titles (including new editions). And weren't NCR in the non-fiction business? Why didn't they award a prize for the best *non-fiction* book of the year?

I was summoned to see Fleet and he bought the idea: the first NCR Book Award for the best non-fiction title of the year was awarded in 1988. The Award is not yet the power in the land that the Booker is, but I'm confident, given time and possibly a major row, that it will be. Silly people (and, it has to be said, some not so silly people) suggest that the name of the prize is a killer, and even sillier people think it has something to do with National Car Parks. NCR Ltd was founded in the States in the nineteenth century and, of course, there were no computers then. There were cash registers. You can see why NCR doesn't care for the initials of its name to be spelt out.

The management committees or administrators of certain literary awards seem to see it as their function to come up with a panel of judges who are likely to disagree strongly among themselves. If you employ as judges five people of totally disparate tastes you are unlikely to end up with universal acclaim for one book. Certainly you are unlikely to end up with the 'best' book, were any such absolute objectivity possible. You will, though, glean much publicity, attended by much controversy, and thus it is assumed that the company or body sponsoring the prize will register in the consumer's mind, and indeed that the winning book or books in dispute will sell in lavish quantities.

NCR sets its sights against this, in an honest endeavour (it can be no more) to pick out and proclaim the best book. First a chairperson of the judges is found – to date they have been Jeremy Isaacs, Magnus Magnusson, Brian Rix (Sir then, now Lord), Ludovic Kennedy, Terence Stamp and David Puttnam. Sue Lawley will be chairperson in 1994. Each year, ten or fifteen people decline, usually because of the amount of reading involved, before white smoke, mixed with more than a little relief, goes up. Which is not to suggest that the judges are usually second or third choice; they're usually tenth or fifteenth. The chairperson is asked if he or she would like to invite the other four judges, or to leave it to NCR. Nearly all have wished to approach kindred spirits and this does tend to lead to strong short lists, even stronger prize-winning books, because the judges' natural inclination is to be in accord. In the case of certain other literary prizes, it seems that judges are chosen with such differing tastes that the winning book is almost bound to be an unsatisfactory compromise. Only once was the NCR system possibly, and certainly inadvertently, abused when the chairperson chose two of his cronies and the three buddies consistently outvoted the other two judges, who were each of more independent mind.

To choose and proclaim *the* best book of the year is impossible when history vies with economics, topography with religion, economics with biography, social history with biology, travel with philosophy, and so on. All the judges can do is to come up with a short list of four titles, chosen from well over 100 books submitted by their publishers, and then, five weeks later, plump for one. The winning books to date have been *Nairn in Darkness and Light* by David Thomson, *Touching the Void* by Joe Simpson, *Citizens* by Simon Schama, *The Invisible Woman* by Claire Tomalin, *Wild Swans* by Jung Chang, and *Never Again* by my client Peter Hennessy.

I took pride in persuading NCR (it was not, surprisingly, difficult to persuade them of this) that another way they could gain plaudits from authors and the book trade was by offering the author of the winning book a larger sum of money than was awarded for any other UK literary prize, and that this should enable the author to buy time to write his or her next book. The philosophy, surely, was admirable, but the first prize of £25,000 went to David Thomson's widow: the poor man had died between his publisher entering the book and the prize being awarded. I nearly cried with frustration at the prize-giving dinner at the Savoy when Mrs Thomson, in a most moving speech, said how grateful she was for the money as it would help her to educate her children. The rules were altered for year two in that the author had to be alive at the time the prize was awarded. Admittedly, if news of the winner leaked an hour or two before the result was announced, one of the other short-listed authors might be tempted to murder. But what publicity for the NCR Book Award!

The prize money, to the winner and the short-listed authors, amounts to £29,500. The overall cost of administering and paying for the award costs NCR Ltd well over £100,000 per annum now, much of the sum going towards a slap-up dinner at the Savoy each May. The prize is increasingly mentioned in the press, not least thanks to the judicious PR exercise undertaken by Dotti Irving, one of the very (very) few intelligent publicists in the book trade. When this happens I do not mean to imply that thousands of individuals or companies charge to their nearest showroom or hardware shop and shriek 'I *must* have an NCR computer', but that advertising of the company's name in this almost philanthropic way has to be subliminally persuasive. The NCR Book Award is industrial patronage of the arts, or at least of scholarship and literacy, at its most intelligent.

# XXXI

I have never fully comprehended the obsession with sport which grips this country, and obviously other countries as well. If politics and current affairs occupy the front pages of our newspapers, sport presides over the back pages. Sport does not play a major, even a minor, part in my life, yet in a strange way I am intrigued that thinking about it, eating it, talking it, reading about it and dreaming it can occupy so much of the lives of so many otherwise reasonably sane people. It is mostly involved with hitting balls of differing sizes and substances all over the place: the history of sport would be much diminished if no one had invented the ball. Of the most popular sports, football and golf, at different ends of the social spectrum, seem to me equally absurd. I can, I suppose, understand the attraction of soccer to its professional players, as if they are good at it they can be paid sums beyond the dreams of avarice.

Conversely, golf seems ideally a game for the middle classes. It takes place in lush and lavish open spaces. Perhaps to play it is to some people more purposeful than taking a walk in the country, or even the town, as the game involves a fair amount of striding from green to green, from tiny hole to tiny hole across mixed terrain.

Croquet is a considerably more arcane and devious game than golf, or of course football. I imagine everyone of an aggressive nature would play croquet if they had a large enough lawn and understood what a brutalising game it is and how bad for the character of those who have mastered it. It makes the boring snooker and billiards seem games almost for gentlemen.

Rugby, which I had to play at school, I am quite indifferent to. It bores me to watch – all kick and run – and I disliked playing it. You get mud all over you, which is not my idea of fun. I was always cowardly at tackling other boys strenuously, and hated the sweaty claustrophobia of the scrummage. I did, though, aged fifteen or sixteen, get pretty excited by the shorts – faded blue cotton, with a slight dusty sheen, quite old and thin – of a pouting, ugly little boy called Kennedy. I insist it was the shorts which excited me and not the boy. Nevertheless, he persuaded me to go camping with him one weekend, somewhere near Edinburgh. We may have gone by bus. I cannot recall. All I remember, the image that comes to mind, is the horror of lying there in a sweet, grassy field with the smell of canvas above and Kennedy and me in our sleeping bags, next to one another. I think it was in the morning. Certainly it was light. He put his hand in my sleeping bag and masturbated me, although I had no idea that this was what he was doing. I knew virtually nothing of the so-called facts of life, and when, in spite of myself, I ejaculated I thought that horrid heavy-breathing Kennedy had somehow caused me to wet my bed; which, in a sense, he had. It was an exquisite moment. Time stood still. It was a combination of a new, unique (it didn't occur to me that what had happened once could conceivably happen again), pleasurable sensation mingled with absolute fear and panic. In the course of the weekend, Kennedy pumped me up and down a number of times. He was, as I remember, very good at it, and must have had some experience. He begged me (I can feel his hot breath close to my face now, like a rasping cow) to do it to him in return, but I couldn't bring myself to. I found the prospect too horrible to contemplate. I fear I have always been selfish sexually.

It was a long time before I realised that what Kennedy had done to me hadn't turned me into a homosexual. I have always associated him, that weekend, and his mouth-watering shorts with rugger, but I don't believe that is why I regard the game, with its ugly goalposts, as so futile. I think it is more to do with the improbable shape of the ball, and the indecisive combination of picking up the ball to run with it, and kicking it. Above all, I suppose I regard games as a waste of time – certainly including most board games – and a way to waste time. Time to me is something not consciously to waste, or while away. Which is not to suggest that I spend my time more 'usefully' than other people.

I know I don't. I love to potter, for instance, spend hours wandering about the house, browsing in books, opening drawers and looking at things, moving pictures and furniture around, playing music. As a teenager I collected Roman coins, but I've never seriously succumbed to stamp-collecting or train-spotting.

On the other hand – and I hope not totally to demolish my strictures above – I am hugely in thrall to cricket, which seems to me a game infinitely closer to art than to sport. I was never any good at the game myself (I think my highest score in a match was eleven runs, and I was a better batsman than bowler) but for three years I was scorer of the Edinburgh Academy's first eleven. I would appear in the first eleven photograph each year, wearing a straw boater, the caption reading: scorer: G. A. E. Gordon. I obtained much satisfaction from keeping the neatest of score books, becoming quite excited as I marked maiden overs, wicket maidens and all the symbols of the score book. I would, when particularly requested by one of our best batsmen, occasionally make 'spiders', those diagrams which indicate where each and every scoring stroke was placed.

The difference between those who revere and relish cricket and those who do not is that the former tend to regard it as the fastest, most intricate game in the world (chess, which I used to enjoy, is more intricate but infinitely slower) and the latter to think of it as the slowest, most enervating. Ne'er shall the twain meet. I once took my elder son to Lord's for the day, when he was in his early teens, but he was bored within minutes. (Rather like the time I took my younger son to the ballet and he said, in the loudest of voices, after about two minutes: 'Dad, when does the speaking start?') He could not comprehend the complexity, the choreography, the poetry of the game. No doubt those who are excited by soccer or rugby would say the same of its detractors.

It has to be conceded that the spectators at, say, Lord's, especially those who sport the hideous maroon and yellow MCC tie, do put you off. They add up to an Identikit cricket supporter, blimpish and wimpish, wearing tweeds or sports jacket or blazer, slate-coloured or fawn slacks, graph paper shirt, pork pie or Homburg hat jauntily perched on the head, and a moustache. Whether they have a fine head of hair or are denuded on top, there's an inheritance of Denis Compton Brylcreem. They carry a shooting-stick or multi-coloured golf umbrella and binoculars, as if they're bird-watching. Their wives will have provided a packed lunch – sandwiches, a slice of cake or even a spot of trifle, a Penguin biscuit perhaps to summon up lost, but never to be forgotten, youth; maybe a half-bottle of claret. More likely they'll be beer men, ordering a foaming (or more probably flat) flagon at one of the drinks tents or taverns, as they are often called, around the ground. It is irretrievably, terrifyingly, self-satisfiedly English, and that our Prime Minister, John Major, seems to spend more time at cricket grounds than in the Palace of Westminster doesn't augur well for his commitment to Europe, which doesn't make a fetish of cricket.

The last time I played, years ago, was in a team captained, if memory serves, by Ronnie Harwood, one of the heroes of these pages. He, like a number of other playwrights including Harold Pinter, Tom Stoppard and Simon Gray, not to mention the late and impossibly great Samuel Beckett (the only Nobel prizewinner to make it into the voluminous pages of cricket's bible, *Wisden*), much enjoys his cricket. There is something in the pages of dialogue in a play, even the breaking of acts into scenes, that corresponds with the inevitable, elegiac progress of a cricket match as the shadows of a declining day lengthen.

When I attempted, in the changing-room, to put on my once white, now yellowing flannels, which I hadn't donned in perhaps a decade, they didn't fit. I like to think that I had lost much weight, that I was thinner than before, but that memory does not serve the circumstances. I had broadened out. I was playing in a writers' team. Luckily, the television playwright and novelist Allan Prior, an affable and generous fellow at all times, happened to have a second pair of flannels with him, and lent them to me for the day. I vaguely remember that I was permitted one over and my bowling, as the over advanced, was increasingly desperate. I think I bowled nine balls because three of them were wides. I didn't bat, presumably because our team had won before I would have had to walk to the crease. I'm sure Allan Prior's flannels were splendid, but they didn't excite me as, years before,

Kennedy's rugby shorts had done. And don't ask me why Mr Prior had two pairs of flannels with him.

The other sport I enjoy watching – surely an anomaly in my character, although I believe there are those who find me aggressive – is boxing, whether in the flesh (especially in the swashbuckling Victorian atmosphere of the Albert Hall) or on television. I am not interested in boxing records, in how many times Muhammad Ali regained the heavyweight championship of the world, or anything like that. I'm stimulated, almost in a sexual way, by the spectacle of two well-matched boxers each trying to gain superiority over the other. I do not enjoy it – indeed, I'm squeamish about it – when one of them gains command over his opponent, but I am elated when the boxer apparently losing regains the initiative. I don't, though reason and humanity tell me I should, find boxing at all degrading to watch. This hardest of sports is to me a ritualistic parallel commentary on life; never a game, never merely a whiling away of time. It is, of course, extremely dangerous, if not cruel; and I wouldn't myself have done it for anything (except at school, where Sergeant McCarron, the gym instructor, insisted ludicrously that it was good for our 'character', an absurd notion which is often employed when people are asked to do what they have no desire to do, particularly in sport). Professional boxers – amateurs, even at Olympic level, seem to flutter about myopically, as if trying to land darts on a dart board – deserve every pound they are paid, and usually a great deal more. Paradoxically, most boxers are not particularly skilled at the sport, which is not to suggest that they aren't the bravest of men, because they are. They are satisfying the voyeurism of the rest of us.

It is all very strange. I just about pass out with horror when I see one man pushing another, or worse still a woman pushing another woman, outside a pub, or in the street, or any kind of unplanned fight. It is the theatrical elements, which are considerable in professional boxing, which are meat and veg to me, no vegetarian.

I have not the courage to be a vegetarian, although, like most people who can afford it, I eat far less meat than I used to. Similarly, I cannot stand up and be counted alongside my client and friend Brigid Brophy in her critique of fishing: How would you like to be a fish, swimming about, when suddenly you feel a hook in your mouth and are jerked out of your environment? Of course I wouldn't, is the only answer. But there's also: I'm not a fish, though if fish were in a position to eat people I might not like it much, but there would be nothing I could do about it except pray that I wouldn't be the one to be caught, cooked and consumed so that fish life might continue. If you are lucky enough to live in a democratic European country, life is substantially about choices, and it is up to each individual who isn't completely downtrodden both to exercise choice and to be aware of why he or she is making such choices.

As I grow older, I begin to obtain much pleasure from gardens, if perhaps not yet from gardening – however hard I try to master the Latin names I am an ignoramus about the identity of most plants. I have, in a manner of speaking, a head start in that I represent those who are, for my money, the best two writers on the subject in the language today. Christopher Lloyd writes about plants, flowers and gardens in the prose of a major creative artist, which he is both as writer and as gardener. Beth Chatto, perhaps more down to earth, the Elizabeth David of gardening, writes a beautiful, practical English. Christopher accepts my ignorance yet comprehends my pleasure in his creations, the garden and the prose. He is a splendidly irascible old gentleman, who wields the language with a scalpel. He lives at Great Dixter near Northiam, West Sussex, in the Elizabethan house that Lutyens adapted for his father, and is a person of the utmost culture and discernment. He rightly scolded me recently for suggesting to Lucy, aged eighteen months, that some of the flowers at Dixter were 'pretty'.

Once Gwenda David, for decades the American publisher Viking's 'scout' in London and surely the best of her breed in the history of publishing, bought some plants from Christopher. He removed them from their red earthenware pot and began to wrap them in some bits of the day-before's newspaper. Gwenda objected, saying she wanted them in the earthenware pot. Christopher pointed out that she had purchased the plant, not the container. Gwenda and Christopher, both with total conviction as to their own rightness, pulled and tugged at the pot which, of course, smashed.

Christopher is also a terrific cook, and a wonderful host. Until a year or two ago he hosted a party at Great Dixter near the end of each Glyndebourne season, for as many of those involved with the opera house as cared to attend, by way of thanking them for the pleasure the season had given him.

I remember in my heady youth being terribly dismissive of opera, believing it to be a mishmash of the theatrical arts – singing, music, acting, dancing – a *mélange* or trifle whose extravagant totality signified less than nothing of substance, an expensive and vulgar bauble. My friend and mentor Jonathan Griffin quietly told me, to my fury at the time (I've never taken such things moderately; moderation was not, I think, a gift with which I was endowed at birth), that when I grew older I would come not only to enjoy opera but to understand that of all the arts it was incomparable, the *crème de la crème*. How right, of course, the dear, gentle man was. Opera is not unlike boxing in that, at its worst, it is appalling, and it is usually pretty awful, at least at the grandest, most ambitious level. The genuinely undersubsidised Royal Opera House at Covent Garden is increasingly hit or miss, and when it's a hit it's usually because Domingo or Pavarotti, in some subfusc ancient production, is in mellifluous, memorable voice, though neither has sung there as exquisitely as I've heard Carlo Bergonzi (in *Ballo in Maschera*).

The English National Opera is a better bet artistically, but no longer the bargain it was. Jonathan Miller's mafioso production of *Rigoletto* there remains the most illuminating single opera production I've witnessed. I cannot keep a tune in my head and when I've played a compact disc of one of my favourite operas – by Mozart, Verdi, Puccini – I cannot tell you whether a particular aria has been sung or not even though I've been in seventh heaven when it was played, if it was played, a few minutes before.

At least opera lovers, when they're not at the opera house, tend to listen to the stuff in the privacy of their homes. You rarely hear opera shrieking out of a leaking head set, because people who enjoy opera are unlikely to listen to it on leaking head sets or to have time for that most horrible invention of the late twentieth century, the Sony Walkman. One morning recently I had to ask a young man – well, yoof – on a bus to turn down the destructive row that was, whether he wished it or not, insinuating itself into the privacy, not to say sanity, of everyone else on the bus. Everybody, I was aware, on the close-packed, lethargic vehicle froze with horror, partly embarrassment, partly relief that someone had popped the request. Everyone, that is, except the youth with the cacophonic, brain-damaged head. His 'music' was playing so loudly that he hadn't heard me.

Yet he was, in this inadvertent clash of the generations, aware of an aggression towards him in the bus, that he was the far from still, quiet centre of attention. He looked up as if to wonder why I was disturbing *his* peace. I repeated my question in an even louder voice. Sullenly he lowered the sound but, as the bus meandered interminably down Gower Street, he sneaked it up gradually in a kind of petty defiance. No doubt he thought angrily that I and everyone else were being anti-social, stuffy and middle-aged and depriving him of his unearned liberty, whereas he, of course, was interfering with ours. The selfishness of most of the young today surely exceeds even my generation's selfishness when we were young, but maybe it was ever thus. A few stops after the scene, the débâcle, another youth prepared to dismount from the bus. As he was about to descend the stairs, he shouted – of course he had to shout as otherwise he would not have been heard – at the youth with the head set: 'Jimi Hendrix is cool, man.' The man with the head set nodded and jerked his thumb in the air.

What would life be like without travel? Much diminished. I am not going to say much about it, because most travel writing is merely nostalgic and vaguely self-congratulatory, as if to endorse how clever you have been in surviving somewhere foreign with all those ever-so-fascinating but quite revolting habits. Paris to me is *the* city of the world, and in any weather or season. I'm not sure about the new, presumably masonic, glass pyramid in the courtyard of the Louvre, though. Shortly after it was erected, I was in the interstices of the gallery and suddenly desperate to relieve myself. Too much wine, no doubt, at lunch. There are fewer opportunities to visit a public lavatory in Paris now than there used to be as most of the stinking street pissoirs have been surgically exterminated, which has improved the smell of the city no end. I noticed, in the bowels of the Louvre, a sign with a symbol of a little man running. In symbolic terms, running as fast as he was, he was obviously as much in need of a slash as I was. I followed the sign (each time I saw it the man seemed to be running more urgently) from the basement of the Louvre, giving the *Mona Lisa* a miss, and up two or possibly three sets of escalators, to find that I'd taken the exit and had been deposited on pavement level and outside the Louvre and the see-through pyramid. I had to queue for some time to descend through the pyramid again like a character in a David Hockney etching, and eventually find a lavatory. Remember, please, the next time you are in the Louvre and no doubt other public monuments in France, that the sign of a little man running does not mean what you may think it does. The EEC might do better to unify its common signs than its currencies. Memo to John Major.

Other essential cities, to the denizen of the planet Earth, are Venice and Istanbul. The Simplon Orient Express from London to Venice, leaving Victoria station at 11 a.m. on a Thursday and arriving at 6 p.m. the following day, provides one of the world's great luxury journeys. Men dress for dinner and women look gorgeous, many of them in twenties outfits. Everyone seems to enjoy themselves except for Americans who, as usual when travelling in Europe, complain about almost everything. Day and night a pianist in the bar plays Scott Joplin, and more Scott Joplin. Only one person, unselfconsciously, is likely to be reading Agatha Christie's *Murder on the Orient Express*. As to Istanbul, the Jules Verne long weekend, staying at the newish Ramada Hotel in the Old City, is one of the greatest travel bargains of our time. The mosques, which seem to float like exotic Arabian Night birthday cakes, are as awesome as Chartres, York, Lincoln and the other great medieval cathedrals.

I'd also rate Jerusalem as an unexpectedly beautiful city, home of four cultures, Armenian, Jewish, Arab and Christian, and the least of these is not the Armenian. Their church services, with much colour and singing, are beautiful, greens and gold everywhere. Somehow, until I went there in 1980, I had the idea that Jerusalem, being such a political hot potato, would be like Baghdad, a city mutilated, bereft of its history. Not so. It is thrilling, simultaneously elating and humbling.

I visited Jerusalem when I took a six-month sabbatical from our agency, which was a benevolent – or possibly self-interested – idea of Anthony Sheil's. We agreed between ourselves that, for each decade notched up by an agent with the firm, he or she could, with the co-operation of colleagues who during the sabbatical would have to work all the harder, have six months away from the office. It only happened twice, the first time with me, the second with Anthony a few years later when he went to his house on the Cycladic island of Andros, a few hours' boat journey from Athens. I spent a month in Israel, assisted in this by the mildly right-wing organisation Friends of Israel, which paid for my air fare from London to Tel Aviv and set me up as writer in residence at a kibbutz in the very north of the country.

I was to keep a diary, and write what else I could. I was, for once, rather pleased with what I wrote, which was turned into an essay for the *New Edinburgh Review*, incisively edited at the time by James Campbell. This piece was political. Most of the rest of what I wrote, apart from a story or two, was lushish travelogue, and travel writing is, like knitting, therapeutic. I say 'lushish' rather than lush travelogue as the landscape up and down the surprisingly modest length of the Holy Land is surprisingly arid. What I didn't realise, because no one had told me in advance, was that I'd have to be up every day at 5 a.m., I think it was, to plant apple trees with the kibbutzim. My 'writer in residence' epithet was no sinecure but had to be indulged after the day's work, physical labour harder than I was used to back home. Not only was planting apple trees back-breaking work but it was, like all manual labour, boring. You might say that when you've seen one young apple tree you have seen them all, and when you've planted two you've planted one too many.

I was billeted on a lovely family at Malkia kibbutz as far north in Israel as possible, bordering Lebanon – which looked exotic across the barbed wire from the kibbutz. At night armoured cars would prowl the narrow road between the two countries, and there would be armed guards on both sides. Until a few years before, Israeli children, putative Romeos and Juliets perhaps, would lob apples across the border at the children of Lebanon and vice versa: an apt and eager image. If anyone was likely to lob anything in 1980 it would be a hand-grenade.

It was disconcerting eating in the refectory (no one ate at home) with these aggressive, handsome, opinionated people, the Israelis of the kibbutz, the young men (and some of the young women) invariably with rifles by their side as endless yoghurt, honey, eggs, fruit and chicken and then more chicken was consumed. At night, against a cyclorama of twinkling stars, the villages to the south of Israel made the Holy Land, the stable, seem very near, very real, although Bethlehem itself turned out to be a cynical tourist trap.

After Israel I flew to India for ten weeks. On my arrival in Delhi, in addition to the instant surprise of my luggage being sent to Australia, I was persuaded out of a considerable percentage of my traveller's cheques and rupees. A pleasant Indian in a Western suit offered me tea, and insisted that he'd be gratified if I attended his daughter's wedding the following Saturday. The reception was being held in the most exotic place I would ever visit, and if I gave him the money now he'd secure me a train ticket. I was, on the day before the wedding, to meet him at a particular place near Connaught Place in the centre of Delhi, and I'd be his family's honoured guest, spend a couple of nights with them and join the feast. When you are abroad on your own you are immediately an innocent, however streetwise you may be at home. Somehow you take 'foreigners', at least in their own country, to be more trustworthy and honourable than you would your fellow country-men back home. Only afterwards, disgusted with myself for having fallen for the smooth Indian's exotic patter (so grateful was I that I'd paid for the tea, too), did I work out that for all the rupees I'd given him I could probably have hired myself a private train.

Some days later, while I was still in Delhi and vaguely hoping to find the conman in the Connaught Place area, a young man sidled up to me. 'You want girl?' he eagerly enquired. I declined the offer. 'You want boy?' Again I declined. And then, in the same matter-of-fact tone of voice: 'You want animal? I get you animal.' India is terrible and beautiful, tragic and exotic, quite unlike anywhere else I've been, including China. China, to me, was bad hotels, bicycles, everyone wearing denim and the Great

Wall looking as if it was constructed yesterday; and some remarkable, surreal scenery. I kept thinking, as I wandered down the Wall, which was infinitely more reconstructed and restored than Hadrian's, that the first spacemen on the moon had said they could identify China by the length of the Wall. Somehow that made the Universe seem a world easier to contemplate.

This book has not been about my private life, my two marriages, my four children. But let me reveal (it is a secret shared by any interested reader of the London telephone directory) that I have lived in a modest, terraced house in a quiet cul-de-sac in Kentish Town for twenty-eight years, and that I paid off the mortgage to Camden Council after twenty-five years. Some people describe the street as being in Chalk Farm and others, if they wish to impress those who wish to be impressed, as in Hampstead, although the postal district is NW5, NW3 being on the other side of Haverstock Hill, or a very few hundred yards to the north.

Later arrivals in a street of but fourteen houses were Ann Leslie, the *Daily Mail* journalist, and her husband, Michael, who is employed by the BBC as a studio manager, frequently going to work in the middle of the night for reasons which I've never altogether understood. Jonathan Ross, the television 'chat show host', didn't survive long, probably because he and his wife had three cars and there was hardly room to park one of them. His house is still for sale, if you want it. Sheila Gish, tragedienne of her generation and a definitive Blanche Du Bois, and the actor Dennis Lawson, invariably spreading a little happiness, live opposite. Richard Lindley, a most serious television person, used to live down the road from us, but it was said that his wife, whom he divorced, or she him, and who seemed always shrouded in a fur coat, didn't enjoy the street.

Merry Archard, who in the sixties and seventies wrote a weekly page for the *Evening Standard* about bringing up children, winsomely called 'Paging all Parents', and her husband Llew Gardner, and their twin sons, moved into the street ten days after we did, although for more than a quarter of a century Llew was claiming in my presence that of all the present denizens of the Gardens they were the first to be established. He had an extremely loud voice and an even louder laugh and was, in his heyday – the sixties and seventies – as well known as any television journalist. He did the top political interviews for Thames Television, and invariably mastered his brief, thus giving politicians with feet of clay a rough ride. Before his employment by television he wrote for *Tribune*. (Michael Foot, once the Labour weekly's editor, was a close friend and orated at his memorial service in 1991. I missed the service as I was recovering from an operation for piles, or haemorrhoids to be more classical. But that is verging on the autobiographical if not anal retentive and I will desist. I whiled away the time at the Royal Free Hospital by reading the first draft of the manuscript of Vikram Seth's masterpiece *A Suitable Boy*, longer than *War and Peace* but, as he pointed out, shorter than Proust. You can't win 'em all.) Although Welsh, Llew regarded himself as something of an expert on the poetry of Hugh MacDiarmid and often claimed a shared nationality with me. He was a large, generous man.

Llew would also claim that he and Merry were the first middle-class people to move into a street of controlled and council tenants. Certainly few in the street owned their houses. When I moved in, in the mid-sixties, there was a controlled tenant on the top floor. But for her presence, my wife and I could not have afforded the house, valued at under £7,000. Mrs Warburton was not the traditional old dear with whom we might have hoped to leave our babies, when they came along, but an old horror. One day she nearly set fire to the building, waving burning strips of newspaper about while trying to light her leaking gas stove on the landing at the top of the house. On other occasions she would have 'black-outs', and once my wife, heavily pregnant, had to pick her up, dust her down, and put her together again. I finally exploded at all this nonsense, especially as my wife had a history of miscarriages, and eventually our sitting tenant's daughter-in-law and her husband took her away to live with them in Borehamwood, a place I've subsequently always avoided.

But that is to digress. One Christmas Eve I opened our front door, which is at the top of a flight of stone steps, on to a scene more common then than now, a white Christmas, with thickish snow like Aero chocolate everywhere. As I bent down to pick up the milk bottles, I glanced down the street and noticed that the lower glass panel in the front door of the next house had been shattered and had a yawning, jagged hole. More than that, a youth was coming out of the house through the hole in the glass. He appeared to be holding, balanced precariously in his hands, half the assets of the Prices, our neighbours, including a pile of record sleeves, presumably containing records.

'What are you doing?' I called out, in my best law-and-order voice. 'Oh, it's all right,' he said, looking up and seeing me. 'I'm just moving some items. The people here asked me to do so.' The scenario, the dialogue of both characters, was already pretty crass, but was to become more surreal. 'I don't think they did,' I said cunningly. 'They are away for Christmas,' which was both true and extremely foolish, if only because the intruder had clearly discovered that satisfactorily for himself.

By this time my wife had overheard the conversation and had come to the door. She took in the scene. 'I'm going to telephone the police,' she announced, mainly, it seemed, for the benefit of the burglar, and went away to do so. I made my way down the slippery steps of our house, feeling somewhat apprehensive but knowing that I must undertake my civic, my neighbourly duty. The thief, for his part, tried to wriggle out of the house and through the jagged glass without doing himself an injury, leaving a trail of blood in the snow, and escaping with our neighbour's household goods before I could bring him down (or so I like to think).

A few inquisitive faces were by now bobbing up and down behind, metaphorically speaking, lace curtains across the street. I was strangely aware of them, the way your senses are somehow heightened when something unexpected and dramatic happens to you and you become, for a while, an unwitting, unwilling third-person participant in your own affairs; a character that is partly yourself, partly someone unknown to you yet harbouring your physical identity. You are both activist and witness, executant and observer.

Then Llew Gardner's door swung open and a gust of powdery snow seemed to jerk in the air as if projected by a wind machine. Llew, who, as I have said, was a big man with an even bigger voice, stood on the threshold like Superman. 'What's the matter,

Giles?' he almost roared as the weedy amateur burglar shuffled down the street, slithering in the snow, which had begun to fall again, with me in pursuit, but not too eagerly. I explained to Llew and he joined me in the chase, which immediately began to assume the dimensions of a film.

The burglar ran into Queen's Crescent, the main street at the bottom of ours and at right angles to it, and slithered his way towards the crammed open-air market up the Crescent which, this being Christmas Eve, and early in the morning, was crushed with people, turkey-laden. By now my breath was heavy and heaving and the thief was still ahead, slithering and sliding as he was and I was.

Llew got to him first, and we both held him outside a butcher's shop. For some reason there were four butchers' shops within a hundred yards of one another. People in Kentish Town ate a lot of red meat. Now there are only three butchers' shops, and the butchers are not as prosperous as they were. There is still no fishmonger, although there is a fish-and-chippy.

The intruder threatened to crash himself through the butcher's plate glass window taking Llew and me with him. Perhaps he was addicted to smashing glass. A crowd gathered round. 'Go on, Llew,' old women crowed and cawed. 'You show it to him, Llew,' they cackled with North London laughter. Some even looked about them to see where the television cameras were.

Although Llew and I together were much stronger than the thief we had difficulty restraining him. If someone decides to throw himself through a plate glass window, provided that the glass yields to the pressure, it is hard to dissuade him. 'Give us a break,' said the man. 'It's Christmas Eve and the wife's expecting a baby.' I was inclined to believe him about the baby, especially as he'd been right about the date. I had a distinct lump in my throat. Doing your duty was not enjoyable, especially if naturally you identified with the underdog. 'The police'll decide about that,' said Llew loudly, and urged the onlookers to seek out a policeman. Actually, I think what he said was not 'the police' but 'the law'.

Eventually the police came strolling up with that maddening air of nonchalance which suggests that everything is rosy in the garden, that there's no hurry in the world. It's a cultivated walk which they must be taught at police college, and which presumably is intended to reassure the goodies that everything is under control, the baddies that it is a fair cop.

The law took the lad away, and still some of the crowd sought out the television cameras, probably prepared to be interviewed and provide a mite of wisdom. I think the assumption was that Llew Gardner was a creature if not a creation of television; they always saw him on the box pop, therefore this was television. That he had a life away from television, that they knew he lived locally and that they frequently saw him in the market was, strangely, disregarded given the high drama of this particular Christmas Eve.

I was reminded of the burglary next door when, on 2 July 1984, I had the disagreeable and humiliating experience of being mugged. I'd been doing my duty as theatre critic of the *Spectator*, attending the press night of Doug Lucie's coruscating play *Progress*. After the production I sat outside the pub theatre (the evening was hot) with the friend I'd taken, Astrid Gillis, whom I hadn't seen for twenty years or so. I didn't have to write my review until the end of the week. A fellow critic had taken her to be my wife and there followed, absurdly, a degree of embarrassment.

As we sat outside the pub, the Shepherd's Bush traffic thundered by. We tried, in a short time, to catch up on our respective lives over the last two decades. We'd both married. A man with a face like an overdone baked potato suddenly lurched above us and asked, courteously if in a sozzled way, whether we could spare him a coin. I dipped my hand into a pocket and gave him 10p, which made me feel both philanthropic and mean. Astrid and I kept talking and the man continued to swing and lurch over us, thanking us profusely.

The press night had begun at seven, the play had been short, and at about 10 p.m. we parted. Astrid lived nearby, and turned into Goldhawk Road. With some difficulty (the traffic is relentless), I crossed Shepherd's Bush Green and began to walk – as I'd done many times before, after visits to the Bush Theatre – across the common towards the Tube. The sky was still quite bright, and I was thinking of Astrid, our lives in Edinburgh all those years ago, when I noticed, without paying particular attention, a man get up from a bench to the left of the path I trod and walk, at a brisk pace, more or less in the direction I was going.

He was stocky, sturdy, scruffy and unshaven and proved to have an Irish accent. In a flash he was in front of me, his face close up to mine: 'Can you give me a pound?' It half crossed my mind that this was no way to beg a coin. I replied that I could not. (For once my wallet was well laden; my wife had slipped me the housekeeping money before going on holiday, and I was doling the cash out to our growing-up children on a daily basis: there lodged about £60 close to my breast.) Whereupon – all this more quickly than I could think or try to rationalise – he jostled me as I attempted to push past, there being no doubt in my mind that I'd succeed. I was, by an inch or two, taller than he but he was heavier. His hand shot out and up and grabbed my Adam's apple, pressed it and pushed and I was thrust backwards down on to the grass, losing my spectacles as I hit the ground.

Somehow the two others who had been sitting on the seat beside him were behind me, and I was pinned to the ground. Swearwords and expletives were spat in my direction with venom and relish. Without my glasses, I could see little. Had I thought rather than reacted, I might have said: 'Take my wallet; let me be.' As it was, I thrashed about angrily on the ground, determined not to lose.

Laughably, my first concern was for the notes I'd taken at the play: the pages of my spiral-bound pad were strewn about. Then instinct persuaded me to turn on to my stomach, and with my right elbow tucked in I tried to protect my wallet. I was surprised, as someone who takes no particular exercise (though being a non-driver I walk a lot), how strong I was, relatively speaking. The first man held my throat, so I couldn't cry out, while the second pinioned my arms. Eventually they rolled me over, and the woman took my wallet. She ran towards Shepherd's Bush Road with it – taking my Barclaycard, cheque-card and various membership cards. The men let go of me (at least I wasn't booted for luck, and wearing as I was a white linen suit I suppose I might have been anally raped) and I scrabbled around, trying to retrieve the notes of my review. Then I saw my spectacles and stood up, groggily. I watched the three run away, towards the distant traffic.

*Declining to play games*

I made it to the nearby police station, and was driven around the area in a police van to see if I could identify the brave trio. I could not. An officer took down the particulars as I described them, and said that he assumed my assailants were coloured. I said they seemed to have Irish accents. 'Are you sure that wasn't a con?' Perhaps, he explained, they were pretending to be Irish. Maybe they were pretending to be white, too, I thought.

They'd left, in another pocket, my Underground pass, and as I travelled home some beleathered Hell's Angels handed out a leaflet. 'Policing London', it began, 'by coercion. The liberties of all Londoners are again under attack. Protect London: oppose the Police Bill.' The somewhat military man sitting next to me muttered angrily and asked what I thought. I hadn't read the new Bill, I said.

At ten to midnight, back home, I tried to telephone Barclaycard in Northampton. The number rang and rang. I dialled once more and woke up some poor man in Northallerton – one digit wrong – who said not to worry, mate; it happens eight times a day.

Such, unfortunately, can be urban life today. But the Northallerton man's lack of irritation, lack of self-righteousness, was reassuring.

# XXXII

One of my children once asked me what my 'best hobby' was. I like to think that I don't have one, in that to confess to a hobby is to suggest that you have time in your life to indulge the inessential, the trivial (although not necessarily so), something that isn't central or 'mainstream' to your life.

If I rode horses or played golf, I suppose, I could claim that as a hobby, although most who play Scotland's national game and talk about it seem to be merely riding a hobby-horse. The nearest I get is the frequenting of second-hand bookshops. But, as I grow older, I find myself visiting increasingly grand second-hand, nay, antiquarian booksellers, and frequently those who 'trade' from their homes rather than from shop premises.

One of those I've found myself calling upon in the last few years is Rick Gekoski, and I mention his name here not to provide him with free advertising, but to tell what I hope you'll agree is an instructive anecdote. When I was visiting him recently he or I made a mention of the dedication to a book, a minor subject which amuses me greatly. Rick, a large bearded American enthusiast who used to teach English at the University of Warwick, asked me if I knew which of our contemporaries had most books dedicated to him. I suggested Christopher Sinclair-Stevenson, if only because he has published so many books. Rick took that to be a reasonable answer, but guessed that Christopher – however many books he has had dedicated to him – was probably the runner-up. The winner, he insisted, with twenty-four books, was Charles Monteith, until recently chairman of Faber and Faber. 'And,' quoth Rick, 'he doesn't just have anybody.' 'He wouldn't,' I muttered, 'being chairman of Faber and Faber.' 'He has Beckett.

And Golding.' Rick beamed over his mug of thick, black coffee. 'Not bad. For starters.'

I told him I thought I had about a dozen books dedicated to me, but I really, truly, couldn't remember for sure. And I had a number of books dedicated to me to the tune of 50 per cent, that is with a co-dedicatee. Does that count as a half or as one? Rick pondered, then pronounced that it counted as one. Iain Crichton Smith's first novel, *Consider the Lilies*, is dedicated to the Scottish poet and BBC radio producer Stewart Conn and to me. My client Alanna Knight's best novel, *The Clan*, is dedicated to me, because she is an author who is most professional – though not remotely Machiavellian – and knows how to massage vain egos. Allan Massie's *Caesar* is dedicated to his wife Alison and to me. I have mentioned the one-fifth (one of five, that is) dedication in *But for Bunter*, but not the 50 per cent dedication in Keith Roberts' *The Grain Kings*. Martin Seymour-Smith's *Fallen Women*, an unnecessarily erudite tome about prostitution as treated in literature, is dedicated to me and to one Harold Brooks. The latter is unknown to me but Hilary Spurling admitted the first time I met her that, given the fulsome nature of Martin's thanks to the co-dedicatees in his acknowledgements, she had assumed Mr Brooks and I were inseparable, not only on the page but, as it were, just good friends. I learned later that Mr Brooks was Martin Seymour-Smith's carpenter and Martin, unable at the time to pay for some bookshelves which Mr Brooks had built for him, offered him half a dedication instead, which was readily accepted.

The dedication, though, that gives me more pleasure than any other is that of Robert Nye's magnificent novel *Falstaff*. It occupies a whole page and reads as follows:

TO. THE. ONLIE. BEGETTER. OF.
THESE. INSUING. FICTIONS.
MR. GILES GORDON
ALL. HAPPINESS. AND. THAT. ETERNITY.
PROMISED. BY. OUR. EVER-LIVING.
POET. WISHETH. THE. WELL-WISHING.
ADVENTURER. IN. SETTING. FORTH.
R.N.

Could any literary agent receive a more handsome present from one of his authors, and that in addition to 10 per cent of the proceeds? I'm not sure about the Polish translation though, where the dedicatee's name becomes Gilesowi Gordonowi.

While chatting to Gekoski, I remembered another title dedicated to me, Peter Ackroyd's *Hawksmoor*. Rick heaved up and down in his armchair, almost sending his coffee flying. 'You mean you have the dedication copy of *Hawksmoor*? he said, clearly impressed. 'You *own* the dedication copy of *Hawksmoor*?' He savoured the thought, and presumably did his rare-book-dealer's calculations. 'Do you realise that is probably the most valuable book you own?'

The meeting concluded with Rick suggesting, albeit tentatively, that I was possibly third in line after Charles Monteith and Christopher Sinclair-Stevenson with regard to the number of books dedicated to me. Myself, I doubt it very much – but it is, indeed, the quality of the books that counts.

None of my books has won a prize, which doesn't surprise me in the least. Maybe having other authors' books dedicated to me is the nearest I'll achieve to this kind of, almost, reflected glory. Being allowed to put a series of initials after my name, relating to books written, is another snare and delusion.

In 1990, I received a letter from the secretary inviting me to become a Fellow of the Royal Society of Literature. I couldn't believe it as I hadn't published a book for more than ten years. The thrill of receiving the invitation was a little diminished by an accompanying note which asked me to fill in (or out) a banker's order so that my annual subscription might more effortlessly be paid. This brought me down to earth, the whole thing seeming analogous to, say BUPA. As well as Fellows, who are elected, there are Members, who file up expressing an interest in literature and send a postal order to the secretary and are then elected. I do not want to labour the point, but what at first seems simply a distinction – and the list of Fellows is indeed distinguished, a roll call of contemporary English letters almost – is a bit of a bribe. It's very English: you do not have to be a Fellow, but if you want to be one you have to pay for the privilege. The President is Lord Jenkins of Hillhead, and the chairman the learned Mortimer, QC.

The offices are in a musty, fusty building at Hyde Park Gate. They appear to be underground, though in fact they are on the ground floor, so dark are they with curtains everywhere, or drapes, and a smell of mouldy mothballs. Somehow incense and inspiration seem to have departed. There is, at the back, a most serene and charming terrace and garden in which Fellows, Members and their guests may, on the Society's high days and feast days, promenade, unless it is pouring with rain, which usually it is.

New Fellows are inducted at the AGM, which takes place in the summer. You have the choice, as Roy Jenkins puts it, of signing your name in the book of Fellows using either Bywon's pen or his, Lord Jenkins', biwo. (Lord Jenkins has a famous speech impediment which I do not intend to mock. It is just so much part of his persona. His inability or disinclination to pronounce his r's rather amusingly suggests that his background is aristocratic, whereas he hails from humble Welsh stock and began his education at Abersychan grammar school.) To use Byron's pen (who would vouch for its authenticity?) is, of course, the most ridiculous conceit, but one I couldn't resist. Fellows are introduced alphabetically, and those before me, including Brian Aldiss who expressed annoyance later, feebly employed Jenkins' ballpoint. When my turn came, and having for much of my life claimed to be related (naturally on the wrong side of the sheets) to Byron, who was, of course, a Gordon, I asked for the favour of my ancestor's plume. The then secretary, Mrs Schute, went into a terrible twitter and confessed, in front of the assembled literati, that there was no ink. 'Then, Mrs Schute, please go and find some ink,' drawled the President, beaming at everyone present over the top of his spectacles. 'We offered Mr . . .' He looked down at the sheet of paper he was holding to remind himself of my name. 'We offered Mr Gordon Lord Bywon's pen and therefore he must have Lord Bywon's pen.' It was like something out of Molière, I thought at the time, the impression being enhanced by the fact that the Royal Society of Literature's room has a stately staircase on one side, very seventeenth-century. As scores of people stood about in keen anticipation (they would only be allowed a drink when the formal proceedings were concluded), Mrs Schute scuttered up the staircase, disappeared into a room, scuttered out again and across the landing, vanished into another room, scuttered breathlessly down the staircase clutching a large bottle of black ink. 'Ah, the ink,' beamed Jenkins, quietly amused. The nib of Byron's pen was tried out on a sheet of paper before I was allowed to embellish the book. The eight or so Fellows introduced after me all, I think, employed the peer poet's pen. 'You do realise,' David Hughes muttered to me, 'that although that may be the old boy's pen' – he was speaking of Lord Byron, not Lord Jenkins – 'the nib was bought at Ryman's yesterday.'

The average age of Fellows – or, to be a little fair, those who turn up to the cobwebby premises of the RSL – must be eighty-three. My wife witnessed my induction while finding the whole business somewhat arcane and irrelevant. Afterwards, when wine was served and people started chatting, she went famous – Fellow-spotting. 'Have you been a Fellow for long?' she asked one interesting-looking woman. The answer, in effect, was since climbing Everest and subsequently writing some distinguished books, principally on Venice and the British Empire as well as being short-listed one year for the Booker with her only published novel. My wife didn't find this brief encounter remotely funny as the crueller I did, but I wouldn't want to go out of my way to ask Jan Morris if, unlike Queen Victoria, she was amused.

And now I must behave decorously where the Royal Society of Literature is concerned, as I have just been invited to serve on the Council and have accepted. I've also agreed to serve on the General Council, as they call it, of a curious body called the Authors' Club, which meets at the Arts Club in Dover Street, mainly for lunch, it seems, and each year to present three prizes. The first is the Sir Banister Fletcher Award 'for the book on architecture or the arts most deserving'; the second, for 'the most promising first novel', the award taking the form of a silver-mounted and inscribed quill – all of which sounds more than a little Freudian – plus £500; the third, the Nelson Hurst & Marsh Biography Award, which sounds like a variety act. I know nothing more about the Authors' Club than this and nor it seems, perplexingly, do the Club's officers.

I sincerely hope that I am not becoming, as my second half-century begins to fast-forward, too respectable or respectful. I think there is little likelihood of that; and if there is, the publication of these irreverent but not, I hope, unsympathetic pages about some of those I've encountered as I go about life's increasingly bewildering business, should dispel any suspicions of complacency and time-serving.

# Acknowledgements

In 1982 I dedicated an anthology I'd edited, *Shakespeare Stories*, as follows: 'To the Royal Shakespeare Company, and especially Peter Hall, John Barton and Trevor Nunn, for having given so much pleasure.' Similarly, I conclude these pages by thanking everybody named herein for enriching my working life, especially the authors for whom I have acted as publisher, editor or agent. I thank in particular those not mentioned by name, although they may well be relieved to be uninvoked.

I especially thank Carmen Callil of Chatto & Windus, who commissioned a novel from me and ended up with the present volume; and Alison Samuel, who easily gives the lie to my long-held prejudice that the skills of editing in London are dead.

Three passages have previously appeared in slightly different forms, and I thank the editors and publishers for permission to reproduce them here. My memoir of Jonathan Griffin is condensed from an essay in *Sage Eye: The Aesthetic Passion of Jonathan Griffin* (Menard Press/King's College, London, 1992); the paragraphs on negotiating with Kevin Maxwell from a Festschrift to Mike Molloy, *Round Up the Usual Suspects* (Sagittarius Press, 1990); and the paragraphs on being mugged originally formed part of an article published in *The Times* (13 July 1984).

I am grateful also to the following for allowing me to quote from letters or other copyright material: Michael Holroyd (p.31); James MacGibbon, executor of Stevie Smith for extracts from her letters to me (pp.35–36); J. G. Links (pp.45–46); J. F. McCrindle for my interview with Joe Orton (pp.115–118); Messrs Methuen for the 'Author's Note' to *Loot* (p.124); G. H. Ballantyne (pp.229–230); Messrs Hutchinson for the extract from *George Thomas, Mr Speaker* (pp.274–275); Lord Weatherill (p.275); and Sir Rudolf Peierls (p.323).

G.G.
*June 1993*

The publisher decided
that there should be no
index to this book . . .